Shylock's Children

Shylock's Children

Economics and Jewish Identity in Modern Europe

Derek J. Penslar

UNIVERSITY OF CALIFORNIA PRESS

Berkeley / Los Angeles / London

The publisher gratefully acknowledges the generous contribution to this book provided by the S. Mark Taper Foundation.

University of California Press
Berkeley and Los Angeles, California

University of California Press, Ltd.
London, England

Parts of the following chapters were previously published: chapter 2, in *Jewish Social Studies* 3 (1997); chapter 3, in Warren Ilchman, Stanley Katz, and Edward Queen II, eds., *Philanthropy in the World's Traditions* (Bloomington: Indiana University Press, 1998); and chapter 5, in the *Leo Baeck Institute Yearbook* 38 (1993).

Library of Congress Cataloging-in-Publication Data

Penslar, Derek Jonathan.
    Shylock's children : economics and Jewish identity in modern Europe / Derek J. Penslar.
        p. cm.
    Includes bibliographic references (p.) and index.
    ISBN 0-520-22590-2 (cloth : alk. paper)
    1. Jews—Europe—Economic conditions.   2. Europe—
Economic conditions.   3. Jews—Europe—Public
opinion.   4. Public opinion—Europe.   5. Jews—Europe
—Identity.   I. Title.

DS135.E83 P46 2001
940'.04924—dc21

                                                            00-048894
                                                                 CIP

Printed in the United States of America
10 09 08 07 06 05 04 03 02 01
10 9 8 7 6 5 4 3 2 1

The paper used in this publication is both acid-free and totally chlorine-free (TCF). The paper used in this publication meets the minimum requirements of ANSI/NISO Z39.48-1992 (R 1997) (*Permanence of Paper*). ∞

To Robin, Joshua, and Talia,
who have made it all worthwhile

Contents

Acknowledgments

As this book has been a full decade in the making, I have accumulated considerable debts to a great many individuals and institutions. A summer fellowship from the Leo Baeck Institute and the Deutscher Akademischer Austauschdienst allowed me to begin research on this project in New York in 1990. Funding from the National Endowment for the Humanities and Indiana University supported summer travel in subsequent years. Most of the research for this book was done during 1993–94 when I was a Yad Hanadiv fellow at the Hebrew University of Jerusalem. A fellowship from the Indiana University Center on Philanthropy and the Ely Lily Foundation in 1996 released me from teaching duties for a semester.

At Indiana University, I received valuable research assistance from Lindsey Barton, a talented undergraduate, and from four graduate students—Tobias Brinkman, Timothy Pursell, Elliot Rabin, and Greg Schroeder—who helped me comb through the microfilm forest of the nineteenth-century Jewish press. Benjamin Laziere, a graduate student at the University of California at Berkeley, tracked down and sent me text from a rare eighteenth-century source in the library of the Boalt Hall School of Law. Drafts of various chapters of the book were delivered at conferences and invited lectures at the New York Leo Baeck Institute, Heidelberg's Hochschule für jüdische Studien, the Historische Kommission zu Berlin, the Institute for Contemporary History and Wiener Library, London, Harvard University's Center for European Studies, the University of Wisconsin at Madison, Hebrew University's

Institute for Advanced Study, the University of Haifa, Tel Aviv University, and Ben-Gurion University of the Negev.

I am grateful to a number of editors and presses for allowing me to make use of previously published material. Chapters 2, 5, and 6, respectively, are revised and expanded versions of "The Origins of Jewish Political Economy," *Jewish Social Studies* 3 (1997); "Philanthropy, the 'Social Problem,' and Jewish Identity in Imperial Germany," *Leo Baeck Institute Yearbook* 38 (1993); and "Ha-tsiyonut ke-tadmit shel mediniyut yehudit modernit," in *'Eidan ha-tsiyonut,* ed. Jay Harris, Jehuda Reinharz, and Anita Shapira (Jerusalem: Merkaz Zalman Shazar, 2000). Portions of chapter 3 appeared in Warren Ilchman, Stanley Katz, and Edward Queen II, eds., *Philanthropy in the World's Traditions* (Bloomington: Indiana University Press, 1998). I also want to thank Stan Holwitz of the University of California Press for his enthusiastic support for this project when it was in its early phases, Rachel Berchten for helping me through the production process, and Sheila Berg for her careful copy editing.

A book that attempts, as this one does, to cover a wide geographic, chronological, and thematic spectrum cannot be written without the insight and support of a sizable community of scholars. Space limitations prevent me from listing the many friends and colleagues who, through informal conversations or comments on oral presentations of my research in progress, deepened this book's analytic framework, sent me off in exciting new research directions, and saved me from embarrassment by pointing out errors. Here, I will limit myself to those who read substantial portions of the manuscript or who have been intellectual mentors ab initio.

Israel Bartal, Nachum Gross, Anita Shapira, David Sorkin, and Steven Zipperstein have nurtured this project over its long period of gestation. Paula Hyman read the entire manuscript and made valuable suggestions for revisions. At Indiana University, I had the great pleasure of working closely with John Efron, whose criticisms of my work combined sound insight with good humor. The Jewish Studies faculty colloquium at Indiana University provided a forum for presenting preliminary versions of some of the book's chapters, and I am particularly grateful to Jeffrey Isaac, Benjamin Nathans, and Hava Tirosh-Samuelson for their penetrating comments. In Indiana's History Department, Bill Cohen, James Diehl, and David Pace helped me to maintain a European-historical perspective and avoid slipping into parochialism. Finally, I want to express warm appreciation of my new colleagues at the University of Toronto, whose History Department and

Jewish Studies Program have provided a stimulating and hospitable environment in which I already feel very much at home.

As I was completing the final revisions on the manuscript, Talia, my ten-year-old daughter, accidentally wiped out some of my computer's operating-system software, and Joshua, my fifteen-year-old son, diagnosed and helped repair the problem. My children have filled my life with joy and meaning. My wife, Robin, is the touchstone for everything I have taught and written. My love and gratitude for her are beyond words.

Introduction

If I can catch him once upon the hip,
I will feed fat the ancient grudge I bear him.
He hates our sacred nation, and he rails,
Even there where merchants most do congregate,
On me, my bargains, and my well-won thrift,
Which he calls interest. Cursèd be my tribe
If I forgive him.
    Shakespeare, *The Merchant of Venice* (1.3)

The moneylender Shylock, Shakespeare's most notorious creation, represents the totality of Jewish otherness in Christian Europe. His livelihood is a synecdoche, representing the inseparability of Jewish religious, social, and economic distinctiveness. Throughout much of European history, Jews concentrated in certain occupations and displayed particular characteristics in the practice of their livelihoods and the spending of their earnings. Gentile perceptions of Jewish economic difference were usually hostile, at times admiring, but always influential in the shaping of government policies toward Jews and social interaction between Jews and Gentiles.

This book is about how Jews in modern Europe perceived and accounted for their economic difference. It examines Jewish responses to Gentile critiques of Jewish economic behavior and, more broadly, Jewish thinking about the relationship between Judaism and economic practice. From the time of the Enlightenment to the early decades of the twentieth century, there developed in Europe a matrix of Jewish economic *mentalités,* a matrix that this book reassembles and represents.

The emancipation of European Jewry has been extensively studied, as has the effect of emancipation on the emergence of new forms of Jewish religious and social identity. But surprisingly, given the centrality of economic themes in modern antisemitism, as well as the very real economic crises that affected much of European Jewry, historians have tended to approach Jewish economic discourse in an indirect fashion at best.[1] To be sure, the economic ideologies behind eastern European, late-nineteenth-century Jewish radicalism—whether in the form of the socialist Bund or the early Zionist Labor movement—have received extensive attention.[2] But the same cannot be said for bourgeois Jews, whose economic distinctiveness was a source of strong feelings, ranging from pride to consternation.

These sensibilities deeply affected the institutional and intellectual life of European Jews. They stimulated the development in the nineteenth century of a network of Jewish philanthropies, which, in their efforts to alleviate Jewish economic distress, developed by the turn of the twentieth century into global vehicles of Jewish social policy.[3] And they produced new forms of Jewish knowledge, beginning in the late 1700s with an identifiably Jewish political economy, developing in the mid-1800s into a secular economic historiography, and culminating in the early twentieth century with the formation of an introspective Jewish social science.

Jewish economic discourse shared a common vocabulary and conceptual framework throughout Europe. It was particularly significant as a source of middle-class Jewish identity in those lands where Jewish populations underwent emancipation and embourgeoisement, that is, England, France, Germany, and much of the Hapsburg Empire. Thus, although this book does pay attention to developments in the Russian Empire, it concentrates on western and central Europe. It is particularly concerned with German-speaking Europe, where incremental emancipation and powerful antisemitism promoted the development of an unusually rich and complex Jewish economic discourse. In the past, scholars made the unfounded assumption that the experiences of German Jewry in the areas of embourgeoisement, acculturation, and religious reform were paradigmatic for European Jewry as a whole.[4] I am arguing quite the opposite: that German-speaking Europe produced unusually deep reservoirs of Jewish socioeconomic thinking and social policies characterized by extraordinary theoretical sophistication. In the early nineteenth century, the particular sociopolitical situation of German-speaking Jews produced unique cultural forms, such as the Jewish political economy that emerged during the last phases of the German Haskalah (the Jewish variant of the European religious Enlightenment). Later in the century, Austro-German Jewry manifested the most developed forms of broader social phenomena, such as the European Jewish philanthropic network.

This is a book about theory and praxis, about a Jewish political economy that catalyzed and guided Jewish social policy. The former originated in Germany and subsequently spread throughout Europe and to the United States. The latter's field of operations included not only Europe and the United States but also much of the Middle East, particularly Palestine. Thus despite its Germanocentrism, this book touches on bourgeois Jewish *mentalités* and philanthropic activities throughout much of the globe.

Although this book contains a good deal of description and analysis of Jewish economic activity, it is not a work of economic history per se. Rather, it seeks to contribute to our understanding of Jewish consciousness and of the relationship between consciousness and the application of Jewish power (which, in the modern world before the establishment of the state of Israel, was primarily of an economic nature). It is not about economic thinkers who happened to be of Jewish origin but about Jewish activists who happened to think about economics. Thus great economic theoreticians of Jewish origin such as David Ricardo scarcely figure here. Karl Marx appears only in reference to economic antisemitism, and Moses Hess's turn to Jewish affairs in his middle age does not, I believe, retroactively instill Judaic content into his earlier, radical writings on the nature of money. Nor does this book systematically address the thinking of the Jewish economic elite, a topic that has been tackled by scholars who have exhaustively chronicled the activities of the Rothschilds, Bleichröders, and other great banking and commercial families in modern Europe.[5]

Instead, this book is about the creators of Jewish political economy, those who thought seriously about Jewish economic life and who attempted to put their programs into action in the spheres of philanthropy and other forms of social politics. These people were rabbis, scholars, publicists, and lay activists in local, national, and international Jewish organizations. They may be defined socioeconomically, employing the terminology of Pierre Bourdieu, as "the dominated fraction of the dominant class."[6] In the late eighteenth and early nineteenth century, they were frequently tutors and clerks to the monied mercantile elite. As the century progressed, these shock troops of the Haskalah gave way to journalists who enjoyed at least marginal economic independence, rabbis with pulpits, established merchants, and, by the beginning of the 1900s, physicians and attorneys. While the great Jewish banking families continued to wield extensive communal power well into the twentieth century, the voice of the communities, as expressed in the bourgeoning Jewish press and in the organs of Jewish associational life, was increasingly that of the Jewish middle class.

I do not claim that the Jewish press or the hundreds of books and pamphlets produced by the subjects of this book necessarily speak for the Jewish public as a whole, or even for its middle-class component. In the mid-nineteenth century, the numbers of subscribers to Jewish newspapers ranged from a few hundred to two thousand. By the early 1900s, some German Jewish newspapers had circulations in the tens of thousands, but one must be careful to distinguish between a newspaper that individuals had to purchase and one that came automatically with membership in a particular community or association.[7] It is likely that a single copy of a periodical was read by many individuals and that its content was transmitted through word of mouth to even more, but still, the impact of Jewish journalism on readers' thinking is often impossible to gauge. Where possible, I have made use of sources, such as unpublished memoirs and the archival records of Jewish associations, that reveal the voices of individuals who were not immortalized in print. For my purposes, however, the most useful function of any source, published or archival, is not representativeness of broad social groups so much as representation of the economic sensibility of the Jewish activist elite and the cultural matrix in which it was formed.

The Jewish press and interlocking networks of Jewish philanthropies created an international community of Jewish activists, a Jewish public sphere. According to Jürgen Habermas's classic formulation, the modern public sphere emerged from the interstices between the state, on the one hand, and the realms of economic and family life, on the other. Originating in late-eighteenth-century Europe, the public sphere represented a collectivity of private individuals, defending their economic interests and cultural autonomy against state power.[8] Like its general counterpart, the Jewish public sphere was the creation of a bourgeois elite, men of property and letters, who, conflating the interests of the Jews as a whole with their own, felt empowered both to speak for the Jews in venues of public opinion and to reshape Jewish society through philanthropic action.[9] The Jewish public sphere's occupation with economic affairs reflected not only the peculiar economic problems of the Jews but also the inextricable linkage of economics, politics, and culture in European society. The Jewish public sphere was a discursive network mediating between the twin realms of Jewish economic life—capitalist production and philanthropic distribution.

This study begins with an analysis of the general discursive framework in which the Jewish political economy took form. The first chapter presents modern economic antisemitism as a double helix of intersecting paradigms, the first associating the Jew with paupers and savages and the second conceiving of Jews as conspirators, leaders of a financial cabal seeking global domination. The first paradigm originated in the rhetoric of the absolutist state. In the eighteenth century, bureaucratic reformers seeking to maximize the human resources of the state considered poor Jewish peddlers economically noxious. There are numerous parallels between attitudes toward the Jews and general conceptions of the poor, who were considered degenerate, unproductive, and in need of improvement through tutelary social policy. Moreover, Jews were the only Europeans stigmatized by the prejudices that Europeans held against Native Americans. Jews, like "savages" in the New World, were thought temperamentally incapable of performing honest labor. Thus modern economic antisemitism arose out of the intersection of the Enlightenment's images of the poor and the savage.

The second paradigm, in which the Jew is conceived of as leader of a financial cabal, also emerged in the era of absolutism and took the form of fear and resentment of the Court Jews who financed the military expansion of the German states. This motif was developed further in post-Napoleonic Europe, which abounded with conspiracy theories seeking to account for the political and social upheaval of the era. Moreover, the onset of Jewish emancipation and economic mobility provoked considerable social anxieties. For both reasons, the rise of Jewish private bankers such as the Rothschilds became a source of popular fear of Jewish economic domination. The twinned motifs of Jewish impoverished savagery and plutocracy were intimately related, for both depicted the Jew as parasitical, dangerous, and dwelling outside the established socioeconomic order. Such imagery persisted well into the twentieth century and provided much of the conceptual fabric of modern political antisemitism.

The second chapter treats Jewish responses to these negative depictions within the framework of Jewish economic thinking of the

Haskalah period. In premodern Jewish society, the intellectual elite valued natural-scientific knowledge (e.g., astronomy and medicine) but was indifferent to social-scientific knowledge, that is, the ascendant discourse of political economy. Between the mid-eighteenth century and the 1780s, central Europe's first generation of *maskilim* (Jews conversant with contemporary European intellectual trends) did not directly engage the Enlightenment's economic critique of the Jews. They did not integrate it into their vision for Jewish regeneration, which was conceived largely in cultural terms. In its later phases, however, the German Haskalah began to employ the rhetoric of cameralism, the economic doctrine of German absolutism. Radical *maskilim* such as David Friedländer and Hertz Homberg diagnosed a profound economic dysfunction among the Jews and prescribed occupational restructuring and philanthropic reform as remedies. Whereas these figures dwelled on the radical periphery of the Haskalah, after 1815, Jewish activists in Germany combined a commitment to the preservation of Judaism with an intense engagement in the economic life of the Jews' host societies. The result was a Jewish political economy, which shaped the social vision of leaders of German Reform Judaism during the decades leading up to the Revolution of 1848.

Whereas the second chapter focuses on Jewish political-economic theory, the third dwells on philanthropic praxis. Between 1815 and 1860, industrialization and urbanization provided unprecedented economic opportunities for western and central European Jews, many of whom became firmly established in the new mercantile middle class. Jewish businessmen developed not only institutional but also ideological affinities for economic liberalism. Precisely because they internalized liberal concepts of self-reliance and diligence, however, the leaders of the new Jewish middle class developed harsh attitudes toward the poor among them. Worried lest Jewish peddlers and vagrants endanger their newfound social status, communal activists strove to outlaw begging and rationalize poor care. Community leaders who were themselves merchants rushed into philanthropic activity aimed at training Jewish youth in handicrafts and farming, occupations thought to be archetypally productive despite their decline in the era of industrialization. Particularly in Germany, where civil rights were made conditional on socioeconomic "regeneration," but also in relatively tolerant France and England, Jewish notables internalized the Enlightenment critique of the Jewish poor as sui generis and in need of drastic corrective measures.

Although critical of the poor among them, Jewish writers and communal leaders also celebrated their coreligionists' economic successes. Chapter 4 analyzes the triumphalist spirit that characterized Jewish economic self-imagery, particularly in Germany and Austria, but also in England, France, and Hungary, over the period 1848–1914. The Jewish press and works on Jewish economic historiography, both scholarly and journalistic, indicate that economic accomplishment was a vital source of Jewish self-esteem and self-definition over the period. Moreover, there is an important connection between economics and a sea change in Jewish historical self-consciousness that began in the 1860s. Breaking away from a theologically dominated Jewish historiography, Jewish writers began to express their historical self-consciousness in secular terms and used economics as the point of departure for their project of reconceptualization. This chapter challenges, therefore, the common assumption that the move among Jews to a secular historical self-understanding came only at the end of the nineteenth century and was wedded to nationalist or socialist ideology or both.

At the turn of the twentieth century, while descriptions of the Jew as economic superman flowed from the pens of Jewish journalists and scholars in western and central Europe, Jewish communal activists tended to the opposite extreme. The latter, I argue in chapter 5, painted a picture of a Jewry in a state of profound socioeconomic crisis. This sense of crisis was induced by virulent antisemitism and a notion of a "Jewish social problem," caused by overcrowding in commerce and an influx of impoverished Jews from eastern to western Europe. Whereas the Jewish economic self-critique before the 1870s had been directed against the poor alone, the "Jewish social problem" was said to affect the Jews as a whole, for even prosperous Jews were alleged to suffer psychically from the strains of modern urban life. And whereas the Jewish response to mid-nineteenth-century economic problems was to encourage self-help and vocational training, the new response was to develop a comprehensive Jewish social policy, inspired by the massive growth of philanthropic services in Europe and the increased role of governments in providing them. (In early-twentieth-century parlance, the terms "social policy" and "social welfare" connoted rationalized, publicly directed social service, administered by experts.) As in European states and municipalities, in Jewish communities social policy was increasingly formulated by experts and was informed by a nascent Jewish social science, which, like the academic sociology that enjoyed burgeoning popularity at the fin de siècle, conceived of itself as a product of crisis and response to it. Indeed, by the 1920s, the sense of crisis and the dense network of philanthropic activity that it engendered provided a powerful form of identity to secular Jews in western and central Europe.

At its most radical, Jewish social policy went beyond education, philanthropy, and refugee assistance. It took on the trappings of social engineering, that is, mass colonization in a region where, it was believed, Jews would be secure from persecution and discrimination and would ensure their economic well-being by establishing a strong agricultural and industrial base. The Zionist project was the most spectacular and successful of these experiments in Jewish social engineering. But there were others, for example, in Argentina and the Soviet Union, and these projects' similarities to and differences from Zionism are analyzed in the final chapter. Despite Zionism's unique qualities, international Jewish social policy and social engineering developed prior to and flourished alongside Zionism. Many of the Zionist project's socioeconomic goals, and the strategies it employed to realize those goals, were adumbrated or simultaneously pursued by other vehicles of Jewish social engineering.

By the 1930s, colonization projects in the Diaspora had reached their peak, and the era of non-Zionist Jewish social engineering came to an end. The Zionist project continued in Palestine, but it became increasingly independent of the European Jewish culture that begot it. The destruction of European Jewry during World War II, the creation of the state of Israel, and the rearrangement of the social and economic bases of Jewish life in the post-1945 Diaspora fundamentally altered not only the practice of Jewish social policy but also its primary, underlying assumptions: the existence of a "Jewish question" and the imperative for Jews to work in concert to respond effectively to it.

Scholars who have written on the origin, meaning, and development of the term the "Jewish question" (or its homologue, the "Jewish problem") have presented it as originating in a primarily political context. According to conventional wisdom, the Jewish question was an expression of unwillingness to admit a body that was still seen as a premodern corporation into an imagined, homogeneous modern nation. The "Jewish question" was thus a political issue, reflecting unresolved tensions between confessional and national identity in modern states.[10]

I conceive the "Jewish question" in a different way. Although the term operated within the particular matrix of the Jews' political relationship with the governments of the lands in which they lived, the term nonetheless shares certain features with other terms in which, throughout the nineteenth century, the word *problem* or *question* was attached to various sources of social anxiety. A hegemonic elite or dominant majority group that discriminated against a subaltern or minority group called the latter a "problem," suggesting that the members of the group were themselves mainly responsible for its disabilities. Thus the constant invocation from the mid-nineteenth century of the "social question," that is, the misery of the pauperized and proletarianized lower orders and the threat they posed to bourgeois society, and the "Negro question," that is, the debate over the fate of slavery. The "women's question" throughout Europe and the "Irish question" in England employed a similar taxonomy of dysfunction.

Conceptualizations of the "Jewish question" partially fit into this framework, yet the "Jewish question" possessed unique features. Unlike the other groups mentioned above, Jews were thought to be fully capable of taking care of themselves. Throughout the centuries, European Jewry had always cared for its own poor and was expected to continue doing so despite the removal in the modern era of virtually all the other functions of the traditional autonomous community. In general, Jewish activists welcomed this arrangement, partly to maintain Jewish communal institutions, and thereby collective identity, and partly to prevent the Jewish poor from embarrassing middle-class Jews and stimulating antisemitism. Thus the nineteenth-century "Jewish problem" was socioeconomic as well as political. In turn, Jews who tried to solve the "problem" did not make a clear distinction between political action (lobbying national and world leaders, appealing to international public opinion) and social welfare work (establishing schools and vocational educational programs, relief and reconstruction, aid to immigrants).

By examining the Jewish question's economic dimensions and attempts by Jews to address the question through organized social policy, I hope to make the readers of this book aware of the power of economic issues in shaping modern Jewish consciousness. The history of Jewish social policy is a largely unexplored subject, but its intellectual underpinnings are even more poorly understood: not merely feelings of compassion, obligation, or anxiety, but also visions of a Jewish political economy, speculation about the nature of Jewish economic difference, and contemplation of the role of economic factors in the shaping of Jewish existence.

CHAPTER I

Jews, Paupers, and Other Savages

The Economic Image of the Jew in Western Europe, 1648–1848

It is always unlawful for men to fornicate, but it is sometimes lawful to do business.

Gratian, *Decretum*, ca. 1150

[These are the seven rarest things on earth:]
A nun who does not sing;
A girl who does not love;
A fair without thieves;
A billy goat without a beard;
A hayloft without mice;
A Cossack without the clap;
And a Jew who isn't cheap.

German proverb

Today, whoever is not rich is poor—this has long been a curse that rests upon us.

Rabbi Isaac Noah Mannheimer, 1835

The irrationality of prejudice, its constant self-contradiction, appears most prominent in the case of antisemitism. Jews, antisemites have claimed, are clannish but eager to assimilate, a teeming mass but an esoteric cabal, capitalists and communists, plutocrats and paupers. The contradictions are so great as to suggest that antisemitism can never be thoroughly understood, only documented. Yet antisemitism can be at least in part understood by placing it in its social context and comparing it with other forms of prejudice. This approach does not belittle antisemitism, nor does it deny its unique qualities. On the contrary, a comparative method points out the uniqueness of antisemitism much better than a mere description of Jew-hating fantasies.

In his monumental *History of Antisemitism*, Léon Poliakov has called economic antisemitism a "detour," claiming that it does not form a legitimate conceptual category. Economic antisemitism, he claims, "remains rooted in theology and only continues to exist by virtue of it, since without the theology, propertied Jews would only have been money-grubbers like any other money-grubber. . . . That is why a history of antisemitism is first and foremost a theological history, however entangled it may be with economic history."[1] Without doubt, antisemitism originated in a theological matrix, and the economic marginalization of the Jews in the later Middle Ages, indeed, the general process in which Jews became a pariah people in Christendom, was driven by the imperatives of religious belief.

That said, the economic element in European antisemitism, particularly in the modern period, is distinct and nearly constant, whereas its theological component is often subdued. One could argue that religiously derived conceptual categories, however occluded or latent they may be, always inform even the most secularized manifestation of antisemitism. But a linear search for the roots of antisemitism must be accompanied by a three-dimensional assessment of the social context in which antisemitism has flourished in certain times and places. Although antisemitic feeling was rooted in Christendom, the forms antisemitism has taken over the centuries, and the relationship between those forms, are the products of specific social realities that change over time and across space. On many occasions, antisemitism has been an expression of cultural anxiety, an outlet for the annunciation of social tensions, and as such, it has shared structural and group-psychological similarities with social discourse about other anxiety-inducing groups, the "dangerous classes" on or beyond the margins of the social order.

I do not intend here to make a totalistic, reductionist argument attributing antisemitism to economic factors alone. Such an approach evinces a naive belief in the rationality of human behavior, and it is no surprise that the first statements of such a view (which I analyze in chapter 4) came in the rationalist and positivist historiography that came into vogue in Europe in the mid-1800s. Rather, I wish here to demonstrate the power of economic themes in antisemitic discourse, particularly in the rhetoric of the modern state, its ruling elites, and its acolytes. Moreover, I wish to demonstrate the intriguing form assumed by modern economic antisemitism, a double helix of intersecting paradigms, the first associating the Jew with paupers and savages and the second conceiving of Jews as conspirators, leaders of a financial cabal seeking global domination. This double helix was formed by the cultural, political, social, and economic revolutions that convulsed Europe over the century between the Enlightenment and the Revolution of 1848.

A note on nomenclature: scholars differ in the terms they employ to describe anti-Jewish sentiment in various times and places. Some use the term *antisemitism* indiscriminately; others restrict their focus to modernity, to the era when Jew-hatred became an "ism"—that is, an all-embracing and all-explaining secular belief system.[2] In between are those who claim the existence of a critical point in European history, ante-dating modern times, when Jew-hatred took a new direction and pointed the way toward modern antisemitic discourse. This point is most commonly mapped onto western Europe during the High Middle Ages, with the birth of stereotypes of Jews as possessed of preternatural and malevolent power.[3] Since this chapter focuses on modern times, with background material from the High Middle Ages, I have used the term "antisemitism" throughout.

Economic Antisemitism in Historical Perspective

Antisemitism has been, in any time and place, a complex phenomenon consisting of many components. In most situations, an economic component has been present, at times dominant. In Europe, where culture was profoundly influenced by Christianity, economic antisemitism was in part the product of the representation of Jews in Christian texts as the embodiment of avarice. This representation began with the Gospels, in which the critique of the Pharisees as legalistic and hypocritical is undergirded by accusations of greed and materialism. Through certain stories, such as that of Jesus driving the moneychangers out of the Temple compound, or of Judas's betrayal of Jesus for thirty pieces of silver, not only the Pharisees but the Jews as a whole were associated with a stifling and pernicious materialism.

Thus the origins of economic antisemitism cannot be confined to a particular social or economic reality, that is, the concentration of Jews in low-status occupations such as commerce or the money trade.

Medieval images of the Jew as oppressor and parasite were nourished by not only Jewish economic activity, and specific anxieties about that activity, but also a generalized belief, rooted in Christian theology, in an inveterate Jewish misanthropy, a misanthropy so great that the Jews killed their own messiah and deny him anew every day. Although this association among Jews, materialism, and misanthropy originated in a theological matrix, it survived intact into the modern period and reso-nated within a number of secular ideologies. This point is noteworthy because not all forms of medieval antisemitism experienced a similar fate.

The more fantastic aspects of medieval antisemitism, which include the demonization of the Jews and accusations of ritual murder and black magic, were, to some extent, suppressed by the combined forces of Prot-estantism and the modern state. Both sought, to use Max Weber's ter-minology, to rationalize and "disenchant" the world, that is, to remove the element of magic from humanity's understanding of the order of things and how individuals can affect them.[4] As is well known, the sup-pression was incomplete and temporary. In Germany, the Protestant movement's attempts to suppress chimeric antisemitism actually pro-duced the opposite effect; the failure of Martin Luther and his followers to bring about a massive Jewish conversion to Christianity led to ex-pressions by some Protestant clerics in the sixteenth century of an in-eradicable and eternal Jewish propensity to evil.[5] A racial element figured in Enlightenment discourse on the Jews in France and Germany; it be-came more pronounced in Germany after the Napoleonic Wars and became virulent throughout much of Europe in the late nineteenth cen-tury.

Economic antisemitism, on the other hand, never experienced eclipse because, over time, it has fit as well into a rationalized worldview as a magical one, into a secular sensibility as well as a theological one. From the thirteenth through seventeenth centuries, Jewish usury was part of a tableau of chimeric accusations such as well poisoning and ritual mur-der. In the eighteenth century Jewish economic behavior became part of a discourse on Jewish poverty, criminality, and parasitism, that is, rationally explicable, albeit noxious, behaviors whose correction was en-trusted to temporal authority for the benefit of civil society.

Economic antisemitism represented an extreme form of the antimer-cantile sentiments that are rooted in pagan antiquity and the early Chris-tian tradition. Plato believed that commercial activity stimulated an im-moderate, hence unhealthy, lust for material gain. Accordingly, his *Republic* accepts merchants as a necessary evil but does not include them among the productive orders of society.[6] This discomfort with commercial activity received systematic treatment at the hand of Aristotle, whose *Politics* begins with an analysis of economics in its literal sense: household management, from the Greek *oikonomika*. Household management is synonymous with agriculture and crafts, which produce "natural riches," limited by the productive capacity of the household and designed to provide only for the family's needs. Retail trade, in contrast, has no limits and no fixed goal save for further acquisition. Whereas household management is "necessary and honorable," retail trade is "unnatural," and trade in money is even more so, because money "was intended to be used in exchange, but not to increase at interest."[7] Aristotle's economic views became a staple of ancient Greek social philosophy. The pseudo-Aristotelian *Oeconomica* praised agriculture as the greatest of the economic arts "because of its justice, for it does not take anything away from men, either with their consent, as do retail trading and the mercenary arts, or against their will, as do the warlike arts."[8] Although classical Roman culture did not share the *Oeconomica*'s critique of the martial arts, it did esteem agriculture and express ambivalence toward commerce; the Latin *negotatio* could mean "cheating" as well as "honest trade."[9]

In early medieval Christianity, Greco-Roman traditions, combined with the moralistic and otherworldly sentiments of the early church, produced a deep hostility toward trade. "No Christian," wrote the fourth-century saint John Chrysostom, "ought to be a merchant, or if he should wish to be one, he ought to be ejected from the Church of God."[10] Such attitudes were common throughout the early Middle Ages, and they were enshrined in a major compilation of canon law, the mid-twelfth-century *Decretum* of Gratian.[11]

The *Decretum* was more a summary of previously held views than a prescription for future doctrine or practice. From the turn of the millennium, the expansion of towns and trade in western Europe pressured the church to alter its economic views, and revisions came in the thirteenth century. Thomas Aquinas perpetuated some of the earlier views when he wrote that trade "has a certain debasement attaching thereto, in so far as, by its very nature, it does not imply a virtuous or necessary end." On the other hand, he observed, trade is not inherently evil, as honest merchants supply real needs, and there is such a thing as *honestus questus*, honest profit.[12] This cautiously approving attitude toward commerce also characterized the new mendicant orders that were housed in urban areas, unlike the rural monastic orders of earlier periods, and, despite their vows of poverty, were sensitive to the rights and interests of tradesmen. Francis of Assisi, the founder of the Franciscan order, was seen as the patron saint of urban merchants. Similarly, the Franciscan friar Bernardino of Siena (1380–1444) claimed that commercial success required not only piety and diligence but also careful bookkeeping and a willingness to take risks.[13]

Ironically, the development of capitalism in the early modern period served to mute as well as strengthen the procapitalist voices among the intelligentsia of Christendom. The onset of capitalism provoked considerable anxiety among many clerics, who projected their insecurities onto Jews, both a necessary and feared component of the new economic order.[14] Anticommercialism could be connected, as shown in a recent study of fourteenth-century Italy, to a visceral antiurbanism, an anxiety about the anonymity of the city and the crassness and self-promotion necessary for successful negotiation of a large, competitive urban space.[15] Or it could be linked to the agrarian ethos of modern utopianism, which emerged in sixteenth-century Italy and England.[16]

On the level of popular, as opposed to elite, culture we do not encounter anticommercialism so much as a fear of instability or rupture in the sphere of mercantile relations. Guild structures, which regulated the production and distribution of goods and competition between economic agents, existed for merchants as well as for craftsmen in early modern Europe. Christian merchants, convinced of the honor and utility of their livelihood, heaped calumny on Jews not because the latter were merchants but because they were competitors. Jewish competition was particularly distressing because of the alleged Jewish practices of cutting profit margins to the bone, selling a wide variety of wares and engaging in many different enterprises simultaneously, and aggressively seeking customers.

Economic antisemitism was not, however, merely an expression of hostility toward a competitor in a trade that in and of itself enjoyed high status. Precisely because Jews were excluded from the merchant guilds, as well as most crafts and large-scale agriculture, they concentrated in low-status forms of trade such as dealing in secondhand goods, peddling, pawnbroking, and, most significant, moneylending. The main forces promoting Jewish moneylending in the Middle Ages were the rise of a Christian bourgeoisie, on the one hand, and the material interests of princes and prelates, on the other. With the growth of towns in the ninth and tenth centuries, Jewish merchants were gradually displaced by Christians. To be sure, Jewish involvement in trade continued throughout the Middle Ages; similarly, despite the exclusion from Christian crafts guilds, many Jews continued to work in a number of crafts. Nonetheless, in the High Middle Ages, most Jews in western Europe engaged to some extent in moneylending.[17]

The economic forces pushing Jews out of other occupations were matched by others pulling them into the money trade. Temporal leaders, including the ecclesiastical rulers of towns and estates, encouraged Jews to practice moneylending in their dominions. Until the thirteenth century, Jews in western Europe were indispensable sources of capital for major construction projects (including cathedrals) and military campaigns. Since the security for such major loans was a landed estate, Jews found themselves at times, as in England in the 1200s, coming into possession, in the case of defaulted loans, of vast properties, thus provoking the wrath of the nobility, which, accurately enough, saw the Jews as the agents of the king. A further source of tension, also developing in the 1200s, came when Jews were gradually displaced by Christians as the lenders of funds to princes and prelates. Jews tended to concentrate in relatively small-scale consumer lending, which involved high rates of interest—often between 20 and 50 percent and at times more than 80 percent—because of the general scarcity of capital, the substantial risk of default or annulment by the authorities, and the Jews' heavy tax burdens.[18]

For medieval clerics, Jewish usury was an evil in itself and a symbol of the corruption of secular authority and, at times, ecclesiastical authority as well. These factors, combined with the profound religious animosity that so many clerics felt toward Jews, stimulated a hysterical anger on the part of many late-medieval clerics toward Jewish usury. That said, even among the highest levels of the canonical theorists there were voices that justified usury and its practice by Jews. They followed the teachings of Saint Ambrose of Milan (340–97) that usury could be legally imposed "against whom you rightly desire to harm, against whom weapons are lawfully carried. . . . From him exact usury whom it would not be a crime to kill. . . . Where there is the right of war, there is also the right of usury." Just as any enemy of Christendom (e.g., heretics, Saracens, or Jews) could be charged usurious interest on a loan by a Christian, by extension, Jews, who were thought to be in a state of war against Christians, were permitted to practice usury against them. At the Fourth Lateran Council (1215), "heavy or immoderate usuries" by Jews, not charging interest itself, were singled out for condemnation.[19]

Jewish moneylending in the later Middle Ages fulfilled a despised but necessary public service. The toleration of Jewish moneylending in medieval and Renaissance western Europe represented a crude form of social policy, for it increased the flow of cash to the poor without having to raise taxes or overhaul the administration of poor relief.[20] Precisely because of the religious barriers between Jew and Christian, the church could more easily tolerate Jewish usury than that practiced openly by Christians. It was commonly argued that because the Jews are already damned, they may be left to commit the sin of usury, thereby saving the souls of Christians who might otherwise engage in this activity. Indeed, Christian moneylenders experienced significant social opprobrium. Merchants from northern Italy who, during the thirteenth century, began practicing usury in France, were denounced in popular literature as devouring monsters, denied Christian burial due to their disregard for canon law, and subject, like the Jews, to expulsions in the fourteenth century.[21]

Not only did some medieval canonists justify Jewish usury against Christians, they also recognized the legitimacy of profit earned on commercial, as opposed to consumer, loans. Canonists formulated dozens of legal fictions that justified the taking of interest through arrangements such as a sham partnership, in which the creditor contributes funds to the debtor's enterprise, earning a guaranteed return on his "investment." And the Franciscans' justification of the taking of moderate levels of interest (5 to 10 percent) on consumer loans, as in the *monti di pietà* (church-sponsored loan banks) in Italy, was overt and unashamed. San Bernardino claimed that "[m]oney has not simply the character of money, but it has beyond this a productive character, which we commonly call capital."[22] This same friar was notorious for his fiery Judeophobic sermons, in which Jewish usury figured prominently.[23] Bernardino's anger stemmed in part from the high interest rates that Jews charged the Christian faithful, but more from the symbolic power of the usurious loan as a vehicle of Jewish domination over Christians.

Both clerics and merchants vilified Jewish usury, but neither party necessarily had contact with Jewish moneylenders. Merchants encountered Jews as business competitors; clerics encountered them as disputants, potential converts, or, most often, chimerical figures—demons who were existential enemies of Christendom and of the church. Associations between the Jews and usury may have originated in the concrete historical reality of the High Middle Ages but thereafter broke from their moorings and entered the realm of fantasy. Jewish usury became the cynosure of a constellation of antisemitic mentalities: a manifest act pointing to esoteric, malignant practices, an allegory for the *bellum iudaeorum contra omnes*. In *The Entire Jewish Belief* (1530), the Jewish convert Anton Margaritha claimed that "the practice of usury was the central obstacle to the conversion of Jews." Only by being forced to perform manual labor could the Jews be weaned of their noxious habit, drained of their inveterate arrogance, and drawn to the Christian faith.[24] The trope of the usurious Jew runs through Martin Luther's notorious screed *On the Jews and Their Lies* (1543), which concludes with thundering demands that the secular authorities not only suppress the Jews' religious practice but also ban usury and compel them to work in agriculture and handicrafts as punishment for their allegedly criminal behavior.[25]

As is well known from the example of Shakespeare's Shylock, the stereotype of the Jewish usurer retained resonance even in lands from which Jews had been expelled in the late Middle Ages. It persisted with a vengeance in the German lands, despite the growing acceptance, from the mid-1500s, of moneylending in Protestant culture.[26] Nor was it affected by the decline in the 1600s of Jewish moneylending in Germany. Reductions in the maximum allowable interest rates from approximately 33 percent to somewhere between 5 and 12 percent made moneylending unprofitable for all but the wealthiest Jews. This factor, combined with steady inflation resulting from the import of specie from the New World, pushed many Jews in Germany into commerce.[27] As the majority of German Jewry fell into poverty, a minuscule minority grew wealthy through international commerce and purveying to armies. The increasingly anachronistic image of the Jewish usurer blended with two developing forms of economic antisemitism: fantasies about the Jewish thief, leeching off the populace from below, and the Court Jew, the manipulator from above.

As a result of the expulsions from the empire in the fifteenth and sixteenth centuries, the percentage of the poor among German Jewry increased dramatically, and there emerged a class of impoverished vagrants known as *Schalantjuden*, or, in Hebrew, *archei u-farchei* (flotsam and jetsam).[28] In the 1500s, this group was relatively small, but by the end of the next century, Jewish vagrancy had become a serious social problem for the Jewish communities of Germany, Austria, Bohemia, and Moravia. High taxes, restricted settlement rights and occupational choices, natural increase, and waves of refugees fleeing persecution in Poland created a mass of what came to be known from the late 1600s onward as *Betteljuden*.[29] In the mid-1700s, as many as two-thirds of the sixty thousand Jews in Germany lived in poverty.[30] The wretched economic condition of the Jews in the empire encouraged criminal activity. Their concentration in pawnbroking and petty trade made burglary particularly enticing because of the relative ease with which purloined goods could be fenced and marketed. The rise of Jewish banditry from the late 1600s added new contours to economic antisemitism, and a new stereotype emerged, that of the Jews as a people of thieves and robbers extraordinaire.[31]

Fear of the Jewish bandit, an emotion mixed with some level of admiration for his allegedly awesome prowess, blended with similar feelings about Court Jews, a cluster of Jews who, from the time of the Thirty Years' War through the mid-1700s, served the royal courts of the German lands as purveyors and financiers.[32] In a time and place when states had only the crudest taxation mechanisms and there was no public credit, Jews were an essential source of funds and services that the state could not provide through its own apparatus. Court Jews flourished in the German lands, where monarchs seeking to rule absolutely were embroiled in conflict with entrenched estates. Social pariahs living on sufferance, Jews were ideal vehicles for royal ambition because they posed no threat to the monarch. The chief impetus for the rise of the Court Jew was the increased number and scope of military operations during the intraimperial conflicts of the mid-seventeenth through mid-eighteenth century. Jews proved useful not only for providing militaristic monarchs with a war chest but also for provisioning the army with victuals, horses, and uniforms. Jewish moneylenders and pawnbrokers in the German lands were an essential source of the specie provided by the Court Jews, just as connections with Jewish grain merchants in Poland facilitated the supply of foodstuffs.

The Holy Roman Empire was not the only site of Jewish purveying to armies and royal courts. Holland, Britain, Spain, and Portugal—all made use of Sephardic financiers and contractors. A mercantile people with a far-flung diaspora, Jews throughout Europe were well situated to import raw materials and luxury goods from Poland, the Levant, and the European overseas colonies to the Iberian Peninsula, northern Europe, and Italy.[33] Yet, despite the ubiquity of the Jewish provisioner, the "Court Jew" remained primarily a German phenomenon. Whereas other, more centralized European lands had only one court, the Holy Roman Empire had hundreds. Here, "enlightened administration stood in the foreground; in Holland and England, on the other hand, private initiative prevailed."[34] Finally, in the German lands, as opposed to the other center of Jewish court purveying, Holland, the Jewish contractor's right of residence was not secure but was rather a privilege bought with service to the court. The Court Jew possessed great wealth and at times wielded influence at court, but his power was evanescent, depending on the goodwill of his royal protector.

The Court Jew's wealth and association with the monarch made him highly visible and vulnerable, an ideal target for popular discontent in the war-torn German lands. Popular literature in early-eighteenth-century Germany conflated the powerful Court Jew with the poor Jewish criminal to form an antisemitic collage of the Jew as manipulator and profiteer.[35] The Court Jew and the Jewish bandit were typologically similar; both were pariahs who, coming from the margins of German society, used unconventional methods to improve their status.[36] Anti-semitic sensibility grasped this similarity but, by placing it within a pre-established stereotype of the Jew as usurer, merely transformed and strengthened preexisting prejudices against Jewish economic behavior.

The thief and the purveyor, the beggar and the banker, form two sides of the same coin, the common currency of modern economic an-tisemitism. The juxtaposition of the two images is not wholly illogical, for they are based on the reality of the Jew as both marginalized and empowered within the European economy. The Jews, excluded from the European corporate order, had by and large fallen into destitution, yet they continued to perform necessary, albeit disdained, services as peddlers and moneylenders. A minuscule minority of wealthy Jews, who, unlike the Gentile elites, placed no strings on their provision of money and material to ambitious monarchs, were accordingly feared, envied, and despised.

Let us speak of two paradigms of economic antisemitism: that of the Jew as manipulating conspirator and as parasitical pauper. Both myths had multiple origins and targets. The first paradigm accommodated not only Ashkenazic Court Jews in the German lands but also Sephardic Jewish merchants and manufacturers in western Europe and in the Ot-toman Empire. (From the sixteenth century, the growing Sephardic presence in the Ottoman Empire, combined with the Turks' political and commercial rivalry with Europe, stimulated in many lands a new myth of Jewish conspiratorial power, based less on religious motifs than on economic ones, drawing on notions of the Sephardic Jewish mer-chant and manufacturer as a mighty economic force behind the successes of the Turkish foe.)[37] And the paradigm of the Jew as pauper, although most often associated with the Jewish usurer or peddler, could take on unusual forms, as seen in a remarkable work of 1700, *On the Diseases of Workers*, by the Mantuan physician Bernardino Ramazzini.

Ramazzini's work on occupational hazards is divided into chapters based on more than fifty livelihoods (mining, wet-nursing, stonecutting, etc.). The one exception is "Jews," who are defined according to their occupations, as if there are certain occupations that only Jews perform and Jews perform only certain occupations. That is, Jews are defined in economic as much as religious or ethnic terms.[38] The occupations, most likely those practiced by the Jews of Modena whom Ramazzini would have had the opportunity to observe, were rag picking, tailoring, the purchase and sale of old clothes, and mattress carding. Ramazzini describes a people living in abject poverty but possessed by avarice: "[T]hey are a lazy race, but active in business; they do not plough, harrow, or sow, but they always reap. . . . They are always open-mouthed for money."[39] No longer a demon, or even a stiff-necked denier of Christ, the Jew has been reduced to a wretched creature, a pest, whose unquenchable greed would be laughable were he not so pathetic.

Significantly, Ramazzini focuses on the environmental origins of the Jews' woes, that is, on the close work and foul vapors that render them infirm. His suggestion that the Jews' wretchedness is at least in part environmentally induced—therefore, that Jews are, to some degree, corrigible—reflects both his own environmentalist approach to pathology in general and his specific contribution to a new, meliorist discourse on the Jews that emerged in the seventeenth century. Mainstream Christian thinking had long held that conversion to Christianity would rid the Jews of their evil inclinations, but this argument rested on a notion of transformation by means of inward, spiritual rebirth, not external, environmental transformation. Conversion, that is, was the necessary and sufficient precondition for improvement of the Jewish character. However, as recent studies of England, Germany, and Spain have shown, powerful voices throughout Christian Europe, from the late Middle Ages through the early modern period, contended that Jewish conversions to Christianity were opportunistic and mendacious and that Jewish malevolence was intractable.[40]

That said, a different approach, advocating toleration of the Jews, was also at work in the seventeenth and eighteenth centuries. This viewpoint employed arguments grounded in moral philosophy and political economy to demonstrate that improvement of the Jews' environment would improve their moral character, rendering them more rational and useful beings. Accordingly, Enlightenment discourse on the Jews focused more on the image of the Jewish pauper and less on the Jewish financier, who was thought to provide useful service for the state.

Moralism, Mercantilism, and Cameralism

During the seventeenth and eighteenth centuries, calls for toleration of the Jews drew on many justifications. The religious wars of the sixteenth century left the champions of Catholicism and Protestantism in deadlock, prompting statesmen and philosophers to accept the principle of religious pluralism. Pragmatically based pluralism stimulated some philosophers to formulate new theories of government, based on a separation of church and state and natural social laws applicable not only to Protestants and Catholics alike but even to non-Christians, foremost among them Jews. Thus pragmatic and idealistic motives were inextricably linked in the creation of the concept of *raison d'état*, that is, of the primacy of the state and the consonance between its interests and those of its inhabitants.[41]

A similar blend of pragmatic, theological, and moralistic justification characterized discussions of the improvement of the Jews through an alteration of their occupational structure. The concept of the Jew as corrigible rests on a broader Enlightenment paradigm of man as a meliorating force and a meliorable object. Central to this paradigm is the constructive power of labor as a means of not only environmental transformation but also internal perfection. The classical and Christian traditions, despite their lyrical praise for agriculture, expressed conflicting views about manual labor, which could be seen as both an act of *imitatio dei* and a punishment for man's original sin. In Germany the Protestant revivalist movement known as Pietism, which originated in the late 1600s, adopted an unambiguous view of labor as a sanctifying and salvific force. Notions of work as a vehicle of spiritual redemption also enjoyed currency in French philanthropic projects of the period. In the following century, Enlightenment philosophy in France and the German lands maintained this veneration for labor, but moral elevation, the attainment of earthly happiness, and social utility blended with spiritual perfection as the consequences of work.[42] Thus German Pietists such as August Hermann Francke campaigned against begging and established workhouses in order to simultaneously salvage and productivize the poor of all faiths.

The association between piety and morality, on the one hand, and productive labor, on the other, was a major influence on programs, first raised in the late 1600s, for the amelioration of the Jews. In the 1680s, the founder of the German Pietist movement, Philip Jakob Spener, called on the Jews to undergo an occupational change from moneylending and peddling to farming. Although complaints about Jewish usury were far from novel, there was a humanitarian quality to Spener's thinking that had been missing from earlier discussion on the subject. Unlike the father of the Reformation, Martin Luther, Spener focused less on the evil effects of usury on the Christian populace than on its adverse impact on the Jewish character. Moreover, unlike Luther, Spener did not dwell on the immorality of usury. The problem with a livelihood centered on moneylending, he wrote, was that it failed to assure the Jews a decent living. Agriculture, he claimed, would grant the Jews an honest and secure existence. This security would elevate them morally and improve their rational faculties; as rational beings, they would perforce perceive the truth of Christianity. Thus, whereas Luther wanted to punish the Jews through labor, Spener hoped to use it to elevate them. When Spener wrote of the need for Jewish "rebirth," he meant an inward, spiritual process with an external manifestation: The reborn Jew would look and act differently; he would practice an honest trade and be thrifty, industrious, and productive.[43] Just as for the Calvinist economic success was an outward sign of divine grace, so for the Pietist it was an outward sign of moral improvement.

We encounter a similarly spiritual justification for Jewish occupational restructuring in France. In the 1680s, Claude Fleury wrote a book titled *The Customs of the Israelites,* which claimed that both Talmudic Judaism and usury represented perversions of the ancient biblical order, in which the Jews farmed the land and practiced a pure religion. A Jewish return to the soil would, of itself, cause Jews to slough off talmudism, return to their biblical roots, and, in time, convert to Christianity.[44] The conversionary impulse remained present in much Enlightenment writing on the Jews. For example, Henri Grégoire's famous *Essay on the Physical, Moral, and Political Improvement of the Jews* (1789), whose economic aspects are discussed below, was inspired by a millenarian fervor that saw in social reform the first step toward divine redemption.[45]

Although grounded in a belief in a universal human potential for perfection, positive evaluations of the Jews during the seventeenth and eighteenth centuries often focused on allegedly distinctive Jewish qualities that could bring a particular benefit to their host societies. For the likes of Spener and Fleury, the conversion to Christianity that would follow on the heels of amelioration of the Jews' status would bring about the Second Coming. More modest goals characterized the growing numbers, from the mid-seventeenth century, of Gentile Hebraists, who considered the Hebrew language and postbiblical Hebrew literature invaluable tools for better understanding of the Christian Scriptures. But by far the most significant, specific feature of the Jews that rendered them desirable to the ruling and intellectual elites in seventeenth- and eighteenth-century Europe was their economic utility.

The question of the Jews' economic utility or noxiousness was central to public discussion and policy making about the Jews throughout this period. Evidence of this centrality appears in an essay of 1714, *Reasons for Naturalizing the Jews in Great Britain and Ireland,* by the Anglo-Irish deist John Toland (1670–1722). Although Toland employed concepts such as freedom of conscience and the separation of church and state in his plea for the naturalization of foreign-born Jews living in the British Isles, he also relied heavily on claims that Jews brought unusual economic benefits to the lands that gave them shelter.[46] If economic argumentation played so large a role in the reasoning of a deist, for whom, one might suppose, the principle of toleration could be justified on philosophical grounds alone, how much more so would the thinking of bureaucrats and other servants of the state be guided by economic considerations.

The economic concept most often employed in scholarship on early modern European Jewry is "mercantilism." Like all abstract classificatory nouns, *mercantilism* lends itself to multiple, and conflicting, definitions. It can refer to all economic policies pursued in the spirit of *raison d'état* or to trade and tariff policies alone. Mercantilist sensibilities can be associated with emphases on commerce or on domestic manufacture and with the promotion of commerce in any form or with a specific policy of encouraging exports and discouraging imports to maximize the amount of specie in the realm.[47] An equally eclectic, but perhaps more useful, term is "cameralism" (from the Latin *camera,* royal chamber), which was widely used in eighteenth-century Germany and Austria to describe the science of economic management. At first referring to the royal domain, by the mid-1700s the term had come to refer to the state's resources as a whole, that is, to the national economy. *Kameralwissenschaft,* a well-defined academic discipline by the late 1700s, sought to maximize the wealth of the nation through all available means, although agriculture and manufacture tended to be favored more than foreign commerce.[48] Economic strength was a precondition for stable, well-ordered government. Thus economic science and administrative science (*Polizeiwissenschaft*) were linked. The deliberate eclecticism of eighteenth-century economic policy, especially in Austria and Germany, but in France as well, has not been fully appreciated by Jewish historians, with the result that specific policies toward the Jews have been analyzed out of context.

In his seminal and widely influential book, *The French Enlightenment and the Jews* (1968), Arthur Hertzberg posited a causal link between general economic doctrines and attitudes toward the Jews in late-eighteenth-century France. He claimed that during the 1770s, mercantilism, which stressed the economic benefits of commerce and thus was appreciative of the Jews, fell out of vogue in France and was replaced by a new economic doctrine known as physiocracy, which favored agriculture and thus criticized the Jews' occupational profile. Not only in France, argued Hertzberg, but also in Germany and Austria, physiocratic thinking contributed significantly to the negative opinion of Jewish economic behavior held by bureaucrats and scholars and added yet another layer to the arguments in support of a Jewish occupational restructuring from commerce to farming and crafts.[49]

Since the publication of Hertzberg's work, historians have described Gentile critiques of Jewish economic behavior as "physiocratic" in nature.[50] Is this true? Let us clarify what physiocracy in fact was: an economic system based on, as its name suggests, "the rule of nature" and therefore emphasizing free trade as opposed to protectionism. It was one of the major intellectual sources for the teachings of Adam Smith. But unlike Smith, the French physiocrats argued that commerce was "sterile," that is, not productive of surplus value (i.e., sale price less the cost of reproduction of the commodity and its producer). Only agriculture and, to a lesser extent, manufacture genuinely contributed to the national economy.

As one might expect from such a rigid economic doctrine, physiocracy played only a minor role in the formulation of economic policy in general, and Jewish policy in particular, in western and central Europe in the second half of the 1700s.[51] In France, where the doctrine originated, its heyday was brief, a decade or so at midcentury. Its principal novel features, an emphasis on free trade and the call for a single tax based on land rent, were rarely implemented on the Continent.[52] Its emphasis on natural economic law and apotheosis of land above all other sources of national wealth went against the grain of cameralism, which was invasive and eclectic.[53] Moreover, eighteenth-century economic doctrines as a whole, not physiocracy alone, tended to favor the productive over the distributive sector of the economy. This was especially so in the German lands; until the mid-1700s, economic literature focused on estate management and the term *economics* referred solely to the products of nature.[54] This concentration on agriculture was not the product of ideological bias so much as it was a response to the very real needs of lands still scarred by the ravages of the Thirty Years' War, lands whose peasantry formed the vast majority of the population and which was, by and large, incapable of any but the most marginal of existences. Conversely, the interest of eighteenth-century absolutist monarchs in Germany and Austria in rural crafts and the foundation of manufactories stemmed from an overarching concern with the plight of the marginalized and frequently pauperized peasant.[55]

It is in this context that we can appreciate the two most important texts on the status of the Jews produced during the late Enlightenment: Christian Wilhelm von Dohm's *On the Civil Improvement of the Jews* (1781–83) and Grégoire's *Essay on the Physical, Moral, and Political Improvement of the Jews.*[56] Dohm's tract on the improvement of the Jews appeared against the background of treatises on sundry ways, such as the promotion of bee keeping and silkworm raising, to increase the productivity of the common folk of Prussia.[57] Grégoire's tract on the Jews was written for a prize essay contest that solicited entries on how to make the Jews "happy and more useful in France." The previous year's contest had requested suggestions for the better utilization of illegitimate children.[58] Bastards, bees, and Jews were all to be mobilized for the benefit of the economy of the absolutist state.

Dohm, a councillor in the Prussian bureaucracy, was a classic cameralist, seeking to maximize the capacity of the state economy through all appropriate means. In his writing, morality and profitability were inseparable; *Sittlichkeit* (morality), independent of religion, is the glue holding together civil society, and corrupt individuals cannot be productive ones. The Jews, Dohm believed, had fallen into corruption due in part to the oppressive conditions under which they had lived for centuries but especially to their occupational concentration in commerce, which encouraged criminality and an overly competitive and acquisitive spirit. In keeping with the meliorist spirit of the Enlightenment, Dohm believed that the Jews were corrigible but that strong tutelary measures would be necessary to bring about the desired reforms in their character. Legislation should limit the number of Jewish merchants in a geographic region or require that one son per family take up a craft for his livelihood.[59]

Dohm's program for Jewish economic regeneration appears, at first glance, to be riddled with contradictions. On the one hand, he attached great importance to handicrafts as an activity that would simultaneously promote Jewish *Sittlichkeit* and profitability. On the other hand, he did not believe that Christian craft guilds should be required to accept Jewish masters.[60] Dohm believed that agriculture should be open to the Jews but offered the curious argument that it would be unlikely to promote Jewish regeneration because agriculture allegedly promoted a "spirit of profit and speculation" akin to commerce.[61] Dohm's program makes sense, however, when considered in the context of his generally cameralist and pragmatic orientation. He favored the abolition of guilds, which hindered the expansion of production, but believed that abolition was not at present feasible. Dohm's remarks about agriculture referred specifically to the ownership and leasing of large estates, which promoted an agrarian capitalism, sustained by a rural wage-earning class and harmful to the interests of a freeholding peasantry. Dohm's opposition to agrarian capitalism, which was one of the goals of physiocracy, is but one sign of his deep hostility to that system. Dohm opposed physiocracy's trade and taxation doctrines, and, most important for his theories about the Jews, he did not believe in the sterility of commerce.[62] For all his fantasies about Jewish corruption, Dohm praised the Jews' commercial abilities, and he envisioned only a reduction, not the elimination, of Jews in the distributive sector of the Prussian economy.[63]

Grégoire, a Jesuit priest from Lorraine, shared Dohm's moralistic utilitarianism, although Grégoire possessed a fervent millenarian and revolutionary spirit that the placid Prussian bureaucrat did not share. As with Dohm, economic issues were central to Grégoire's critique of the Jews; one-fourth of his book-length essay is devoted to a harsh and relentless attack against Jewish moneylending in Alsace and Lorraine. Arguing against the popular cameralist notion that the national wealth increases with population growth, Grégoire claimed that the Jewish population grows disproportionately rapidly because of their avoidance of celibacy and military service and that they bring the national economy little benefit because they are a nation of traders, not producers. To promote the moral improvement of the Jews and save the peasantry from a cycle of debt, Jewish usury must be heavily regulated and Jews must be allowed to sell goods for cash only. Increased Jewish participation in crafts production will lower prices, and a Jewish return to the soil will foster "pure manners" and probity.[64]

Despite his religiosity, Grégoire was very much a progenitor of the French Revolution, not only because of his social reformism, but also because of his belief in the power of the state to mold, uplift, and improve human beings. Grégoire was a French patriot, but as a native of a German-speaking province under French rule, he openly acknowledged that the French nation was still to be created. The Jews constituted one of many distinct bodies, including ethnic minorities and socioeconomic estates, to be first disbanded and then integrated into this new nation.[65] The Jews, like all others in France, were to undergo a process of regeneration.

The term *régénération,* which Jewish historiography tends to associate with the Jews alone, enjoyed wide currency and had multiple applications during the revolutionary period. It had vitalistic, moral, and economic qualities, connoting a "reborn race," "energetic and frugal."[66] In Germany, the notion of *Verbesserung* (improvement) was applied in liberal circles in the early 1800s not only to the Jews but also to the poor, the nobility, and ultramontane Catholics. Like the poor, Jews deserved certain basic rights, such as the protection of the rule of law, but needed to undergo a process of elevation and embourgeoisement before they could be worthy of political equality.[67]

The term *bürgerliche Verbesserung* (civil improvement), on the other hand, was only occasionally used outside of a Jewish context, but these rare cases are of interest nonetheless. It was used in the title of a pioneering work on the amelioration of the status of women, Theodor Gotlieb von Hippel's *Über die bürgerliche Verbesserung der Weiber* (1792). It is possible that Hippel borrowed the title phrase from Dohm, but the two works have little in common save for a generally environmentalist and meliorist approach to human imperfection. Hippel's portrayal of women is far more positive than Dohm's depiction of Jews; women are not described as morally degenerate but rather as unfulfilled. Hippel's evaluation of women's potential contributions to society is far higher than Dohm's opinion of the Jews' potential; at the same time, Hippel is far less utilitarian than Dohm, appealing primarily to notions of universal rights and obigations.[68]

Hippel's lack of utilitarian argument points to an important difference between Enlightenment discourse on Jews and on women in western Europe. Whereas the emancipation of the former, however problematic and painful, was widely discussed and, eventually, partially implemented, the emancipation of the latter rarely encountered serious consideration. Jewish emancipation, like that of the peasantry, was a necessity given the modern state's abolition of corporatist structures, reliance on free labor, and striving for a religiously neutral public sphere. The modern state depended, however, on the maintenance of patriarchal domination and the relegation of women to circumscribed spheres of economic activity and cultural expression.[69] Jews, like peasants, produced wealth for the state and, if emancipated, might create a great deal more, whereas women produced children and, if emancipated, might (or so it was feared) have many fewer.

An additional, neglected, yet highly significant application of the terminology and conceptual framework of civil improvement appeared in public discussion in the German lands about internal reform within the Catholic Church. The Catholic Enlightenment was in good part a theological movement, dedicated to rationalist theology and open to historical analysis, but it featured a pronounced political-economic strain as well. Educational reform in the Hapsburg Empire under Joseph II was spearheaded by Johann Ignaz von Felbiger, a Reform Catholic who rationalized the church calendar and established spinning schools for the rural folk to increase their productivity.[70] The monastic orders were a prominent target of criticism, and in 1783, the year the second volume of Dohm's tract was published, there appeared *Über die bürgerliche und geistliche Verbesserung des Mönchwesens,* by Peter Adolph Winkopp (1759–1813), a Benedictine monk who, in the spirit of the radical Catholic Enlightenment, broke away from the order, became a bureaucrat and publicist, and wrote novels and tracts exposing the compound evils of the cloistered life.[71]

In his book of 1783, Winkopp excoriated the monastic orders, employing language remarkably similar to that employed by critics of the Jews. Monastic orders, he argued, constitute a state within a state, and the monks' vows of obedience to their superiors render them incapable of being citizens of the state in which they live. *Mönch* and *Mensch* are mutually exclusive; "the man who would be a perfect monk would be the most imperfect man."[72] They are simultaneously both wealthy and impoverished—wealthy in that they amass vast amounts of capital but poor in that most of their members lead a beggarly life. The vast treasures sequestered in the monastery's vaults constitute dead capital, of no benefit to the state. Winkopp's description of the *Bettelmönche* resembles popular images of *Betteljuden:* possessed of an "unquenchable thirst for money," savage and rapacious.[73] Unproductivity and immorality are closely linked; the monk's vow of poverty leads to laziness and avarice, and his dedication to chastity, in addition to denying the state the next generation of peasants and laborers, promotes onanism, that is, the spending of seed, the most egregious and shocking form of waste.[74] (Grégoire accused the Jews of a predilection for onanism, although he did not fret that their fertility might suffer thereby; quite the contrary, he and his contemporaries perceived Jews as threatening for their alleged fecundity.)

For Winkopp, the radical Reform Catholic whose gaze was fixed firmly on the monastery, the Jews are vastly preferable to his erstwhile brethren. The Jewish religion, he argues, does not in any way work against the interests of the state; more important, the Jews are "useful subjects." "Monks can certainly not demand as much tolerance as Jews. For the latter are loyal and active citizens, bearing the burden of the state; monks, on the other hand, are subjects of a foreign lord, inactive freeloaders, who enjoy all the advantages of the citizen, even more so, and yet do not help carry even one of the latter's burdens."[75]

Thus monks, for Winkopp, should become more like Jews. Monasteries should become state property; some should be turned into workhouses for the poor, others into schools. A new generation of monks and nuns will arise, industrious and patriotic. They will marry and sire offspring, and in both their intimate life and daily labor they will fulfill the original function of the monastery, that is, to help the poor. Especially valued among the monks will be those with economic knowledge, for they will extend help to the simple rural folk in the face of an increasingly complex market economy.[76]

Winkopp's paean to Jewish utility was unusual, perhaps unique. It was more common for writers in the German lands to invoke utilitarian argumentation against the Jews than on their behalf. A number of writers in Germany disputed Dohm's central claim that Jews could be rendered useful beings. Occasionally one encounters an argument, such as that offered by Johann August Schlettwein several years before Dohm's book appeared, that the Jews are economically useless because middlemen are by definition noxious, lowering the profit margin of the producer and raising costs to the consumer.[77] More common views did not condemn commerce as such but questioned whether Jews were capable of becoming productive and enlightened subjects of the realm.[78] In a work of 1795, Ernst Traugott von Kortum argued not only that their faith and constitutions rendered the Jews incapable of any livelihood but commerce, but also, and more important (and in this he paralleled Winkopp's screed), that Jewish commerce is harmful because it removes wealth from general society and concentrates it in a separate Jewish entity.[79] The application of this latter argument to the Jews is as old as political economy itself, being made as early as 1615 by the individual who coined the term *political economy,* the mercantilist Antoine de Montchrétien.[80]

Economic theorists were of varied opinions regarding the value of the Jews, but the rhetoric on Jewish utility was more uniform among those social strata most likely to benefit or suffer from the Jewish commercial presence. Merchants did not want Jewish competition, and there are numerous examples from the late seventeenth through the early nineteenth century of merchant groups throughout Europe complaining that the Jews were ruining them, and by extension the nation as a whole.[81] Bureaucrats, by contrast, particularly in the upper echelons, tended to see Christian merchants as defending entrenched and localist interests and appreciated the lower prices and larger variety that the Jews brought to market.[82] This positive view, however, was usually restricted to prosperous Jewish manufacturers and wholesale merchants engaged in long-distance, particularly international, commerce.

Thus in France, the international economic activity of the Sephardim of Bordeaux and Bayonne endeared them to the Crown, and they were granted full commercial freedom in 1763. Policies toward the poorer Ashkenazim of Alsace and Lorraine were far more hostile. The 1784 *lettres patentes* from Louis XVI to Alsatian Jewry granted freedoms that few impoverished Jews could enjoy, such as the right to open factories and engage freely in large-scale commerce or banking. Traditional Jewish occupations such as the cattle and grain trade and moneylending required governmental approval.[83] Thus a pattern was set that would extend well into the revolutionary period and thereafter. In 1808 Napoléon Bonaparte issued the infamous *decret infame,* which severely restricted Jewish moneylending and commercial activity. Although it had various aspects, the *decret infame* was primarily a piece of economic legislation, directed against the poor Jews of the northeast; it exempted Jews from elsewhere in France and in French-occupied Italy because they were thought to be prosperous and productive.[84]

In Austria and Prussia, as in France, state policies on the Jews displayed far greater Judeophobia toward the poor Jewish masses than the minuscule economic elite. Even the policies regarding the Jewish economic elite, however, were dictated by a complex mix of rationally derived economic doctrine and irrational Judeophobia.

In the Hapsburg Empire, prosperous Jews who served the state as purveyors, leaseholders, tax farmers, manufacturers, and exporters enjoyed royal favor. Despite her intense Judeophobia, Empress Maria Theresa (r. 1740–80) encouraged Jewish commercial and industrial activity. Her successors esteemed Jewish bankers and *Grosshändler,* some of whom were ennobled, but the monarchs strove (with incomplete success) to limit the number of Jews in Vienna to a few hundred and did not authorize Vienna's Jews to constitute a public community until the Revolution of 1848.[85] Emperor Joseph II's Edicts of Toleration, issued for various parts of the empire between 1781 and 1789, were designed, like the French *lettres patentes* for Alsace, to maximize the Jewish contribution to large-scale commerce and enforce an occupational restructuring of the poor Jewish masses through tutelary legislation. Thus, although all forms of wholesale trade were now open to Jews, retail trade remained subject to strict quotas, as did family size. The 1789 extension of the edict to Galicia outlawed Jewish involvement in innkeeping, brewing, and leaseholding, thus sending streams of rural Jews into the towns. The emperor hoped that such Jews would take up crafts and agriculture, although the edicts placed many restrictions on Jewish purchases of rural property, and they failed to guarantee rights of residence or guild entry for Jewish craftsmen.[86]

At the same time, Galicia's backward economy occasionally forced Austrian officials to appreciate the essentiality of Jewish peddling in that region. Thus a district administrator in Sambor in the early days of Austrian rule in Galicia wrote:

Were it not for them, it would be impossible to procure even a strand of cotton or silken thread in the cities for the price of a few pennies. The estate owners would not sell their grain and linen, the peasants would be unable to buy on credit and thus obtain their most vital commodities. In this land, which is so lacking in diligence, they are the ones who influence its economy with a breath of life and serving all classes of the population.[87]

Similarly, the emperor Franz stated in 1795 to an imperial commission studying the status of the Jews:

Since peddling promotes and multiplies the more rapid trade of manufactured products in the hereditary lands for the benefit of the producers, and also creates the advantage for the greater part of consumers that they may obtain some wares more cheaply than in stores, and given that each individual is free to buy from a peddler or merchant, peddling thus belongs among the useful trades and livelihoods; thus one does not put an end to it because of abuses, which can creep into all human interactions, but rather only the abuses are to be dealt with.[88]

Such realistic evaluations of the Jews' distributive functions were not the norm, however, and Hapsburg bureaucratic discourse on Galician Jewry spoke more of parasitism than of economic benefit.

Bureaucratic animosity toward Jews was even stronger in Prussia. True, the Prussian kings Frederick William I (r. 1713–40) and his son Frederick II (r. 1740–86) looked to Jews as well as Huguenots to fund and manage the royal manufactories. Of the forty-six royal manufactories established under Frederick II's rule, thirty-seven were managed by Jews.[89] Unlike his father, Frederick II appreciated the necessity for a strong commercial network to promote the export of domestic produce and manufactured goods. As Jews dominated the commercial sector in Poland, and Poland was the natural target for Prussian luxury goods and a major source for necessary raw materials, Frederick accepted the necessity of their presence in Breslau, Königsberg, and other Prussian commercial centers.[90] But royal and bureaucratic ill will toward the Jews was palpable. The General Patent of 1750, which remained in force until the emancipation edict of 1812, severely limited the number of Jews admitted to the realm, and only a handful of the wealthiest Jews could purchase a perpetual right of residence for themselves and their families. Jews paid a variety of discriminatory taxes and were held collectively liable for their payment. Berlin's Huguenot colony, whose occupational structure was similar to that of the city's Jewish community, enjoyed a far securer and more equitable legal status and was not a target of opprobrium.[91]

Discrimination against Jewish merchants in Prussia took exceedingly complex forms, such as the careful enumeration of wares permitted or forbidden to them to purvey and the compulsory purchase of Prussian wares, which were often of inferior quality. The intricacy of this legislation indicates not only the obsession with order and detail that characterized cameralism as a whole but also a sense of the Jew as an essential but dangerous economic force that must be contained lest he wreak havoc. Jews, like overpowering thoroughbreds, were to be handicapped. So doing would protect Gentile merchants, benefit the state treasury through the taxes Jews paid, and, finally, force Jews to perform the riskiest of ventures that Gentiles could not or would not undertake.

In the cameralist worldview, the wealthy Jew was an accepted, albeit often despised, figure. The poor Jew, however, was rarely thought to play any useful economic role, and the level of vituperation directed against him was, therefore, all the greater. Enlightenment-era texts about the Jews abound with references to Jewish peddlers and moneylenders who not only fail to contribute to the national economy but also weaken it through theft, fraud, and usury. Let us keep in mind, however, that the poor as a whole, not only impoverished Jews, were a source of fear and worry to the elites in eighteenth-century Europe. Accordingly, governmental policies on the Jews must be set in the context of policies against the poor in general.

The Jew as Pauper

Pauperism was a major social problem in late-eighteenth-century western and central Europe. Overpopulation and the introduction of capitalist agriculture created a rural proletariat, whose members streamed into the cities, only to find access to crafts stymied by the urban guilds. In France, one-third to one-half of the population was poor or indigent; one-sixth of the population consisted of vagrants. In Germany, three-fourths of the peasantry led a marginal existence; one-seventh of the total population of Prussia were propertyless rural laborers.[92] The absolutist regimes, not content to allow hordes of beggars to roam the countryside, strove to limit their numbers through incarceration in closed institutions, antivagrancy legislation, and marriage restrictions.

These policies represented a culmination of centuries of gradually shifting attitudes toward poverty and the poor. In the classical Christian tradition, wealth and poverty were both thought to be the result of divine decree more than human agency. The church taught that those who were materially poor enriched humanity, first through their own suffering, but even more by giving the well-to-do the opportunity to gain salvation through the generous giving of alms. As early as the thirteenth century, however, canonists developed conceptual distinctions between the worthy and the unworthy poor, the former including the infirm and the "shame-faced poor" (upper-crust folk who had fallen on hard times), the latter including vagabonds and layabouts. It was only in the 1500s, however, when inflation and overpopulation sent hordes of starveling paupers into the cities, that rationalized poor care began to replace the indiscriminate distribution of alms. Throughout western Europe, municipalities centralized poor relief, expelled the alien poor, banned begging, and employed the able-bodied poor in public works. By the mid-1600s, poverty was likened to a crime, punishable by incarceration in a workhouse, where hard labor was seen simultaneously as a form of punishment and as a vehicle of salvation and moral regeneration. In the eighteenth century, these harsh views were softened somewhat by Enlightenment meliorism, but government officials and the

European intelligentsia continued to look upon the poor with fear and suspicion.[93]

Well into the nineteenth century, the Jews were among the poorest of the poor. The majority of Holland's Jews were poor Ashkenazi immigrants from Germany and Poland; in 1799, 80 percent of Amsterdam's Ashkenazim as well as more than half of the Sephardim received public assistance.[94] Most Jews in eighteenth-century England, too, were impoverished immigrants.[95] In France, Jewish vagrancy was a serious social problem not only in Alsace but even in smaller and generally more prosperous southern communities such as Carpentras and the Comtat. (In the latter region, in 1773 Jewish vagrants beat and stoned local Jews who had denied them assistance.) Until the mid-1800s, the majority of Paris's Jews were poor, requiring public assistance for the burial of their dead.[96] And in Germany, the *Betteljuden* formed a desperate and dangerous class feared by the Jewish communal leadership and Gentile authorities alike.

Thus it is not surprising that early-eighteenth-century German legislation prohibiting begging and vagrancy does not single out Jews from the "Gesindel" (rabble), the general object of concern. One such decree from Ansbach deals with "Land-Streicher, Vaganten, fremde Bettler, blessirte Soldaten, fremde Juden, Zigeuner, Jauner" (vagabonds, vagrants, foreign beggars, wounded soldiers, foreign Jews, gypsies, thieves). Similarly worded decrees were issued in Baden, Württemberg, and Hamburg, also using the adjective *fremd* before the Jews, thereby implying a conceptual separation between vagrant "foreign" Jews and less objectionable resident ones. (A Franconian decree of 1711 focuses "primarily on the foreign impoverished Jews roaming the countryside.")[97]

An excellent example of the meshing of the Enlightenment discourses on the Jew and the poor comes from an obscure German preacher and writer named Johann Kaspar Bundsschuh. A tireless scholar, Bundsschuh wrote multivolumed gazetteers about the geography, flora, and fauna of upper Franconia.[98] In the early 1790s Bundsschuh switched his documentary gaze to the Jews of Franconia. He began to publish under the name Josef Isaak and claimed to be a Jew from the tiny hamlet of Gochsheim. His writing reflects an intimate knowledge of the affairs of this and other Franconian Jewish communities. Bundsschuh's Jewish writings focus on problems of Jewish begging and vagrancy. He is, in general, sympathetic with the plights of both the beggars, whose numbers in Franconia he estimates at five thousand, and the Jewish villagers who lack the resources to contain this flood of human misery. Although he is harsh in his demand that foreign Jews—that is, those who are not residents of Franconia—be expelled, he argues passionately for the better treatment of the resident Jewish poor. He calls on communities to give up their habit of spending charitable funds on meal tickets and short-term accommodations, which only encourage a life of vagrancy, and work instead to find employment for the beggars and incorporate them into the fabric of communal life.[99]

The economic crises that accompanied the revolutionary and Napoleonic Wars allowed for little ebbing of pervasive fears of paupers. During the period between the Revolutions of 1789 and 1848, countries that limited the Jews' freedom of movement and occupation also acted similarly toward the Gentile poor. The 1794 Prussian legal code restricted the ability of the poor to move freely or marry. At the end of the Napoleonic Wars, such restrictions were lifted in Prussia, only to be introduced, in even harsher forms, in the southern German states.[100] In Baden, until 1831 Christians were divided into "protected citizens," whose freedom to marry was restricted, and "residents," who were not so fettered. Marriage restrictions of some type remained in place until 1851. Similar limitations existed in Würtemburg. And Bavaria had the toughest marriage and movement legislation in Germany. Legislation of 1834 sought to prevent the poor from marrying and bearing children in order to limit population growth, business competition, and demand on the communal poor chests.[101] It is often mentioned in works of Jewish history that after 1815, the southern German states introduced authoritarian and pedagogic policies toward the Jews. But these states were authoritarian and pedagogic vis-à-vis the majority of their citizens as well. The attempts to limit population growth among paupers and Jews had a common motive: fear of the teeming "dangerous classes," which could, if allowed to multiply unchecked, overthrow the social hierarchy.

There are, to be sure, limits to the analogy between Jews and the Gentile poor. After the turn of the nineteenth century, the status of Jews was often worse than that of poor Christians. In southern Germany, for example, it was much harder for Jews to overcome or circumvent marriage and residency restrictions. After 1831 only Jews in Baden retained the inferior legal status of "protected citizens," and Jews alone were denied freedom of movement. (Jews were allowed to move only into communities with preexisting Jewish populations; a mere 11 percent of Baden's communities qualified.) And in Bavaria only Jews lived within the confines of the *Matrikel,* a quota that strictly limited the number of Jews allowed in any given community.[102]

Poor and foreign Jews exacerbated antisemitism; they did not create it. A memorandum of 1813 from a police official in eastern Prussia, anticipating a flood of Jewish immigrants from the Grand Duchy of Warsaw, did not oppose the entry of Polish Christians but urged that "the foreign Jew must not be admitted at all, [for] his settlement is recognized as an evil in itself." Four years later, a memorandum from a municipal official in Memel urged that prosperous as well as poor Polish Jews not be allowed right of entry.[103] As one recent study of Germany over the period 1789–1848 has noted, "granting or refusal of right of entry to foreigners [followed] the criteria Jew/Gentile and poor/rich. The rejection of poor Jews was thereby doubly motivated and unambiguous, whereas in the case of well-to-do Jews their property or their occupation could annul the criterion for exclusion, 'Jew.' "[104] But whereas this statement implies that poverty and foreignness are distinct conceptual categories, in fact, the two concepts overlapped considerably in the European sensibility of the period. The image of the poor as constituting a separate nation was employed by writers throughout western Europe, for example, Alexis de Tocqueville and Friedrich Engels, and it gained currency with the publication of Benjamin Disraeli's social novel *Sybil, or, The Two Nations* (1845).[105] The Jew, often poor, was always, in the eyes of Gentile observers, to some degree foreign, even if he held a right of residence in his land of domicile. And the sort of foreignness attributed to Jews was not merely the difference in culture and society that separated the civilized nations, but rather the barbarism of the heathens and savages who dwelled beyond Christendom.

The Jew as Savage

The Age of Enlightenment developed not only modern economic science but also anthropological inquiry. Dohm and Grégoire, the two most significant Enlightenment authors on the Jews, wrote as well about a variety of exotic, non-European peoples. (Dohm wrote on, among others, the subcontinental Indians, and Grégoire, who was an ardent abolitionist, wrote tracts glorifying black African civilization.)[106] In European consciousness, Jews were the most marginal of many marginal groups at the far end of a social spectrum with many gradations. Jews suffered not only from poverty but also from otherness and were hence subject to all the prejudice that late-eighteenth-century society felt about the outlandish, the alien, and the savage.

There are intriguing similarities between European views of Jews over the period 1750–1850 and the images, depicted by Europeans and their descendants in the New World, of Native Americans. The similarities emerge out of the Enlightenment's theories of civilizational development, which themselves were influenced by the encounter between the Old World and the New.[107] Jean-Jacques Rousseau, Adam Smith, and many other thinkers proposed that human progress was linked to changes in the mode of subsistence.[108] As Rousseau wrote, "The savage is a hunter, the barbarian is a shepherd, and the civilized man is a husbandman."[109] In a lecture of 1840, John Quincy Adams elaborated on this point: The hunter, who leads a nomadic life and eats what he can find, lives in a random, meaningless, and godless universe. The shepherd, however, who tends his flock, has begun to rationalize and order his world. But the settled, hardworking farmer possesses "the three essential conditions of happiness: a unity and fixedness of habitation, a unity of conjugal affection, and a unity of worship."[110] Moreover, it was widely believed in the mid-1800s (by, among others, Adams and the German political economist Friedrich List) that with rational, settled farming comes the division of labor, the growth of trade and financial technology, and, eventually, a modern commercial society.[111]

The main point here, made over and over again by writers on both sides of the Atlantic, is that morality and civilization are consonant with agriculture and that one can judge the level of a civilization by its proximity to or distance from a settled, agricultural way of life. Not surprisingly, white observers usually depicted Native American society as based on hunting and thus morally degenerate. Native Americans were said to be idle, shiftless, and cunning, incapable of the hard labor that agriculture demands.[112] (This observation was accurate for some tribes, although many Indian tribes in the eastern United States farmed as much as they hunted.) More important than the issue of accuracy, however, was the need of the white observer to negate the native, to deny him his place on the land. And in a society where productivity was sacred, the most natural means to delegitimize others was to call them unproductive.

European discourse on the Jew and on the savage employed the language of moral economy; both conjured up an Other who was sly, parasitical, and vagrant. The similarities become even stronger when we compare the programs of Jewish "civil improvement," introduced in Europe during the first half of the nineteenth century, with contemporary "civilization" programs of the United States government toward the natives. In the 1820s Jews in central Europe often found residency and citizenship rights contingent on taking up farming or a craft. At the same time, the American Congress appropriated funds for missionary activity and agricultural and crafts education among the Indians. In Germany Jews founded crafts associations to encourage their young to adopt respectable occupations. In America missionaries built large manual-labor boarding schools for the Indians. Throughout Europe the authorities saw Jewish occupational restructuring, along with the abandonment of Yiddish in favor of the national vernacular, as important steps toward Jewish assimilation into the Christian body politic. In America missionaries taught handicrafts, English, and Christianity to the natives in the hope of transforming them into farming, churchgoing, and bourgeois white Americans.[113] Throughout Europe improvement of the Jews' civil status was thought to be conditional on and conducive to the surrender of Jewish particularisms and, depending on the place and time, varying levels of assimilation into the host society. This concept was embodied in the famous phrase of Count Stanislas de Clermont-Tonnere before the French National Assembly that "the Jews should be denied everything as a nation, but granted everything as individuals." Similar thinking motivated American policy toward Native Americans from the late 1700s onward. This sentiment was pithily summarized by a missionary among the Sioux, who exclaimed that "as tribes and nations the Indians must perish and live only as men!"[114]

The comparative net can be cast even wider. In early-nineteenth-century Colombia, liberal meliorism dictated that the indigenous population would be morally regenerated through Hispanicization, miscegenation with whites, and the practice of agriculture on individually owned holdings.[115] And back in Europe, gypsies as well as Jews occupied the imagination of reformist bureaucrats and missionaries. The Austrian emperor Joseph II's gypsy regulations, issued the year after his Edicts of Toleration for the Jews, aimed to settle this nomadic people on the soil. At the same time, and continuing into the 1800s, proposals were made in Germany for special agricultural colonies for gypsies and Jews alike; although no Jewish colonies were established, a zealous missionary founded a gypsy farming village in Magdeburg in 1829.[116]

Jews and savages were to undergo a process of "cultivation" in both meanings of the word: cultivation of the soil, producing, in time, a cultivated, civilized being. But, in fact, for Jews and indigenous Americans alike, cultivation did not lead to social acceptance. The Cherokee and other members of the so-called five civilized tribes, who took up farming along with a white American way of life, frustrated white settlers in Georgia who coveted their land. Unable to accuse them of not adopting American folkways, settler activists declared that the Cherokee were racially incapable of farming and leading a settled, virtuous life.[117] A similar set of circumstances stimulated the rise of racial antisemitism, which was provoked by Jewish acculturation far more than by ongoing manifestations of Jewish separateness. In early modern Spain, for example, racial antisemitism rose precisely after Jews had converted en masse to Christianity, that is, had done what medieval Christendom had been demanding from them for centuries.[118]

Nonetheless, as in the association between Jews and poverty, here too there are distinctions to be drawn between conceptions of the Jew and the savage. Discourse on the savage was more ambivalent, more inclined to praise as well as condemn, than rhetoric on the Jewish question. Grégoire's *Essay on the . . . Regeneration of the Jews,* for example, is far more hostile to its subject than his later work, *Enquiry Concerning the Intellectual and Moral Faculties, and Literature of Negroes.* In the latter Grégoire praises black Africans for their virtue, bravery, and independence. In the former Jews receive a few compliments for their communal solidarity and perseverance, but these characterizations are two-edged swords that, elsewhere in the text, cut deeply.[119] In Grégoire we encounter a common phenomenon among observers of Native American culture: the opposition to the myth of the savage hunter of a counter-myth of the Noble Savage. For Tocqueville, for example, the Native American embodied the values of the dying European old order: independence, chivalry, and valor. Tocqueville saw the native as a free soul, indifferent to or bewildered by the European commercial ethos. The Indian, he wrote, radiates "a pride not yet vitiated by commerce or central authority." Tocqueville sympathized with their "noble prejudice against regular, settled work as unworthy of a free human being." In other words, for Tocqueville, it was the native's nobility that made him unfit for "civilization," not his ignobility, as other observers believed.[120] Discourse on the Jews was usually not so fissured. There was a far clearer association between the Jew and the ignoble savage: crass and venal, lacking honor and virtue, in thrall to a slave religion or unrestrained passion.

The Jew dwelled in the discursive nexus between the pauper and the savage. To be sure, there was always much conceptual overlap between the two; notions of the poor as not merely outlandish but also barbaric date back to the early modern period, and the image of the benighted peasant or urban proletarian with low forehead and lantern jaw was a staple of early-nineteenth-century representations of the poor.[121] In such characterizations the intelligence of the subject was ambiguous; he could be presented as a dim-witted hulk or an artful dodger. Antisemites uniformly described Jews as the latter, and they did so with a vehemence that is unique in the history of prejudice and xenophobia. Moreover, there is no real equivalent in the discourse on the pauper and the savage to the antisemitic belief in Jewish power. True, the pauper and the savage were thought to have awesome strength, but it was the strength of the masses, the might of a stampeding herd. Jews, however, were seen as a cabal, possessed of astonishing financial acumen, power as vast as it was obscure. Thus the pauper/savage paradigm of antisemitism coexisted with its opposite, that of the Jew as conspirator and economic master.

The Jew as Master

Beliefs in Jewish conspiracies predate the modern era; they are manifest in the medieval chimeric accusations of ritual murder, host desecration, and poisoning by Jews allegedly seeking to wreak havoc on a hapless Christendom. And beliefs in innate Jewish avarice and shrewdness enjoy an at least equally venerable pedigree. But only in modern times did there develop a secularized vision of an international Jewish conspiracy to achieve world domination through the deployment of economic might. This vision was first articulated in England, during the controversy over the 1753 "Jew Bill," which proposed to offer naturalized status to foreign-born Jews. Whereas proponents of the bill claimed that wealthy Sephardic merchants would bring great benefit to the English economy, opponents warned that said merchants were conspiring to dominate the country by, among other things, buying up England's ancestral estates, then parceling and reselling them at inflated prices.[122] On the Continent the notion of far-ranging Jewish financial machinations developed only in the wake of the political and economic changes unleashed by the French Revolution, peasant emancipation, and early industrialization.

Whether out of devotion to the ideals of human liberty, equality, and brotherhood or to the needs of a modern centralized state, the French Revolution brought emancipation to the Jews of the western part of continental Europe.[123] "Emancipation" meant many things: the right to political participation, the abolition of discriminatory taxes, and varying levels of freedom of movement, occupation, and domicile. For most Jews, the economic consequences of emancipation were far more significant than the political ones. Taken as an aggregate, Jewish economic mobility between 1815 and 1848 was modest,[124] but there were certain spectacular and highly visible developments that shaped nineteenth-century discourse on Judaism and the Jews. Jews played a highly disproportionate role in many of the European stock exchanges. For example, the Berlin stock exchange, founded in 1803, featured equal representation of Jews and Christians among its elders and jobbers.[125] And in Germany, as well as in France, England, Italy, and Austria, descendants of the eighteenth-century Court Jews founded private investment banks that, during the first half of the 1800s, provided the lion's share of the public debt and industrial investment capital. In 1812, out of thirty-two banking houses in Prussia, seventeen were owned by practicing Jews and seven more by converts. In the Prussian state loan of June 1812, bankers of Jewish origin provided 670,000 taler, whereas Christian sources provided 90,000.[126] In Italy, in a forced loan of 1815, the Jewish community of six thousand provided 300,000 lire, whereas the Gentile population of three million provided another million lire.[127] In France James de Rothschild's wealth in 1828 was estimated at 37 million francs out of a total of 102 million francs of banking capital in the country (the Bank of France had 60 million).[128]

The highly visible role of Jewish bankers in high finance in the first half of the 1800s caused worries about Jewish financial power to overshadow the previous century's fears of demographic inundation by Jewish paupers.[129] A number of sources fed this new stream of antisemitic sensibility. The revolutionary and Napoleonic Wars catalyzed the development among the intelligentsia of nationalist sentiment, which often featured a liberal or radical political slant. Because Jewish bankers supplied credit to the reactionary regimes of the Restoration period, it was possible for nationalists on the left of the political spectrum to associate Jews with the oppressive ancien régime. Moreover, both radical and conservative nationalists were often hostile to industrial capitalism, and because Jewish bankers were prominent promoters of early industrial ventures such as the laying of railroads, Jews could bear the blame for the new economic order as well. Finally, on the Continent, the domination of the market by British industrial goods stimulated a xenophobic economic protectionism, and, as we have seen earlier, the notion of the Jew as archetypal foreigner had a venerable pedigree in European sensibility.

All these factors do much to account for the pungent antisemitism of the first theoreticians of socialism. A pioneering work of modern economic antisemitism, Alphonse de Toussenel's *Les Juifs: Rois de l'époque* (1845), like the subsequent writings of Pierre-Joseph Proudhon, paint a dire picture of a France whose Catholic and French core is being destroyed by Jewish, Protestant, and other alien forces.[130] In Germany and Austria, radical discourse was no less antisemitic. As one scholar has recently argued, much of the German philosophy produced from the late 1700s through the mid-nineteenth century possessed a "revolutionary antisemitism" that saw the dissolution of Judaism as a precondition for human redemption.[131] In the 1830s, a group of philosophers known as the Young Hegelians began to produce a stream of texts critical of the existing order. Their focus was largely theological, centering on a critique of revealed and established religion, and although they accused Judaism of an exceeding materialism, they did not dwell on the issue of contemporary Jewish economic activity. The great exception among them was Karl Marx, whose notorious screed of 1844, *On the Jewish Question,* fits well into the framework of conspiratorial antisemitism of the 1840s. Although Marx was of Jewish origin, he did not identify himself as a Jew; he neither advocated nor worked on behalf of the amelioration of Jews. Thus, although Marx was the greatest political economist of the nineteenth century, his writings must be treated here and not in the discussion of Jewish political economy.[132]

Marx's *On the Jewish Question* was a response to an essay by the theologian and fellow Young Hegelian Bruno Bauer. Both men saw the contemporary controversies over Jewish emancipation as pointing to a deeper structural social problem. Bauer claimed that Jewish emancipation must be conceived within the framework of a general emancipation of society from established, heteronomous religion. But Marx claimed that emancipation from religion can only occur within the framework of social emancipation from property. Marx noted that even in a land such as the United States, where the state has separated itself from religious affairs, that is, has emancipated itself from religion, religious life flourishes. Even in its privatized form, Marx argued, religion is an epiphenomenon, a smoke screen of fictitious brotherhood that bourgeois man requires to conceal the cruelty inherent in the capitalist environment. Marx did not argue that Jews engendered capitalism but rather that they embodied it. That is, whereas other antisemites of his generation saw Jews as particularly shrewd and successful traders, Marx claimed that the essence of commercial capitalism bore all the characteristics that had long typified Jewish religious culture: egoism, materialism, and a cold, instrumental view of nature.[133]

Marx's critique of Jewish egoism was common not only among the Young Hegelian philosophers but also among less illustrious people. In a rather pedestrian antisemitic work of 1828, a Bavarian civil servant complained that "all his [the Jew's] strivings and activity unmistakably demonstrate the drive to want to be only himself and for himself, and to view the collectivity as foreign."[134] Similarly, notions of a peculiar Jewish "commercial spirit" (*Geschäftsgeist*) were popular during the *Vormärz*, the years preceding the revolution of March 1848. An intriguing source of information about this issue is a long article on Jewish emancipation that appeared in a Brockhaus encyclopedia of 1848 and which focused almost exclusively on Jewish economic activity.[135] It begins with an ironic quote from a noble member of the Prussian provincial diet:

We wish to guarantee them the capital of complete civil freedom through emancipation so that they can flourish [*wuchern*, which also means to lend money at interest], act honestly and with industry in order to bring benefit to themselves and to the state. I believe that we are speaking of a people which has demonstrated that it knows how to put its capital out at interest and to extract good earnings therefrom.

The article quotes as well from the Prussian minister of justice who, in a report of 1841–42, argued that the Jews possess an inborn cleverness and industriousness that, combined with their proclivity for frequently moving from one place to another, reduces their moral level. The author agrees with these sentiments, noting that "the religious convictions of the Jews cause them to prefer any livelihood over agriculture, cattle breeding, crafts, or domestic service for Christians, thus their proclivity for petty trade and peddling." Nonetheless, the author claims to have a liberal view on the issue of Jewish emancipation. He believes that with emancipation the Jews will alter their occupational profile, and he criticizes the punitive and discriminatory legislation of the southern German states that restricts Jewish access to petty trade. Such laws, he argues, "damage the general sense of self-worth; they are unworthy of the modern state."

This article, along with many other writings on the Jewish question in Germany, used words such as *Schleichhandel* (slippery dealing), *Schacher* (huckstering), and *Wucher* (usury) so often that they came to signify the Jew himself.[136] One 1824 dictionary explained that the word *Schacher* came from the Hebrew *mishar* (commerce) and meant trade of a "Jewish, profit-seeking type."[137] These terms point to an interesting conceptual paradox. On the one hand, they conjured up images of poor Jewish peddlers who could barely make ends meet. The term *Nothandel*, for example, which was coined in the early nineteenth century to describe Jewish peddling, referred to the *Not,* or distressed state, of peddler and customer alike.[138] On the other hand, these terms suggested, and at times bureaucrats and merchants said outright, that Jews had exceptional financial ability. Thus in southern Germany in the 1840s, merchants sent streams of petitions to the authorities, urging that Jews not be allowed to compete with them lest they be ruined.[139]

In northern France and southern Germany, economic antisemitism flourished among the peasantry as well as the urban population during the half century after 1789. During the revolutionary and Napoleonic periods, residents of Alsace and Lorraine complained that they were virtually enserfed to the Jews, who controlled the purchase of agricultural produce, livestock trading, and, most infamously, the provision of credit at high interest.[140] In post-Napoleonic southern Germany, there were pervasive fears that Jews were buying up vast amounts of property. Germans used the term *Güterschlächterei* to describe the alleged Jewish practice of descending on indebted peasant holdings and wresting them from their rightful owners.[141] Similarly, in Alsace, Jews were accused of monopolizing the purchase of nationalized church lands.

Underneath economic antisemitism lay genuine fear, fear of the shrewd, glib, and tenacious Jew who could dance circles around the Gentile, buy the shirt off his back and the ground under his feet, without the Gentile ever knowing what hit him. How much of this fear was justified? In revolutionary Alsace, it is true that Jews purchased nationalized estates and that they did so for speculation, reselling the properties quickly, at times for a tidy profit. But between 1791 and 1811, Jews accounted for only 2 percent of the firsthand purchases of nationalized estates in the Lower Rhine *département*; if secondhand purchases are included, the figure may be as high as 10 percent, but still nothing near what the antisemitic imagination perceived it to be.[142] In *Vormärz* Bavaria, Christian peddlers far outnumbered Jewish ones.[143] And in Westphalia, virtually all indebted peasant parcels were bought by nobles, not Jews.[144]

But the myth of the powerful Jewish *Landfresser* (landgrabber) served important psychological functions among the peasantry. It made sense of the unstable economic situation in the wake of peasant emancipation and mandatory redemption payments to erstwhile lords. In the new order, peasants experienced a great need for credit, either for redemption payments or for real estate to expand their meager holdings. Lacking the collateral for a bank loan, and with no infrastructure of rural credit institutions (these would come only after midcentury), peasants turned perforce to Jewish moneylenders, dependence on whom they bitterly resented. A similar case of economic dependence in an atmosphere of crisis and want accounts for the strikes and revolts against Jewish grain merchants in Bohemia in the late 1840s.[145]

Moreover, the stronger the negative image of the Jew, the easier it was to justify not paying back loans from him. Surely, one could think, it is not immoral to deny a swindler his ill-gotten gain. Finally, the myth of Jewish power legitimized exploiting the Jews' very real weaknesses. One could threaten or refuse payment to a Jewish moneylender without bringing on the sort of physical retribution that would come from an affronted Christian neighbor. The state's legal mechanisms were slow and capricious, especially in cases involving a Jewish creditor. In one case in which the courts worked in the Jew's favor, in Westphalia in 1782, a debtor who had welshed on his debt to a Jew was so shocked and angered that a district court ordered him to pay that he murdered the Jew just outside the courtroom.[146]

After 1789 Jewish emancipation presented to European society as a whole a psychological threat similar to that experienced by this enraged Christian debtor. In the postrevolutionary atmosphere of peasant emancipation, urbanization, and increased vertical social mobility, antisemitism reflected a longing for an older, hierarchical society in which the Jew's ossified pariah status symbolized social stability and affirmed the Christian identity of the majority population. It is this environment that accounts for the rise, beginning at the turn of the century and crystallizing in the 1840s, of theories of international Jewish conspiracies to achieve global economic domination. The cataclysmic political and economic changes that were occurring on the Continent appeared too great to be accounted for through natural causality alone, yet the Enlightenment had successfully weakened many intellectuals' faith in supernatural intervention, whether divine or satanic, in history. And so the Revolution was blamed on sinister cabals, comprised of the likes of Freemasons, Illuminati, and, of course, Jews. Of the Jews, the French conservative thinker Joseph de Maistre warned darkly, "Everything leads to the belief that their money, their hatred, and their talents are in the service of great conspirators."[147]

Conspiracy theories, formed out of emotional need, seek evidence to sustain them. For antisemites, the incontrovertible proof of Jewish economic collusion was the Rothschild banking dynasty. I discuss the Rothschilds' economic activities and their role and image in Jewish society later. Here I merely wish to point out the traumatic impact of the Rothschild dynasty, linking much of the European continent, on the antisemitic imagination.[148]

This dynasty had humble beginnings in the Frankfurt ghetto, where Meyer Amschel Rothschild served as a financial agent for the Elector of Hesse-Cassel. During the Napoleonic Wars, Meyer Amschel sent four of his five sons to set up banking operations in London, Paris, Vienna, and Naples. By 1815 the family had earned a fortune through the provision of war loans to the Allied forces. In addition to the Rothschilds' great wealth and periodic involvements in international crises, the Damascus Affair of 1840—or more accurately, the organized Jewish response to it—stoked antisemitic hysteria. At that time, James de Rothschild, the Paris-based son of Meyer Amschel, led the defense of Jews in Damascus who had been accused by the French consul there of the ritual murder of a Capuchin monk. Afraid that Rothschild was undermining French interests in the Middle East, the prime minister, Adolphe Thiers, publicly accused the Jews of wielding their international financial influence to the detriment of France. Much of the French press followed suit.[149] Not surprisingly, the cosmopolitanism and power of the Rothschilds figured prominently in the literature of secular antisemitism, literature that flourished in the 1840s, when the wealth and power of the Rothschilds was at its zenith.

To be sure, economic elements did not dominate all forms of antisemitic rhetoric or sensibility during the period from the French Revolution to the Revolution of 1848. The German philosopher Immanuel Kant may have called the Jews "a people composed solely of merchants,"[150] but his criticism of Judaism centered on the Jews' lack of moral freedom due to their alleged slavish obedience to heteronomous authority. The chauvinist antisemitism of German nationalists in the early 1800s certainly had economic elements, but more important was a theological and political critique of the Jews as comprising what they called a "state within a state," a foreign body within the Germanic-Christian polity. Finally, the anti-Jewish riots that swept through Germany and Denmark in 1819 can only be partially ascribed to economic factors.[151]

Modern antisemitism is far more than a manifestation of economic anxieties. But it does, like all forms of bigotry and paranoid fantasy, have powerful economic motifs. Like the pauper at home and the savage in distant lands, Jews were conceived of not only as numerous and uncouth but also as dangerous because of their alleged lack of utility and parasitical nature. In what appears at first glance to be a contradictory paradigm, Jews were also associated with Freemasons and other congeries of conspirators in being few, subtle, and threatening due to their awesome economic power. But the social reality of Jewish life in western and central Europe between the mid-eighteenth and the mid-nineteenth century provided a basis for both of these stereotypes. Most Jews in the eighteenth century were impoverished, and many engaged in occupations of low repute. Thus not only did the Jew resemble the savage, in that neither was Christian, he also resembled the pauper, because neither was a burgher. By the mid-1800s there had developed a significant Jewish commercial bourgeoisie and a financial elite with enormous wealth. But the Jews' ongoing religious alterity and economic distinctiveness, combined with postrevolutionary Europe's traumatic encounter with agrarian and industrial capitalism, stimulated the association of the Jew with malevolent and uncanny economic forces.

It is difficult, if not impossible, to imagine modern antisemitism without the twin paradigms that I have analyzed in this chapter. The paradigms in place by the mid-1800s flourished throughout the Continent and enjoyed currency well into the twentieth century. Although the focus in this chapter has been antisemitism in western Europe, one can easily apply the "pauper" paradigm to the east; Russian economic antisemitism from the time of the partitions of Poland through most of the 1800s was based in the stereotype of the impoverished Jewish parasite.[152] What one scholar has referred to as a late-nineteenth-century European stereotype of Jews as "opulent capitalists and impoverished revolutionaries"[153] was already established in the eighteenth century, in the topoi of the Court Jew and the hawker. The later manifestations of these forms will be examined in chapter 4. For now, it suffices to have demonstrated their power in European society during the time when the question of the role of the Jew in the modern state was first posed and debated. We can now proceed to ask what effects, both psychic and social, this powerful economic critique had on its objects.

CHAPTER 2

The Origins of Jewish Political Economy, 1648–1848

Ben Menahem [Moses Mendelssohn] was the first in Israel to introduce the novelty of seeking a purpose and reward for one's actions. . . . He taught his children and disciples not to toil in vain. He himself was an accountant . . . and accounting is what he taught them. . . . The word went forth from Ben Menahem that we must seek reward for our labor, and that it is therefore in vain to toil for Torah.

Peretz Smolenskin, 1877

In premodern Jewish thinking, religion and economics were inextricably linked. During the heyday of rabbinic Judaism, the economic life of the Jewish community was no less subject to halakhic authority than any other aspect of Jewish life. Contracts, business partnerships, and relations between employer and employee all were subject to rabbinic supervision. Not only the pursuit of profit, but even the pursuit of a livelihood, were subordinate to the fulfillment of commandments.

From the mid-seventeenth century, economic life in western Europe began to remove itself from the sphere of Jewish religious authority. This separation of the religious and economic spheres was an important harbinger of Jewish modernity, because it marked the diminution of communal authority and a secularization of Jewish consciousness. In the later phases of the Jewish Enlightenment (Haskalah) in Germany, the two were rejoined, but in an entirely modern form that constituted a distinctly Jewish political economy. At first, speculation about Jewish political economy came from the radical periphery of the Jewish intellectual community in France and Germany. In the early 1800s, however, the notion of a Jewish political economy migrated from the periphery to a core of Jewish communal leaders committed both to acculturation and to the preservation of Judaism and the Jews. This chapter traces the dialectical process, taking place over a period of some two centuries, of unity, rupture, and fusion between Judaism and the economic practices of Jews.

I must offer a caveat from the outset. In any field of study in Jewish history, the concept of a Jewish author is ambiguous, and this problem is especially vexing in the case of Jewish economists.[1] Among the most celebrated individuals of Jewish origin who pioneered modern economic theory were converts or lapsed Jews. Joseph von Sonnenfels (1732–1817), a founder of the discipline of cameralist economics, was baptized as a child. David Ricardo (1772–1823), one of the fathers of modern political economy, was born into a Sephardic Jewish family and may have received a traditional Jewish education, but he married a Quaker and, like his siblings, abandoned Jewish observance.[2] The urban and mercantile orientation of Jewish society was no doubt one of many influences on the thinking of these and other individuals of Jewish origin who wrote on general economics. Far more important, however, were specific social factors, such as the fact that Sonnenfels was raised in the court of the empress Maria Theresa, whom Joseph's apostate father served as court interpreter. Living at the very center of a classic absolutist state, Sonnenfels became the theoretician par excellence of state-supervised economic development.[3] Ricardo's thought, in contrast, bears the influence of the relatively noninvasive British state, the individualistic socioeconomic theory of the Scottish Enlightenment, and the good fortune of being the son of a prominent member of the London stock exchange. Besides, Ricardo's theoretical genius cannot be confined within any set of sociological factors.

My inquiry here is limited to those economic thinkers who identified as Jews. Moreover, although I am interested in how and why Jews began to think about political economy in general, my particular concern is the onset of Jewish political economy, that is, reflection about the economic structure, behavior, and utility of the Jews within the framework of the society in which they lived.

Judaism and Economics

Jewish civilization does not possess a tradition of systematic economic thinking. The legalistic texts of Jewish antiquity—the Torah, Mishnah, and Gemarah (the last two comprising the Talmud)—contain a great deal of economic material, as they do material on all aspects of daily life. But, in keeping with the exegetical and discursive quality of rabbinic thinking, the Talmud offers no coherent economic philosophy. Nor does medieval Jewish thought, although it developed systematic analyses of Jewish belief and ritual and flourished in an increasingly mercantile Jewish society. This lack is not due to a denigration of economic affairs or a reluctance to deal with them. Rather, according to the historian Salo Baron, "a belief in the exclusiveness in the Torah's guidance in social philosophy" led to a "conscious attempt to prevent the Greco-Arabic social philosophy from modeling the economic relations among Jews."[4] Moreover, the Jews' existence as a dispersed minority, dependent for their economic well-being on external forces in their host societies, discouraged the formation of a comprehensive economic philosophy.

Although Rabbinic and medieval Judaism lacked an economic philosophy, it had identifiable economic sensibilities. One was the rejection of the idea of poverty; wealth, when properly and ethically acquired, was to be enjoyed. In this the Jewish tradition corresponded more to Islamic civilization than to that of Christendom. The same is true for attitudes toward private property, which medieval Christian thought did not esteem but was accepted by Jewish and Muslim jurists as eternal and divinely sanctioned, albeit subject to regulation. Finally, Rabbinic Judaism, like medieval Islamic thought, did not share the church's ambivalence toward commerce, the money trade, and the exchange of goods in the open market.[5]

Other economic conceptions were subject to change across space and time. One celebrated example is the evolution of Jewish attitudes toward the lending of money at interest. The Mishnah and Toseftah (the latter contains legalistic material not included in the Mishnah), composed in the largely agrarian society of second-century C.E. Palestine, contain stringent legislation against the lending of money at interest, which could easily ruin an unfortunate or imprudent peasant. The Talmudic rabbis in Babylon, however, lived in a more mercantile culture; some of them appreciated the benefits of moneylending and sought to weaken

Mishnaic limitations on it.[6] This tendency was strengthened by Maimonides, who lived in the urban, commercial realm of medieval Islam. His monumental code of Jewish law, the Mishneh Torah, sanctioned lending at interest by Jews to Gentiles and vice versa. He went beyond the rabbinic consensus by interpreting Deuteronomy 23:21 (*la-nokhri tashikh*, normally rendered, "To the foreigner you may lend at interest")[7] as a positive commandment: "We have been commanded to burden the Gentile with interest, and thus to lend to him, not to help him, nor to deal graciously with him, but rather to harm him, even in the case of a loan at interest of a sort which we have been cautioned against making to Israelites."[8]

It is not clear if the motive for this statement was animosity against Gentiles or a literalist construction of the imperative *tashikh*. In medieval Europe, some notable rabbis justified moneylending as a vehicle of Jewish revenge against an increasingly hostile Gentile environment.[9] In so doing, they were merely reflecting the classic Christian notion, enunciated by Saint Ambrose, that "where there is a right of war, there is a right of usury": just as Jews may lend to Christians at interest, so may Christians, in principle, practice usury with Jews in order to do them harm.[10] Both the Jewish and the Christian view give credence to Max Weber's assertion that in a precapitalist society "every foreigner [is] originally an enemy in relation to whom no ethical restrictions apply; that is, the ethics of internal and external relations are categorically distinct." The "dual ethic" described by Weber for all societies was especially prominent in Christendom because of the doctrinal conflict between Christianity and Judaism.[11]

No medieval halakhist, however, went as far as Maimonides; Moses ben Nahman (Nahmanides) and other rabbinic luminaries objected that Maimonides had misinterpreted rabbinic discussions of this verse, which simply permitted the lending of money at interest to non-Jews. Moreover, most medieval juridical opinion on usury represented an attempt to form *halakhah le-'ahar ha-ma'aseh*, that is, a legal basis for what had become an omnipresent socioeconomic reality. From the twelfth century, Jews, particularly in northern Europe but elsewhere as well, engaged increasingly in moneylending. This practice required legal justification, which duly came in the halakhic writings of the Tosafists, the Franco-German Talmudic commentators of the twelfth through fourteenth centuries. The Tosafists combined pragmatic arguments (e.g., the Jews' need to make a living) with theological ones. On the one hand, they claimed that Christians were not idolaters, thus circumventing

Mishnaic limitations on doing business with pagans. On the other hand, the rabbis maintained the Christians' essential Otherness, thereby avoiding halakhic prohibitions against lending at interest to one's "brother." True, by the end of the Middle Ages Jews regularly lent to each other at interest, employing a legal fiction known as the *heter 'iska,* which disguised the loan as investment in a business partnership.[12] But the rabbis felt no need for such casuistry in justifying loans between a Jew and a Gentile.

By the end of the Middle Ages, the Jews in both Christendom and the realm of Islam were an overwhelmingly urban and mercantile people. Although Jews in some lands, such as the Holy Roman Empire, were mostly extruded from commerce and banking and reduced to petty moneylending, in other lands, such as the Polish-Lithuanian kingdom, Jews combined the lending of money at interest with a wide variety of lucrative occupations such as commerce, leaseholding, estate management, and tax farming. There is little doubt that Jews contributed disproportionately to the economic development of their host societies. The more vexing question is whether there is some causal or correlative link between the Jews and the rise of modern capitalism.

According to the classic conceptual framework established by Weber, in capitalist environments, labor and profit become central and inextricably linked aspects of an individual's life. Although the search for material gain is as old as humanity itself, modern capitalism is unique for its rationality, manifesting itself in the search for steady and long-term profit. The use of free, that is, wage labor, and the separation of home and workplace are further indications of capitalist economic rationality.[13] For Weber, the crucial, and paradoxical, quality of modern capitalism was its "worldly asceticism," a drive, originally motivated by Puritan sensibilities, to accumulate material wealth but not to indulge in luxury or let one's wealth rest idle once it has been obtained. Weber's thesis about the relationship between spirituality and economic activity is the subject of eternal controversy, but it is clear that a strong sense of altruism motivated the eighteenth-century political economists who pioneered the conceptualization of modern capitalism. Adam Smith and his contemporaries argued for the essentiality of the free market and open competition, not to maximize individual material wealth, but to limit the harmful effects of avarice, which seeks the unlimited accumulation of capital to the detriment of the common good. Underlying many streams of classical political economy was a notion of a unitary society linked by human sympathy and promoted materially by rational, collective economic policy.[14]

Medieval Jewish culture displayed no precocious interest in these concepts. Let us return to the example of Maimonides. Despite his openness to commerce and profit, Maimonides considered the pursuit of profit entirely secondary to the pursuit of religious knowledge. Although he called on all capable men to pursue a livelihood so as not to burden society, Maimonides' notion of a twelve-hour workday consisted of three hours at one's livelihood and nine studying religious texts. Maimonides showered praise on those rabbinic sages who engaged in crafts or physical labor, but he did so to demonstrate that poverty and hard work need not, in fact must not, lessen one's devotion to learning.[15] (This interpretation would be reversed by modern, apologetic views that the laboring sage demonstrated that a life of learning need not lessen one's devotion to productive labor.)

But what impact did classic medieval texts such as those of Maimonides have on ways of thinking several centuries later, during the epoch of early capitalism? To assess the relationship between Jewish mentalities and the rise of capitalism, we must avoid generalisms and the culling of choice citations from the vast corpus of Rabbinic texts. Rather, we should focus on Jewish texts composed during capitalism's formative centuries.[16] One scholar who undertook such a study demonstrated convincingly that Weber's characterization of the Calvinist work ethic in no way applied to Jewish attitudes of the period.[17] Great halakhists such as Isaiah Horowitz (1565?–1630) and Jacob Emden (1697–1776) called on men to devote as little time as possible to their occupations. Emden favored the employment of business partners or wives to run a man's business, thereby allowing him more time for study. These and other rabbis praised abstinence, but their motives had little to do with a Weberian, ascetically driven work ethic. Rather, they considered ascetic behavior to be a proper sign of mourning for the destroyed Temple.

The rabbis assumed no connection between labor and wealth, nor was wealth perceived as a sign of worthiness to enter the world to come. In eastern Europe, this slighting of labor continued well into the nineteenth century, with texts by both Hasidim and their Orthodox opponents agreeing that the biblical command "to live by the sweat of your brow" entailed zealous study and the production of Talmudic novellae. Because commerce was perceived as being less time-consuming than crafts, it was considered by Emden, Horowitz, and others as enjoying a higher status than crafts. A communal functionary, Emden argued, must not be a craftsman. Coming from a different perspective, Horowitz's monumental didactic work, *Shnei Luhot ha-Brit* (Two Tables of the Covenant), argued that commerce is a more ethical occupation than crafts because it involves personal negotiations, based on trust, instead of simply working with raw materials.[18]

In central and eastern Europe throughout the early modern period, Jewish society displayed no movement toward free trade or unrestricted competition. In fact, rabbinical writings in eastern Europe showed a growing concern with limiting rights of residence (*hezkat ha-yishuv*) and protecting the privileges of the holder of a monopoly.[19] Because of their social isolation from Gentile society, Jews, writes Jacob Katz, "were little involved with the broad problems of the national or regional economy, and did not decide what was forbidden or permitted for themselves out of concern for the general welfare."[20] Jews had no concept of a common economic good, and, as I have argued above, a sense of social unity characterizes modern capitalism no less than individual pursuit of material gain.

Early modern rabbis displayed no awareness of the ascendant discourse of political economy. This lack of engagement deserves further scrutiny. After all, in many ways early modern European Jews were intimately involved in the culture of their host societies. One historian has recently demonstrated the Jewish intellectual elite's "acute awareness of and positive attitude towards contemporaneous medical and scientific discoveries."[21] But there are important differences between astronomy, medicine, and other aspects of natural science, on the one hand, and economics and other forms of social science, on the other.

For Jews in early modern Europe, natural-scientific knowledge was eminently practical and assimilable into Jewish culture. Astronomical innovation lubricated the mechanisms of the Jewish calendar, and medical knowledge was an essential livelihood and source of communal well-being. Natural-scientific inquiry entailed reflection on the majesty of God's universe, an activity easily justifiable in the Jewish tradition. True, over the seventeenth and eighteenth centuries Jewish scholars detached science from the realm of the sacred, but the separation of physics from metaphysics actually stimulated scientific inquiry by placing science into an isolated matrix that appeared not to challenge Jewish theology, theosophy, the corporate nature of Jewish society, or Jewish particularism in its various forms. Social-scientific discourse, on the other hand, demanded thinking about the Jews and their hosts as a single social unit, a notion that few Gentiles espoused before the mid-1700s and with which Jews began to experiment only toward the end of that century.

One might argue that as most Jews were not jurists, rabbinic rumination tells us little about the thoughts of any but the rabbis themselves.

Is it possible to go beyond the rabbinic elite and grasp the economic sensibilities of the great and middling Jewish merchants in the communities of early modern Europe? I believe so, but there are different ways of trying to do so, some more successful than others. In his masterful recent study of Renaissance Italian Jewry, Robert Bonfil offers a sweeping assertion about differences between Jewish and Christian concepts of time and space and about the relation between these differences and mercantile culture. Bonfil claims that whereas Christian society posited a clear distinction between the church's sacred space and the profane realm of the marketplace, and between the autochthonous "time of the church" and the "time of the merchants," such a distinction did not exist for the Jews of Renaissance Italy, because of the synagogue's mixture of sacred and profane functions. Thus "the secular 'time of the synagogue' was in harmony with the 'time of the merchants,' the bankers and all those who worked, and in contrast to the 'time of the church.' "[22] This is an intriguing argument, yet it was precisely the *separation* of the sacred from the profane sphere in the western European Jewish communities in the seventeenth and eighteenth centuries—a separation that Bonfil himself acknowledges—that facilitated the expansion of Jewish economic activity.

Before Jews could think about themselves in political economic terms, two things had to occur. Jewish economic life needed to free itself from halakhah, and Jews needed to conceive of themselves as integrally linked with the economy of their host societies. The first condition was forced on Jewish communities throughout western Europe during the second half of the eighteenth and beginning of the nineteenth century. The 1750 Prussian General Jewry Code abrogated rabbinic authority over civil affairs. In Napoleonic France, Jewish representatives at the Assembly of Notables and the Sanhedrin, convoked in 1806 and 1807, respectively, could not resist governmental pressure to formally proclaim the separation of the civil and religious spheres of Jewish life. Henceforth, the former would fall entirely under secular authority, and only the latter would remain within the purview of the Jewish community.[23]

There is evidence, however, that the separation between the economic and religious spheres of Jewish life occurred as the result of developments within Jewish communities, as opposed to external pressures on them, and that this process began as early as the turn of the seventeenth century. In a pioneering book, Azriel Shohat made such a claim, pointing to a general weakening of religious observance and obedience to rabbinical authority. This process was spearheaded by the

Court Jews, the economic elite of purveyors, financiers, and mintmasters to the princes of the Holy Roman Empire. Shohat noted how prosperous Jews in Germany made increasing use of Gentile courts to resolve business disputes and ignored rabbinic sumptuary legislation.[24] No doubt, some members of the Ashkenazic economic elite did these things, but it is not clear how widespread such practices were, or whether those who engaged in them explicitly rejected existing social norms in favor of a new, secular matrix of mentalities.

Shohat derived much of his evidence from the memoirs of Glikl (1646–1724), a successful merchant and moneylender, commonly known as "Glikl of Hameln," although she spent most of her life in Hamburg and Altona. (Her first husband was from Hameln.) There are many references in the memoirs to the growth of the personal fortunes of at least some German Jews, the use of Gentile courts, and increasing materialism, manifested in ever-larger dowries and growing expectations by children for parental munificence.[25] But contrary to the thrust of Shohat's argument, Glikl's own economic behavior and values display important signs of continuity, not a break with, traditional concepts of inextricable links among piety, providence, and the marketplace.

The memoirs, which Glikl wrote for her children, must be understood as an extended ethical will, a pietistic and moralistic text intended to guide her descendants along the path of righteousness. The memoirs convey statements about the meaninglessness of material things and exhortations not to strive after gain for its own sake. At the same time, there is a profound appreciation for money as the most precious of resources. Thus Glikl carefully documents the cost of an enforced six-month absence from Hamburg but notes, "Of the money we thought little." On another occasion, a harrowing journey cost her and her husband more than 400 talers, but, she writes, "we did not weigh the price."[26] Money never lies idle; dowry money intended for her children is immediately set aside and lent out at interest. On her deathbed, Glikl's grandmother revealed that she had for years been saving up small gifts of money that she had received and had lent the money out at interest in order to provide for her grandchildren.[27]

For this successful merchant and moneylender, God, sin, and heavenly reward and punishment were as much a part of her balance sheet as her debits and credits. The careful documentation of expenditures and constant assessment of the cost of things testify not to a growing materialism so much as an appreciation of the ephemerality of riches. Glikl might note the value of all things but possessed a value system suffused with deep piety.[28] The diaries of Christian merchants of the early modern period evidence similar sentiments, along with meticulous documentation of financial affairs and a sense of a divine presence behind them. The idea of wealth as evanescent derived from the great instability of mercantile life. Jewish and Christian merchants alike endured losses from war and brigandage, bankruptcy from overextension, and the incompetence or criminality of business partners. For Jews, the situation was particularly bad because of discriminatory taxation and the constant threat that their worldly goods would be confiscated by the authorities. Moreover, Jews were not able, as Christians were, to diversify their holdings and purchase real estate and farms, sources of steady rental income and food. For Jews, material well-being was wrapped up entirely in their inventory, whose value shifted constantly, and which might have to be sold—at a substantial loss—on a moment's notice to cover pressing debts.[29]

Modern Jewish economic sensibilities did not originate among the Ashkenazic economic elite in the early eighteenth century but rather among its western European Sephardic counterpart a few decades previously. These communities were founded in part by Spanish Jews who left Spain before or at the time of the expulsion of 1492 and largely by converts to Christianity ("New Christians," or *conversos*), descendants of the victims of the enforced mass conversion of the Jews of Portugal in 1497.[30] Although small, the Sephardic communities of Amsterdam and other western European port cities have long been looked to by historians as the cradle of Jewish modernity. Classic works of Jewish history, focusing on the intellectual-historical aspects of modernity, have analyzed the contribution of seventeenth-century Sephardim to the development of theological skepticism, the rejection of the idea of Jewish existence as one of physical and cosmic exile (*galut*), and the growth of complex dual identities melding attachments to Jewry and one's host society.[31] But most of the western Sephardim were men of affairs, not of letters, simultaneously benefiting from and contributing to revolutionary changes in commercial technology.

Mercantilism and Jewish Modernity

Many Sephardic Jews made little conscious effort to transform Jewish life, redefine Judaism, or reconfigure the patterns of textual study. What made the Sephardic Diaspora modern was the unselfconscious development of a new form of group identity based on ethnicity. To the Sephardim, particularly those of Portuguese origin, the Jews comprised a "corporation" (*naçao*) that united practicing Jews with New Christians. And the tie that linked together the members of the *naçao* was largely an economic one; the Sephardic trading network united Jews in Danzig, Livorno, and London with New Christians in the Iberian Peninsula. That is, Jews knew that they were Jews because of the economic bonds between them.

Precisely as the bonds of mercantilism between western Sephardic Jews grew stronger, the power of the halakhah to direct and reflect Jewish economic life grew weaker. The *takkanot* (regulations) of the new communities neglected the economic issues that were of such concern to the Polish rabbinate during the same period. Perhaps the Sephardic communities' *converso* founders internalized the Roman Catholic distinction between the sacred and the profane at the expense of the traditional conception of Judaism as a comprehensive way of life. More likely, the Sephardic elite, unable to regulate economic, and hence social, interaction between Jews and New Christians scattered throughout Europe and the New World, chose to ignore the matter altogether. Whatever the reason, for western Sephardic Jews, economic life was disconnected from the halakhah.[32]

Thus it will come as no surprise that the first general economic analysis by a Jew was the work of a Sephardi in Amsterdam: *Confusion de Confusiones* (1688), by Joseph Penso de la Vega (1650–92). De la Vega was born to a New Christian family that, under duress from the Inquisition, had fled Spain for northern Europe. His father, who adopted Jewish practice more than a century after the family had been forced to abjure it, was a prosperous banker and an active philanthropist in the communities of Antwerp, Hamburg, and Amsterdam. Perhaps because of his father's wealth, de la Vega worked primarily as a litterateur, composing a Hebrew drama while still in his teens and going on to become heavily involved in the Spanish-speaking cultural community of Amsterdam. Along with poems, treatises, and panegyrics to people in high places, de la Vega wrote the *Confusion de Confusiones,* a description of the Amsterdam exchange that focused on trading in shares in the Dutch East India Company or options to purchase stock therein.[33] His book is the first thorough description of the workings of the modern stock exchange.

Nothing about the book's format or content is overtly Jewish, although the writing does have certain classic Marrano characteristics, such as the heavy use of imagery from the Old Testament and classical antiquity while shying away from any Christian references.[34] More significant is that the book was written in Spanish, meaning that it was intended for Amsterdam's Sephardic Jewish community. But for the author "the stock exchange, like other aspects of economic life, was considered to be outside the bounds of Jewish life."[35] What makes the book modern is not only its lack of pietism but also the complete separation between its subject and the religious and communal life of its author.

The book's title was a reference to the "Year of Confusion" in ancient Rome when the old lunar calendar was replaced by the new Julian solar reckoning. "This year too," writes de la Vega about recent scandals in the exchange, "was a *year of confusion*[,] for many unlucky speculators declared in one voice that the present crisis was the labyrinth of labyrinths, the terror of terrors, the *confusion of confusions*."[36] In good classical fashion, the book takes the form of a conversation, here between a philosopher, a merchant, and a shareholder. Speaking through the shareholder, de la Vega is frank in his criticism of the exchange's unethical activities, including insider trading, short selling, and wild speculation in "ducaton" stock, which (not unlike the derivatives that rocked the bond and money markets in the United States in the mid-1990s) were not bona fide securities but rather a mere device to gamble on rises or falls in the price of shares on the exchange. Although hostile to speculation, the shareholder is adamant that one can make a relatively risk-free and honest profit through practices such as the purchase of options contracts, wherein one risks only the premium paid to the broker, or the sale of one's own stock on a future basis, where the buying price is guaranteed. Despite the risks, the shareholder notes that people are compelled to invest in stocks because the rate of return on loaned cash is quite low, approximately 3 percent. The book ends with both the merchant and the philosopher agreeing about the probity of a modest investment in shares with a long-term perspective.

Only an antisemite could find anything "Jewish" about de la Vega's economic sensibilities, which simply reflect those of any prudent investor trying to turn a profit in the hectic world of the securities market in the late seventeenth century. Thus we encounter the conceptual and methodological problem of whether there is anything intrinsically Jewish about a text penned by a Jew but lacking any overt Jewish content. I have argued that the Jewish quality of the text may be subtle, as in de la Vega's language and style, and that the lack of explicit references to Jewish affairs is significant for its demonstration of the author's engagement with the political-economic discourse of his environment. This last point is important for an understanding of the Franco-Sephardic Isaac de Pinto (1717–87). De Pinto is remembered in Jewish history as a philosophe who eloquently defended Sephardic virtue, while all too freely admitting Ashkenazic corruption, against the antisemitic onslaughts of the French philosophe Voltaire. But de Pinto was also a prominent economist and director of both the East and West Indian Companies. He was a classic mercantilist in his support for colonies and a strong manufacturing and commercial sector; purely agrarian countries like Poland, he argued, are bent on ruin. De Pinto's economic writings, in particular his *Traité de la circulation et du crédit* (1771), offered, far more than *Confusion de Confusiones,* a positive view of the securities market and speculation. He also supported the issuing of national debt, which, as proven by England's issuing of government bonds, provided the state great resources and enriched the population through interest.[37]

De Pinto is a significant figure not merely because he was among the first Jews to think systematically about political economy. He was also a pioneer in the creation of a specifically Jewish political economy. We encounter this sort of thinking in a pamphlet of 1748 composed by de Pinto himself, *Reflexoens politicas tocante à constituição da nação judaica.* In his capacity as treasurer of the Amsterdam Jewish community, de Pinto was among those most responsible for the provision of charity to Amsterdam's Jews, who had, since the end of the previous century, experienced economic decline along with Holland as a whole. In his pamphlet, employing concepts adumbrating the celebrated theories of the early-nineteenth-century English economist Thomas Malthus, de Pinto analyzed the demographic forces leading to exponential increases in the Jewish population. He called for the establishment of public workshops for some of the Jewish poor in Amsterdam and for the transportation of others to Surinam, Holland's most prosperous overseas colony. Although de Pinto was able to win a reduction of the tax burden on the Jewish community, it is not clear if his pamphlet led to significant practical results or if it stimulated an ongoing discourse among the Sephardic elite about Jewish political economy.[38]

Ironically, precisely at the time that de Pinto was dissecting the economic woes of Amsterdam Jewry, Isaac Wetzlar (1680?–1751), a prosperous merchant from Celle (near Hanover), was praising the Sephardim's economic prowess and attributing it to their superior educational practices as compared with those of the Ashkenazim. His *Libes Briv* (1749), an early Haskalah tract, could be seen as adumbrating the later German Haskalah's economic dimensions, to which we shall turn below. Wetzlar claims that the Ashkenazic educational system's emphasis on Talmudic dialectic engenders a sophistic worldview, which leads to moral relativism and thence to corruption, thus meriting divine punishment in the form of grueling poverty. In contrast, the Sephardic emphasis on the Hebrew Bible and Hebrew grammar instills morality, which generates virtue, which is then rewarded by wealth. Despite its raising of economic questions, however, this tract cannot be seen as a product of Enlightenment social or economic thinking. Its conceptual framework is entirely pietistic and moralistic. Education is a process of ethical formation, not vocational development. The *Libes Briv* is disconnected from the non-Jewish body politic and does not consider the Jews' benefits or responsibilities thereto.[39]

The first Ashkenazic Jew to write about economics in the fashion of de la Vega or de Pinto was Moses Wessely (1738–92). Wessely was a younger brother of the famous educator Naphtali Herz Wessely, discussed below. Epitomizing the experience of Jewish merchants of this period, Moses experienced great economic insecurity and repeated cycles of success and failure.[40] Moses's unhappy business experience may account for his conservative economic views, expressed, inter alia, in his essays "Money and Circulation" and "State Debt."

In the former essay Wessely strongly favored currency made from precious metal over notes, for whereas the former existed in limited amounts and required labor to extract, thus bestowing on it intrinsic value, the latter represented only a promise of a future satisfaction of needs. In language reminiscent of Montesquieu, but much more conservative than the celebrated philosophe, Wessely described paper money as a mere abstraction, nothing but "a representation of a representation," a "symbolic sign."[41] A similar conservatism underlies Wessely's essay on state debt. Wessely urged utmost caution in issuing state debt, claiming that such a practice should be limited to times of national emergency. Like de Pinto, Wessely admired the flourishing English economy, but unlike de Pinto, Wessely did not see state debt as the key to England's successes. Rather, he admired England for its public discussion of debt issues; a vigorous exchange of public opinion, he argued, boosts the morale of the bond-buying public.[42]

Wessely's essays were written in German and published in various journals of public opinion in Prussia. They were intended for a Gentile audience and sought to make contributions to the social and economic weal of the state. The separation of economic from religious life made possible an engagement with the political-economic discourse of the states in which western European Jews lived. Yet only a handful of Jews in the seventeenth and eighteenth centuries wrote political-economic tracts. Far more common was the inclusion of economic material in apologetic texts submitted by European Jewish merchants or their representatives to Gentile authorities. The apologetics invoked economic arguments to preserve or improve the residency or occupational privileges of Jews in a particular place. The earliest, and most elaborate, examples of this genre of apologetics were produced by Sephardic and Italian Jews in the mid-seventeenth century.

Whereas medieval apologetics had, in response to Christian attacks, focused on the defense of Jewish scriptural interpretation, their seventeenth-century counterparts stressed the Jews' economic usefulness. Medieval Jews were of course aware that their rights of residence and well-being depended on their economic utility and, on occasion, referred in polemical works to the essentiality of Jewish loans for all sectors of Gentile society.[43] In seventeenth-century apologetics, economic threads are omnipresent. Isaac Cardoso's *Las excelencias de los hebreos* (1679), a panegyric on all aspects of Jewish life both sacred and profane, touched on a number of economic issues, ranging from King Solomon's public works to Diaspora Jewry's exemplary philanthropy.[44] And economic arguments are central to the two most significant producers of Jewish apologetic texts of the century: Simone Luzzatto (1583–1663), a rabbi in Venice, and Menasseh Ben Israel (1604–57), a Sephardic scholar in Amsterdam.

Luzzatto's *Discorso circa il stato de gl'hebrei et in particolar dimoranti nell'inclita città di Venetia* was an appeal for continued Jewish rights of residency in the face of opposition from Gentile merchants on Venice's Board of Trade. Like Luzzatto, Menasseh Ben Israel also petitioned for Jewish residency rights, in this case in the form of readmission to Britain, in his *Humble Addresses* to Oliver Cromwell (1655). The similarities between the works derive not only from the analogous environments in which they were produced but also from the fact that Menasseh Ben Israel read and was influenced by Luzzatto's *Discorso*.[45] Both works placed the issue of Jewish rights squarely within the framework of utility, although the *Humble Addresses* are undergirded by the millenarianism that was central to Menasseh Ben Israel's earlier, more elaborate work, *The Hope of Israel* (1649).[46]

The argumentation of the *Discorso* and the *Humble Addresses* is similar: Centuries of persecution and enforced wandering have made the Jews into a people of enterprising, innovative merchants. Internationally linked and multilingual, Jews promote the flow of imports and exports, which, in addition to being a good in itself, enriches the national treasury through tolls and customs. Politically powerless, they are docile and obedient subjects, whose presence requires no expenditures for state security. Finally, prosperous Jewish merchants, who are unable or unwilling to commit their wealth to real estate, continue to benefit the national economy long after their Gentile counterparts have given up trade, bought estates, and taken on the quiet and respectable life of country gentlemen.[47]

Two additional points on Luzzatto's *Discorso* are worth noting. First, Luzzatto did not speak merely for himself but echoed or expanded on arguments made by Jewish merchants on the Venetian Republic's Board of Trade. The piece was written during a period of Venice's decline as a port, and Jewish merchants conceived of themselves as pillars shoring up its declining economy. Second, although the piece is primarily a defense of the Jewish role in promoting trade, it is also, by extension, a defense of trade as such. At a time when Venice was changing from a republic of merchants to one of estate and piazza owners, Luzzatto defended commerce as a vehicle of civilization, whereby not only merchandise but also artistic and scientific knowledge were transmitted through commercial exchange.[48] (One encounters the same concept in the *Humble Addresses:* "The Commerce and reciprocall Negotiation at Sea, which is the ground of Peace between neighbour Nations, and [is] of great profit to their own fellow-citizens."[49]) Thus the *Discorso* is a pioneering work in a number of respects: as a treatment of the Jews' role in international commerce, as a socioeconomic justification for Jewish rights,[50] and as an early testimony to the economic values of Jewish merchants differing, at least to some degree, from those of their Gentile counterparts.

We encounter views in the spirit of Luzzato and Menasseh Ben Israel in memorandums composed by Sephardic Jews in France in the mid-1700s. These *mémoires* were part of the Sephardic Jews' effort to obtain complete commercial freedom, which they did receive in 1776. But the trumpeting of Jewish utility was not limited to Sephardim. In 1716 a petition from Alsatian Jewish leaders requested that Jews be allowed to move beyond the livelihoods to which they were currently limited by law—trade in old clothes and cattle and moneylending—and into all branches of business. The petition claimed that "the more merchants there are in a province, the richer it is, the better able it is to pay taxes."[51] The presence of Jewish merchants in Strasbourg, they averred, will provide badly needed competition with Christian traders, hence lowering prices for the good of the consumer. (The demand for economic equality was central in the representations of Alsatian Jews to the French crown up to the eve of the Revolution.) Similar arguments came from Jewish merchants in Trieste, the Hapsburg Empire's most important port city,[52] and from Prussian Jews beginning as early as the reign of Frederick William of Brandenburg, the "Great Elector" (r. 1640–88), and continuing through the eighteenth century.[53]

In their memorandums to the authorities, Jewish merchants in Germany offered rationalist and mercantilist responses, claiming that they and their business methods were bringing only benefit to the state, whereas the Gentile merchants were a burden on the national economy. These themes would be repeated over and over until Jewish emancipation was secured in the mid-nineteenth century. So, for example, in 1819 Munich's Jewish community boasted that whereas Gentile merchants demanded a 30 to 50 percent profit margin, their Jewish counterparts were content with one-tenth that amount, thus bringing maximal benefit to the people of the city.[54]

Taking together the apologetic and general analytic works written by Jews on economic issues, we see that during the age of mercantilism, Jewish economic speculation, reflecting the Jews' occupational structure, focused on commerce and its benefits for the national economy. (As the radically "enlightened" philosopher and educator Lazarus Bendavid wrote, "[When I was a child] to be a merchant . . . was the highest ideal which I knew and strove to attain."[55]) An ethos of utility, a positive view of trade, and innovation and enterprise in the distributive sector characterize the economic sensibilities of the Jewish economic elite. Many Gentile policy makers shared this orientation and, like the Jews, favored economic freedom over a corporatist, guild-based system.[56]

Unlike the economic thinking of Jews, however, mainstream economic science, whether in the guise of central European cameralism or British political economy, devoted considerable attention to, and frequently centered on, agriculture. The reason for the difference is that the Jewish texts were composed by merchants or rabbis defending the Jews' economic interests, whereas general works of economic science were penned by bureaucrats, who made policy for countries with prominent, even dominant, agrarian sectors. The failure of Jewish apologists in the age of mercantilism to engage the full matrix of the economic life of their host societies demonstrates the limitations on Jewish economic thinking of the time.

European economic thinking in the eighteenth century consisted of far more than the debate over the relative benefits of manufacture and commerce versus agriculture, or of free trade versus corporatism. Underlying the discourse of political economy was anxiety about the poor and a search to render them more productive. Members of the Jewish economic elite shared this concern. In Berlin in the 1760s, Jewish-owned textile factories began to employ Christian children from the royal orphanage as laborers. In the next decade, when the exploitation of orphans came under attack, Jewish manufacturers reduced working hours and added educational facilities for them.[57]

Under pressure from the state as well as its own personal ambitions, Berlin's Jewish economic elite served as the communal leadership, one of whose long-standing functions was the supervision of poor care. The authorities' obsession with the general problem of poverty and vagrancy was internalized by the Jewish elite, which bore the responsibility for whatever poor, wayward, and criminal souls the Jewish community contained. The Jewish elders acted on a governmental recommendation of 1743 that a lodging house for the traveling poor be constructed outside one of the two gates through which Jews were allowed to enter the city. The Jews also posted their own guards at these gates to discourage the entry of foreign Jewish paupers. In the early 1760s, the time when Jewish factories were employing Christian orphans, Daniel Itzig and Veitel Heine Ephraim proposed the establishment of a "jüdisches Armen-Kinderhaus," wherein poor Jewish children would be molded into productive subjects through instruction in German, arithmetic, and science.[58] These ideals were realized in the Berlin Jewish Freischule, founded in 1781 by members of the Jewish economic elite, including Itzig and his son-in-law David Friedländer (1750–1834), a silk manufacturer and prominent figure in the late phases of the German Haskalah.

The Berlin Jewish economic elite provided the impetus for an economic reconfiguration of the Jews. But that impetus faded after the 1770s, as the leadership role of the elite began to weaken and that of Jewish publicists and educators began to increase. In Berlin, as throughout western Europe, the rise of an educated reading public of ministers, litterateurs, doctors, and bureaucrats brought about the rise of published journals that purported to communicate "public opinion," an intellectual presence that overlapped with, but existed separately from, government policy. Accordingly, the principal vehicle for discussion about Jewish issues shifted from the bureaucratic memorandum to the published journal. A small Jewish circle, the most famous representative of which was the philosopher Moses Mendelssohn (1729–86), emerged as the source of Jewish public opinion. True, the Jewish entrepreneurs continued to play a crucial role as financial supporters of that circle's literary and educational projects. And as the case of Friedländer shows, some overlap between the Jewish publicists, known as *maskilim,* and the Berlin Jewish economic elite would remain. But the *maskilim* came from diverse social backgrounds; their ranks included entrepreneurs, rabbis, physicians, clerks, and tutors.[59]

Ironically, despite the powerful economic critique of the Jews in Gentile public opinion of the late eighteenth century, and despite the *maskilim's* close ties with the Berlin Jewish mercantile elite, the Haskalah movement that flourished during Mendelssohn's lifetime avoided or at best subordinated economic issues in its writings. The next generation of *maskilim,* coming of age after Mendelssohn's death in 1786, loosened its connections with the Jewish upper class, which had become increasingly diverse, religiously polarized, and contentious. Paradoxically, the lessening of the Berlin Jewish elite's ability to bankroll the Jewish intelligentsia's operations further stimulated the radicalization of the Haskalah, one of whose manifestations was systematic reflection on Jewish economic behavior.[60] This speculation represented the beginnings of a bona fide Jewish political economy.

Educating Shylock: Economics in the German Haskalah

The science of Jewish political economy originated in Germany. Germany's *maskilim* undertook a systematic reconceptualization of all aspects of Jewish life, including, over time, economic behavior. Although the mercantile elite of French and English Jewry initiated a number of philanthropic projects designed to alter the occupational profile of poor Jews, they offered little justification for their action save for humanitarianism and the alleviation of pressure on the communal poor chests. Even in Germany, Jewish political-economic thinking was limited to a few members of a small circle of intellectuals who produced what is known to history as the Berlin Haskalah.

There were substantive distinctions between the first generation of the Berlin Haskalah, associated with Mendelssohn and Naphtali Herz Wessely (1725–1805), and the second, dominated by the likes of Friedländer, Lazarus Bendavid (1762–1832), and Herz Homberg (1749–1841). The first generation favored Hebrew, the second German; the first proposed moderate reforms in Jewish life, while the latter was more radical; the former focused on the renewal of Judaism, while the latter addressed the improvement of the Jews' status.[61] Accordingly, the writings of Mendelssohn and Wessely contain relatively little economic material, whereas later *maskilim* possessed of a more secular worldview devoted substantial attention to economics.

It is intriguing that Mendelssohn, a savvy and successful industrialist who wrote thoughtful memorandums on silk manufacture, all but neglected economic issues in his Jewish writings. Mendelssohn rose from serving as tutor to the children of the silk manufacturer Bernhard Isaac to Isaac's bookkeeper, then his manager, and finally co-owner as well as director.[62] In this capacity he wrote, first in 1771 and then in 1782, about the disadvantages of governmental regulation of the silk industry. The latter work was a series of responses to a memorandum by a Huguenot silk manufacturer who favored a bureaucratized workplace environment, featuring a highly specialized labor force and mandatory apprenticeship in silk manufacture for any aspiring merchant of the precious fabric. Taking issue with these views, Mendelssohn argued against occupational compulsion of any sort, noting that pigeonholing workers into particular tasks stifled their creativity and productive potential. A multiskilled workforce, he contended, would be able to manufacture a variety of products in a single plant, thus increasing the marketability of the factory's wares, and hence its profits.[63]

This emphasis on economic freedom is apparent in the only sustained piece of economic speculation that can be indubitably attributed to Mendelssohn, a six-page section of the introduction to the 1782 German translation of Menasseh Ben Israel's *The Salvation of Israel*. Here Mendelssohn argues that state intervention in the economy works against natural economic laws that dictate population movement out of unprofitable livelihoods and into lucrative ones. Expanding on the themes in Menasseh Ben Israel's work, Mendelssohn argues for the utility of commerce: "Producing is not only *making*, but also *doing*. Not only he who works with his hands, but also absolutely anyone who does something . . . initiates, facilitates," is of benefit. Agriculturalists are "an indeed estimable but yet lesser [*geringerer*] portion of the population."[64]

(This is an eyebrow-raising statement for a land three-fourths of whose population lived on and off the land.)

However brief, this section was referred to by subsequent generations of *maskilim* and Jewish journalists, who invoked it to defend Jewish mercantile activity and attack those who would associate productivity with production alone.[65] But such a reading misses Mendelssohn's point. When read in the context of the essay as a whole, the section's defense of economic freedom becomes one component of Mendelssohn's general program for the maximization of human freedom. The section begins and ends on a moral and philosophical note. All individuals have worth and dignity, writes Mendelssohn at the beginning: "for a wise government no beggar is superfluous; no cripple is fully useless."[66] And the section is immediately followed by a discussion of the abrogation of communal autonomy, another limitation on individual freedom.

Mendelssohn's economic views must be understood in the broader context of his attitude toward the relationship between Jews and politics. If Mendelssohn dealt with economics briefly, and only then as part of a plea for civil rights, it was because his political involvement was circumscribed and his approach to the state characterized by caution, even trepidation. On the one hand, during the 1770s Mendelssohn did intercede on behalf of Jewish communities in Germany and Alsace when discriminatory legislation threatened to throttle their religious practices and economic life.[67] On the other hand, Mendelssohn believed that so long as Jews were deprived of civil rights, that is, effectively extruded from the body politic, there was no reason for them to engage in issues of concern to the general public. It made little sense to urge Jews to serve the state, wrote Mendelssohn, when the only service allowed to them was to be milked for cash. Mendelssohn claimed to have little knowledge of politics and statistics; he claimed to be far removed from the corridors of power and contented himself to watch from the sidelines.[68] Thus for Mendelssohn, Haskalah was associated with religiosity, philosophical speculation, and aesthetics.

One encounters a similar contrast between a vigorous mercantile life and a marginalization of economics in theory in Naphtali Herz Wessely. Like his brother Moses, Naphtali Herz was a merchant, raised in Copenhagen, where his father was a purveyor to the Danish king. Also like his brother, Naphtali Herz ascended and slid down the ladder of success with dizzying speed. Having made and lost a fortune in precious stones, Mendelssohn and other Berlin *maskilim* came to Wessely's assistance;

Mendelssohn commissioned him to contribute the portion on Leviticus to the Bi'ur, the translation of and commentary on the Pentateuch that Mendelssohn supervised.[69]

Wessely was a prolific writer, producing didactic poetry, biblical and Rabbinic commentary, and works on Hebrew philology. Wessely's programs for Jewish reform were based on a notion of universal, secular knowledge, which the current Jewish educational system failed to instill. Whereas many Orthodox rabbis of the time saw secular education as a useful supplement to the traditional Talmudic curriculum, that is, as a source of vocational training or an aide to sacred textual study, Wessely considered such education essential, for in it lay the root of universal morality and civility. Wessely's notions about the interdependence of education, morality, and utility represent an internalization of the social values of the German Enlightenment, the Aufklärung.[70]

Wessely's devotion to the study of language and his belief in the relationship between purity of expression and moral elevation left their imprint on his most celebrated work, *Divrei shalom ve-emet* (Words of Peace and Truth, 1782–85), which was the Haskalah's first systematic tract on Jewish educational reform. These tracts do suggest some understanding of the Jews' material needs and the function of Jewish education as a means of economic reform. Wessely notes that out of every one hundred pupils in a Jewish lower school, perhaps two are destined to become Talmudists and another five have the ability to become truly learned Jews.[71] To earn their living, most Jewish youth will need to learn a livelihood (*melakhah*); Wessely specifically mentions medicine, engineering, architecture, the nautical sciences, and various kinds of handicrafts as sources of social benefit, status, and benefit to the polity (*ha-kibbutz ha-medini*).[72]

These matters take up only a minuscule portion of Wessely's tract, however. The first section of *Divrei shalom ve-emet* barely touched on practical matters, and even the fourth, which is by far the longest section and offers the most detail about Wessely's educational program, devotes scarcely five pages out of one hundred to the issues discussed above. Throughout the work, Wessely subordinates economic issues, or places them within a framework of questions about the language of instruction, the training of teachers, and the form and content of instruction in sacred Jewish texts. Central to Wessely's pedagogical project is instruction in Hebrew and the Gentile vernacular, the mastery of which will, Wessely believes, promote inner cultivation, moral elevation, and an aesthetic sense.[73] Wessely identifies education, even for small children, with *Bildung,* the Germanic ideal of self-cultivation, which itself over-lapped with traditional Jewish concepts of morality (*musar*). But this equation led Wessely into a highly contradictory position. On the one hand, his educational program centered around language and literature, but on the other hand, he campaigned against the formation of a surplus of textually learned Jewish youth. Wessely left unclear why a generation of young Jews fluent in German and able to appreciate the beauty of the Hebrew Psalter would necessarily be any more employable than precocious Talmudists. Moreover, Wessely envisioned only a reform, not a dismantling, of the traditional curricular fare of sacred texts.[74]

Indeed, if we move beyond Wessely to the educational program of the early Haskalah as a whole, we encounter little interest in vocational training and an overwhelming concentration on Torah education. Most of the articles about education in the Haskalah journal *Ha-Me'asef* (The Gatherer)[75] dealt with religious and linguistic instruction, ethics, and hygiene. Typical was an article of 1786 by Elia Morpurgo, a silk manu-facturer in Gradisca, near Trieste. Focusing mostly on sacred textual and ethical education, Morpurgo acknowledged the need for practical edu-cation, but only from the age of fourteen, when boys should learn some German, arithmetic, history, and geography to prepare for their "going out into a craft or commerce."[76] The only programmatic article in *Ha-Me'asef* to deal substantively with vocational training was a piece of 1788 by Hertz Homberg, whom we shall turn to in our analysis of the radical Haskalah below. *Ha-Me'asef*'s neglect of vocational issues is but a symp-tom of a more significant phenomenon — the early Haskalah's failure to engage the political-economic discourse that was no less integral to Eu-ropean public opinion of the era than the linguistic and moral-philosophical literature that the *maskilim* took so much to heart. To be sure, *Ha-Me'asef* did offer, in addition to its philological and belle-lettrist material, information about the natural sciences — botany, zoology, mineralogy, and so on. But these discussions about *Naturwissenschaft* only highlight the neglect of *Polizeiwissenschaft,* the science of social and economic organization.[77]

The mid-1780s marked the beginning of the radicalization of the Ber-lin Haskalah, and with it the onset of serious speculation about Jewish economic reform and the means to attain it. With the death of Men-delssohn and the subsequent loss of his restraining influence, as well as that of the Prussian king Frederick II, who had opposed wide-ranging reforms of the Jews' civil status, came a new dynamic to the Haskalah, a dynamic with a distinctively political element. A royal commission was appointed to study the reform of the Jews' status, and between 1787 and 1792 a committee of Prussian Jewish notables led by David Friedländer submitted a series of petitions for the expansion of Jewish rights. The open discussions about the civil reform of the Jews catalyzed some *maskilim,* including Saul Ascher and Lazarus Bendavid, to ruminate on the need to radically transform Jewish religious practice.[78] As the possibilities for civil reform grew more real, and notions of substantive religious reform gained popularity, the goal of amalgamation with the Gentile body politic became thinkable. As such an amalgamation would have to take place in the economic as much as the cultural realm, the later *maskilim* moved economic reform from the periphery of the Haskalah project and pushed it toward the center.

Bendavid is well known to students of the Haskalah as a philosopher and educator, director of the Berlin Jewish Freischule, and an extreme rationalist and radical reformer. What has been overlooked, however, is his complex attitude toward economic affairs, an attitude produced, at least in part, by childhood trauma.

Bendavid was born in Berlin to a family of moderate means, sufficiently well-to-do to educate him with private tutors. Bendavid's mother's family was involved in textile manufacture, and as a child he spent time in weavers' workshops, where he learned about the craft. Just before his bar mitzvah, Bendavid's Polish Talmud tutor persuaded him to go to the weavers with whom his grandfather worked on a putting-out basis and offer to sell their products on commission. The lad sold the cloth in the Huguenot colony in Berlin and split the profits with the tutor. Bendavid soon encountered a truculent customer, who threw the boy out of his store and into the street. He was further traumatized by his tutor, who beat him when the boy announced that he was breaking off the arrangement. The experience convinced Bendavid that he "would never peddle again." Shortly thereafter, Bendavid was put to work as a clerk; he left his position after a year, determined to have nothing to do with commerce. He tried, unsuccessfully, to become a carpenter and glazier and then found a patron to sponsor the mathematical and philosophical studies on which he would base his career.[79] Bendavid's distaste for commerce would continue throughout his adult life. In 1797 circumstances forced Bendavid to take a position as manager of a business firm, but his autobiography assures the reader that the job involved "no commercial activity, rather, merely accounting and bookkeeping."[80]

Bendavid's philosophical and other writings reflected both discomfort with the association between Jews and trade and an appreciation of economic science as a pillar of the modern state. Whereas Mendelssohn's sense of solidarity with his fellow Jews inspired sympathy for Jewish economic activity and trepidation toward the state, Bendavid's sense of alienation from Judaism led to critiques of Jewish economic behavior and an engagement with the political-economic discourse of cameralism. While at the university in Göttingen in 1795–96, Bendavid obtained notes for a lecture course titled "Polizey-und Kameralwissenschaft."[81] He wrote an essay, "On Money and the Value of Money," an outline for a series of lectures that he planned to give on Adam Smith, whose writings were the object of debate in Germany in the late 1700s. The essay, which criticized Smith's support for paper currency, employed arguments common to cameralist thinking of the era.[82] Bendavid also accepted as valid the cameralist critique of Jewish economic behavior, and he incorporated that critique into his best-known work on a Jewish theme, *Etwas zur Charakteristick* [*sic*] *der Juden* (1793). Here, economic themes, so muted in the earlier *maskilic* works, are woven into the fabric of the text.

The work begins with an account, which conflates ontological with historical analysis, of the process by which the Jews have attained their current degraded state. First, in antiquity the Jew was enslaved, and slaves do not respect, but fear and despise, one another. Then, with the triumph of Christianity, Jews threatened by the dominant faith adhered all the more fanatically to their laws and practices. Searching for reconciliation with the God who, the Jews believed, was punishing them, Jews came to scorn their brethren, suspecting them of insufficient piety and therefore holding up redemption. The Jews' hostile, defiant, and public display of piety, which made no effort to conceal their hatred for Christianity, aroused fear and anger in Christians, thus resulting in a further degradation of the Jews, who were robbed of personal and communal freedoms and forced into the most despised of occupations, small-scale commerce.[83]

Now the Jew stood in reference to his brethren in a threefold relationship: as a fellow slave, as a coreligionist, and as a participant in the same livelihood. All three relationships could not increase the love of Jews for other Jews. As a fellow slave he had no respect for him as a person, as a coreligionist he had no trust in him as a Jew, and as a fellow merchant [he felt] no joy in his prosperity, because he primarily feared being ruined by him.[84]

Bendavid goes on to argue that the Jews' status as a despised merchant promoted an unhealthy avarice and misanthropy. Scorned by Gentile society and unable to feel affinity with his own people, the Jew becomes an egoist, scorning human approval and finding solace only in his riches. But, paradoxically, the Jew's egotism causes him to crave approval and recognition of his accomplishments. Seeking public approval, the Jew gives heavily to charity. Thus the free-spending Jewish philanthropist is actually motivated by deep-seated misanthropy![85]

This is the mise-en-scène for Bendavid's work. The text then goes on to cover such classic Haskalah topics as the critique of talmudism and the Jews' linguistic deficiencies, and it ends with a call for Jews to abandon the ceremonial law and embrace a natural religion. Nonetheless, the essay brings the Jews' economic dysfunction to the forefront of the discussion. Bendavid's disassociation from the realm of Jewish observance and textual study, his attempt to loosen the bonds that had united the Jews for more than a millennium, forced him to confront the undeniable, material, ongoing distinctiveness of the Jews in the economic realm.

The correlation between an abstract, universalist religious reformism, on the one hand, and a concrete, particularist economic analysis, on the other, is found among the radical *maskilim* as a whole, not only Bendavid, but also such figures as David Friedländer and Herz Homberg.

Friedländer, who saw himself as Mendelssohn's closest disciple, did not possess his master's intellectual depth and breadth. But during the decade after Mendelssohn's death, he was perhaps the most influential leader of Prussian Jewry. A prosperous silk manufacturer, Friedländer augmented his wealth considerably through marriage to the daughter of the banker Daniel Itzig. Like Mendelssohn, Friedländer was a respected figure in government circles, and, like his mentor, Friedländer produced governmental memorandums on the silk industry.[86] Not surprising, given his firsthand experience with the labyrinthine Prussian mercantilism bureaucracy, Friedländer shared Mendelssohn's taste for economic freedom. Freedom of trade and occupational liberty, Friedländer wrote, are prerequisites for national wealth; merchant and crafts guilds are comparable to "unproductive common lands" and must be abolished.[87] But unlike the most famous representative of the Berlin Haskalah, Friedländer accepted the Gentile critique that many Jews were economically unproductive, and he made the direct association between morality and economic utility that was central in the political-economic imagination of the period. This difference between the two men, as several historians have argued, was in part class based. Friedländer's acceptance of the Gentile stereotype of Jewish unproductivity was made possible by his elite social standing, which caused him to look on the poor Jewish masses as utterly alien.[88] But neither Bendavid nor Homberg, who is discussed below, originated in Friedländer's lofty social stratum. Rather, there is something inherent in the structure of these men's worldviews that attracted them to the economic problems of the Jews.

Whereas Mendelssohn saw virtually any laboring Jew as useful, Friedländer's writings distinguish between those who are at present useful and those who have the potential to be so. Clearly, Friedländer considered elite merchants and manufacturers like himself to be of the utmost utility, but his feelings about commerce were nonetheless complex. Significantly, Friedländer composed a treatise on business ethics, *Briefe über die Moral des Handels,* published in 1785.

In this epistolary exchange between Friedländer and a young aesthete who has decided to become a merchant, Friedländer follows the lines of earlier apologetics by portraying commerce as vital to the national economy and the spread of culture between peoples. After paying homage to Mendelssohn, the epitome of the virtuous, cultured merchant, Friedländer goes on to undermine his own argument by unfavorably comparing "trade," the exchange of tangible objects, with "philanthropy," the exchange of intangible for tangible objects. Intangibles, such as health and good sense, are inherently moral, and their value cannot be easily measured: "The more the value of the object to be exchanged is indeterminable, the more noble and moral considerations enter into the transaction of this type." The doctor and the teacher do not provide their services out of a desire for personal gain alone but rather for personal satisfaction and a sense of brotherly love. It is up to the recipient to determine payment. In turn, the recipient responds to *philanthropy* with *generosity.* "Er belohnt, nicht bezahlt"; he gives because he wants and not because he must.

In the world of commerce, on the other hand, philanthropic attitudes are as out of place "as pineapples in a cold climate." Everything has its price, and the bottom line determines all. Friedländer depicts the businessman as a heroic figure in that he must constantly struggle against greed and other lowly drives. It is the triumph of reason over feeling, of nobility and honesty over the temptations to behave dishonorably, that makes the merchant worthy of praise.[89] Let us keep in mind that a belief in commerce's corrupting qualities was common in moral philosophy of the period; the father of capitalist theory, Adam Smith, favored the free market precisely because it would impede the formation of cartels and combinations that would raise prices and unfairly enrich the merchant.[90] But even so, Friedländer's tone is unusually dark and ambivalent.

Petty trade, Friedländer writes toward the end of the essay, is no less than a war of all against all. The peddler is scorned and disreputable; he does not have a well-established clientele; the market out in the hinterlands is not large enough to put a lid on prices, and so gouging ensues. Here the Jews, "despised and despicable" petty traders, make their appearance.[91] Skeptical as to whether petty traders can ever be reformed, Friedländer casts an unusually long shadow over the prospects for Jewish civil improvement. But there is a ray of hope, he concludes; perhaps every merchant can aspire to be like Mendelssohn.

For Friedländer, the justification and one of the primary goals of Jewish civil improvement is utility. One encounters the call for service to the "body politic" (*kibbutz medini*) in Wessely, but Friedländer emphasized it far more strongly. A concrete example of this shift comes from Friedländer's German rendering of the first part of Wessely's *Divrei shalom ve-emet*. Throughout, Friedländer's text is less a translation than a paraphrase of the original. Of interest to us here is a passage in the Hebrew original that praises secular learning, argues for its universal character, and claims that it will "shore up the breach in the house of Israel," "so that [the Jews] might be successful, to assist in [the monarch's] kingdoms with their deeds and labor and wisdom."[92] In Friedländer's hands this passage becomes a manifesto for Jewish mobilization on behalf of the absolutist state:

[Joseph II sees] that we are only a dislocated [*verenktes*], but not mutilated [*verstummeltes*], limb in the body politic, and from the first glance he recognizes with sublime insight how it can be once again put into action and can operate for the best of the whole. . . . His far-reaching glance sees how through encouragement, assistance, and forbearance, long-unused powers become active, and the state achieves new bloom and splendor through new industry and zeal.[93]

Friedländer's words were repeated in a petition of 1787, in which a deputation of Prussian Jewish notables, including Friedländer, described the Jews to a royal commission as a "dislocated, but not useless, limb in the state machine. With childlike longing we await the moment of mobilization."[94]

How will this mobilization take place, and what form will it assume? We find answers to these questions in the *Akten-stücke*, a collection of petitions and other documents produced over the years 1787–92 by the deputation of Prussian Jews for the royal commission on the improvement of the Jews' civil status. Friedländer, who published the collection in 1793, was undoubtedly the principal author of its contents.[95] At the end of the volume is a summary of the Jewish deputies' requests in fifteen sections, eleven of which dealt with economic freedoms: six called for freedom of occupation and movement, four for the abolition of extraordinary taxes and collective liability for their payment, and one for the determination of poor care policies on the local, communal level. Three demands dealt with equality before the law, and one with educational freedoms. In other words, economic freedom was, for Friedländer and the Jewish notables in whose name he wrote, an essential component of Jewish civil improvement.[96]

For the most part, on Friedländer's view, Jewish economic freedom will translate into the expansion of commerce, the money trade, and manufacture. But Friedländer also considers it essential for Jews to take up livelihoods in crafts and agriculture, for their own benefit as much as that of the state. Reflecting the experience of his own mercantile background, Friedländer notes that commerce, however rewarding, is not stable and that many Jews who inherit sizable sums from their merchant fathers go bankrupt due to commercial misfortune. The dizzying financial ascent of Berlin Jewry during the Seven Years' War was a windfall, not to be repeated. Moreover, Friedländer cautions, in recent decades commerce has become an overcrowded field among Jews and Gentiles alike. Economic freedom, therefore, will not only allow the Jews greater access to the marketplace, it will also allow them to choose viable alternatives to commerce.[97]

These writings by Friedländer reflect an eclectic cameralism. He makes no specific appeal to physiocracy, mercantilism, or any other economic theory but rather offers a bald assessment of the Jews' economic needs and asserts that these needs correspond with those of the state. As we saw in the previous chapter, physiocracy played a relatively minor role in the Jewish policies of the central European absolutist states, so its failure to inform Friedländer should come as no surprise.

The late German Haskalah's correspondence between radicalism and an economic orientation was not unique to Friedländer, or to the Berlin Jewish elite to which he belonged. Herz Homberg, a *yeshiva bokher* from Bohemia, embraced the Haskalah as a young man and, throughout his career, held a variety of positions in the Hapsburg Empire that involved close collaboration with the government and a harsh critique of Jewish practices. In 1788, while serving as superintendent of German-language Jewish schools in Galicia under Joseph II, Homberg published a critique of traditional Jewish education, which included a call for instruction in "household management" (*hanhagat ha-bayit*) and practical livelihoods (*melakhot*) in the broadest sense of the term. Underlying Homberg's educational program was the claim that the Jews are an integral part of the polity in which they live and so must act for its good.[98] The tone of this article is unremarkable, but over time, Homberg's economic thinking became both more systematic and dogmatic.

Between 1807 and 1814 Homberg published three catechistic works for Jewish youth. The first, *Imrei Shefer,* composed in Hebrew, went far beyond Friedländer in arguing that agriculture and crafts are the "pillars of civil society" on which all other classes are dependent. Perhaps alluding to differences between the western European maritime powers and central Europe, Homberg argues that whereas "sea peoples" have extensive contact with foreign markets, and so can import many of their necessities, land-based nations must depend on their own people to provide sustenance.[99] Homberg made his argument more forcefully in the later catechisms, *B'nei Tsiyon* and *Ben Jakir,* both of which were written in German. In an outburst of classic physiocratic argumentation, Homberg claims that although merchants are useful as distributors, their numbers must be limited, because they are supported by those who produce goods (farmers and fishermen) and those who transform raw into finished products (craftsmen and manufacturers).[100]

The German catechisms contain extensive economic discussions, which amount to between 10 and 15 percent of the total text. This is remarkable given the all-embracing nature of these works, which purport to present the essence of all useful and edifying knowledge to Jewish children. Beginning with general exhortations to diligence, the catechisms offer a detailed analysis of the productive and distributive sectors of the economy. Employing an argument that is as old as Plato, Homberg argues that merchants are economically beneficial in that they save producers and consumers the trouble of having to market and locate goods, respectively.[101] Excessive numbers of middlemen, however, reduce the market share per merchant; profit margins increase in an attempt to make up for the lost turnover, and thus prices rise, to the harm of the economy. Accordingly, Homberg urges Jewish parents to train their children in crafts or agriculture.

The catechisms had little impact. The first was widely distributed in the new state-sponsored Jewish elementary schools, but these schools were not well attended; in Lemberg in 1795, 389 Jewish children attended the new schools, while 1,574 attended traditional ones. In 1811 a governmental decree proclaimed that any betrothed Jewish couple in Galicia and Bohemia would be required to take an examination based on the text of *B'nei Tsiyon* before their marriage could be licit. But connections and bribery often circumvented this policy, or Jews simply avoided getting a governmental license.[102]

Most Jews in Galicia saw the catechisms as yet another loathsome act by a man who was already heartily detested. In 1794 Homberg had called for strict censorship of Jewish books, effectively banning most Jewish literature, including Talmudic commentaries and kabbalistic works. Moreover, in 1797 he supported the imposition of a dreaded tax on Sabbath candles.[103] It is no surprise, therefore, that the rational aspects of Homberg's project for Jewish economic restructuring were ignored. Rather, he became a demonological figure in the imagination of Galician Jewry. A folk legend related:

Guarded by dragoons, [Homberg] sat in front of the synagogue in the center of the Jewish quarter [of Lemberg], eating pork sausages; he wanted to lead the Jewish children to baptism and indoctrinate them with the Torah of "Moses the Glutton" [Moshe Fresser, a popular derogatory name for Mendelssohn]. The emperor Joseph sorely regretted his decision to have sent this "Homburg" to Lemberg, for Rabbi Leib Sure's [*sic*] flew every Friday from Brody to Vienna and punished the monarch for the conscription of Jewish youth and compulsory education.[104]

Although not subject to as much visceral hatred as Homberg, Bendavid and Friedländer are not beloved figures in Jewish history either. All three men are often portrayed, accurately enough, as extreme reformers who sought to dismantle all Jewish particularities, religious and social, meld the Jews into the body politic of their ambient societies, and preserve little of their heritage save for a strong ethical sense and a passion for social justice. But it is precisely this politicized agenda that accounted for their interest in economic speculation. Jewish acculturation in central Europe at the turn of the eighteenth century occurred along a spectrum. At the lower end of the spectrum were those forms of non-Jewish knowledge most easily reconciled with traditional Jewish practice and society. Literary German and the practical arts and sciences are examples of this sort of knowledge. Natural and moral philosophy were further along the spectrum; early modern Ashkenazic Jewish society had disengaged itself from philosophy precisely because it was seen as a threat, and the grand project of the Mendelssohnian Haskalah was to reengage Judaism with philosophy without cutting the former loose from its moorings. But the science of state policy, *Polizeiwissenschaft*, was only absorbed by Jews who had thrown in their lot entirely with non-Jewish society and who hoped to be emulated by their brethren. Thus it is no coincidence that Jewish political economy originated not at the German Haskalah's center but at its radical periphery.

Economics in the Eastern European Haskalah

The significance — and uniqueness — of the German case may be demonstrated via a comparison with developments in eastern European Jewish culture over the same period, that is, from the 1780s to 1815. Over this period, Russia experienced a proto-Haskalah, with a number of rabbis asserting the value of the medieval Jewish rationalist heritage and proclaiming esteem for natural sciences such as astronomy and medicine.[105] But Russian and Polish Jewry before 1815 expressed virtually no interest in political economy in general and the question of the Jews' socioeconomic transformation in particular. There were few displays or portents of Jewish integration into general society, which remained a foreign entity in Jewish eyes.

There were fascinating exceptions. Shklov, a small city in eastern Belarus, became in the 1780s a beehive of Jewish cultural activity, thanks to the town's position on the Russo-Polish border and its economic and cultural vitalization at the hands of its owner, Semion Gavrilovich Zorich. Nota Khaimovich Notkin, a prominent merchant, contractor for Zorich, and *shtadlan* (community intercessor with the Gentile authorities), penned a memorandum in 1797 that one historian has called "the first contribution by a Jew to the political debate on the Jewish question in Russia." The memorandum called for a program of massive Jewish agricultural colonization. In subsequent years Notkin modified his position, and came to favor the establishment of communally owned factories that would put impoverished Jews to work in industrial enterprise. Neither form of Notkin's economic vision, however, found an echo among the rabbis and communal leaders of Shklov; their engagement with general cultural currents was limited to mathematics, the natural sciences, and geography.[106]

A more influential figure than Notkin was Menachem Mendel Lefin

(1749–1826), a Podolian Jew who, while living in Berlin in the early 1780s, came to know Mendelssohn and other *maskilim* and began a life-long engagement in the production of translations and manifestos for the reform of Jewish life. In 1791, as the Polish Sejm discussed numerous proposals for the improvement of the Jews' status and living conditions, Lefin submitted an essay that focused on the need to combat what he believed were the pernicious influences of kabbalah and Hasidism and to introduce Polish-language instruction in Jewish schools. One means to regenerate the Hasidim, he believed, was to settle them as farmers; and Jewish society in general would benefit from tougher charitable regulations that would force Jewish beggars to work. Also in the early 1790s, Lefin composed a Hebrew essay on the flaws of contemporary Jewish society. The essay contained stinging criticisms of the Jews' economic behavior and outlook:

At present a foolish notion has slipped in among our ignorant and common folk that since we see that the limbs of our bodies were created weaker than those of other peoples . . . [God] did not create us for hard physical labor at all but only for lofty occupations and spiritual values, except for a few men of low worth among us to whom somewhat stronger bodies were given, as if it were allowed to them temporarily, by implication, to engage in hard physical labor. Strenuous crafts and working the land remain for the horses and asses and for people like a beast, [people] who were created only to follow their bellies; food alone shall be their wage. And so the merchants and entrepreneurs are the elite and important among us, and behind them the students and the idlers receiving their sustenance from the public, and the craftsmen and their like are the least of them all.[107]

The Jews, Lefin claimed, are excessively materialistic, addicted to luxuries and status symbols. They crave money more than do Gentiles, but they cannot satisfy even their basic needs, for they are overcrowded in petty commerce and in selected crafts, such as tailoring, baking, and shoemaking. The solution is the development of new forms of cottage industry, especially the spinning and weaving of cloth, which can be sold to a wide market and hence always fetch a good price.

Lefin was unique among Jewish writers in late-eighteenth-century Poland in his call for a thorough socioeconomic transformation of the Jews. He was influenced by the economic orientation of the late Berlin Haskalah, although he shunned its radical, assimilatory quality. In this Lefin, who moved to Galicia in 1808 and lived there until his death, was prototypical of the post-1815 eastern European Haskalah, which, although cautious on issues of religious reform, accepted the radical Berlin

Haskalah's diagnosis of Jewish economic dysfunction and prescriptions for its cure.

Maskilim in Galicia displayed activist economic sensibilities that contrasted sharply with traditional rabbinical views of wealth and poverty as determined by divine decree alone. Joseph Perl (1773–1839) saw "wealth [as] a natural reward for economic initiative, energy, and education; while poverty [was] the result of indolence, inertia, and illiteracy."[108] As the philosopher Nachman Krochmal (1785–1840) put it sharply, "All that is called the fortune or misfortune of a man is not something that comes upon him from without, but from his inner nature, and the man who is God-fearing, who has learned a profession or trade and strenuously opposes, from his youth, the inclination that is evil, may be assured of succeeding on his way in this world, if he desires no luxuries."[109]

This was indeed a bourgeois ideology in its advocacy of a worldly, as opposed to a pietistic, asceticism. The origins of this ideology lay less in the economic realities of early-nineteenth-century eastern Europe, whose Jews had not undergone embourgeoisement, than in the influence of the German Haskalah, whose project to enlighten Judaism and reform the Jews had begun a half century earlier. Eastern European *maskilim* admired Germany as a bastion of economic rationality and German Jewish merchants as models of prudence, modesty, acumen, and moderation.[110] This idealization of Germany was, of course, unjustified in many respects, and was no more realistic than the eastern European *maskilim*'s bilious attacks against the Hasidim as uniformly wasteful, parasitical, and unproductive.

The same combination of religious conservatism and bold economic vision characterized the Russian Haskalah's first fruits, such as Isaac Baer Levinsohn's *Te'udah be-Yisra'el* (1828) and subsequent works by *maskilim* in Russia's eastern provinces. In 1847, for example, the Lithuanian *maskil* Mordechai Aaron Günzburg composed a tract expressing deep admiration for the British industrial and agricultural revolutions and agreeing fully with the gloomy assessment of small-scale commerce that Friedländer had offered in his *Briefe über die Moral des Handels*.[111]

The magnitude and traditionalism of the eastern European communities, as well as the lack of integration between the Jewish and the Gentile elites, ensured that from its start the eastern European Haskalah would lack the radical agenda of its German predecessor's last phases. At the same time, *maskilim* in eastern Europe, looking on the poverty of their fellows and hoping for an eventual improvement in their civil status, found much merit in the Berlin Haskalah's economic discourse. In Germany, however, precisely because of the assimilationism with which the Haskalah had flirted, the synthesis of Jewish political economy and a commitment to corporate Jewish continuity was longer in coming, arriving only on the eve of the conflagration of 1848.

From the Periphery to the Center: Political Economy in German Jewish Social Thought, 1815–1848

During the three decades following the end of the Napoleonic Wars, economic issues assumed a growing importance in German Jewish consciousness. By 1848 German Jewry had produced an identifiably Jewish strain of modern social thought, and throughout central and western Europe Jews had begun to transform traditional charities into modern philanthropies.

The idea of a "Jewish mission" to embody rational religion in its purest form was integral to the Haskalah. In the decades surrounding the Revolution of 1848, the mission assumed a specifically political connotation, calling on Jews to fulfill their religious obligations by being exemplary citizens.[112] Although this version of the Jewish mission was most fully developed in Germany, it also existed in France, where it had adherents even among relatively traditionalist rabbis in Alsace.[113] Parallel to this development came a reworking of traditional concepts of Judaism as epitomizing social morality. Whereas medieval rabbis conceived of Jews as commanded to pursue justice and understood many of the commandments to be of social benefit, the ultimate source and justification for the commandments was the divine will. In modern Jewish social thought, although the source of Jewish law remained the divinity, its justification was shifted to its eudaemonistic effects. Moreover, the ancient Israelite polity, rather than rabbinically generated halakhah, was held up as a blueprint for a state based on socioeconomic justice. This was done partly because of the Haskalah's biblicism, but even more because the state-building fervor of the early nineteenth century inspired some Jews to legitimize their faith by reference to their own glorious political heritage.

Characteristically, this vision emerged out of the radical Haskalah, as we see in Herz Homberg's *Ben Jakir* (1814), which featured a long paean to biblical society and its social legislation. Ancient Israel, Homberg argued, was a simple, self-sufficient land, with "no significant commercial traffic" and little recourse to money or moneylending. The Mosaic code, Homberg claimed, promoted industry, moderation, and a reasonable level of prosperity without allowing for an accumulation of wealth.[114] In the decades to come, this simple theme would be embellished by rabbis and Jewish activists, particularly in the German-speaking lands. This theme became as central to Jewish apologetics as arguments about Jewish utility had been during the previous century.

In France, a political-economic approach to the study of Judaism and the Jews remained the purview of the radical periphery. Joseph Salvador (1796–1873), a biblical scholar from a Marrano background, had little Jewish learning and appears to have been unobservant, yet he wrote a pioneering, dithyrambic account of the ancient Mosaic polity. In his book *Loi de Moïse ou système religieux et politique des Hébreux* (1822), Salvador presented ancient Israelite society as a nomocracy, an archetypal liberal republic. The book contained a detailed discussion of Mosaic social legislation, which allegedly fortified the republican spirit by preventing the accumulation of individual wealth. Moreover, Israelite republicanism was maintained by the ancient Hebrews' veneration of agriculture and their engagement in it.[115] Although Salvador's work was hailed by French Jews as a masterpiece of scholarship, its social gospel did not have visible effect, whereas in Germany it inspired the young Ludwig Philippson (1811–89), a prominent rabbi and editor of the *Allgemeine Zeitung des Judentums,* an influential and long-lived newspaper representing a moderate reformism.[116]

In the decade before the Revolution of 1848, Philippson and other Jewish activists in German-speaking Europe made Judaism's social ethos central to their self-conception. The reasons for the highlighting of this theme were twofold: the ongoing struggle for Jewish emancipation in the German lands and the general social tensions pervading the region. Partially emancipated by edict in 1812, Prussian Jews after 1815 sought to extend the boundaries of emancipation to include regions, such as Posen, that were excluded from the 1812 edict and liberties, such as public office holding, that the edict had not granted. In the western and southwestern German states, Jews who had enjoyed increased political and economic freedoms while under Napoleonic rule were dismayed by the abrogation of much of the emancipatory legislation under the Restoration. In the battle for emancipation, Jews searched for arguments that, they believed, would appeal to their Gentile interlocutors. And during the decades after 1815, the most pressing domestic issue, in the German lands as elsewhere on the Continent, was the wretched state of the laboring population. Peasant emancipation produced a landless, rural proletariat. Early industrialization disrupted older forms of crafts production and created intolerable conditions for those who labored under the new ones. A series of bad harvests during the mid-1840s raised tensions to the boiling point. It was at this time that the term "the social problem" and its equivalents in other languages gained currency.[117]

Whether for instrumental reasons or out of genuine conviction, rabbis in central Europe during the "hungry forties" made much of Judaism's social teachings. At the third and last of three Reform-oriented rabbinical assemblies, held in Breslau in 1846, the "social meaning" of the Sabbath was a topic of discussion; one delegate called the Sabbath a "social regulation." Two years later the young Bohemian rabbi Adolph Jellinek (1820–93), who would become a celebrated preacher, scholar, and publicist in Vienna, wrote of the Jewish mission to work for social progress.[118] As in the case of Salvador, discussions about Judaism's social ideals invariably hearkened back to ancient Palestine, thus fostering a particularistic association with the ancient Jewish homeland while proclaiming sympathy with the woes of the general society. Thus in 1838 a six-month-long series of articles in the *Allgemeine Zeitung des Judentums* embedded a discussion of Jewish social legislation in a detailed geographic and ecological survey of ancient Palestine. The author wrote that the ancient Israelites' social morality derived from the agricultural base of the Hebrew national economy. Only an agricultural people, he wrote, would be fit to receive divine teaching. As a sign of his engagement with contemporary political economy, he quoted at length from the contemporary German economist Albrecht Thaer, a prominent champion of the primacy of agriculture, on spiritual, moral, and economic grounds, even in a modern state.[119]

Ludwig Philippson brought a crusading temperament, a journalistic flair, and indefatigable energies to his efforts to combine the spirit of Judaism with substantive social reform. Philippson was a widely respected public figure in Magdeburg, where he held a rabbinical post and engaged in a wide variety of journalistic activities, including editing the *Allgemeine Zeitung des Judentums*. The uprisings in Berlin in March 1848 affected Philippson deeply. The plight of the German people, he wrote his brother Phöbus, is rooted deeply in the land's social structures, which "political freedom cannot ameliorate, for this, at best, will ease the way to a total revolution." "I do not foresee," he continued, "any calm for a long time; when there will be a constitution—only then will the real struggle begin[,] . . . will the social question burst forth."[120] Philippson broadcast this radical message at public gatherings in spring 1848 and took particular interest in the plight of craftsmen threatened by the import of industrially produced goods. He edited and contributed heavily to periodicals catering to artisans and promoted the local master craftsmen's association. Philippson was also respected by Magdeburg's teachers and merchants, who elected him to the boards of their professional associations. Twice he was a candidate for election to the Frankfurt Parliament, which labored unsuccessfully in 1848–49 to create a unified and liberal Germany during the upheaval of 1848.[121] Philippson's humanitarianism, eloquence, and charisma were powerful indeed, given their ability to overcome the pervasive antisemitism of the German lower middle class of the time.

Philippson's fiery reformism clearly left its mark on the *Allgemeine Zeitung des Judentums* during the years leading up to the Revolution of 1848. His lead articles looked back to ancient Palestine as a model of social justice. Projecting his own economic liberalism onto the Palestinian landscape, Philippson argued that Mosaic law demanded legal, but not economic, equality, for the latter would violate the sanctity of private property and hence of personal freedom. Nonetheless, social equity was promoted through legislation, such as the sabbatical and Jubilee years that impeded the accumulation of wealth and the descent into dire poverty. Referring to the ideas of the contemporary social thinkers Charles Fourier and Robert Owen, Philippson stressed the sociological significance of the Sabbath as "the first labor regulation," a day of rest and spiritual renewal. Philippson admitted that biblical precepts were not necessarily observed in antiquity, nor are they fully observable today, but he urged contemporary society to grasp the spirit behind them and act accordingly.[122] In 1845 Philippson made only a vague proposal for state intervention in the economy, but by 1848 his social thinking had taken a concrete, and quite surprising, turn.

Reacting to the economic as well as political chaos unleashed by the Revolution of 1848, Philippson demanded a radical reconfiguration of society based on a massive return to the soil—a return to be carried out by all the peoples of Europe, including the Jews. The "social problem," he wrote, cannot be solved in a mercantile or industrial society, which promotes crushing competition, avarice, and waste. The land-hungry rural proletariat of Europe, as well as the land-deprived Jews, must, like the Hebrews of old, be anchored in the soil, where they will form a "natural corporation," that is, a social entity defined by their livelihood and not by distinctions imposed from above. Echoing the sentiments of liberal reformers in *Vormärz* Germany, Philippson concluded that a prosperous, freeholding peasantry will be receptive to religious enlightenment and will guarantee lasting democratization.[123]

Philippson's economic views of the 1840s would change, even reverse entirely, in subsequent decades. But the inconsistency of his economic views is less important than the fact that he considered economic affairs worth thinking and writing about. This was not the case for most of the founders of the Wissenschaft des Judentums, or Science of Judaism, which was in its first flower at the time. This scholarly project was initiated in the immediate post-Napoleonic years by a handful of German Jewish intellectuals seeking to grasp the essence of Judaism through a historicist approach to the Jews' religion and culture. The founders of the Wissenschaft des Judentums conceived of Jewish history primarily in intellectual terms, whereas German historiography of the time operated within political and institutional frameworks as well.[124] Thus the founding father of modern Jewish historiography, Isaak Jost (1793–1860), neglected economic matters. Jost's ten-volume *Geschichte der Israeliten* (1820–47) yields valuable information, but, in keeping with the harsh, self-critical tone of the work as a whole, economic data are invoked only to demonstrate the corrupting effects of commerce on the Jewish character.[125]

Following suit, the most important literary fruit of the Wissenschaft des Judentums, the *Monatsschrift für die Geschichte und Wissenschaft des Judentums,* displayed, from the time it began publication in 1851, a preference for philological and religious-historical inquiry. Yet there were fascinating exceptions. The first number of the *Monatsschrift* included an article by Zecharias Frankel (1801–75), the journal's editor and principal contributor, on those aspects of Jewish law that deal with "questions of social policy [*polizeilich sociale Frage*]." Frankel defines policy as "the content of those public institutions and establishments which purport to prevent action in the legal arena, be it that of the state or of the individual, and is distinguished thereby from justice, which has as its duty the restoration of the action that has occurred, of violated law."[126] Claiming that ancient Judaism had a well-developed social policy, Frankel examines Talmudic laws of the marketplace; these proscriptions supervise and provide "care for the national economy." He relates Talmudic disagreements over the preferability of fixed versus market-determined prices to contemporary debates about guilds, whose lingering power, he argues, violated the Jewish social-political ideal that price-fixing must not be tolerated if it works against the interests of the community as a whole.[127]

In part, this article was an apologetic, an assertion that Jewish antiquity, like Greco-Roman civilization, had a well-developed sense of the public good and the means to attempt to achieve it. But the very fact that Frankel, a university-trained scholar of Jewish law and legal interpretation, would think to raise this issue and to put it in the framework of contemporary concepts of social justice points to an elevation of economics in Jewish public discourse. Philippson, too, represents this phenomenon but on a far vaster scale. Philippson's engagement with political economy was as full and rich as that of the members of the radical Haskalah but, unlike Bendavid and Homberg, Philippson sought to create a healthy modern Jewish community that was both stable and dynamic. Liberal Judaism in Germany developed a notion of a Jewish mission to serve the state in all arenas, including economic productivity. Jewish acculturation and embourgeoisement justified an identification with the German *Volkswirtschaft* (national economy). At the same time, a distinctly Jewish religious and social life remained essential.

Thus the period from the radical German Haskalah of the late 1700s to the Revolution of 1848 witnessed the forging among certain influential Jewish intellectuals of an identity that fused the religious and economic spheres. This fusion no longer took place, as in previous centuries, within the framework of the autonomous community, which regulated all aspects of its members' lives. The autonomous community was a thing of the past, the victim of the modern state's search for legal uniformity and administrative efficiency in the interests of maximizing productivity and hence state power. The fusion now took place within the host society. Attempts by Jews to engage general economic issues, to identify their economic interests with those of the state, indicate the depth and breadth of the Jews' encounter with modernity in a particular situation, as here in *Vormärz* Germany.

Philippson's articles extolling ancient Palestinian agrarianism represented the beginning of a lifelong engagement in Jewish political economy. Nor, as we shall see in the next chapter, was he alone. An attempted occupational restructuring of the Jews was a pillar of Jewish philanthropy in much of Europe, in particular in the German lands, throughout the first half of the 1800s. The practice of Jewish philanthropy, motivated by certain conceptions about the economic needs of the Jews, in turn stimulated a deepening of those concepts. The dialectic of theory and praxis, and the ongoing movement of political economic thinking from the Jewish periphery toward its center, will do much to account for the rise of modern Jewish philanthropy in the nineteenth century.

CHAPTER 3

The Origins of Modern
Jewish Philanthropy, 1789–1860

On the first day — a guest
On the second — a pest
By the third he has fled
Or he stinks like the dead.

Judeo-German proverb about housing vagabonds

With this inspection facility, nothing can pass undetected by the
vigilant eye of the director, be it for surveillance of the staff, be it for
surveillance of the patients.

Newspaper description of the Paris Jewish hospital, 1852

Like all other aspects of Jewish society, Jewish philanthropy is an arena of clashing approaches to the study of the Jewish past.
I will call these approaches "essentialist," "contextualist," and "comparative."

The essentialist line of thinking dates to the early nineteenth century,
when Jewish reformers began to conceive of *tsedakah* (the traditional
Hebrew term for charity) as a manifestation of an eternal Jewish social
ethos. Ever since, the essentialist approach has characterized the pedagogic and apologetic literature of the liberal movements in Judaism in
the Western world. This approach depicts Jewish civilization as the first
to conceive of charity as a religious obligation. Moreover, so the argument goes, from antiquity to the present Jewish philanthropy has been
characterized not only by exceeding compassion, generosity of spirit,
and communal solidarity but also by a preventive, as opposed to a

merely palliative, approach and a desire to foster the economic independence of the poor. Jewish writings in this vein focus on ancient Israelite social legislation, ostensibly for its function as a preventive against pauperization. Talmudic sources as well are combed for appropriate citations demonstrating the rabbis' solicitude for the poor and respect for their dignity. These arguments tend to be as anachronistic as they are apologetic. For example, Ephraim Frisch's classic *Historical Survey of Jewish Philanthropy* (1924) depicted the medieval *gabbai* (synagogue treasurer) as a modern-day social worker, employing "enlightened and wide-awake measures of treatment, with rehabilitation as the constant goal in view."[1]

Underlying the essentialist approach to the study of Jewish philanthropy is a heavy reliance on the Hebrew Bible and halakhic literature as explanatory sources for the Jews' remarkable levels of charitable action and philanthropic cohesion over time. Yet we must be cautious about drawing direct causal links between the charitable practices of the Jews in a particular time and place and the exhortations to care for the needy found in the Jews' textual canon. For one thing, the corpus of biblical and halakhic literature, composed over a period of more than two millennia, contains widely different dicta on charity and directives for their implementation. Moreover, throughout the long period from the completion of the Talmud to the seventeenth century, it was not so much the Jews' textual heritage as the specific conditions of the Jews' social, legal, and economic status that shaped the practice of Jewish charity.

Medieval European Jewry was primarily urban and mercantile. The Jews lived in close-knit communities, in close physical proximity. Prosperous Jews were unable to translate their wealth into landed property and so retained large amounts of liquid capital, much of which went to tax payments and poor care for the community. Lacking the characteristics of the Gentile nobility, wealthy Jews lived cheek by jowl with their poorer brethren. The Gentile authorities demanded that this elite care for the Jewish poor, and, out of both compulsion and a sense of obligation, the Jewish elite fulfilled this demand. The Jews had to care for their poor because the two principal sources of medieval charity, the church and the guilds, were closed to Jews. As a sign of the hostile environment in which medieval Jewry lived, among the most vital philanthropic services provided by the medieval communities was the ransoming of Jews taken captive in wars and acts of brigandage.[2]

What does this picture of medieval Jewish charity have to do with its modern manifestation? There have indeed been some lines of vertical, diachronic transmission of Jewish philanthropic sensibility across the centuries. But influences from the ambient environment have been at least as strong, and understanding modern Jewish philanthropy is impossible without a contextualist approach, operating horizontally and synchronically, which places the practice of *tsedakah* within the framework of the modernization of philanthropy on the Continent as a whole. At the same time, I do not intend a contextual analysis to reduce Jewish philanthropy to a mere echoing of Gentile practices. If the philanthropic strategies of the Jewish leadership elite frequently resembled those of their Gentile counterparts, the reason is not that the former were mimicking the latter but rather that the two shared similar problems and a common pool of resources, technological and intellectual, with which to solve them. Moreover, although the social problems affecting Jews and Gentiles in modern Europe often overlapped, and thus did the solutions they set forth, the problems and solutions at times diverged as well. Thus my approach here is best described as comparative rather than merely contextual.[3]

Rationality, Morality, and Philanthropy

Beginning in the sixteenth century, there was a dramatic shift in attitudes toward poverty and the poor in Europe. Because of both a real increase in the number of poor and the rise of a more activist way of thinking about poverty and its treatment, from the middle of the 1500s municipalities throughout western Europe attempted to centralize and rationalize the distribution of alms. This process quickened in the eighteenth century with the rise of Enlightenment concepts about the eudaemonistic value of work and mercantilist policies to productivize the poor as a means of maximizing the wealth of the nation.

The demographic increase and geographic diffusion of European Jewry during the early modern period promoted a notable increase in philanthropic activity. There was an expansion of traditional private charities for dowering poor brides, redeeming captives, and sending money to the Holy Land. The *hevrah kadishah,* a burial society consisting of communal notables who receive no compensation for their services, came into existence in the sixteenth century. In addition to these charities, which had no exact parallels in the Gentile world, there was a growth of institutional relief, taking the form of almshouses and hos-

pitals (i.e., shelters for the itinerant as well as the ill). For example, the
first Jewish orphanage appeared in Amsterdam in 1648.[4] Along with this
material increase came attempts to rationalize poor care along lines similar to those observed for Gentile society.

As in Europe as a whole, the rationalization of Jewish poor care had
medieval roots. In the thirteenth-century Ashkenazic *Sefer Hasidim,* one
encounters a distinction, also made in canon legal sources of the time,
between the "worthy" (*mehugan* or *hagun*) and the "unworthy" poor,
the latter deserving of only sparing and carefully supervised aid, if any
at all. Although most medieval legal sources permitted door-to-door
begging, they were less likely to accept Talmudic exhortations to Jews
to take beggars into their homes (e.g., "the poor shall be as members of
your household [Avot 1:5]). This text was interpreted by medieval commentators such as Rashi as a command to Jewish householders to employ paupers and not to accord them the hospitality one would bestow
on honored guests. Rashi's comment, however, did not necessarily reflect social reality. It is true that as early as the 1200s poor and vagrant
Jews were at times housed in communally supported hospices. But
throughout the early modern period, the most common form of support
for the vagrant poor was the distribution of tickets valid for a fixed
number of nights of lodging and food in a community member's home.[5]
The texts from Rashi and *Sefer Hasidim* are significant, nonetheless, for
they attest to a sense that charity is separate from hospitality and that
the former is subject to strict limits and controls.

An excellent source of information about Jewish poor care practices
at the cusp of the modern period comes from the Christian Hebraist
Johann Buxtorf (1564–1629), whose massive tome *Synagoga Judaica* (1st
ed. 1603) scrupulously documents the customs and society of German
Jewry. In a chapter on begging and poverty among the Jews, Buxtorf
notes, "Where there is a man who suffers from noticeably great poverty,
his rabbis, who know him, give him a begging-letter, in which they
document his want and poverty; they demonstrate also that he is pious
and of the Jewish faith, etc. They call this letter a *kibbutz,* a gathering-
letter, and the beggar is called a *kabhzan* [sic], a gatherer." When the
beggar arrives in a town, he presents the letter to the Jewish authorities
and requests permission to beg. Accompanied by two Jewish males of
that community, he stands by the synagogue entrance and begs, or the
two Jews take his letter from door to door and collect alms for him.
There are similar procedures for a poor father who needs to dower his
daughter.[6]

Buxtorf's account suggests that although begging by poor strangers was tolerated, it was controlled as well. The presence of a two-man escort assured the members of the community that the beggar was worthy of aid and ensured that he would not harass his benefactors. A similar sort of cautious and limited poor care characterized the distribution of food and lodging tickets to vagrants as well. "When poor Jews travel long distances, and come across others, they are accepted for a day or two as guests; one does not like, however, for them to stay long in one place, and so they write in their rooms: *Bejóm rischon orach, Bejom schéni thórach, Bejom schelischi barach* or *sarach*, that is, on the first day a guest, on the second a pest, on the third he has fled, or he stinks [like the dead]."[7]

By the late 1500s Jewish communities throughout Europe had moved beyond the regulation of begging and were undertaking serious efforts to move the locus of charitable giving from the individual donor to the communal institution. A statute issued by the Avignon Jewish community in 1558 requested individuals to give the poor only small amounts of aid and instituted a certificate system for the receipt of communal alms. A *takkanah* (communal regulation) in Cracow in 1595 outlawed begging door to door. But it was the flood of Jewish refugees created by the Thirty Years' War and the Russo-Polish-Cossack wars of the mid-1600s that prompted wide-ranging efforts by Jewish communities to stanch the flow of beggars and limit communal resources on care for the foreign poor. In Poland in 1623, for example, a synod of the Council of the Four Lands sought to divide the Polish-Lithuanian kingdom into districts for the regulation of itinerant begging. The synod's *takkanah* declared that beggars were to be housed for only one day and then sent on their way: "A man shall give nothing to any beggar except the ticket to send him from here."[8] Employing a similar logic, between 1622 and 1634 the Jewish leadership of Amsterdam shipped some one hundred Jewish paupers to southern Europe, Poland, and Palestine.[9]

Communal officials feared that Jewish vagrants would commit crimes against Gentiles and thereby bring the wrath of the authorities down on the Jewish community as a whole. The conceptual distinction between the worthy and the unworthy poor, first made in the Middle Ages, became sharper and assumed ever-increasing amounts of public attention. A 1649 *takkanah* from Moravia referred to "vagabonds, worthless people, robbers, and cut-throats who endanger the entire Jewish community" and who must be either expelled or handed over to the Gentile authorities.[10] A 1639 regulation of the Portuguese community of Amsterdam branded the refugees from Poland "dangerous people"; they were to be encouraged to return to their homes, and if arrested by the Gentile authorities, the Sephardim were not to intervene on their behalf.[11] This harsh language was repeated in the German lands in the next century, when demographic increase and strict residence requirements created a sizable class of Jewish vagrants, a class augmented by an influx of Jewish refugees from the Ukraine in the wake of the Haidamack uprisings.[12]

Fear alone does not account for the devotion to and rationalization of poor care that occurred in the Portuguese diaspora communities in the seventeenth century. The impoverishment of Ashkenazic Jewry occurred simultaneously with the establishment or reestablishment of communities in western Europe by prosperous Sephardic merchants. As a result, the western communities had the means as well as the motive to expand their philanthropic activity. Moreover, fear of Gentile wrath was not the only motive prompting the Sephardic elites to care for the poor among them. In part, the Sephardim were perpetuating those characteristics of the traditional autonomous community that were still available to them. For example, although the Portuguese Jews in southern France were organized as merchant guilds, not as legally autonomous communities, they took care of many of their own needs, including not only religious affairs and education but also poor care. Although the practice of autonomous poor care reached deep into the Jewish past, the methods employed by the Sephardim in France were new. From the mid-seventeenth century, for example, the almoners of the Bordeaux Jewish community had a central poor register, regularly inspected the recipients of aid, and made efforts to locate gainful employment and interest-free loans for the poor.[13]

A similar striving for efficiency characterized the Portuguese community in Amsterdam. A regulation of 1664 forbade, under pain of excommunication, all private donations to the "Ashkenazic" (i.e., of German origin) and Polish poor. Although fear of the Jewish poor as potential criminals was one motive behind such actions, there was also a strong element of ethnic prejudice, in that Ashkenazim were singled out from the resident Sephardic poor and accused of "vices, foreign to the morality and ways of Judaism."[14] The language employed by the Sephardic leadership in Amsterdam is significant for its emphasis on the alleged moral degradation of the poor Ashkenazim, who were said to be as impious as they are dangerous. Conceiving of poverty as a moral as well as an economic problem, the leaders of the Portuguese community shared in the contemporary general currents of thought about poverty. As morality was closely associated with productivity in the social thinking of the era, it is not surprising that the Sephardic elite sought to moralize the Ashkenazic poor by teaching them a useful trade. The society Avodat Hesed, founded in Amsterdam in 1642, emphasized vocational training for the poor, but only so long as its purview was the Ashkenazim; after 1670, when its focus switched to the Sephardic poor, productivization dropped from its agenda.[15]

The modernization of Jewish philanthropy, like the modernization of Jewish economic perceptions, may have had roots in many lands across a broad swath of time, but it was most clearly adumbrated by the western Sephardim. This modernization was the result of many factors: the economic dislocation of large segments of Ashkenazic Jewry, which brought them under the care of relatively prosperous Sephardim; changes in sensibility among the Sephardim about poverty, labor, and charity; and, finally, the vast and tenuous nature of the Sephardic diaspora, which encouraged the development of a Jewish identity defined more by economic and philanthopic activity than halakhic discourse and ritual observance. According to one historian, economic ties linking the members of the Portuguese diaspora, although a necessary precondition for the construction of group identity, "were primarily instrumental, and did not give spiritual or emotional value to collective existence. It was in the realms of welfare and proselytizing activity that the value of the group was affirmed."[16]

The centrality of philanthropy as a source of collective Jewish identity is indeed a hallmark of modernity. The development of this ethos among western and central Europe's Ashkenazic Jews, along with movement toward the rationalization and moralization of philanthropy, can be traced to the late eighteenth century. Exposed to Enlightenment ideology and the prospect for improvement of their legal and political status, communal leaders in England, Alsace, the German lands, and Bohemia sought to rationalize poor care by reducing the number of Jewish vagrants, centralizing the distribution of alms, and forming strict criteria for the receipt thereof.

The origins of modern Anglo-Jewish philanthropy may be traced to 1788, when the governors of the Ashkenazi Talmud Torah, a school for poor boys, altered the curriculum by cutting down on rabbinics and adding reading and writing (in English) as well as arithmetic. Associating morality with utility, the school instilled in its pupils a respect for cleanliness and propriety, and at the age of thirteen the boys were apprenticed to craftsmen. Similar motives were at work behind the establishment in 1807 of the Jews' Hospital; it combined an old-age home with a trade school, which inculcated moral values along with artisanal education. The first sustained attempt to centralize Anglo-Jewish philanthropy came in 1801, when the surgeon Joshua Van Oven proposed the establishment of an autonomous Jewish poor-relief board. In addition to policing the foreign-born Jewish poor, the board would oversee the construction of a home for the elderly and infirm, a medical hospital, an artisanal workshop, and a workhouse for the able-bodied poor. The plan was never realized, in part because of protests from London's Sephardim who were, in general, better off than the Ashkenazim and did not want to be saddled with the economic burden of supporting them. Moreover, the British government did not sanction the establishment of an autonomous private agency in the British body politic.[17]

Discussion of the need for centralized poor care continued, however, and it intensified during the mid-1840s. Harsh winters, poor harvests, and a constant stream of immigration from the Continent made the Jewish variant of the "hungry forties" especially acute. Each synagogue and charitable society operated independently, thus producing considerable overlap and waste. The methods of distribution were capricious. At times money was simply thrown into crowds. Recipients of more substantial sums were chosen by ballot, elected by the subscribers to the charity to which the supplicants had appealed.[18] Responding to this chaotic situation, in 1844 Henry Faudel called for the establishment of a central Jewish board of poor guardians; this proposal was vigorously supported by Joseph Mitchell, editor of the Anglo-Jewish weekly, the *Jewish Chronicle*.[19]

The notion that vagrancy could be combated only at the national level gained currency in the wake of the Crimean War, which brought to Britain a wave of Russian Jews fleeing the Crimea or dodging military service.[20] Abraham Benisch, owner and editor of the *Jewish Chronicle* between 1855 and 1868, used the newspaper as a bully pulpit from which to preach the gospel of philanthropic centralization. In 1857, for example, an article claimed that whereas in the past year Jewish charities in London had spent at least £ 30,000, the Parisian Comité de bienfaisance, the umbrella agency for Paris Jewish charity, spent only £ 5,240 to provide for a similar number of claimants. Thus the article endorsed earlier calls for the creation of a board of guardians to coordinate Anglo-Jewish charity.[21] Discussions about the structure and purview of such a board proceeded for two years, and the Jewish Board of Guardians (JBG) was founded in 1859. The JBG included only Ashkenazic synagogues and societies; the Sephardim remained aloof, forming their own board some twenty years later.

As we shall see in chapter 5, the JBG did not put an end to philanthropic anarchy. Lionel Cohen, the initiator and first leader of the JBG, encountered stiff resistance to his centralization efforts. Nonetheless, the JBG was in many ways an innovative institution, practicing careful selection and inspection of applicants, regular visitations, and diligent record keeping. This innovative quality had complex origins. On the one hand, the JBG was loath to make use of that most fearsome of Victorian charitable institutions, the workhouse. Until 1871 Anglo-Jewry lacked its own workhouse, and although communal officials occasionally sent Jewish paupers to the parish workhouses, they were reluctant to do so because of pressures to convert and the difficulties of observing the Jewish Sabbath and dietary laws. Thus deprived of the workhouse, Anglo-Jewish charity emphasized various forms of outdoor relief, such as cash allowances, social services, and vocational training, arguably more humane than incarceration in the workhouse.[22] On the other hand, the activity of the JBG, and of mid-Victorian Anglo-Jewish philanthropy as a whole, was stimulated by profound embarrassment and unease about the Jewish poor. As shown by recent analyses of London and Manchester Jewry, the Anglo-Jewish elite considered it essential to keep poor Jews away from the statutory welfare services and out of the public eye so as not to provoke antisemitism and thus impede Jewish integration.[23]

The rationalization of Jewish philanthropy in Britain was predicated on mixed feelings about the Jewish poor. On the one hand, there was an undeniable humanitarianism and an acknowledgment that the Christian character of much public charity forced the Jews to care for their own. On the other hand, there was a common assumption that the poor, particularly the foreign poor, were parasitic and noxious. In an editorial of 1860 in the *Jewish Chronicle*, Benisch wrote, "The Board of Guardians in its operations evidently proceeds on the correct view — that mendicancy is only a symptom . . . of a deeply seated moral disease, with which it is in vain to battle while the disease is not removed."[24] An article in the same newspaper, discussing the immigration of poor Ashkenazim to Britain during the previous century, noted that the newcomers, knowing that "their co-religionists dared not leave them to the relief of the then Christian world, revelled in all the delights of well-fed idleness, and thus formed the first link of that now weighty chain, girdled round

the attenuated form of Jewish political economy."[25] This distinction between the domestic and the foreign poor, as well as the complex issue
of relations between Jewish and Gentile charity, stand out when we turn
to the modernization of Jewish philanthropy on the Continent.

In France, the rationalization of Jewish poor care began in 1809 with
the establishment by the Paris Consistory of the Société d'encouragement et de secours to supervise and, it was hoped, centralize all charitable activity on behalf of Jews in the capital. (Reorganized and laicized
in 1839, the society took on the name Comité de bienfaisance.) From
the start, the society denied aid to those whom it considered drunks and
idlers. In 1812 the society assisted the government in the location of
foreign indigent Jews for deportation, and eight years later it responded
to a flood of poor Jewish vagrants into Paris by clamping a two-year
residency requirement for the receipt of alms.[26] Comparable principles
were at work in Alsace-Lorraine. The Alsatian Jewish leader Beer Isaac
Berr wrote in 1806 that while each community must provide for its own
infirm, the indiscriminate giving of alms must stop, and vagrants must
not be given money to continue their wanderings. Berr called for state
action to solve the problem of Jewish vagrancy.[27] From the early 1820s,
the Upper and Lower Rhine Consistories labored to limit the number
of beggars in any given locality and the amount of aid to be distributed
to them. The problem of begging remained unsurmountable, however,
and the economic troubles of the mid-1840s only aggravated the situation. (After midcentury emigration abroad and the gradual economic
ascent of those who stayed did much to resolve Alsace's Jewish crisis.)

Attitudes among the Franco-Jewish leadership toward the poor
among them were sharply divided. The most hostile views tended to
come from those in the progressive camp championing educational reform and social integration. Such Jews had accepted the connection,
drawn first in the thought of the Enlightenment and then transmitted
to nineteenth-century liberalism, between poverty, on the one hand, and
unproductivity and immorality, on the other. Jews of a more traditional
bent, including rabbis in Alsace-Lorraine, criticized the new Jewish philanthropic practices as inhumane; they saw the poor as deserving unfortunates and charity as a religious commandment to be practiced un-
grudgingly.[28]

This bifurcation between the progressive and traditional camps regarding poverty and poor care existed in Prussia as well. The radical
maskil David Friedländer compared foreign Jewish beggars to ill, and thus
presumably dangerous, vagrants. He urged that "all foreign incoming

beggars be held back, by the strongest means, already at the border of the Prussian state."[29] In 1809 the board of elders of the Berlin community, which was dominated by Friedländer and other supporters of the Haskalah, claimed that pregnant unmarried women are "an extraordinary burden on the community and its charitable institutions" and thus urged the chief of police to keep poor pregnant Jewish women from the city. Four years later Friedländer attempted to eliminate the subsidies paid to bastard children receiving aid from the Talmud Torah, which provided traditional education to poor children. The relatively lenient Orthodox Jews who ran the Talmud Torah, however, refused to hand over the names of the recipients of their services.[30]

The rationalist spirit motivating the modernizers among the Berlin Jewish leadership was present throughout Germany during the first half of the nineteenth century. The German Jewish press was filled with hostile depictions of the Jewish poor as cheeky beggars and con artists, a "cancer," as one correspondent put it, that requires radical treatment.[31] A particularly grim example of the new Jewish philanthropic ethos comes from proposals, published in the *Allgemeine Zeitung des Judentums* in 1840, to establish Jewish "industrial schools," which would combine military discipline, spartan living conditions, and rigorous labor. Beginning with five-year-olds and keeping students from five o'clock in the morning until seven o'clock in the evening, the schools would teach children a useful craft that they would practice on completion of their education. Uniform clothing, extended periods outside in cold and inclement weather, simple food, savings funds, and moral instruction, the author proclaims, would bring about a far-reaching transformation of the Jewish lower orders.[32]

Although this Dickensian vision was never realized, treatment of the Jewish poor could be harsh indeed. In Fürth, for example, from the mid-1820s to the time of German unification, the community provided very limited aid to strangers and vagabonds and strove to keep nonresident Jews out altogether. Poor Jews were sent to the general workhouse, where kosher food and Sabbath rest were not available. Moreover, poor Jewish suicides were sent to the local hospital's dissecting theater despite Jewish religious prohibitions against autopsies. Seeking to prevent the poor from bearing children, the community prohibited marriages if the groom was not deemed able to support a family, expelled pregnant unmarried women, and did not allow bastards into the communal orphanage.[33]

Harsh though they were, these policies were in keeping with the general tone of policies toward the poor in mid-nineteenth-century Bavaria, which featured the most stringent antipauper legislation in Germany. Not only among the Jews of Fürth, but in Bavaria as a whole, the receipt of charity was predicated on *Heimatsrecht,* a legal status that could be acquired only by birth in the municipality in question or legislative decree therefrom. (This was an even stricter requirement than the three-year residency required for the receipt of public charity in *Vormärz* Prussia.)[34] One should also take into consideration the precarious economic condition of Bavarian Jewry during the first half of the nineteenth century. Under these circumstances, the harshness of Jewish philanthropy in Fürth was the product of both real economic needs and a sharing in popular bourgeois prejudices regarding the poor.

The rationalizing philanthropic spirit had undeniable positive as well as negative manifestations. One was the creation of centralized poor care commissions; in addition to the London JBG and the Paris Comité de bienfaisance, institutions were established in Amsterdam in 1825 and Vienna in 1839.[35] In Berlin a poor care commission, which brought together representatives from all the Jewish charitable associations, was created in 1837. The commission, one of its champions explained, is a necessary product of the age of occupational freedom, in which those capable of work can and must be found employment and the truly invalid can be cared for separately. An applicant for aid from the Armenkommission was visited and examined by two of the commission's members. Whenever possible, the commission located work for those capable of it. Within a year of its establishment, out of 192 recipients of aid, almost half had been put to work, many in a communal laundry subsidized by the commission and others in cottage-industry weaving, for which the commission supplied the materials.[36]

In Hamburg the move toward modern Jewish philanthropy began as early as 1788, in the wake of the creation by the municipality of a unifying institution for the Gentile poor (Allgemeine Armenanstalt) and a ban against indiscriminate charity. The city compelled the Jewish community to assess its members a monthly contribution to charity. The Jews, beset by beggars demanding direct payment, refused to make the contribution, which was thus transformed into an obligatory poor tax in the first decade of the nineteenth century. In the wake of the French conquest of Hamburg in 1813, the community developed a wide-ranging philanthropic system with an emphasis on preventive measures, especially loans.[37] Attractive repayment terms were offered to Jewish craftsmen, and loans were refused to the invalid poor. By midcentury, the credit society had made more than twenty thousand loans worth some 1.8 million Hamburg taler.[38]

The Berlin Armenkommission's public works projects and the steady climb in Jewish philanthropic spending in Hamburg point to an important economic change affecting German Jewry during the first half of the 1800s. Although there were substantial numbers of paupers and vagrants, as an aggregate German Jewry was gradually becoming more affluent. The enormous gap between the handful of very rich court factors and the masses, which had existed in the eighteenth century, was slowly narrowing as the result of the creation of a German Jewish commercial bourgeoisie. It was the growing wealth of the Jewish communities, as much as the poverty within them, that stimulated the growth of Jewish philanthropy throughout Germany.[39] In this sense, Ashkenazic Jewry in the nineteenth century replicated the experience of western Sephardic Jewry in the seventeenth. The stark opposition of poverty and affluence, combined with rationalist and utilitarian sensibilities about the poor, provided Jews with the means as well as the motive to revolutionize the way they thought about and cared for the poor among them.

The embourgeoisement of German Jewry stimulated the formation of philanthropic sensibilities similar to those of the Gentile bourgeoisie. Jewish and Gentile philanthropists shared the corporate-voluntarist spirit of mid-nineteenth-century Germany. Among Christians as among Jews, ecclesiastical, communal, and private philanthropies sought to work in concert in order to rationalize and centralize poor relief. This rationalization process took place outside the parameters of the state, which philanthropists, whether Jew or Gentile, did not see as a source of funding or guidance. Moreover, the principal goal of Gentile philanthropic action, like that of the Jews, was the integration of the able-bodied poor into a market economy, not the establishment of elaborate programs of social maintenance. The "Elberfeld system," developed in that Westphalian town in 1853 and later implemented in other communities, consolidated poor relief into a single body similar to the Berlin Jewish Armenkommission. A staff of volunteers, each responsible for a small number of cases, closely supervised its charges in order to separate the able-bodied, employable poor from the invalid. For the former, the caseworkers functioned as a labor exchange, finding work in the private sector and occasionally providing public-sector employment or long-term financial aid.[40]

Jewish and Gentile philanthropists also shared the view that charity should be centralized on more than the local level. In 1848 the Lutheran minister Johann Wichern founded the Innere Mission, a federation of Protestant charitable and educational institutions.[41] The following year, a long article in the *Allgemeine Zeitung des Judentums* by a Dr. Rothschild from Hamm explained that the problem of Jewish vagrancy was too great for individual communities (*Gemeinden*) to solve on their own. To achieve "Festhaltung und Fesselung" of the poor, that is, to effectively deny them freedom of movement and enroot them in their home communities, there must be coordination of local Jewish charitable associations on the district and regional levels. The regional bodies would elect representatives, who would in turn be attached to the provincial diets. Although nothing came of this proposal at the time, some twenty years later came the formal establishment of the first national German Jewish organization, the Deutsch-Israelitischer Gemeindebund, which considered the problem of the vagrant poor one of its principal concerns.

Underlying the growth of modern Jewish philanthropy in Germany was a complex, and at times contradictory, relationship with charity offered by Gentiles. Until the middle of the nineteenth century, Jewish leaders assumed that they had to take care of their poor because no one else would. In the late 1780s Friedländer remarked that Prussian Jews received no benefit from public charitable institutions and were not admitted to the royal hospitals, although they were required to contribute to them.[42] In Hamburg Jews were excluded from the purview of its almshouse when it was created in 1788. In Munich, beginning in the 1820s, if not earlier, the Jewish community contributed to general charity while shouldering the burden of supporting its own poor. During the Revolution of 1848, opposition to Jewish emancipation by municipal officials throughout Germany stemmed at least in part from a fear that emancipated Jews would demand public charity.[43] After midcentury, Jews began to be allowed access to public charity, but its availability varied from one locality to another.[44]

The uneven availability of public charity was not the only factor maintaining the independence of Jewish philanthropy, however. For one thing, the confessional quality of so much of what passed for "public" charity in nineteenth-century Germany, and in Europe as a whole, provides an additional reason for the maintenance of this independent network. Fear of missionary activity is well known to have stimulated modern Jewish political activity. The Mortara Affair of 1858, in which the Vatican did not allow for the return of a Jewish child who had been baptized by the child's Catholic maid, led to the creation two years later of world Jewry's first international political lobbying organization, the Alliance Israélite Universelle. Concern about proselytism could also be a catalyst for the development of Jewish philanthropic institutions such as hospitals and orphanages. There is evidence for this in England, France, and Austria.[45] Even if they did not suspect the Gentile authorities of harboring ulterior motives, Jewish philanthropists preferred that their poor and sick be cared for within their own community. The motivation for this sentiment could have been self-interest, in that providers who kept the Jewish poor out of the public eye promoted their own strivings for social acceptance. If Jews cared for their own poor, anti-semitism would lose a powerful source of support; moreover, well-to-do Jews could demonstrate through their philanthropic institutions how thoroughly they had imbibed bourgeois social ethics. But there were other forces at work as well.

When Hamburg Jewry was formally emancipated in 1864 and the community's legal status was redefined, the majority of the *Gemeinde* leadership wanted to maintain control over poor care rather than cede it to the municipality. The members of the Jewish poor care commission claimed that they could provide more effective preventive welfare services than the state. Over the protests of the Jewish leaders, the Hamburg Senate did, in fact, shift responsibility for poor care from the Jewish community to the municipality. But the community was allowed to, and did, impose a voluntary annual levy so that it could maintain its philanthropic network. It did so not merely to keep the Jewish poor away from Gentile scrutiny, but also, as one scholar has recently argued, to preserve Jewish collective identity in an era when the Jewish community had been deprived of its autonomy.[46]

This sentiment was explicated by Ludwig Philippson, who was unusually sensitive to the socioeconomic structures of Jewish life. For Philippson, the preservation of a separate Jewish philanthropy was essential not merely for instrumental reasons but for substantive ones as well. Protesting a call by an extreme liberal to dissolve all separate Jewish charity and meld it with public institutions, Philippson argued that Jewish charity must continue, partly because general charity does not suffice, but even more because the Jews require an outlet for their charitable spirit and sense of obligation to their coreligionists.[47] In an article of 1847, "The Essence of the Jewish Community," Philippson defined the community as a "corporation," which takes charge of not only its religious and educational life but also its poor care, which he described as a border zone "where religion and society adjoin." Although the philanthropic spirit is universal, Philippson contended, it carries a confessional stamp; Jews operate in this spirit no less than Roman Catholics or Protestants. Stressing the "unity of religion and society," Philippson claimed that "[t]he mission of Judaism is therefore: not merely to teach the unity of God, but also the unity of religion and society, the idea and life." Until now, he wrote, the religious reform of Judaism and the social reform of the Jews have gone along separate tracks, but the time has come to combine the two. The *Gemeinde,* argued Philippson, is responsible for changing the poor economically and morally, that is, altering their entire way of life, including all their customs and habits.

Philippson was a pioneer not only in his conception of Judaism as realizing itself through social action but also in his awareness that such action would constitute a new, powerful, and viable source of modern Jewish identity. In 1842 he spoke of international Jewish activity as a source of solidarity among the increasingly secularized and culturally divided Jews of the Western world.[48] Interestingly, and at first glance surprisingly, Philippson chose Palestine as the site of his envisioned project. There is a conventional notion that the Haskalah and Reform movements among nineteenth-century Jews weakened much of the traditional attachment to the Land of Israel. After all, the general tendency of Jews in western and central Europe was to adopt the culture of the country in which they lived and to consider that land not merely a temporary host but a true homeland. Among some Reform congregations in Germany, prayers for the return of Jews to the Land of Israel and the restoration of the Temple were deleted from the service. But ironically, the major intellectual movements among nineteenth-century European Jews, along with the increasing social and economic mobility that they enjoyed, in some ways strengthened Jewish bonds with the Land of Israel, although the nature of those bonds underwent considerable change.

Central to the Haskalah was the notion that Jews needed to undergo a process of transformation in order to render them acceptable to Gentile society. Jews were to obtain a modern Western education, and the poor among them were to be channeled out of peddling and money-lending and into respectable occupations like crafts and agriculture. Progressive Jewish leaders believed that this transformation must take place not only in Europe but in the Holy Land as well. Palestine's small Jewish community (the Yishuv) was for the most part deeply Orthodox and wretchedly poor—dependent on charity (*halukkah*) from abroad for survival and engaged primarily in the study of sacred texts rather than a remunerative livelihood.[49] The poverty of the Yishuv disturbed European Jewish philanthropists and stimulated them to abandon the traditional disbursement of alms in favor of constructive activity in Palestine. This activity began as early as 1839, with attempts by the Anglo-Jewish leader Sir Moses Montefiore to promote crafts and agriculture among the Jews of Jerusalem.[50] Its pace quickened after the Crimean War of 1852–54, during which the supply of *halukkah* from eastern Europe was cut off and the Yishuv became even more deeply mired in poverty. To be sure, Jewish philanthropic activity in Palestine had other motivations besides purely socioeconomic ones. The growing presence of European Christians in Jerusalem stimulated Diaspora Jews to contribute vast sums to build Jewish workshops and hospitals so that destitute, sick, or otherwise vulnerable Jews would not fall into the clutches of the church. Philippson was the first to suggest the establishment of a Jewish hospital in the Holy City. The first one was founded in 1854; the German conservative rabbinical leader Zecharias Frankel reported that it kept ill Jews out of the hands of missionaries.[51] More important, an ongoing sense of the sanctity of the Land of Israel impelled Jews to contribute to its welfare; and as western European Jews became more politically secure and affluent, so did their public display of attachment to Palestine increase. In 1854 Frankel wrote, "The time is behind us, in which cowardly, ignominious self-abnegation sought to supress any mention of the Holy Land and a connection of the Jews [to it]. We desire a spiritual connection, mediated and rooted in faith; and we are not ashamed of our faith, so there is nothing in this attachment that can be brought as an accusation against us."[52]

Although Frankel acknowledged the benefits that European Jewish philanthropy could bring to Palestine, he emphasized the benefits that Palestine would bring to the Diaspora: "The Orient has many millions of Jews, who are almost cut off from the West. . . . These Jews have, however, one central point, to which they cling with pious love: Palestine. . . . This central point alone can mediate between occidental Jews and those scattered across Asia."[53] The founders of the Alliance Israélite Universelle held similar views; Palestine held pride of place in a vision of international Jewish unity through philanthropic activity.[54] Much of the Alliance's vision was already contained in Philippson's original call of 1842: he envisioned an international Jewish union that would replace the practice of philanthropy by isolated notables like Montefiore with mass mobilization, not necessarily for the betterment of the Yishuv, but to promote the strengthening of Diaspora Jewish identity.[55]

The centerpiece of Philippson's envisioned philanthropic project, both in Palestine and in the Diaspora, was to be vocational training to promote occupational restructuring (*Berufsumschichtung*) among the Jews. Vocational training, he wrote, has a religious base in that it morally and spiritually improves the poor, allowing them to attain a truly "bourgeois existence."[56] Philippson's placement of vocational training at the center of modern Jewish philanthropy was not idiosyncratic. Throughout the first half of the nineteenth century, efforts by Jewish elites to alter their poorer coreligionists' occupational profile were sincere, earnest, and concerted. These efforts have been noted by many historians of modern Jewry, but the existing scholarship does not do the subject justice.[57] Unintentionally reading history backward, scholars have paid relatively little attention to Jewish attempts at occupational change because such projects swam against the tide of history; they tried to send Jews into artisanal and agricultural careers at the beginning of an era of industrialization and rapid expansion of the commercial sector. But there is no necessary connection between the feasibility of a project and its popularity, or between its intended and actual consequences. Moreover, an event with relatively minor immediate ramifications can produce significant consequences over the long term. For all these reasons, we will focus now on the beginning of the Jews' attempts to reshape themselves economically, attempts that would continue for some one hundred fifty years, and whose later manifestations included the most sweeping attempts at Jewish social engineering in modern history.

The Theory and Practice of Jewish Productivization

At the end of the eighteenth century, there were three overlapping but distinct justifications in Europe for increasing the economic productivity of a state's subjects. The first was utilitarian, the second soteriological, and the third eudaemonistic. Mercantilist striving to enhance economic efficiency shared a common language with Christian preaching that labor and productivity were means and signs of salvation. At the same time, enlightened, secular thinkers argued that pleasure taken in a job well done was an end in and of itself; moreover, the more efficiently one labored, the more one could enjoy leisure time, which could be devoted to cultural pursuits. All three forces were at work behind the economic policies of the absolutist monarchies. In Josephinian Austria, educational reform was the province of Johann Ignaz von Felbiger, a Reform Catholic who had been influenced by the German Pietists. The reduction of holy days and processionals, as well as the development of spinning schools for the rural folk, was thought to enhance the populace's piety as well as its productivity.[58] For Anne-Robert-Jacques Turgot, director of financial affairs under King Louis XVI in France, *raison d'état* and eudaemonism were intertwined. As Arthur Hertzberg has noted, "Economic liberty itself was more than a tool for increasing the power of the state; it was a necessary precondition for realizing the happiness of the individual."[59]

Jewish leaders possessed a similar set of justifications for occupational change. The goal of utility to the state was paramount for the German radical *maskilim*. In France as well, there was a general agreement, among the Ashkenazic as well as the Sephardic elite, that the Jewish masses in eastern France were a "negative phenomenon" and harmful to the national economy. But there was also a frank expression of self-interest, a feeling that the Jews' concentration in petty commerce was causing them great misery and that, if only for their own benefit, the Jews must expand their occupational horizon. This sort of pragmatic appeal came from traditionalist Jews throughout Europe, from Alsace to Lithuania. Moreover, although the Pietist concept of work as a salvific force was not directly applicable to Judaism, given the religion's relative lack of soteriological focus, the idea of labor as a source of morality, and especially of a specifically Jewish piety, was common among Jewish philanthropic activists.

Although there was widespread agreement among Jewish leaders that the Jews must undergo an economic transformation, it was not always clear what new occupational profile the Jews should assume. On the one hand, the writing of the German Haskalah, like that of its later, eastern European counterpart, praised commerce, and the Jewish schools founded by *maskilim* emphasized the inculcation of mercantile skills such as math, bookkeeping, geography, and languages. On the other hand, there was a strong anticommercial note in *maskilic* writings, and calls for occupational restructuring from commerce to crafts and agriculture were common. The apparently contradictory stance can be explained in terms of the Gentile stereotypes that viewed Jews as a people of parasitical paupers and conspiratorial bankers. Middle-class Jewish philanthropists felt themselves charged with the responsibility to dismantle both of these stereotypes. The first would fall away once the Jewish poor had been refashioned into respectable craftsmen and farmers. And the second would be proven false by constant displays of probity, honesty, and virtue by Jewish tradesmen. Philanthropic activity was, in and of itself, a means of demonstrating middle-class virtue and thus accomplished both goals simultaneously. Thus the display of a commercial or artisanal orientation by Jewish philanthropists depended on the income level of the targets of philanthropic attention.

Jewish educational reform in western and central Europe from the 1780s to the Revolution of 1848 devoted considerable attention to the preparation of youth for commercial careers. For example, Wessely's momentous work, *Divrei shalom ve-emet,* called for commercial and technical training. In 1784 a proposal brought by the *maskil* Isaac Euchel for the establishment of a Jewish school in Kiel envisioned separate tracks of study: commercial, rabbinic, and (secular) scholarly.⁶⁰ The Berlin Freischule, founded in 1778, attracted Christian as well as Jewish pupils for its commercial training, which was superior to that offered in other schools in Berlin at the time. In 1789 the Jewish school in Mantua described reforms in its curriculum for the education of "lads intended to be merchants"; the new subjects to be taught included "the study of states and their management [*Finanzwissenschaft*]" and "the history of commercial peoples." In 1794 the new Wilhelmsschule in Breslau claimed to teach, in addition to the three Rs, natural science, history, geography, and "the division of the land among kings and princes, and their ways of governing."⁶¹ The Frankfurt Philanthropin, after its reorganization in 1813, featured an educational track similar to a *Realschule,* with an emphasis on modern languages and other subjects of practical benefit to an aspiring merchant. In 1817, in the premier issue of the journal *Jedidja,* the editor J. Heinemann proposed the establishment of a school in Berlin where "particular attention should be paid to commercial science." During the 1820s, the Hamburg Freischule emphasized commercial training. Of the school's 280 graduates by 1830, 200 had gone into commerce, and the school had gained a reputation as an excellent preparatory facility for merchants.⁶²

This emphasis is not surprising, given the sources of most German Jews' livelihoods. As a document of 1819 from the Munich community, responding to complaints about overcrowding from the Christian merchant guilds, avers: "Many merchants, much trade, and much trade, much profit—something about which many retailers have no conception."⁶³ Similar expressions came from the Jewish merchants of Fürth in 1821.⁶⁴ Michael Benedict Lessing's apologetic work of 1833, *Die Juden und die öffentliche Meinung im preussischen Staat,* admitted that peddling and petty trade were ignoble occupations and called on Jews to practice more honorable ones, but it held up as an example the Jewish community of Stockholm, all of whose members engaged in commerce but were free of criminal activity. Lessing praised commerce for demanding calculation and industry and saw it, along with the provision of credit, as indispensable in the industrializing states of Europe.[65]

Beneath Lessing's praise for commerce, however, lay a profound discomfort with the Jews' occupational profile. Necessary though commerce may be, he wrote, he derived far greater satisfaction from the Jews' participation in industry, science, and cultural production. He expressed pride in the increasing numbers of Jewish craftsmen and the remarkable achievements of the handful of Jews who had purchased estates and were rationally farming their lands. In general, Lessing admitted, occupational restructuring can only affect the poor, because the well-to-do will not abandon secure commercial careers.[66] One encounters this notion of separate occupational paths for the prosperous merchant and the struggling peddler in much of the Jewish journalism and educational literature of the early 1800s.[67]

One could argue that the Haskalah schools' commercial training programs represented a form of vocational training for the poor, for the bulk of the children who attended these schools came from poor families. (Well-to-do Jews hired private tutors.)[68] But judging from the important German Jewish journal *Sulamith,* most of whose issues were published between 1807 and 1827, many adherents of the Haskalah in central Europe did not see things that way.

Sulamith presented itself as a vehicle of enlightenment for cultivated Jews and as a mediating force between modernism and traditionalism and between Jew and Gentile. Appealing to mercantile subscribers, it offered essays on economic and technological developments, "particularly those of concern to the merchant," as well as religious, ethical, and pedagogical matters. Yet David Fränkel, who along with Joseph Wolf edited the journal, contributed strongly anticommercial essays, including one lamenting commerce's "corrupting spirit" which had possessed the Jews and must be driven out if the Jews were ever to be truly happy or useful.[69] Many pieces in the journal expressed similar sentiments. But as one contributor noted after a grim depiction of the immorality of the tradesman's life, "We are not speaking about the educated merchant." In a revealing passage, the author of this piece wrote:

Scholars and artists will take the place of pedantic dandies; merchants the place of the many small traders, artisans the place of peddlers, farmers the place of idle beggars, and brave warriors the place of vagrants. Then many of us will have all the less need to be ashamed of our oriental facial features, and we will have among us no more Christianizing Jews and no more baptized Jews.[70]

In this construction, prosperous merchants belong at the top of an idealized social hierarchy whose lower elements will, by engaging in venerable, productive tasks, do nothing to shame their betters and hinder their social advancement.

Publications about artisanal training for Jews in *Vormärz* Germany seldom failed to specify that poor children were their intended beneficiaries. The same association was made in France. In 1789 the Polish Jew M. Zalkind-Hourwitz claimed that once Jews are granted economic freedom, the wealthy among them will invest in large-scale commerce and real estate, middling Jews will manage retail shops, and the poor will go into crafts and agriculture where, given the Jews' celebrated sobriety, they will work harder and produce more cheaply than Gentiles.[71] The restriction of occupational restructuring to the poor was taken for granted in the activity of the Société pour l'encouragement des arts et métiers parmi les Israélites de Metz, founded in 1824, and the Société de patronage des apprentis et ouvriers Israélites de Paris, established in 1853.[72] The gospel of productivization of the poor traversed the Mediterranean and worked its way to Algeria; in 1854 the chief rabbi of Constantine called on those unable to advance in the mercantile world to farm the soil, gaining thereby not only a livelihood but also the undying admiration of their coreligionists.[73]

There were a number of reasons for assuming that only poor Jewish children should be shunted into crafts and farming. On one level, there was a simple pragmatic claim that there was no room for them in commerce but that they could aspire to a satisfactory livelihood in manufacture or farming. On another level, the project of Jewish regeneration relied on pedagogy as the chief vehicle of reform, and it was led by self-styled educators who sought to uplift and reform their brethren through the dissemination of enlightenment. Most of their brethren were wretchedly poor, and an association between poverty and immorality was a staple of modern European sensibility. Many *maskilim* in Germany, adopting this way of thinking, argued that poor Jews needed to be productive to be moral beings. It was told of Salomon Heine, the Hamburg banker and philanthropist, that he agreed to give a poor Jew a loan only after paying an unexpected visit to the supplicant's home and ensuring that his children had clean hands and combed hair.[74]

Even though French Jewry did not produce a literary Haskalah on a par with German Jews, many of the German Haskalah's pedagogic and social concepts were shared by French Jewry's liberal activists. As Gerson Lévy, president of the Metz vocational association, put it, vocational education's "purpose will be social, which is a synonym for moral." Such moralism informed the words of Jacques Weill, a teacher in Alsace, who, under the Second Empire, touted a project for an agricultural colony for Jewish orphans and abandoned children: "Convinced that the poverty of the majority of the unfortunate stems from the general intellectual and moral inferiority in which they live, we have thought that, in order to raise them from their level of abasement, we must engage in education and instruction. . . . Thus, attacking at the root moral poverty, the normal source of material poverty, is the best form of preventive assistance."[75]

The discourse of productivization was ubiquitous in the liberal Jewish press during the first half of the nineteenth century. The topic of *Berufsumschichtung* was a staple in journals such as *Sulamith* and *Der Orient*. A statistical survey of Prussian Jewry published in *Der Orient* in 1840 attributed grave economic and moral problems to the approximately half of Prussian Jews living in communities with fewer than two hundred fifty inhabitants. Such small communities, the article argued, cannot support the educational facilities needed to wean Jews away from their "particular aptitude" for commerce.[76] More striking, the call for Jewish occupational restructuring came from pulpits throughout the lands of the German Confederation and the Hapsburg Empire. As might be expected, champions of the reform of Judaism also zealously advocated reform of the occupational structure of the Jews.

Support for Jewish *Berufsumschichtung* spanned the spectrum from radical reformers to more moderate sorts. Mendel Hess, the *Landesrabbiner* of Saxony-Weimar, set forth extreme reformist views in the newspaper he founded in 1839, *Der Israelit des 19. Jahrhunderts*. In the 1840s, in a Passover sermon on the Song of Songs, Hess found contemporary economic implications in the biblical phrases "Do not look down upon me; a little dark I may be because I am scorched by the sun. My mother's sons were displeased with me" (1:6). The Jews, he said, suffer from "blackness," a proclivity for commerce and an unhealthy love of gain; and this stain is the result of discrimination and persecution by Gentiles, the "mother's sons." Fortunately "the winter is past; the rains are over and gone" (2:11–12); that is, the warm winds of enlightenment have carried the Jews back to honorable occupations in crafts and agriculture. Adopting a similar tone, the more moderate reformer Salomon Herxheimer, *Landesrabbiner* of Anhalt-Bernberg, sermonized in 1837 that "our contemporary widespread [economic] activity *did not exist* among our blessed forefathers, *should not exist* according to our written and oral teachings, and *cannot remain* given the demands of the time."[77]

What are these demands, and who makes them? They come from the fatherland, which demands service and productivity from all its citizens. Noah Mannheimer, the celebrated Viennese preacher and a cautious reformer, sermonized in 1834 that the present age "measures the worker according to his work, the thinker according to his thoughts, the man by his strength and the tree by its fruit, and does not ask from which tribe or soil it sprang up." Until now, Mannheimer noted, the Jews' economic energy has gone in only one direction, toward commerce, and although some Jews have grown wealthy therefrom, such wealth is "sterile" and robs the Jews' lives of "worth and sanctity and grandeur." To be sure, Mannheimer expressed sympathy for the diligent Jewish peddler, who, as he hauls his heavy pack, dreams of becoming another Rothschild. But such hard labor, said Mannheimer, yielded little; a craft would give the poor Jew a secure and honest living, thereby infusing him with moral virtue (*Biedersinn*).[78]

All agreed that occupational restructuring would improve the Jews' status in the eyes of the Gentiles, but the emphasis was on the material and moral benefit that Jews would derive from engaging in secure livelihoods. As Leopold Braun, a teacher in Altofen, Hungary, sermonized in 1841, by abandoning commerce for agriculture and crafts, Jews will no longer be subject to the "currents of time and the whim of happenstance" and will become masters over their own fate.[79]

The ideology of productivization inspired concerted, albeit unsuccessful, efforts among educators to alter the Jews' occupational profile. Although Jewish schools established in Germany in the early 1800s had a commercial orientation, crafts featured prominently in their agendas as well. Lazarus Bendavid, director between 1806 and 1826 of the Berlin Freischule, believed that the children from well-to-do as well as struggling families should turn to productive occupations. Victor Jacobson, founder of the Jewish school in Seessen, saw vocational training as central to the school's educational mission. More typical, however, was the philosophy of the Hamburg Freischule, founded in 1816 and intended mainly for poor children. The pupils' socioeconomic standing, rather than a desire for a universal Jewish *Berufsumschichtung,* led its directors to focus on crafts education during the school's first four years. Unable to place the children with masters and facing opposition from parents, who wanted their children to take up commercial occupations, the school took a new tack after 1820 by developing a commercial orientation and began to accept children from well-to-do families. A special track for future craftsmen remained in place, however, as was the case at the Frankfurt Philanthropin.[80] In France, schools for Jewish vocational education were founded in Strasbourg (1824) and Mulhouse (1842). Opinions of these schools varied: Jewish liberals lauded vocational training, as the *Archives Israélites* put it, as the "only means to regenerate Jewish Alsace"; and traditionalists tended to suspect any program put forth by their progressive opponents.[81]

In addition to the Jewish schools, voluntary associations devoted to the training of Jewish youth in crafts and agriculture sprang up throughout western, northern, and central Europe from the 1790s through 1848. The first was founded in Copenhagen in 1793, five years after a royal decree opening up the crafts to Jews in Denmark; in 1798 Amsterdam's For Work and Industry association was founded by a small number of modernizing Jews seeking to alleviate the appalling poverty of that city's Jews.[82] In Germany, a number of crafts associations were established between 1815 and 1848; no major community lacked a *Handwerkverein*.[83] There were similar associations throughout the Hapsburg Empire, in Vienna, Prague, Pest, and Lwow.[84] The associations shared a common modus operandi: contributions by the societies' members paid for the *Lehrgeld,* or fees, charged by a master craftsman during the period of apprenticeship. At times, a stipend for room and board was provided as well. Some of these associations were entirely new creations; others grew out of older charities, such as the one in Hechingen, a town near Tübingen. In 1777 a society was founded in that community to provide dowries for poor brides and to meet on the Sabbath to hear edifying sermons. In 1839 its members decided, due to the needs of the time, to change the society into a support mechanism for the vocational training of poor youth.[85] Similarly, in Lyssa (Posen), in 1847 an old society for the provision of clothing to poor children changed its name to the Verein für die Heranbildung jüdischer Handwerker and to select children worthy of financial support during the apprenticeship required to become a craftsman.[86] Thus traditional charities transformed themselves into modern constructive philanthropies. As a report of the Mecklenburg crafts association put it, "Thereby support for the association is

and remains a matter of the utmost importance for anyone who sees in
the suppression of poverty with its dismal consequences, on the one
hand, and on the other hand, the promotion of industry, which is one
of the primary sources of all civil virtues, a goal worthy of the effort of
noble men."[87]

This quotation from the Mecklenburg association, like the publications by and about the crafts associations in general, specified that their
intended beneficiaries were poor boys. But during this same period there
was a good deal of effort to "productivize" Jewish girls, and these programs featured a greater ambiguity regarding the relationship between
class and curriculum. The first efforts at vocational training for Jewish
girls focused on the poor. Such was the case in Prague, whose Jewish
German school, which opened in 1782, added a section for girls two
years later. One hundred forty girls enrolled at the school, about 40
percent of the total enrollment for that year. According to *Ha-Me'asef,*
the girls were instructed in crafts and the three Rs in order to provide
"the Israelite nation with a significant aid for the support of the truly
poor among them."[88]

A similar focus on poor girls characterized the first school for girls in
Germany, established in Hamburg in 1798, and the Frankfurt Philanthropin's girls' section during the first decade after its founding in 1810.
Over time, though, as the Jewish schools moved toward catering to the
children of middle-class, mercantile families, crafts training retained a
position of honor in the education of middle-class girls far longer than
in the boys' curriculum. David Fränkel's girls' school, established in Dessau in 1806, drew on a wide socioeconomic base, yet its primary emphasis was on home economics, with additional instruction in the arts
and sciences. Crafts education remained part of the Frankfurt Philanthropin's girls' curriculum until midcentury. A school intended for middle-class girls, founded in Berlin in 1809, devoted fifteen of its thirty-
seven hours of weekly instruction to crafts. A decade later, Jeremiah
Heinemann's school for middle-class girls in Berlin featured a broad
curriculum of secular studies, but afternoons were devoted entirely to
crafts.[89]

The middle-class parents who sent their daughters to these schools
may not have approved of the emphasis on crafts, as indicated by the
gradual reduction of crafts instruction at the Philanthropin and other
girls' schools and by the fact that Heinemann's school closed in 1825, to
be replaced by an institution specifically for poor girls. But the schools'
directors were motivated by an ideology that caused them to project the

idea of vocational education for girls onto a broad social base. They associated productive handwork with the bourgeois ideal of the *mère-éducatrice,* the modern equivalent of the biblical "woman of valor," whose loving weaving of flax and linen is traditionally evoked by Jewish husbands chanting Proverbs 31 on the Sabbath eve. On this point there was little distinction between *maskilim* and Christian pedagogues. As Heinrich Würtziger, a Gentile, wrote in *Sulamith,* "[If] Jewish heads of households from the middle and lower classes complained about the clumsiness and laziness of their daughters, the reason therefor lay in no way in ill will on the part of female youth, but rather merely in the lack of opportunity for a purposeful training."[90] Instruction in handicrafts would serve poor girls by making them employable as domestic servants; it would benefit middle-class girls by instilling a work ethic, which would make them effective managers of the domestic economy.[91]

The training of poor Jewish boys to be artisans, like the teaching of home economics to Jewish girls of all classes, paralleled educational trends in European society as a whole. In *Vormärz* Germany and France under the July Monarchy, there were many similarities between Gentile and Jewish associations for the promotion of handicrafts among poor youth.[92] There was also a broader economic and cultural context behind attempts to settle Jews on the soil.[93] Discussions about the agricultural colonization of Jews in late-eighteenth-century Prussia and Austria were part of a broader effort to increase the agricultural productivity of the realm through the improvement and farming of uncultivated land. In 1787 the Jewish deputies to the Prussian royal commission on the improvement of the Jews' civil status claimed that Jews would be more useful than the French and Bohemian colonists whose settlement on empty land the government had encouraged to date.[94] The new province of South Prussia, created in 1794 from land acquired in the partition of Poland, witnessed a brief attempt by the authorities to encourage Jews to settle on wastelands.[95] In 1789 the Hapsburg emperor Joseph II turned to Jews to colonize Galicia after his experiments with German Protestants had failed.[96]

In these cases, however, the goal of turning Jews into farmers clashed with the Gentile authorities' prejudices. In South Prussia, Jews were not allowed to acquire land previously held by Christians but could only obtain virgin tracts. They were allowed the use of Christian hired help for just three years. Lacking means and experience, it would have been difficult for Jews to become successful farmers even under the best circumstances, and these conditions made the transition to agriculture all but impossible. As to Galicia, Joseph II's plans to settle Jews on the soil were intended less to maximize the value of his land than to enroot them in one spot and prevent their migration into western parts of the empire. Opposition from the bureaucracy, the poor quality of land offered, high taxation, and insufficient credit, all conspired to doom the colonization program to failure.[97]

Jewish activists in France and Germany made occasional attempts over the years 1815–48 to turn Jews into farmers, and their proposals clearly bore the influence of the social reformist spirit of the era as well as the Jewish ideology of emancipation. In 1847 one of the elders of the Breslau community proposed founding a *colonie agricole* for poor Jewish children, to be modeled along the lines of a colony near Tours that had been set up eight years previously by Christian philanthropists. In 1844 the Alsatian industrialist Léon Werth began a quarter century of campaigning for agricultural education for poor Alsatian Jews.[98] A supporter of Werth's plan described it as a boon for the orphan and the abandoned child; his language strongly resembled that of French social reformers of the Second Empire who sought to solve the problems of rural depopulation and child abandonment by enrooting abandoned children in state-supported *colonies agricoles*.[99] Mid-nineteenth-century Jewish discourse on agriculture was part of a broader phenomenon analyzed by the historian Malcolm Chase, whose book on radical agrarianism in late Georgian and early Victorian Britain differentiates between what he calls "agrarian" and "pastoral" thinking. The former was pragmatic, seeking to elevate the impoverished individual's standard of living and social status; the latter was romantic and escapist.[100] Jewish agricultural projects of the period fell squarely into the former camp.

Unlike the crafts associations that sprang up throughout western and central Europe, however, attempts to turn Jews to agriculture were scattered and unpopular. Werth's decades of effort to establish a *colonie agricole* came to naught; agriculture, unlike crafts training, was widely perceived by the French Jewish elites as infeasible and unappealing.[101] The most concerted Jewish agricultural initiative of the mid-1800s came in Posen, where the province's chief rabbi, Salomon Eger, claimed that 1,064 Jewish families had committed themselves to the pursuit of a new life on the soil. Only 64 of them, however, could or would pay for the land and inventory; this project's publicity clearly stated that it was intended for the "shamefaced poor" among the Jews. Unable to raise the necessary funds, the project folded.[102]

Although agricultural projects for the poor were not popular among

European Jewry, the Jewish estate owner became a much discussed and admired figure in liberal Jewish circles. Michael Benedict Lessing praised the "not unconsequential number of Jewish estate owners who, at times fully equipped with the theoretical and practical knowledge of their occupation, at times supported by good [Gentile] gentleman farmers, promote the tilling of the soil."[103] *Sulamith* sang the praises of Moses May, a businessman in Vosges, who bought an old estate, drained, forested, and parceled the terrain, and leased the parcels out to local peasants.[104] The Prague *maskil* Ignaz Jeiteles contributed a stirring obituary for Israel Hönig Edler, a Bohemian tobacco leaseholder who had been ennobled by Joseph II.[105] The *Allgemeine Zeitung* detailed the legal quandary faced by a Jewish estate owner in Gleissen (Neumark) who paid for the construction of a church on his estate but, because he was not a Christian, was legally denied the right to choose the pastor and inspect the church's accounts.[106] And after 1850, when Jews in Hungary took on a prominent role in the ownership, and especially the leasing, of large estates, the Hungarian Jewish press noted these accomplishments with unabashed pride.[107]

Because the agricultural projects proposed an even more radical alteration of the Jewish economic profile than the crafts associations, they attracted especially strong reactions from those seeking to alter or maintain traditional Jewish observance, that is, from Orthodox and Reform Jews. Although Eger claimed that his agricultural project enjoyed support from Orthodox and Liberal Jews alike, he was accused of promoting a decline of ritual observance, which could not easily be maintained by one engaged in agricultural labor.[108] In upper Silesia, during the second half of the 1840s, a Jewish estate owner named Berliner, who was active in political reform societies in Berlin and Breslau, announced his intention to found an agrarian colony for Jewish "proletarians." Berliner argued that religious reform will only be possible if Jews return to nature and take up agriculture, for "living as a countryman in the circle of Jewish country folk, many [religious] laws must take on a quite different form."[109] Not surprisingly, Berliner was attacked viciously by a local Orthodox rabbi.[110] A similar radical-reformist philosophy was expressed by an anonymous newspaper article arguing that the greatest barrier to the Jews flourishing in agriculture and crafts is observance of the Sabbath and dietary laws. Jews pursuing these livelihoods, the author argued, should receive a special dispensation from rabbis to forgo these observances.[111]

The proposition that Jews should turn to crafts was far less divisive, largely because there were already sizable numbers of Jewish craftsmen in east-central and central Europe. Eighteenth-century Polish Jewry had featured a prominent artisanal class, organized into craft guilds separate from those of Christians.[112] Well into the nineteenth century, the Polish territories acquired by Prussia had a large number of craftsmen; in 1836, 30 percent of Jewish males in the city of Posen were craftsmen.[113] During its first decades, the Prussian *Handwerkverein* concentrated its efforts in the province of Posen because there was an existing artisanal class on which to build. Most of Posen's Jewish artisans were concentrated in a few areas, especially tailoring and shoemaking, thus leading the crafts associations to try, with little success, to divert Jewish youth into other fields. The overcrowding of Jews into a limited number of crafts stimulated a large-scale emigration of Posen Jews during the middle decades of the nineteenth century.[114] Nonetheless, the percentage of Jews engaged in handicrafts in Prussia as a whole climbed from 9.8 to 14.8 percent between 1834 and 1852.[115] This increase had less to do with the activities of well-meaning crafts associations than with the struggle by Jews in the newly acquired Rhineland provinces for economic improvement.

Greater problems confronted Jews in the southern German states, where between 1815 and 1848 citizenship, and even the right of residence, was made conditional on what the authorities deemed a productive occupation.[116] In these lands there was the utmost incentive for Jews to take up handicrafts. (Areas of southern Germany that did not feature such strongly tutelary legislation did not witness as much occupational restructuring or philanthropic activity to that effect.) In 1813, 3.3 percent of Munich's Jewish workforce was in crafts; the figure had risen to 15 percent by 1833 and 22 percent by 1839.[117] In 1822, 1.8 percent of Bavarian Jewry as a whole engaged in crafts; by 1848 the figure was 24 percent. This figure may be misleading, however. Jews often combined agricultural or artisanal pursuits with commerce; a Jew who was officially registered as a "peasant" could well be a cattle trader, and a "weaver" might function primarily as a woolen merchant.[118]

The Jewish entry into crafts was fraught with difficulties. Christian master craftsmen were generally unwilling to accept Jewish apprentices and journeymen; and outside of Posen, there were not enough Jewish masters to assume the burden alone. (In Berlin in 1844 there were 100 Jewish masters and 41 journeymen out of a total Jewish population of some 8,200.)[119] Guild opposition effectively barred Jews from producing for the market in many communities; cases of Jewish-Christian cooperation were rare.[120] Thus Jews in southern Germany, as in Posen, crowded into selected nonguild crafts, such as tailoring, only to find themselves denied admission to settle in a community because the Gentile authorities judged that their field was overcrowded. Young, fit, and skilled Jewish artisans emigrated, either to other parts of Germany or westward, to Great Britain and the United States.[121]

Dutch Jews faced problems similar to their German counterparts. In Amsterdam, since the late 1780s craftsmen and shopkeepers suffering from Holland's economic decline strove to eliminate Jewish competition and deny them admission into the guilds. Although guilds were dissolved in 1808, Jews continued to encounter difficulties joining the new crafts and commercial corporations that replaced the guilds.[122]

In the Hapsburg Empire, additional obstacles were posed by the very same authorities who had demanded Jewish occupational change in the first place. In Vienna, the noted Jewish philanthropist Joseph Ritter von Wertheimer (1800–87) found his plans to establish a crafts association blocked by officials unwilling to allow young Jewish apprentices the right of residence in Vienna. In 1840 Wertheimer succeeded in establishing the Verein zur Beförderung der Handwerke unter den inländischen Israeliten, but Jewish craftsmen in the city were required to pay a special residence fee, and there was no chance that they could obtain the right to settle there permanently as masters.[123] One could argue that the Viennese case was exceptional because the Jewish community, although counting several thousand members and possessed of a synagogue and other institutions, was not officially recognized until after the Revolution of 1848. But the same problem cropped up in Tarnopol, where the Galician *maskil* Joseph Perl attempted in 1829 to obtain official approval to found a crafts society; because of the reactionary regime's fear of association or combination in any form, approval came only in 1848.[124]

Even if the crafts had been wide open to Jews, however, the occupational restructuring of the Jews would have been of limited scope and duration. Guild antisemitism was only one of the obstacles blocking the path to occupational restructuring. As is well known, handicrafts and agriculture experienced protracted crises during the Restoration and *Vormärz* periods. The gradual breakup of the guilds and population growth conspired to produce overcrowding in the crafts. In the countryside, recently freed former serfs, unable to survive on their holdings, became rural proletarians or migrated into the towns.[125] Moreover, during this period of early industrialization and the rapid expansion of the

distributive sector, those Jews whose circumstances did not force them
to emigrate naturally gravitated to commercial, rather than artisanal or
agricultural, careers. The Jews of Alsace and Germany definitely underwent an economic transformation, but it was a change from peddling
to stationary commerce, not crafts.[126] In Posen, the number of craftsmen
in the Jewish workforce declined from nearly 30 percent in 1836 to 21
percent in 1849.[127] In Prussia as a whole, the percentage of Jews in
handicrafts reached its peak in 1843 and thereafter declined.[128] In Hamburg, interest in handicrafts waned after the resolution of the economic
crises of the late 1840s.[129] In Munich, Jews obtained full freedom of
movement and occupation in 1861; in turn, the number of craftsmen in
the Jewish workforce declined from 22 percent in 1860 to 15 percent by
1870.[130]

Jewish proponents of occupational restructuring rarely showed the
slightest awareness of these statistics or of the macroeconomic trends to
which they pointed. Even opponents of Jewish vocational training were
unlikely to refer to the broad economic picture and instead focused on
the threats that an occupational shift from commerce would pose to
religious observance. But on this issue Jewish activists were not significantly more obtuse than their Christian counterparts.

First, the distributive sector, particularly in the countryside, was
shaken up by the introduction of industry and railroads, and it was not
easy for a German Jew in the 1820s to see that commerce stood on firm
ground. Moreover, there was strong sentiment in post-Napoleonic Germany to preserve the independent peasantry and artisanate. This sentiment had a number of motivations. One was a continuation of cameralism; another was an anticameralist conservatism that saw in the
peasant and artisan a bulwark against the rationalizing, absolutist state.
But most important for our topic was a third motivation: a liberal view
that the common folk needed to be economically stable and propertied
in order to be participants in the new political order.[131] Before and even
during the Revolution of 1848, German liberals from the new industrial
and mercantile middle class were loath to separate themselves from the
older middle class of independent craftsmen and peasants.[132] In other
words, one could be a German liberal, supportive, as the Jews were, of
economic freedom and freedom of movement, while at the same time
believe in the limited expansive capacity of the distributive sector and
the ultimate primacy of production.

After 1848, however, it was not merely the number of Jewish craftsmen in western and central Europe that declined, and with it the

numbers of youth supported by the crafts associations. Jewish public interest in the issue lessened; it took up decreasing amounts of space in the Jewish press. After 1848, as Jewish emancipation became increasingly accepted as part of the German liberal platform, the notion of a quid pro quo for rights in exchange for regeneration waned. The impetus for religious reform, which had been so strong over the period 1815–48 and which had stimulated the introduction of radical reforms of Jewish practice, lost force thereafter.[133] The same may be said for the economic sphere, where the vigorous vocational activity of the first decades of the century slackened.

In the early 1800s Jewish philanthropy in western and central Europe was directed almost entirely inward. Jews in England, France, Germany, and Austria cared for their own; the era of systematic philanthropic activity on behalf of eastern European and Middle Eastern Jewry would come only later in the century. The centralization of poor care did not extend beyond the communal level, although on the national plane the makers of Jewish public opinion did create a unified and unifying philanthropic discourse, in which the rationalization of charity was associated with a simultaneous economic and moral elevation of the poor, on the one hand, and a concomitant recognition by Gentile society that Jews are worthy of emancipation, on the other.

Despite the specific political agenda of Jewish reformers, the resemblance between their philanthropic sensibilities and those of Gentiles did not arise from mere mimicry of the values of a dominant elite. Nor was it simply a matter of an unreflective internalization of Gentile criticism by Jews seeking to distance themselves from the lowest orders of Jewish society and enhance their status in Gentile eyes. Rather, Jewish and Gentile philanthropists were cut from similar social cloth, the commercial and industrial bourgeoisie, and their champions drew from a common (although in the case of the Jews, larger) literate and literary elite of clergymen, functionaries, and publicists. The origins of modern Jewish philanthropy may be understood in terms similar to those proposed by the eminent historian Fritz (Yitzhak) Baer in his study of the *hevrah kadishah*, which he depicted as a product of the medieval world of confraternal association: "There is little sense . . . in posing the question whether such statutes were first set forth from the Jewish or the Christian side, then to be copied by the other side and recast in a different spirit. For institutions do not arise out of patterns, but rather out of general, human forces and roots."[134]

From the mid-1800s, not only in England and France, but also in much of German-speaking Europe as well, the commercial and industrial bourgeoisie displayed increasing pride in its accomplishments and confidence in the universality of its values. This atmosphere dampened economic antisemitism and enhanced the economic self-image of Jewish activists, who turned from criticism to complacence, or even, as we shall now see, to self-congratulation. The solidarity born of economic crisis and the common effort to overcome it, the sense that the common fate that knits the Jews into a single community (*Schicksalgemeinschaft*) is a troubled one, gave way to a sunny triumphalism, an image of the Jew as a trailblazer of capitalism.

CHAPTER 4

Homo economicus judaicus and the Spirit of Capitalism, 1848–1914

> *Israel owes its wealth solely to that lofty, godly belief to which it has been devoted for millennia. The Jews worshiped a highest being that rules unseen in heaven, while the heathen, incapable of elevation to the purely spiritual, made themselves all sorts of gold and silver gods, to which they prayed on the earth. If these blind heathen had transformed all the gold and silver that they wasted for such vile idol-worship into hard cash and lent it out at interest, they would have become as rich as the Jews—who knew how to place their gold and silver advantageously, perhaps in Assyrian-Babylonian state loans, in Nebuchadnezzar bonds, in Egyptian canal shares, in 5 percent Sidon and other classical notes—whom the Lord blessed, as he takes care to bless the modern ones.*
>
> Heinrich Heine, 1846

The flourishing of commercial and industrial capitalism in nineteenth-century Europe strengthened the historic association between Jews and trade. For Jews, as for any ethnic minority that falls into a particular economic niche, economic distinctiveness may engender or reinforce group identity. "Economic factors," writes one sociologist, "play an important role in the retention of ethnic ties.... [E]thnic groups often act as economic-interest groups, and when they cease to do so, they tend to dissolve."[1] This can be an unselfconscious, functional phenomenon, the result of constant interaction in the workplace and marketplace with members of one's own ethnicity. Indeed, scholars of European and American Jewish history have argued that the Jews' concentration in particular economic sectors created a structural dam against the loss of collective identity.[2]

For the Jews, however, the relationship between economic distinctiveness and ethnic identity was more than functional: it was self-conscious and reflective. Constant antisemitic pressures, on the one hand, and the Jews' yearnings for social acceptance, on the other, ensured that Jewish economic behavior would occupy the thoughts of the Jewish leadership elite. Chapter 2 demonstrated the growth in the late eighteenth and early nineteenth century of a distinctly Jewish political economy, characterized by a diagnosis of the Jews as economically dysfunctional and in need of occupational restructuring. In the second half of the nineteenth century, however, Jewish economic discourse took on a decidedly triumphalist tone in response to Jewish emancipation and increased social mobility. This discourse was more than an exercise in apologetics. At least for certain influential individuals, it indicated a sea change in Jewish self-understanding. *Homo economicus judaicus* became, in Jewish eyes, a distinct being, defined by and much valued for his contributions to the capitalist order.

As elsewhere in this book, the discussion that follows covers much of Europe but focuses on the German cultural sphere and on the liberal, Germanophone Jewish bourgeoisie. Few of the voices evoked here were steeled by expertise in economic theory. Reflecting continental, particularly German, cultural influences, Jewish writers saw political economy as a science of state, not, as in England, a largely mathematical enterprise. Economic relations were described in historical narrative: economics, economic history, and other forms of historical inquiry formed a seamless web. In an environment in which economic knowledge was accessible to any educated individual, and in which the marvels of capitalist society and the search for its origins were of universal concern, it is no surprise that Jews far removed from academic economics eagerly contributed their opinions on the nature of *Homo economicus judaicus*. Among the most visible generators of Jewish economic discourse were two internationally prominent rabbis, Adolph Jellinek of Vienna and Ludwig Philippson of Magdeburg. Neither man had any business experience or scholarly training in political economy, yet this did not prevent them from passing judgment on the great economic issues of the day, or even, in Philippson's case, from writing articles for business and trade journals. The goal of this chapter is to evoke visceral sensibility rather than invoke learned opinion; thus the dilettantish quality of much of nineteenth-century Jewry's economic writing is more a help than a hindrance.

I begin with an account of ongoing Jewish economic distinctiveness from the mid-nineteenth century until World War I. I then trace Gentile perceptions of Jewish economic difference before analyzing the development, by Jewish activists, publicists, and scholars, of a triumphalist vision of Jewish economic life, a vision that had gained sufficient focus and clarity by the early twentieth century to facilitate the production of pioneering and insightful scholarly inquiry into the economic bases of Jewish civilization.

Economic Mobility

Before the nineteenth century there was no particular correlation between geographic and socioeconomic divisions among European Jews. The differences between Ashkenazic and Sephardic Jews within a singe political unit, such as Holland, were at least as great as those between Ashkenazim in far-apart lands such as Alsace and Poland. Moreover, Jews in western Europe were only somewhat less likely to be pauperized than those in the east. (In 1800 at least half of Amsterdam's Jewish community, the largest in western Europe, was on the dole.) A handful of wealthy purveyors and court factors aside, Jewish breadwinners in Alsace and Germany barely eked out a living. The Polish-Lithuanian kingdom certainly had its share of needy Jews, but many Jews, serving as the lifeblood of the kingdom's rural distributive sector, made comfortable livings through grain and livestock dealing, leaseholding, tax farming, and estate administration.

Although Jews in eighteenth-century Germany and Poland conceived of themselves as belonging to different communities with distinct cultural profiles, the *economic* dimension to that distinction — the notion of a prosperous "western Jew" opposed to an impoverished "eastern Jew" (Polish, Romanian, or Russian) — has its origins in a series of developments that began at the turn of the eighteenth century and accelerated in the mid-1800s. The most important was the incorporation of much of the eastern portion of the Polish-Lithuanian kingdom into Russia, which, in a series of legislative decrees beginning in 1804, limited Jewish settlement to the formerly Polish territories (plus some Black Sea territories conquered from the Turks). Confined to this legally delimited zone, or "pale," of settlement and denied access to many livelihoods, Russian Jews crowded into petty commerce and crafts, only to find even these threatened by prohibitions against settlement in the Pale's rural hinterland and other forms of harassment. The astonishing demographic increase among Russian Jews throughout the century (from one and a half to five million) added greatly to their misery, as did competition from former serfs who, after their emancipation in 1862, began to compete with Jews as traders in agricultural produce.[3]

Even in eastern European lands where anti-Jewish persecution was less widespread, the overall economic backwardness of the region, combined with massive Jewish population increase, promoted Jewish misery. The Jews of Galicia, unlike those in Russia, were emancipated at the time of the creation of the Dual Monarchy in 1867. But the removal of legal disabilities had little practical effect. Over the nineteenth century, the Jewish population of Galicia increased more than threefold, from 250,000 in about 1800 to 870,000 by 1910. Railroads were slow to penetrate the region, industry was almost nonexistent, and trade in imported manufactured goods was throttled by Austrian tariffs. Cultural and economic backwardness were mutually reinforcing. Galician Jews failed to develop either a modern educational system or an effective alliance with the Polish gentry elite. Locked in their Yiddish vernacular and Talmudic studies and estranged from the nobility, Galician Jews fell into a cycle of economic deterioration. Meanwhile, their Hungarian brethren, many of whom adopted the Magyar language and developed political and commercial ties to the Magyar landowning elite, wove themselves into the fabric of the Hungarian economy, which expanded significantly during the second half of the 1800s.[4]

In western Europe and the German lands, rapid economic growth provided abundant opportunity for Jewish merchants, bankers, and, to a lesser extent, industrialists. For Jews, as for millions of impoverished Gentile peasants and craftsmen, immigration to the New World bled off much of the underemployed population. Urbanization promoted the rise of a settled merchant class as well as a "new middle class" of clerks and commissioned salesmen. In general, however, the entry of western and central European Jews into the middle class preceded their urbanization. By the end of the 1860s Germany's *Betteljuden* were virtually a thing of the past, yet only 17 percent of Germany's Jews lived in the seven largest urban communities. Moreover, Alsatian Jewry was largely situated in small towns and villages. Prosperous rural Jews worked as cattle traders, estate managers, moneylenders, and grain dealers. Some went into manufacture; rag peddlers amassed enough resources to start paper and textile factories.[5]

The economic historian David Landes has proposed a multitiered profile of the Jewish mercantile economy in modern Germany, and with a bit of modification this profile can be applied to western European Jewry as a whole for the period 1848–1914.[6] The wealthiest Jews were primarily bankers, such as the international and interlinked Rothschild dynasty, the Goldsmids in London, the Foulds in Paris, and the Bleichröders, Oppenheims, and Warburgs in Germany. Then came prosperous, upper-bourgeois Jews — primarily merchants and, to a lesser extent, industrialists. These men (and all were men) amassed considerable wealth and honors, such as ennoblement in the Hapsburg Empire and, in Germany, the title Commercial Counselor (Kommerzienrat).[7] They were active in chambers of commerce and professional associations and figured prominently in organized Jewish life, whether on the communal or supracommunal level. Toward the end of the nineteenth century, as Jews increasingly entered law, medicine, and (in France) state service, there developed a Jewish professional, as opposed to commercial, bourgeoisie, some of whose members acquired sufficient independent wealth to engage most of their energies in Jewish public affairs. Next were the small-scale merchants, white-collar workers, and craftsmen of the Jewish petty bourgeoisie, followed by an underclass that, although highly visible, was proportionately smaller than that in the general society.

The banking plutocracy that constituted the top rung of the Jewish economic ladder was weakened somewhat in the nineteenth century as private banks, the descendants of the purveying operations of eighteenth-century Court Jews, gave way to publicly financed joint-stock banks. In France, the banking practices of James de Rothschild and his son Alphonse remained conservative, leery of granting long-term credit to infant industries. Although under the Second Empire some Jewish bankers, such as the Pereire brothers and Jules Mirès, were early and forceful champions of joint-stock and industrial banking, the Crédit Mobilier, which they founded in 1852, went bankrupt fifteen years later, whereas the long-lived Crédit Lyonnais was the product of Gentile capital. Over this period, only two of the thirty-seven members of the directorial board of the Bank of France were Jews, and the vast bulk of new banking capital was supplied by Protestant and Catholic firms.[8]

Farther east, the picture was different. In Germany, Jews figured prominently in the managerial elite of large corporations and played a leading role in the founding of joint-stock financial institutions such as the Dresdner Bank, more than one-third of whose first stock issue in 1872 was bought by four Jewish financiers.[9] Jews remained the financial linchpin of financial enterprises in Austria, although antisemitism drove many to convert to Christianity or to disguise their involvement behind Gentile-dominated directorial boards. Jewish wealth continued to be highly visible; in 1910 at least twenty-nine of Prussia's one hundred richest individuals were of Jewish origin. As the economic historian Werner Mosse has remarked, "The wealth of the elite group of Jewish capitalists . . . was actually . . . almost as imposing, collectively, as public opinion presented it."[10] As opposed to the situation in France, the German Jewish banking elite provided the Reich's young industries with much of its start-up capital. In both Germany and Britain, groups of perhaps a dozen Jews (in the case of Britain, German immigrants) pioneered the development of the hallmarks of the second industrial revolution: electric power, motors, chemicals, and dyes.

Taken as a whole, however, the economic profile of late-nineteenth and early-twentieth-century Jewry remained overwhelmingly mercantile, not industrial. Jewish dominance in British industry was limited to textile production (and only that up to the early 1870s).[11] In Germany, despite the stunning achievements of a handful of Jewish industrialists, most Jews were not economic pioneers. In an age of concentration in the production and distribution of goods, Jews were slow to enter the industrial workforce as entrepreneurs, managers, or workers. They preferred self-employment in small, independent shops or workshops. In Munich in 1882, 70 percent of Jews worked independently.[12] In Germany as a whole, they were three times more likely than Gentiles to be self-employed, overwhelmingly in petty commerce.[13] The definitive work on this subject concludes, "[T]he course of industrialization in Germany would have scarcely run differently had there been absolutely no Jews there."[14]

Jews were most effective at promoting capitalist forms of production in those parts of Europe where they remained most closely tied to rural occupations. In the Hapsburg Empire, where Jews had traditionally served as agricultural middlemen, the liberalization of access to rural real estate allowed Jews to begin to purchase estates in Hungary from the mid-1840s and in Galicia from about 1860. The pace of acquisition increased markedly after full emancipation in 1867. By 1899 in Galicia, Jews, who comprised 11.7 percent of the population, were 12.4 percent of the estate owners in the region and owned 11.1 percent of total estate acreage. In Hungary in 1910, one-fifth of landowners with more than 500 hectares were Jews. More important, Jews were strongly overrepresented in estate leasing. In Galicia, Jews were 48 percent of the leaseholders and rented 54 percent of the total leasehold territories. And in Hungary, nearly half of all tenant farmers were Jews, as were virtually all the lessors of major estates — 500 hectares (approximately 1,200 acres) or more.[15] Whereas in western Europe Jews bought or leased estates primarily as status symbols, in Hungary and Galicia the estates were business propositions, rationalizing the production of grain and livestock for export to the provinces of the empire. And it was in Hungary, where industrialization's leading sector was foodstuffs, not textiles as in the West, that Jews played a conspicuous role in the mechanization of flour milling and sugar beet refining.[16]

It was a sign of the backwardness of a nation, rather than of its wealth, if a sizable percentage of its Jews were engaged in manufacture. This statement is true for both industrialists and those who labored for them. Jewish manufacturers were barely noticed in a wealthy country such as England, which welcomed industrial innovation and was well supplied with capital and technical knowledge. Similarly, in lands with rapidly expanding economies, where hard-pressed Gentile peasants flocked to cities to become the new urban industrial proletariat, poor Jewish peddlers preferred if at all possible to become established merchants or traveling salesmen, working for small outfits and profiting from the increased supplies of and demand for finished goods. Thus in Germany as a whole in 1895, only 19 percent of Jewish breadwinners worked in manufacture, while in the poor, formerly Polish territories of eastern Prussia, as well as in Galicia and the Russian Empire, 33 percent or more of Jews were engaged in crafts.

On the other hand, there was an inverse correlation between the proportion of Jews in a country's commercial sector and that country's overall economic development. The more prosperous the country, the larger its commercial sector. As the commercial sector expanded, so did the percentage of Jews engaged in commerce relative to the overall Jewish population. Simultaneously, the percentage of Jews in the commercial sector as a whole declined. Thus between 1895 and 1907, although the number of Jews engaged in commerce in Germany increased, thanks to the overall growth of the German economy the percentage of Jews in the empire's commercial sector fell from 11 to 8. By the early 1930s, 63 percent of Germany's Jews were in commerce, yet they made up barely 3.4 percent of Germany's total commercial labor force. This situation can be contrasted with Poland at the same time: only 39 percent of Polish Jewry worked in trade, but more than half of Poland's merchants were Jews.[17]

In addition to independent commerce, salaried employment was a major source of Jewish social mobility in the major urban centers of Germany and Austria. In fin-de-siècle Vienna, although independent commerce continued to dominate the Jewish occupational profile — accounting for some 40 percent of gainfully employed Jews in this field — white-collar employment accounted for another 25 percent, and as much as 35 percent by 1910.[18] The figures were similar in Munich; over the period 1882–1907 some 40 percent of Jews in commerce worked as clerks and other kinds of salaried employment.[19] In the Kaiserreich as a whole, Jews figured prominently in commercial employees' unions. Although the largest of the three organizations, the 100,000-member, Berlin-based League of German National Commercial Employees, was overtly antisemitic, the other two had a sizable number of Jewish members. One-fourth of the 80,000 members of the Leipzig-based League of German Commercial Employees were Jews. Considering that the total number of Jews employed in commerce at that time was approximately 145,000 and that Jews also figured among the members of the third union, white-collar employment accounted for a significant proportion of Jews in German private enterprise.[20]

On one level, the entrance of Jews into white-collar employment represented a step away from their distinctive concentration in commerce and toward a more normal economic profile. Yet even here the Jews remained occupationally distinct. In Germany and Austria, Gentile white-collar workers were often employed by the civil service, which discriminated against Jews. In about 1900 only 4 percent of Vienna's Jews worked for the massive government bureaucracy, whereas ten times that many were independent merchants.[21] At the same time, entire sectors of the white-collar labor force — for example, in retail sales — were overwhelmingly Jewish.[22] One of the major issues dividing Germany's associations of clerical and bank employees was whether to admit Jews. For several years German Jewish white-collar activists debated the merits of founding a separate union. Although by 1914 none had been founded, the mere presence of the debate points to ongoing senses of vulnerability and distinctiveness on the part of Jewish white-collar workers.[23]

The higher echelons of the civil service were often closed to Jews or were perceived by Jews as hostile to them. True, in France under the Third Republic, Jews rose to positions of prominence in the district bureaucracy and national ministries. But in Germany Jews had to content themselves with the civil service's less prestigious branches, such as the Prussian state railway. Discrimination also kept Jews away from many of the late nineteenth century's most rapidly growing professional fields, such as architecture, engineering, and bench science, which were practiced in government offices or large private firms that preferred not to hire Jews. At first glance this claim might appear to be refuted by statistics, such as those provided by Germany's 1907 census, which showed that 5.5 percent of the German workforce was in the civil service or professions while 6.5 percent of Germany's Jews were so employed. But if one takes into account German Jewry's prosperity and educational attainments and compares the Jews with their true Gentile counterparts—the urban bourgeoisie—the glass ceiling blocking certain forms of Jewish social mobility becomes more visible. Even in the Weimar Republic, when Jewish access to the professions loosened up somewhat, only 1.7 percent of Prussia's engineers, architects, and chemists were Jews.[24] The low involvement of Jews in these fields should not be attributed to antisemitism alone; a culture of small-scale, independent commercial activity and ingrained distrust of state and large corporate enterprises may well have kept Jews from attempting to enter these fields and pushed them, instead, into professions in which technical skill could be sold, like goods, on the open market.

Medicine and law were often practiced independently. Both enjoyed high status in Jewish culture, and in the late 1800s Jews began to flock to these professions. By 1900, 60 percent of Jewish university students in Prussia were studying medicine and 16 percent of Germany's doctors were Jews. Startling though these statistics may be, they should not disguise the relatively small number of German Jews—5 to 6 percent—employed in the professions or state service. In Vienna, the figure was somewhat higher (12 percent), but here, as in Germany's major Jewish communities, more than two-thirds of the working Jews were in business.[25]

Not all the Jews of western and central Europe were part of the middle classes. Except for Galicia and parts of Hungary, the pauperism that had plagued communities in previous centuries was largely gone, but the major communities in Germany, France, and England had sizable populations of lower-class Jews. Many were recent immigrants from eastern Europe, but significant levels of Jewish poverty existed even where the number of foreign Jews was quite low. In the early twentieth century, about one-fourth of the Jewish population of Aachen, Düsseldorf, and Duisberg were exempt from tax assessments because of their low incomes. In Breslau, where scarcely 7 percent of the city's twenty thousand Jews were not German citizens, 57 percent of male Jewish and 87 percent of female Jewish taxpayers had an annual income of less than 3,000 marks (an amount that would allow for a comfortable, middle-class lifestyle), and at least three-fifths of female taxpayers had to get by on less than 1,200 marks per year. Single, divorced, and widowed women were particularly vulnerable to hardship. It is important to keep in mind, however, that even here Jews were heavily overrepresented among the city's well-to-do—only 5 percent of the city's population but a quarter of its middle class and a third of its economic elite.[26]

Eastern European Jewish immigrants concentrated in crafts and manual labor. Three-fourths of the Jewish immigrants who entered England in the late 1800s claimed to work in one these areas. For Paris over the years 1906–12, the figure was even higher, and although one-third of the immigrants found their way into commerce, the rest found employment in manufacturing.[27] In Germany around 1910, one-fifth of the 63,000 Jews engaged in manufacture were wage laborers, and the total number of Jewish laborers may have been as high as 23,000, or about 6 percent of the German Jewish labor force. (In Vienna at this time, the figure was about 4 percent.)[28] During World War I, some 65,000 eastern European Jews were either enticed or forced to come to Germany as laborers; this number remained constant into the 1920s. Although some worked in large enterprises, such as construction and mining, most clustered in traditionally Jewish trades such as the manufacture of leather goods, cigars and cigarettes, and, most famously, textiles.[29]

The Jewish lower class in cities such as London, Paris, and Berlin did not form a true industrial proletariat. Many of its members were independent craftsmen, and others were peddlers. In London the laborers toiled in small workshops, such as textile sweatshops, which, however miserable the working conditions may have been, offered workers the prospect of saving a bit of money and buying into a small workshop of their own. Unionization was stymied by the small scale of the enterprises and their razor-thin profit margins, which rendered strikes ineffective.[30] Finally, there is the controversial, unquantifiable, but undeniably present role of Jewish economic culture, which valued independence and stimulated Jewish wage earners to go into business for themselves. This cultural element was discussed long before the immigrant invasion; one encounters it in the *Jewish Chronicle* as early as 1848. And in 1879, two years before the immigration wave sparked by the pogroms of 1881, a letter to the editor of the *Jewish Chronicle* observed that Jewish employers were reluctant to hire Jewish laborers: "[T]hey are not satisfied like other men to drudge all their lives for a moderate salary. They betray too great an anxiety to set up in business for themselves, to the detriment of their masters' commercial interests, as soon as they have accumulated sufficient experience and capital."[31]

Both the Jews' economic successes and their self-confessed determination to succeed were objects of wonder in fin-de-siècle European public discourse. Although economic antisemitism flourished throughout the nineteenth century, and indeed accelerated after 1870, in many situations Gentiles expressed unalloyed admiration for the Jews' economic accomplishments. Similarly, unlike the self-critical tone of the Jewish political economy of the Haskalah period or the diagnosis of economic dysfunction central to Zionism, there was a time, from the mid-nineteenth century until the outbreak of World War I, when discussions among Jews about their economic life were more likely to be celebratory than anxious. A crucial difference between critical and celebratory economic discourse on Jews is that while the former conceived of the Jews as abnormal, the latter portrayed Jews as distinct. Abnormality and distinctiveness are related yet separate concepts, and we need to disentangle them before proceeding further.

Abnormality and Distinctiveness

Like many ethnic minorities, throughout their long history Jews have often occupied specific economic niches in the lands in which they have dwelled. Therefore, their economic distinctiveness has been completely normal, that is, typical of an ethnic minority. Jews are the archetypal representatives of what social scientists call a "middleman minority," concentrated in commercial occupations considered by the dominant elites to be low status or overly risky. In modern history, middleman minorities (e.g., ethnic Chinese in Southeast Asia, Indians in southern Africa, Greeks in the eastern Mediterranean) have concentrated in small, family-run enterprises, made use of extensive family and ethnic links to markets and supply sources abroad, and had low operating expenses and profit margins. They have enjoyed high income levels but low status, stimulating the minorities to perform Sisyphean labor to win social approval through ever-higher levels of commercial success.[32]

This line of analysis is useful for the comparative study of minority group consciousness, as it helps us understand that Jews are hardly alone among ethnic minorities in their historic striving for social acceptance through the acquisition of wealth and celebrity. But it neglects certain specific aspects of nineteenth-century European culture that informed Jewish thinking about the Jews' place in their host societies. Not only Jewish prosperity, but the very nature of Jewish acculturation in nineteenth-century western Europe, ensured an ongoing Jewish social distinctiveness. The Jews' rapid social mobility, continuing over-representation in commerce, and accelerating involvement in the arts, sciences, and free professions, combined with other unusual qualities, such as high rates of urbanization and low birthrates, separated Jews from the Gentile societies into which they wished to integrate and from which they dearly desired acceptance.[33] Jewish writers frequently expressed awareness of the Jews' archetypal bourgeois qualities and reveled in them. They claimed that Jewish economic gifts, and the benefits that Jewish commercial acumen brought to civilization, were unique.

Moreover, when Jews of this period claimed to be distinct, rather than abnormal, they were frequently thinking in terms of the ethnic heterogeneity of the lands in which they lived. To be sure, confessional diversity — the coexistence in a single state of Catholics and Protestants, and of numerous denominations within Protestantism — had been a powerful justification for the inclusion of Jews in the European body politic since the seventeenth century, and Jews in the late nineteenth century continued to define themselves and their relationship with the state in terms of the natural right to freedom of worship and the state's obligation to guarantee that right without favoring one faith over another. Yet a more materialistic and ethnic discursive strategy was employed as well, particularly in the Austro-Hungarian and German Empires — the former because of its multinational nature and the latter because of its relatively recent creation out of independent states with strong regional identities.

The idea of the "Jewish mission," which originated in *Vormärz* Germany, justified Jewish particularism in terms of a universal mission to humanity. Beginning about 1870, the dialectic between the universal and the particular, on the one hand, and between Jewish particularism and the multiplicity of nations, on the other, figured with increasing prominence in the writings of Liberal (i.e., neither Orthodox nor Zionist) rabbis and activists in the German cultural realm.

In his book of 1869, *Der jüdische Stamm*, Adolph Jellinek, Vienna's most prominent rabbi, freely employed the term *Stamm* (literally, "tribe," but more accurately translated as "ethnic group," or, to employ Anthony Smith's useful term, *éthnie*) to describe the Jews.[34] Although Jellinek denied that the Jews formed a distinct nation, he claimed that they possessed a unique *Stammeseigentümlichkeit,* or ethnic particularity, which required and was amenable to ethnographic study like any of the world's *éthnies.* The Jewish *éthnie,* Jellinek claimed, represented a blend between the obsessive particularism and pragmatism of the Hungarians and the supreme cosmopolitanism and unworldliness of Germanic culture. The result is that Jewish civilization embodies a healthy, humane individualism, possessed of equally strong urges for service to humanity, political involvement, and self-preservation. For Jellinek, the "Jewish mission" was largely a secular one: to benefit the state through the practice of law and administration, to solve the diplomatic "Eastern Question" through cooperation with the Jews of the ailing Ottoman Empire, and to enrich people's lives through contributions to journalism and the fine arts. (Jellinek's secularist particularism is epitomized by his glorification of the revival of literary Hebrew, among whose achievements he praises not only Hebrew belles lettres and journalism, but also the translation of lurid, popular entertainment like Eugène Sue's 1843 potboiler, *Les mystères de Paris*.)[35] Although Jellinek did not write specifically about Jewish economic life in this book, we will see below that his writings on economic affairs in the Viennese Jewish weekly *Die Neuzeit,* to which he frequently contributed and which he edited during the 1880s, operated within the framework laid out in *Der jüdische Stamm.*

Two years after the publication of *Der jüdische Stamm,* the freshly established German Empire presented Jews with what appeared to be a model of inspiring unity without crushing uniformity. Rabbi Elkar Weimann of Buchau (Württemburg) claimed that "all German *Stämme* are one and will build a single, powerful family of states." Unification had brought together culturally diverse *Stämme,* such as Prussia and Bavaria, into one nation, and each *Stamm* was a justification for the continued existence of a separate Jewry, no less German than any of the empire's component parts. Friedrich Wachtel, a champion of national German Jewish organization, praised the level of autonomy granted to individual states in the empire's constitution, and he considered a union of the Reich's various Jewish communities in keeping with the constitution's spirit. The ethnologist and communal activist Moritz Lazarus claimed that the new empire would be as culturally and confessionally diverse as the Holy Roman Empire of centuries past.[36] This concept of a Jewish ethnic collective identity, nourished and justified by the diversity of the empire, lived on throughout the days of the Kaiserreich and enjoyed currency among Liberal Jewish activists in postwar Germany and Austria.[37]

This self-perception did not exist in a vacuum. German, and all the more so Hapsburg, collective identity could and did celebrate the diversity of the German cultural realm (*Kulturbereich*). In the years leading up to unification, German scholars glorified the geography and folkways of various regions and associated the vigor of Germany with the ongoing distinctiveness of its constituent parts. As the folklorist Wilhelm Heinrich Riehl wrote in his *Natural History of the German People* (1851–69), "[T]he very nature of the German community precludes attempts at homogenization, whether social or political."[38] Thus when Jews called themselves a *Stamm,* they were not perverting, but rather adapting, the current usage of a term that Germans used to describe themselves. The notion of Jewish ethnic particularity could justify Jewish distinctiveness in all its forms, including economics. Wachtel himself demonstrated this linkage when in 1871 he wrote of the dispersion of the ancient Jews as marking the onset of the "world-historical, religious and economic mission of Judaism."[39]

Granted, in the eyes of Liberal Jews, what made them particular was, frequently, the universality of their monotheistic faith and their mission to be models of ethical behavior. Yet this idea was also an echo of a prevalent cultural discourse: the notion of German cosmopolitanism that was central to the German Enlightenment and whose values remained dear to German Jews throughout the nineteenth century and beyond.[40] Thus German Jews could draw on two, somewhat contradictory but satisfying sources to justify their ongoing distinctiveness — an idealist celebration of their universality and a materialist depiction of the particularities of their culture.[41] In discussions of economic matters, the two sources were joined, as the production and distribution of goods were invariably linked with the advancement of enlightenment, culture, and morality.

A view of commerce and industry as the modern saviors of humanity was hardly unique to Europe's Jews. In the mid-1800s the Gentile bourgeoisie frequently saw Jews as natural allies in a common struggle against the nobility and the clergy, the forces of reaction. In western Europe the period 1850–80 brought about a sharp decline of the pauper/savage paradigm of economic antisemitism. This was a result partly of Jewish social mobility and partly of the pro-commercial spirit of the era of high capitalism. After 1880 immigration of eastern European Jews into the West's major urban centers revived the image of Jew as barbaric pauper, a drain on the state's resources, a tenacious and unscrupulous competitor with the indigenous laboring class, and capable of unspeakable criminal acts. (Consider the popular notion in London in 1888 that Jack the Ripper, the terror of Whitechapel, was a Jew.)[42] At the same time, the forces that transformed western European Jews from paupers into burghers, and from strangers into citizens, made possible the strengthening of the notion of the Jew as economic master. Admiration of the Jews could easily mutate into awe, and from awe into fear.

Gentile Visions of *Homo economicus judaicus*

The exchange and the salon were the first social spaces in which Jews and Gentiles interacted on equal terms. The latter, the literary Enlightenment's most precious flower, was a product of the 1780s, but the former and Jewish involvement therein go back a century or more. In 1657 a Sephardic Jew was admitted to the city of London's Royal Exchange, through whose brokers all wholesale trade was transacted. Over the next twenty-five years, another five were admitted, so that the southeastern corner of the open-air colonnade became known as "Jews' Walk." In 1697 the admission of brokers came under the jurisdiction of the Court of Aldermen, which decided to allow on the exchange 100 English brokers, 12 Jews, and 12 aliens. This was the "first grant of freemen's privileges to dissenters and non-freemen which the Corporation had ever made. It placed the Jews in a better position than even the alien Protestants," according to a nineteenth-century source. Admission to the Amsterdam exchange soon followed, and when the Berlin exchange was founded in 1803, it featured equal Jewish and Christian representation. In Breslau, where Jews were at first denied permanent membership, a threatened boycott soon led to their admission.[43]

In Germany and parts of the Hapsburg Empire, the Jews' relative prosperity ensured that they would be disproportionately represented in chambers of commerce and municipal assemblies. (For example, the Karlsruhe chamber of commerce, founded in 1819, had two Jewish and six Christian members eight years later.) The franchise for town councils was heavily weighted in favor of a town's highest taxpayers, that is, its wealthiest residents. After 1840, and especially during the Imperial period, Jews were strongly represented in the merchant corporations of many German cities, although there were certain areas, such as Saxony, where they were largely excluded. In Posen, West Prussia, and Silesia, there were towns where Jews dominated commercial life; they were heavily overrepresented among the highest taxpayers and thus among the town councillors. In Breslau under the empire, at least 20 percent of the city councillors were Jews, as was, most of the time, the city council chair (5 percent of the city's population was Jewish). In Hungary as well, Jewish prosperity translated into higher than average rates of enfranchisement and overrepresentation in instances of local government.[44]

In general, local government in nineteenth-century Germany was more open to leadership by men from commercial backgrounds, as politics in most of the German states was the domain of aristocrats and the *Bildungsbürgertum,* the "educated bourgeoisie" of bureaucrats, academics, and clerics.[45] The commercial bourgeoisie commands our attention here, because it was the reference group for Jewish acculturation and because of its historic support for Jewish emancipation. In the Rhineland, already in the early 1840s an aggressively pro-commercial bourgeoisie championed Jewish emancipation, expressed admiration for Jewish accomplishments in banking and trade, and dismissed the notion that Jews need to undergo an occupational transfer into agriculture. This spirit strengthened in the 1860s, the heyday of political liberalism in many of the German states and a time of liberalization for France's Second Empire. During this period, the German middle class's most popular journal, *Die Gartenlaube,* portrayed Jews in a most positive light, in keeping with its generally high opinion of commerce as an ennobling activity and its association of parasitism not with Jews but with the idle aristocracy. Also at this time, Jews were accepted into executive positions in the Deutscher Nationalverein, an association that championed unconditional Jewish emancipation as part of its liberal agenda.[46] Meanwhile, in France the national government, which historically had been less hostile than the German states to Jews, went so far as to praise Jewish moneylending operations in Alsace as a necessary source of scarce commercial credit.[47] All in all, in the 1860s a Jew in Germany, especially in lands west of the Rhine, could logically infer that equal rights would no longer be conditional on socioeconomic regeneration.

The European Jewish press diligently searched for flattering depictions of Jewish economic behavior from Gentile publicists and politicians. Although the motives behind this fishing for praise were apologetic and attest to ongoing Jewish insecurity, the sources bespeak a deep, yet often double-edged, appreciation of Jewish business success. Some of these sources were paeans to the Rothschild dynasty, depicted as a true aristocracy of birth whose vast capital breathes life into industrial and scientific development throughout the Continent. This financial aristocracy was favorably compared with the allegedly spendthrift and unimaginative Gentile landed elites.[48] More generally favorable comments were in line with the chorus of assent that greeted a proclamation by a member of the Hungarian diet that "the Jew is an essential component of economic life, . . . an essential, prominent component of Hungarian bourgeois life. . . . Whoever damages this organ damages the body of the nation itself."[49] In 1913 a Jewish scholar could happily insert into his history of Austrian Court Jewry the following bit of gushing praise offered by Leopold Ritter von Sacher-Masoch, a Galician aristocrat who wrote frequently and sympathetically on Jewish themes (and also on erotic ones; hence the origin of the word *masochism*):

A court factor is a Jew in the court of a Galician nobleman, who must manage all affairs from diplomacy to cobbling. It is he who connects the estate, lost in the sea of grain, with the world, so that he serves simultaneously as caravan, postman, and telephone. There is nothing that he does not know how to bring forth. He fills food chests and cellars and also the cash box when it is empty. To that end he sells all that there is to sell, even, not seldomly, the harvest itself before it has been brought in, and the calf before it has been born. It is difficult to say what he is, for there is nothing that he is not.[50]

An ominous undercurrent could underlay many such statements. In 1849, in what may be considered one of the first systematic studies of Jewish economic behavior, a series of articles, first published in a German literary journal and then reproduced in the *Allgemeine Zeitung des Judentums,* traced the story, "Joseph, Son of Tobias, and his Sons, the First Jewish Businessmen." The article alleged that the wealthy Tobiad family, which rose to prominence as tax farmers in Palestine during the Ptolemaic period, was the first to see in money a vehicle for gaining power, a way to endear oneself to political authority and win special treatment. The author sees the era of Greek rule over Palestine as one when Jews developed their special relationship to money, their "conviction, more lively than in almost any other people, of the power of money and the commercial and speculative spirits that flow therefrom."[51] Even more disturbing is the half-admiring, half-derisive tone of a French

Catholic newspaper that in 1869 mocked the plans of a French Jewish philanthropist to found an agricultural school for Jewish youth. Farming and crafts, ran the piece, are dull and mindless jobs, best performed by people fettered by centuries of thralldom. Jews can be neither content nor successful in such labor, and "it is much more logical to push them into the field of commerce, which better develops their best faculties and even to direct them towards banking, where they have shined for so long, where they are destined to become the highly intelligent and highly accepted masters of all the enterprises of Europe and, perhaps, of the entire world."[52]

Thus even in the optimistic third quarter of the nineteenth century, when continental European liberalism was at its zenith and there was great confidence in the growth of capitalism and the benefits it would bring to humanity, in public discourse the Jew remained separate, somewhat suspicious, abnormal rather than merely distinct. The consistent and persistent association between Jews and one particular set of economic characteristics testifies to the ongoing hold of venerable stereotypes on the link between Jews and money.[53] The Jew continued to serve, as he had in the 1840s, as a symbol of the revolutionary, transformative qualities of capitalism. The more quickly the old order changed, the more seriously particular social groups felt threatened and oppressed, the more virulent antisemitic sentiment would be.

There was no necessary correlation between official antisemitism — that is, state sponsored and serving as a justification for state policy — and renewed outbursts of literary antisemitism that began in eastern Europe in the 1860s and then spread westward. In Russia, the 1860s witnessed partial Jewish emancipation, yet the same liberalizing forces that made this possible also threatened the stability of the country's social order, thus stimulating the formation of antisemitic fantasies similar to the conspiracy theories dreamed up in western Europe during the chaotic 1840s. The emancipation of the serfs in 1861 caused widespread social dislocation, and the legalization of land purchase by Jews augured, in the eyes of Russia's elites, the collapse of the nobility and the rise of a new serfdom, capitalist rather than manorial, in which the knout would now be wielded by Jews.[54] In western Europe, a series of crises beginning in the early 1870s produced a great escalation in the quantity of antisemitic rhetoric, although Jewish emancipation was never in serious danger of being revoked.

Moreover, the nature of late-nineteenth-century antisemitism did not fundamentally change. True, antisemitism of the late 1800s sometimes employed the language of scientific racism and traditional theological justifications for Jew-hatred lost their élan and explanatory force.[55] But the use of the word *antisemitism* (popularized, if not coined, by Wilhelm Marr in 1879) was motivated by a desire to transmute Jew-hatred into a political ideology, an *-ism,* rather than a form of scientific inquiry. On the purely discursive level, nineteenth-century antisemitism was very much of a piece across both time and space. Thundering denunciations of acculturated Jewish capitalists and immigrant paupers could be found in England and throughout the Continent. There was not a substantive difference between Alphonse de Toussenel's tirades of the 1840s against Jewish capital and Edouard Drumont's notorious antisemitic compendium of 1886, *La France Juive.* Similarly, the fear of the vagabond Jew that gripped *Vormärz* Germany was manifested anew in the historian Heinrich von Treitschke's depiction in 1879 of hordes of pants-selling Jewish youth descending on Germany from the east.

The most important differences between late-nineteenth-century antisemitism and its predecessors were not rhetorical but operative. In an era of mass politics, where victims and malcontents demanded a hearing, antisemitism in the West became, simultaneously and paradoxically, more powerful in the sense that it inspired political movements and less so in that, unlike the period before 1848, it rarely influenced government policy. What began in the 1870s as a purely literary affair — a series of articles in German periodicals (among them, the formerly philosemitic *Gartenlaube*) attributing to Jews the woes of capitalism, including the stock market crash of 1873 — became by the end of the decade a political movement in Germany and Austria. In Germany during the 1890s, small parties whose raison d'être was limited to antisemitism won seats in state parliaments and the Reichstag, and the platform of the German Conservative Party contained a plank protesting Jewish domination of German economic and cultural life. In Austria, political antisemitism's economic base was clear from the popularity among lower-middle-class voters of Karl Lueger, elected mayor of Vienna in 1895 and finally seated, despite opposition from the Imperial bureaucracy and some Catholic clerics, two years later. France, too, experienced a development from literary to political antisemitism; the Dreyfus Affair transmuted Drumont's paranoid fantasies into the political sphere with the formation in 1897 of the Ligue antisemitique française, led by Jules Guérin.[56]

Small shopkeepers losing custom to department stores, craftsmen threatened by factory-produced goods, investors ruined by stock exchange speculation, peasants starved of credit, aristocrats fearful of losing power to the bourgeoisie, clerics and intellectuals worried by the secularization and commercialization of modern life—all of these were vulnerable to the charms of antisemitism, which accounted for the evils of the new economic order without casting doubt on the viability of the old. The actual levels of popularity and institutionalization of antisemitic sentiment, however, depended on factors unique to each country's political and social order. Moreover, despite its sound and fury, fin-de-siècle political antisemitism accomplished little.

No government in western Europe desired or was able to push Jews out of the national economy or revoke emancipation. Demonstrations, manifestos, roughings-up and mob violence (in Vienna in the early to mid-1890s), blood-libel accusations (in Germany and the Hapsburg Empire), and even full-scale riots (in France in 1898) were, in retrospect, merely brush fires in the relatively nonflammable ecology of the era of emancipation. Ironically, the only European country that passed legislation before 1914 that could be defined as antisemitic was England, which did not feature a political antisemitic movement. (The 1905 Aliens' Act was designed to reduce the entry of immigrant Jews into the country, although its actual effects were unclear.)[57] To cite Shulamit Volkov's memorable phrase, antisemitism of the pre-1914 period in western Europe was more a cultural code, a symbol of discontent with the bourgeois order, than a stimulus to direct action. Even in Vienna, the avowedly antisemitic mayor Lueger provided Jews with municipal contracts, and attempts by Christian-Socialist radicals to boycott Jewish businesses failed.[58]

Jews in western Europe were far more secure than antisemitic rhetoric alone would suggest. They lived in constitutional states, ruled by law, and committed to the principles of freedom of occupation and of movement that are the bedrock of modern capitalism. They were part of a prosperous and confident bourgeoisie that, even in Germany, where political power lay largely outside the middle classes' grasp, felt superior to the forces of reaction, both aristocratic and clerical, and believed that time was on its side.[59] Antisemitism, however disturbing, was perceived as an atavistic force that would be defeated by a combination of the state's own judicial mechanism and, when needed, lobbying by Jewish interest groups.[60] When Jews expressed pride in their economic accomplishments, they were doing so not only as members of a middleman minority, striving for success and social acceptance, but also as bourgeois, possessed of Promethean strength and beneficence, bearers of the fructifying gift of capitalist development.

Burghers of the Mosaic Persuasion

In 1885 Adolph Jellinek offered the following observation about the relationship between Jews and commerce:

People are ungrateful. We do not mean toward the Jews; that is an old story. It is the social world-reformers who are ungrateful toward commerce. It is not simply a great benefactor of humanity, because it mediates the exchange of agricultural and industrial products among the most distant lands, but also because it frees men of diverse faiths and nationalities from prejudice. Men of commerce have always been more open-minded and have had a wider view, independent of their own turf, than men in agriculture and crafts. It certainly cannot be denied that trade, which has to endure competition, produces a certain slickness, develops shrewdness and expands the conscience of certain merchants so much that it creates room for a laxer morality. It is therefore no surprise if the portrait of Jews engaged in commerce is not always very flattering. It remains, however, a consolation for them that in terms of shrewdness and slickness Jews are far exceeded by other peoples. In lands in which Greeks and Armenians traffic, Jewish merchants are valued as better and more upright than any other.[61]

The text's blend of triumphant and apologetic tones is typical of Jewish economic self-imagery after 1848. The self-criticism in this passage is hardly new; we encountered it in Jewish economic and philanthropic discourse of earlier times. What is significant here is the positive association among Jews, trade, and economic freedom — an association made briefly by Moses Mendelssohn in the early 1780s but not widely accepted among the Jewish intelligentsia until after 1848.

Throughout a run of more than forty years (1861–1903), the Viennese Jewish weekly *Die Neuzeit* consistently supported economic freedom as a value in and of itself and as the wellspring of Jewish sustenance.[62] In its first volume, the editor, Simon Szanto, addressed freedom of occupation and freedom of movement, pillars of economic liberalism and Hapsburg Jewish life. Although Jews do not suffer from "a surplus of intelligence," as their enemies claim, they have "a certain commercial talent . . . which has furnished the Jewish entrepreneurial spirit with such brilliant success throughout the globe." These talents are stifled in closed economic systems, such as the old order in Bohemia, where Jewish residence rights were restricted to small towns and villages, far from commercial centers, and where the right to live even in these undesirable locations had to be bought at a dear price. As testimony to the mercantile orientation of the journal, in 1873 it introduced a business affairs section, providing financial news and investment tips, as part of the omnipresent "mercantile movement of the era."[63]

In other lands the Jewish press featured a similar tone. Jewish civilization was presented as inherently liberal, in both the economic and the political meanings of the term. In his first years as editor of the *Allgemeine Zeitung des Judentums*, Ludwig Philippson argued forcefully for occupational freedom throughout the German states, while his brother Phoebus, making a claim that Ludwig would repeat over and over in the next half century, asserted that Mosaic social legislation was designed to protect private property. As Ludwig put it in 1862, ancient Judaism allowed for no monopolies or price controls, and unlike other ancient lands, it had no caste system, thus making the Davidic kingdom an archetypal liberal state. In that same year, he published an article in a general business journal on the political virtue of the merchant class, which, he claimed, brought out the best in humanity because of its cosmopolitan and meritocratic nature. Ten years later, Philippson produced a five-part series of articles titled "The National Economy of the Jews," in which biblical Israel was presented as a paradise of free trade and a sophisticated, export-based agricultural economy. Israel Abrahams made similar, albeit less effusive, arguments in the *Jewish Chronicle*.[64]

This is a particularly obvious case of history being mobilized in the service of ideology. The traditional Jewish community, like the medieval city, had its guilds, monopolies, and limited rights of residence. This system unraveled in the eighteenth century. In central Europe, the Court Jews operated outside the autonomous community (the *kehillah*); instead, they constructed a new, vertically concentrated apparatus, which assembled specie, foodstuffs, and textiles from the humblest strata of the Jewish communities and transmitted these goods to royal treasuries and armies. In the Polish-Lithuanian kingdom, Jews seeking a leasehold no longer sought the *kehillah*'s permission but instead negotiated directly with the magnates, who encouraged cutthroat competition among the aspiring Jewish agents.[65]

By the early nineteenth century, Jewish communities throughout Europe had been deprived of economic regulatory power, as the ideals of freedom of movement and of occupation became widespread among liberal mercantile circles throughout Europe. Jews, who had for centuries tended to seek customers more aggressively and operate with a lower profit margin than Gentile merchants, were eminently suited for this new, highly competitive marketplace. So it is no surprise that Jewish communal leaders now attempted to define Judaism as a religion that was, on the one hand, inherently supportive of free enterprise and healthy competition and, on the other, opposed to tariffs, which guaranteed manufacturers a home market but endangered the livelihood of merchants engaged in import and export.[66]

The Haskalah's image of the Jews as originally, and essentially, a people of farmers and shepherds did not fade away altogether, but it was now safely compartmentalized, regarded as one, time-bound, manifestation of the Jewish creative spirit. The Jewish press featured a marked drop in discussions about vocational training in agriculture and crafts; one piece that did appear in *Die Neuzeit* in 1878 decried the declining appeal of vocational societies throughout the Hapsburg Empire.[67] Articles on Jewish productivization were as likely to be critical as supportive of the concept. For example, the 1869 proposal to create an agricultural school for Jewish youth in France was vigorously opposed by a Jewish businessman who described it as running counter to the principles of contemporary science and political economy. Not only will mechanization of agriculture and manufacture reduce the need for manpower in these sectors, he argued, Jews can best fulfill their divine mission to serve humanity as a priest-people "not by attaching ourselves to the soil [but through] industry, the spirit of commerce and enterprise, which pushes us to leave our native soil (too often due to persecution) and to become the bond between peoples."[68] The recrudescence of antisemitism in the 1880s and 1890s stimulated new forms of Jewish economic self-critique, and in the decades surrounding the fin de siècle Jewish leaders and publicists offered conflicting views about the propriety of commerce. Most often the envisioned alternative was not simple, productive labor but the arts, sciences, and, above all else (in the words of one French writer), "the golden book of industrial Judaism."[69]

The clearest, and most impressive, sign of the decline of Jewish economic self-critique and the rise of an aggressive, triumphalist spirit was Ludwig Philippson's abrupt volte-face on the subject of Jewish vocational training. Philippson had flirted with social radicalism in the 1840s and called for a return to the soil not only for the Jews but for all of humanity. Yet the failure of the Revolution of 1848 left a bitter taste in Philippson's mouth. Adopting a tough and weary tone, in 1852 Philippson dismissed his earlier calls for massive occupational change as part of the romantic worldview that had flourished during the decades up to 1848 and that now lay in ruins. The world had become irrevocably commercialized, he wrote, and the Jews, a primarily commercial people, were ideally suited to catch the wave.[70]

In an 1861 article, "The Industrial Mission of the Jews," Philippson noted that although Reform rabbis rush to speak of the Jews' religious mission to embody pure monotheism, the Jews have fulfilled an equally great social mission of being the primary founders of modern banking, without which the modern state and industry could not have developed. And, like the Jews' spiritual mission, their economic one exacts a heavy toll—antisemitism, persecution, and ruin. In fulfilling their industrial mission, the Jews are "here, as well, in part the sacrificial victim for all mankind." Like Jellinek, this classically trained rabbi, whom one would imagine to be more familiar with (and interested in) comparisons of Greco-Roman and rabbinic literature than the yield of government bonds, attributed to the Jews an essentially secular mission with a strong economic component. Philippson went even further, claiming that the Jewish future lies not in the fields of scholarship or belles lettres—the occupations most often exalted by Liberal rabbis of the period—but in industry.[71]

Philippson saw the Jews as Germany's finest liberals, perhaps its only true liberals. Disappointed by the failure of the bourgeoisie to create a united, liberal Germany in 1848, Philippson concluded in the 1850s that the only two important social forces in the land are the nobility and the Jews. The former govern the country, and the latter "are the highest sources of control in industry. Neither the crooked stock exchange nor bungling brokering—rather, the great banks, the great industrial and financial societies, the most significant manufacturing establishments are in great measure in their hands, are founded and run by them, indeed, to the blessing of all Europe, for the financial salvation of the greatest states."[72] Addressing the notorious series of articles in the conservative *Kreuzzeitung* blaming Jews for the 1873 financial crisis, he attributed the crash to Germany's antiquated securities legislation and adherence to the gold standard, as opposed to the progressive bimetallism of France and other members of the Latin monetary union.[73]

The Jewish press in each country in western Europe featured a similar interest in general economic affairs and an apologetic depiction of Jews as not only good bourgeois, but the very pillars of the contemporary economy. What is more, just as Liberal rabbis proclaimed the superiority of Judaism to Christianity (as a religion of pure ethical monotheism, untainted by Christianity's allegedly idolatrous, ascetic, and superstitious qualities), so did the liberal Jewish press portray Jewish civilization as having engendered and nurtured capitalist sensibility while medieval Christianity produced, in the words of an editorial in the *Jewish Chronicle* in 1870, "idle monks who live on eleemosynary aid." "In religious systems other than ours," according to this same piece, "indolence and sanctity are confounded; in our religion, on the contrary, industry is especially sanctified."[74] As early as 1848, articles in the *Jewish Chronicle* claimed that medieval Jews invented the bill of exchange, the sine qua non for capital transfer, and that the readmission of Jews to England under Cromwell's Protectorate made possible that happy land's rise to global economic domination in the centuries that followed.[75]

In France, Jewish economic triumphalism took the form of echoes of or direct references to the Saint-Simonian movement of the 1820s and 1830s, many of whose leaders were Jews. University-educated, highly assimilated, but socially blocked by the antisemitism of the immediate post-Napoleonic period, the brothers Olinde and Eugene Rodrigues, Leon Halévy, and the brothers Emile and Isaac Pereire were mesmerized by the universalistic utopianism of Count Henri de Saint-Simon. The Jewish Saint-Simonians hoped to develop commerce into a vehicle of universal brotherhood: the railroad would unite humanity, and the joint-stock bank, by vastly augmenting the amount of capital in circulation, would lower interest rates, thus creating a terrestrial paradise for the common man. Signs of this spirit were present in the dramatic courtroom testimony of Jules Isaac Mirès, a Sephardic banker from Bordeaux and, along with the Pereire brothers, a founder of the revolutionary joint-stock bank, the Crédit Mobilier. In 1861, bankrupt and brought to court by his creditors, Mirès spoke in his own defense. He drew a distinction between the Sephardic Jews of southern France and the Ashkenazic Jews of the north. The former, he claimed, have absorbed the noble instincts of the Latin race and have responded to their full admission into French society by tying their interests fully with those of France, that is, with the promotion of industry, while the "northern French" Jews (he was referring here specifically to the Paris Rothschilds) have no identification with the state and tie neither their wealth nor their fate to it.[76]

Compared with Germany and Austria, the Jewish press in France produced relatively little apologetic literature about Jewish economic puissance. George Weill contributed a glowing piece on the Jewish Saint-Simonians to the *Revue des Études Juives,* and, after 1900, the *Archives Israélites* featured a number of essays on economic themes by Hippolyte Prague, who boasted of the Jews' role as a "source of public prosperity": "They were, as [Jules] Michelet justly called them, the carriers of civilization, and they prepared, in the misery and mystery of their ghettos, this superb economic expansion to which an astonished and enchanted world is witness in our day." Moreover, concluded Prague, since global economic linkages make the outbreak of world war unlikely, Jews are forces for a lasting universal peace.[77]

These sorts of statements were made far more frequently in Germany and the Hapsburg Empire, in part because of higher levels of antisemitism, which stimulated the production of apologetic literature, and in part because of the actual economic significance of Jews in certain sectors of the economy in these lands. In 1864, five years before publishing his book *Der Jüdische Stamm,* Jellinek opened the door to a solidly materialist definition of the "Jewish mission" by waxing lyrical about the recent opening ceremony of the Spanish northern railway, at which Isaac Pereire sat next to the Spanish queen. The ceremony represented the "triumph of industry," which had done at least as much to promote Jewish emancipation as liberal ideals: "Jews must therefore look upon industrial activity, in which dwells a liberating power, with a certain piety, and as adherents of a religion, which recognizes, structures, and regulates real life, they can do so as well." In later years, Jellinek went further, calling the Jews "the representatives par excellence of capitalism" and seeing in backward Russia's dependence on foreign, Western loans the defeat of Mars by Mercury, the guiding star of capitalism.[78] David Löwy, who after Jellinek's death in 1893 took on the editorship of *Die Neuzeit,* wrote in the same vein; Jews have been "forerunners and pathbreakers of most branches of manufacture" and the "cornerstone of a great national-economic structure."[79]

The editors did not speak only for themselves; they reproduced lectures on economic themes by Jewish professionals and merchants, including one businessman whose remarks concluded curtly: "We are not dispensable. Our commercial spirit, initiative, and ability know no equal. We are not a *quantité négligeable;* one cannot shrug us off; the Monarchy needs us."[80] This triumphalist spirit also animated the writings of Sigmund Mayer, a prominent Viennese merchant whose literary oeuvre consists of paeans to commerce and industry and the Jewish contribution thereto.[81] We encounter similar, albeit more narrowly focused, sentiments in memoirs produced by German and Hapsburg Jews in the late nineteenth and early twentieth century. Such memoirs, written by elderly businessmen or their admiring children, are filled with stories of ascent from rags to riches through commerce, which is depicted as an ennobling occupation, requiring and instilling diligence, orderliness, resourcefulness, self-control, thriftiness—in short, the very essence of bourgeois rectitude.[82]

Beginning in the 1890s, among Jewish activists this undiluted enthusiasm began to give way to more nuanced approaches, as the entrenchment of antisemitism in German and Austrian society caused even Liberal Jews who felt deeply attached to their homeland and proud of their contributions to it to question the virtues of Jewish economic exceptionality. In 1893 the Liberal German Jewish elite established the Central Association of German Citizens of the Jewish Faith (Centralverein) to combat antisemitism. (Its Austrian equivalent, the Österreichisch-Israelitisches Union, had been founded in 1886.) In 1909 Ludwig Holländer, an attorney and the chief counsel for the Centralverein, published a highly sophisticated analysis of antisemitism and its relation to Jewish economic life. Holländer depicted the Jews as constituting a separate economic stratum and as having done so since the early Middle Ages, when they were the sole bearers of commercial skill and liquid capital. Their prosperity, indeed their viability, now depended on the fortunes of economic liberalism, for legal protection and political rights alone could not guarantee them a livelihood; only the free flow of goods and capital could. Despite his vigorous defense of Jewish economic activity, Holländer agreed with the German sociologist Werner Sombart that Jews have been inured by centuries of commercial dealing to materialist and rationalist ways of thinking, thus stunting their psyches, which do not properly appreciate the sentimental and Dionysian qualities in humanity.[83]

Thus far the focus has been the sensibilities of Jews who have combined faith in political and economic liberalism, on the one hand, with a liberal, accommodating approach to Jewish observance and its place in the modern world. This is not to say, however, that Orthodox Jews did not reflect on their position within the general body politic and their economic role therein. In Germany, the Orthodoxy associated with Sampson Raphael Hirsch (1808–88) and Azriel Hildesheimer (1820–99) demanded Jewish engagement with secular culture, and the newspapers linked with their communities, in Frankfurt am Main (*Der Israelit*) and Berlin (*Die jüdische Presse*), respectively, expressed views not unlike those we have already encountered, with the difference that strict ritual observance is cited as a necessary prophylactic against descent into dishonest behavior in the marketplace.[84] Perhaps because large numbers of Orthodox Jews in Imperial Germany still lived in rural areas, where they engaged, inter alia, in moneylending, German Orthodoxy expressed particular concern over the so-called *Wucherfrage,* the problem of usury, which attracted a great deal of attention from lawmakers and experts in social policy in Germany and Austria-Hungary.

Hirsch's understanding of this issue was less than acute and was clouded by piety, but it is interesting that he employed the language of the nineteenth-century "social question" to defend the ancient Israelite prohibition against the taking of interest from one's fellow Jew:

If this prohibition is strictly kept, all capital is in itself dead and unproductive, and can only be of use by wedding it to labor. It raises labor to the primary and essential factor of social well-being. Capital is forced to recognize the equality of labor. The rich man must either bring his otherwise dead capital to production by his own powers of work, or he must associate himself with the power of labor of the poor man, share profit and loss with him, and in his own interests further the interest of labor. Every crisis of labor becomes to an even higher degree a crisis of capital, and capital can never make profit from the ruin of labor.

This view contrasts sharply with that of Philippson, who claimed not only that the lending of money at interest was a pillar of the economic order but also that attempts to artificially limit interest rates would discourage lending, thus starving enterprise of badly needed capital.[85] Moreover, when in 1887 *Die jüdische Presse* devoted four issues to the subject of rural usury (in response to a recently published book on that subject by the august German Association for Social Policy), there was no attempt to deny the existence of or need for lending at interest, merely an apologetic claim that the rate of Jewish involvement was declining and that Jews were not heavily overrepresented among rural usurers.[86] (Considering that in Germany in 1884, 103 Christians and 29 Jews were accused of usury, and of these 49 Christians and 12 Jews were convicted, Jewish overrepresentation was quite apparent.)[87]

The issue of Jewish usury was an especially painful one for Jewish activists, whether Orthodox or Liberal. Antisemites published lurid pamphlets detailing the trials of accused usurers, who lent at rates as high as 24 percent. In one case, in Mainz in 1883, a Marcus Loeb was put on trial for dozens of usurious loans going back some two decades; among other things, he was accused of tricking a Gentile into proving his literacy by writing a pledge to pay Loeb 600 marks at interest! Speaking to an overflowing auditorium, Loeb's defense attorney claimed that Loeb was performing a vital social service. The prosecutor then received tumultuous applause when he suggested sarcastically that a public monument be erected in the town square to commemorate the good deeds of this proven parasite.[88] Bad publicity such as this, along with the general hemorrhaging of literary antisemitism of the 1870s, provoked a volley of Jewish apologetic literature and attempts to disassociate Jews from the odious practice. As early as 1846, Jews in Pest had attempted to

boycott Jewish businessmen engaged in usury, and the similarly motivated Anti-Usury Association was founded in 1889 under the auspices
of the German-Jewish Communal Federation.[89] The apologetic literature essentially continued in the line of the 1806 Paris Sanhedrin, which
sought to refute charges of a Jewish double standard, in that Mosaic law
prohibited the exaction of interest when lending to a fellow Jew but
allowed it when lending to a Gentile. Like the members of the Sanhedrin, Jewish and sympathetic Gentile writers of the 1880s and 1890s
claimed that the Israelites of antiquity prohibited lending to each other
at interest to protect their simple, rural way of life. Jewish law, they
claimed, had long abandoned distinctions between Jew and Gentile in
lending transactions; moderate interest could be exacted from both, and
in the contemporary money economy such a practice was fully justified.[90]

The problem of providing adequate consumer credit, particularly in
the rural sector, was a small part of a much greater crisis, the "social
question" that, if unresolved, threatened to topple bourgeois society and
replace it with some form of socialism. As Philippson claimed in 1867,
"[T]he *social* question is the religious idea of our time."[91] Before midcentury, when Philippson was filled with youthful radicalism, he had
looked to the utopians Robert Owen and Charles Fourier for answers
to the social question. But as he aged Philippson was more likely to cite
the liberals Adolphe Thiers and Thomas Macaulay in his editorials. The
"social question" would be solved, Philippson wrote, not through political revolution but through the inevitable improvements in living
standards wrought by the commercial and industrial bourgeoisie. In
the 1870s, as the German labor movement gained strength, Philippson's
liberalism grew fearful as well as aggressive. Enthusiastically supporting the anti-Socialist laws of 1878, he claimed Social Democracy was
a degenerate, corrupting force, preaching hatred of labor as opposed
to the authentic Jewish (read bourgeois) love of honest work. Once
again, Philippson hotly denied any socialist or communist ethos in
Judaism. "Jedem das Seine," he wrote, was a watchword of the faith of
our fathers, whose biblical homeland had been a sanctuary for laissez-
faire economics.

Philippson, the embattled liberal, faced enemies on both sides of the
political spectrum. His ultimate enemy was not Social Democracy but
the premodern German political elite, the aristocracy and the clergy.
These forces, he argued, have maintained Germany's ancient caste system into the industrial era. Thanks to the German legacy of "law of the

jungle" (*Faustrecht*), these castes take on the form of political parties that fight aggressively for dominance. Jews are considered a caste, as are laborers. The latter, sensing an unbridgeable chasm between them and the rest of German society, are attracted to socialism and translate their caste spirit into political behavior in the form of Social Democracy. Moreover, a harsh and alienating religious orthodoxy aggravates the situation by driving laborers away from the church and into the arms of materialist heresies.[92]

Philippson's vision of an alliance between reactionary and socialist forces against the bourgeoisie, on the one hand, and his solid identification of the German bourgeoisie with the Jews, on the other, meant that it was impossible to separate the Jews' economic position from their political vulnerability. The "social question" incensed Philippson because of its potential to be manipulated by the Jews' political enemies. Just as his switch from a romantic-agrarian to a realpolitik-commercial ethos after 1848 was conditioned by political upheaval, so was his hostility after 1871 to the Junker agrarian elite and to Social Democracy the product of anxiety about the Jews' political status in the new German empire. There was an inextricable bond between the political and economic strands that, in turn, tied Philippson to liberalism; free trade, for example, both benefited Jewish merchants materially and struck a blow against the tariff-hungry Junker elite.

Philippson's feelings about the Jewish plutocracy were more complex and conflicted than his unalloyed scorn for the German aristocracy. In general, Jewish publicists looked on the Jewish economic elite with a volatile mixture of hope and awe that could quickly turn to disillusion, scorn, and anger.

Until the late nineteenth century, the Jewish financial aristocracy played a vital role in Jewish communal leadership. In the 1700s this active stance was partly a product of compulsion, as the ruling authorities made Jews corporately responsible for the payment of taxes, and unless a Jewish plutocrat converted to Christianity and cut all ties with his community, he was essentially forced into a position of responsibility and leadership in communal affairs. Financial power not only conferred a responsibility to lead but also stimulated a taste for leadership. Germany's Court Jews and their counterparts in France and England comprised an aristocracy of merit, one that, in some cases, survived more than one generation to become a financial aristocracy of birth, to which lesser Jews willingly deferred. After all, until the late 1800s political leadership in European society as a whole was limited to a minuscule propertied elite. Thus throughout much of the century there was a virtual consonance between Jewish communal leadership and the Jewish financial elite. Anglo-Jewry was dominated by its banking and mercantile elite, the "Cousinhood"; in France, despite the widening of the franchise for consistorial elections after 1848, the Central and Paris Consistories continued to be dominated by the bankers of the July Monarchy: Rothschild, Fould, Cerfbeer, and Rodrigues. The situation was similar in Germany on the eve of unification and Austria after the creation of the Dual Monarchy in 1867.[93]

Not surprisingly, Jewish literature and journalism in the nineteenth century often portrayed the Jewish economic elite, particularly the Rothschild dynasty, in glowing terms. The Rothschilds were seen as the royal family of international Jewry; they demonstrated to Jews the world over that they, too, could be as powerful as Gentile kings. In the 1830s and 1840s Jewish radicals, the most celebrated among them being the writer Heinrich Heine (whose conversion to Christianity failed to separate him emotionally or physically from the Jewish world), saw the Rothschilds' financial triumphs as a vehicle of Jewish revenge against centuries of oppression by "Edom," a rabbinic appellation for Christendom. More important, Heine considered the Rothschilds the instruments of a great socioeconomic revolution that would destroy the old aristocratic order and institute a meritocratic, and eventually egalitarian, society. "Richelieu, Robespierre, and Rothschild," he wrote in 1840, "are the three most terrible levelers of Europe." Baron James's pioneering of the French rail network proved that the Rothschild dynasty "now places itself at the head of great national undertakings, devoting its enormous capital and its immeasurable credit to the advancement of industry and the prosperity of the people." Young Ludwig Philippson, going through his radical phase at approximately this time, offered a similarly stirring tribute to the involvement of the Frankfurt Rothschilds in the infant industries of Germany.[94]

The Rothschilds' steadfast adherence to their faith, their massive contributions to philanthropic causes in their respective communities (and, eventually, to the Jews of the Middle East, particularly Palestine), and their occasional intercession on behalf of persecuted Jews caused them to be seen as the Jews' mightiest worldly power. Their familial solidarity, although based on a premodern paradigm of an extended aristocratic family, spread out over a vast geographic area, became a metaphor for bourgeois family life, which, Jewish apologists believed, their faith nurtured and treasured. Perhaps most important, the Rothschilds' munificence to the Jewish community could be staggering. In 1852 James de Rothschild contributed three-fourths of the building costs for the new Jewish hospital in Paris, and twenty years later Salomon Albert provided a similar service for the Jewish sick of Vienna.[95] No wonder that the first Zionists of the 1860s and 1870s looked to the Rothschilds to buy Palestine for the Jews. As the Hebrew journalist Peretz Smolenskin, who was living in Vienna at the time, wrote in 1881, "The House of Rothschild is with us and if they so wish they can work miracles overnight, for with a mere fifth of their wealth they could buy the country and resettle in it all the hungry and all those thirsting for salvation."[96]

No less awe-inspiring were their philanthropic contributions to humanity as a whole and to the advancement of the arts and sciences. In 1888 Baron Albert Rothschild of Paris donated a colossal reflector telescope and auxiliary building to the Vienna observatory. Jellinek's dithyrambic account of this gift, and of a similar endowment two years previously for a different observatory, suggests that the association between financial and celestial luminaries was not idiosyncratic.[97] For what could be more central to the nineteenth-century imagination than the relationship between the capitalist order and the Newtonian universe? Both were infinitely complex yet comprehensible, dynamic yet constrained by inexorable natural law. Let us not forget that in James Conrad's classic novel *The Secret Agent* (1907), obscurantist, reactionary Russia, seeking to undermine the very foundations of order in the West, sends a terrorist into England to blow up the pillar of that nation's vast empire based on invisible power (the imperialism of free trade, global insurance, and banking): not the Bank of England but the Greenwich Observatory.

Jewish literary depictions of the Rothschilds were indeed often hagiographic, from the first biography of the dynasty's founder, Meyer Amschel, published a year after his death in 1812, to a play, produced in Germany a century later, on the ennoblement of Meyer Amschel's five sons. The centenary of Meyer Amschel's death produced an outpouring of praise for the doughty banker from the Frankfurt ghetto, in whom "wealth and status fulfilled their greatest mission: they were dedicated to the service of the Jews." His son Nathan, who established the English branch, was exalted as "king of the exchange and a sovereign of governments [,] . . . more than once the saviour of states."[98] Some evaluations were more cautious, although still motivated by respect and appreciation. Writing in 1883, the historian Heinrich Graetz expressed deep admiration for the accomplishments of the Rothschilds, as he did those of the Jewish economic elite throughout history. Graetz considered the bill of exchange, whose invention he attributed to Sephardic Jews, a product of divine inspiration, for it allowed the persecuted Jews of the Iberian Peninsula to take great wealth with them; such is "the rectifying justice of history." The Rothschilds as well had transformed mere paper into staggering wealth and the power to determine whether there will be war or peace in Europe. Yet paper empires, Graetz worried, could be over-thrown in an instant. Gentiles may imagine that Jews are invulnerable, but Jews know better.[99]

Opposed to this trepidation that the power of the Rothschilds might be too ephemeral were critiques from French Jewish activists that the Rothschilds' control over their communities was permanent and stifling. In France and Germany alike, there were protests that the Jewish eco-nomic elite did more harm than good to ordinary Jews because of the antisemitism they attracted and the spotty nature of their munificence to their coreligionists. There was even a dyspeptic tone in the *Archives Israélites'* obituary for James in 1868: "[O]ur religion bore the backlash from a fortune which, naturally, did not benefit each and every one of us."[100] Although Ludwig Philippson continued to praise the Rothschilds and a handful of other philanthropically active Jewish plutocrats throughout his life, he had harsh criticism, bordering on contempt, for most members of the Jewish economic elite of his generation. Their showy lifestyle and shady financial practices, Philippson wrote in 1867, arouse envy and antisemitism among the Gentiles. Worse, few Jewish bankers identify closely with the Jewish community and contribute sub-stantively to its welfare. In general, he claimed, Jewish political activists such as Gabriel Riesser and Adolphe Crémieux have done far more for the Jewish welfare than all the wealthy Jews put together.[101] Thus Phil-ippson distinguished in his journalism between the Jewish financial elite's great benefit to humanity and its ambiguous, even noxious, effect on the Jewish communities of Europe. Moreover, in his attempts to distinguish between a heroic "banking Jew" and an unscrupulous, nou-veau riche "stock-market Jew," Philippson walked a very fine line be-tween honest self-critique and internalized antisemitism.

In fact, the great Jewish financiers, the Rothschilds included, were not wont to sacrifice business interests for Jewish communal benefit. Despite Meyer Amschel Rothschild's assistance in the collective pur-chase by Frankfurt Jewry of their emancipation in 1811 and his son James's outspoken stand in defense of Damascus Jewry at the time of the blood libel of 1840, the subsequent record of the dynasty as a protector of Jewish interests was spotty at best. In 1849 James and his brothers in Naples and Vienna considered, but decided against, making a papal loan conditional on the improvement of the status of Roman Jewry. The English and French Rothschilds' withdrawal from an 1891 loan to the Russian government was not connected to the expulsion of thousands of Jews from Moscow in that year, although the Rothschilds used this as a pretext. A decade later many of the major Jewish banking houses in Europe—Mendelsohn, Bleichröder, and Rothschild—floated Russian bonds and at the time of the Russo-Japanese War refused to heed the American Jewish banker Jacob Schiff's call to starve Russia of credit and bankroll Japan instead.[102] Even when the Rothschilds refused to lend to Russia, other Jewish bankers provided credit. In Vienna in 1905 a storm of controversy ensued when Theodor Ritter von Taussig, a member of the Jewish communal directorium and president of an Austrian bank, assembled a loan to the Russian government. Mass protests of Viennese Jews called for Taussig's resignation from the directorium and for the abolition of its curial system of election that disproportionately weighed the votes of the wealthiest members of the community, thus guaranteeing access to plutocrats such as Taussig.[103]

This public explosion over the affairs of the Jewish economic elite points to an important change in the nature of Jewish communal leadership that was occurring in Germany and Austria. Although the Jewish economic elite continued to have a stranglehold on communal politics in France into the twentieth century, beginning in the 1870s control over the communal affairs of German-speaking Jews began to fall into the hands of middling merchants, physicians, attorneys, academics, and journalists. This process unfolded slightly before, and in tandem with, demands for democratization of communal politics that would be made increasingly after 1880 by eastern European immigrants to major Jewish centers such as London, Paris, and Vienna. The former phenomenon was not so much democratization as the replacement of one elite by another. It was in good measure the result of the economic elite's abandonment of communal leadership, particularly in Germany and Austria, where assimilatory pressures and blandishments led many Jewish bankers away from their former communities and even from their faith altogether. At the same time, growing numbers of Jews raised in mercantile homes chose to pursue socially more respectable, and intellectually more challenging, professions such as law, medicine, and scholarship. Finally, the increased accessibility to political power in fin-de-siècle western Europe for individuals from beyond the narrow propertied elite set the stage for a quiet revolution in Jewish political life. Although a number of prominent millionaire bankers and merchants continued to take an active role in Jewish life, managerial functions fell increasingly to the new Jewish educated bourgeoisie.[104]

This new elite revolutionized Jewish communal life. As chapter 5 shows, at the time of the great immigration of Jews from eastern Europe members of this elite conceived and implemented a coherent Jewish social policy that drew on the social theory and praxis of the lands in which they lived. Moreover, they refined and expanded on the investigations into Jewish economic life that Philippson and a handful of other farsighted Jewish publicists had undertaken at midcentury. Jewish professionals with a taste and respect for scholarship, who had internalized the investigatory and taxonomic ethos of the late-nineteenth-century university, displayed increasing interest in the material, as opposed to the spiritual, conditions of Jewish existence.

Thus the period after 1900 witnessed an explosion of economic historiography by and about Jews. This historiography testified to both the growing numbers of Jews with serious academic training in the historical and social sciences and the increasing access of Jewish scholars to a reading public of both Jews and Gentiles. Jewish economic historiography, moreover, points to a sea change in the way that Jewish scholars defined Jewish civilization and conceived of its relations with humanity as a whole. An increasingly materialist worldview was in keeping with broader cultural trends, in particular, the mobilization of academic resources for the study of capitalism: the attempt to understand its origins, nature, and future; the search for the strand, like primal DNA, that transmuted the static medieval economy into an endless spiral of economic growth.

Wirtschaft and *Wissenschaft*: Economics and Jewish Historiography

In an incisive, fascinating, and long-forgotten article of 1938, the Jewish historian Bernard Dov Weinryb lamented Jewish scholarship's long-standing neglect of economic themes. Nineteenth-century Jewish studies (in Germany, *Wissenschaft des Judentums;* in eastern Europe, *hokhmat yisra'el*) was, he claimed, romantic and idealist in its method and apologetic in its goals. It shied away from economic subjects in favor of literary texts and philosophical ideas. When Jews wrote on economics, they did so primarily in reaction to Gentile treatments of the subject, and Jews used materialist arguments selectively to maintain their idealist position. For example, biblical prohibitions on interest were presented as the eternal, lofty ideal, with Jewish usury in the Middle Ages apologetically chalked up to environmental factors. That the biblical prohibition itself may have been no less environmentally conditioned did not enter into consideration. Similarly, high levels of charitable giving (*tsedakah*) in the medieval community were seen as embodying the Jewish philanthropic spirit, whereas restrictions on rights of residence and oligarchical communal rule were dismissed as necessary evils, responses to material constraints.[105]

Weinryb's critique is in large part valid. The pioneering products of Jewish *Wissenschaft* were primarily philological; and Isaak Jost's comprehensive work of Jewish history, produced between 1820 and 1847, placed economics in the service of apologetics. In a brief 1822 essay, the founder of Jewish *Wissenschaft*, Leopold Zunz, did call for a comprehensive study of the conditions of Jewish life, including economics. The term employed in the essay is a *statistical study,* with the word *statistics* having its contemporary German meaning of the current status of a polity, that is, a cross section at a particular point in time, as opposed to a study of historical development. More important, Zunz's essay does not clarify what use these "statistics" would serve, or what benefit would be gained from the study of Jewish material life.[106] Economic themes were muted in the greatest nineteenth-century work of Jewish history, Graetz's *Geschichte der Juden,* produced between 1853 and 1876. To be sure, this encyclopedic work boasts about Jewish economic accomplishments such as the wealth of Solomon's empire, Jewish dominance in commerce in the Carolingian Empire, and the contribution of Marranos to the prosperity of seventeenth-century Holland. But the material is relatively meager, and Graetz asserts that the Jews' favorable legal position in certain historical situations owed far more to their scientific skills and "refined conception of God" than to their access to hard cash.[107]

German Jewish scholars in the last quarter of the nineteenth century produced mounds of communal and regional histories as well as accounts of medieval German Jewry's legal and political status. But their fundamental approach remained what Salo Baron described as the *Wissenschaft des Judentums'* "lachrymose view of Jewish history." This conception stressed the tragic aspects of Jewish mistreatment at the hands of Gentiles in premodern times. Moreover, it presented high culture as the most essential factor in the shaping of Jewish history and great individuals as the wellsprings of cultural growth.[108]

Weinryb claims—and most scholars today would agree with him—that the turn to an expressly materialist approach to Jewish history came first and foremost from eastern European Jews, particularly those inspired by socialist or nationalist ideologies. The Diaspora nationalist Simon Dubnow and the Labor Zionist theoretician Ber Borochov are the best known of these figures, but others include Chaim Horowitz, a Russian Jew who wrote a pioneering Hebrew text on economics and who, at the turn of the century, justified his political Zionism through a scholarly historical demonstration that modern capitalism, by denying the Jews their traditional monopoly over certain commercial and financial functions, would result in their complete marginalization in Europe.[109] The Polish Jewish historian Yitzhak Schipper, who began to publish on medieval Jewish economics history in 1906, was attracted to the study of economics because of his strong Labor Zionist sentiment as well as concern about the plight of the Jews in his native Galicia. Although Graetz was a hero to him, Schipper believed that a purely religious history could not speak to the needs of at-risk Polish Jewry: "We know the Sabbath Jew with his holiday spirit, but it is now high time to become acquainted with the history of the weekday Jew and the weekday ideas, and cast a beacon of light upon Jewish labor."[110]

Schipper sought in economics the source of the Jews' resourcefulness, strength, and perseverance that had enabled them to survive over time and that would engender their national revival. This sense of crisis and mission, this transition from a conception of the Jews as a nation to a passionate interest in their national economy, would characterize a number of Jewish economists, statisticians, and demographers during the interwar period. Most were eastern European and Yiddish speaking, although they often were educated and employed in Germany; such individuals included Jakob Lestchinsky and Bernard Weinryb himself.[111]

Diaspora nationalism, Bundism, and Labor Zionism are thus well-known manifestations of a materialistic worldview, as are the social-scientific inquiries into the material bases of Jewish life that these movements inspired. But whereas these movements were radical and emerged only at the end of the nineteenth century, it is in fact the case that the materialistic outlook on Jewish history and civilization had a liberal heritage, originated in the mid-nineteenth century, and dwelled within the

very heart of bourgeois German Judaism. We have seen above how the
concept of the Jewish mission in German Judaism had a prominent
economic dimension in the writings of Philippson, Jellinek, and an array
of lesser-known Jewish activists. Moreover, Philippson explicitly demanded that the course of Jewish history and civilization be conceived
in materialistic, economic terms, as opposed to purely spiritual ones. As
early as 1853 Philippson argued that Jews were the lifeblood of the medieval economy, and he accused Jewish writers of neglecting the Jews'
economic greatness in favor of rabbinic accomplishment: "The Jews
were the masters of the European peoples in industry and commerce.
They contributed more to the civilization of Europe than all the bookish
bookmakers [*bücherlesende Büchermacher*] ever imagine."[112] In his 1861
piece on the Jewish "industrial mission," he claimed that this mission is
"so essential a component of their existence, that the closer study of it
can henceforth no longer remain distanced from their history."[113]

   Unlike Graetz, Philippson read and reacted quickly to German economic historiography. The 1860s marked the beginning in Germany of
serious scholarly work on the history of Jewish economic activity. Indeed, Philippson's remarks on the essentiality of economic factors to an
understanding of Jewish history came as a reaction to Wolfgang Kies-
selbach's *The Course of World Trade and of the Development of the European
Peoples in the Middle Ages* (1860), one of the early examples of this new
genre.

   Scholarly examinations of Jewish economic life first appeared in
France (e.g., George Bernhard Depping's work of 1821, *Les juifs dans le
Moyen Age*), but the lion's share of historical research on Jewish economic life was done in Germany. Whereas English classical political
economy emerged from moral philosophy, and thus approached questions of value, production, and consumption in terms of the abstract
individual, German economics grew out of the eighteenth-century "sciences of state": practical inquiry into human behavior and organization
for the benefit of the polity. Like German legal-historical studies, which
analyzed the historical development of institutions and of "positive"
law, that is, the actual juristic practices of groups of individuals acting
in history, German economics, although inclusive of value and price
theory, "opposed . . . the belief that there were ultimate causal laws in
economics that transcended historical time and place."[114] The fields of
history, political economy, and law all came together in the study of
the Jews, whose juridical position and economic performance during
the Middle Ages were considered of the utmost importance for the

understanding of the genesis of modern capitalism. Thus the central questions posed by the first German scholars of Jewish economic history were the extent of Jewish domination of commerce in early medieval western Europe, on the one hand, and when and why Jews were pushed from commerce into moneylending, on the other. In 1866 the medieval historian Otto Stobbe published a tome attributing the change in status to religious persecution during the eleventh century. Nine years later, Wilhelm Roscher, who had pioneered German economic historicism in his *Outline of Lectures on Political Economy by the Historical Method,* published a pathbreaking article claiming that Jews enjoyed a monopoly on long-distance trade until the rise of a Christian bourgeoisie in the twelfth century displaced them and led to their eventual economic degradation.[115]

Jewish responses to this first wave of scholarship were meager. In 1879 Levi Herzfeld, who had written a general history of the Jews of antiquity, produced a substantial monograph, the first of its type by a Jewish author, on the economic history of ancient Jewry. Herzfeld's main motivation appears to have been an apologetic desire to demonstrate that Jews entered the stage of world history as neither parasites nor natural-born hucksters but rather as farmers, craftsmen, and, increasingly over time, sober and useful merchants. He did, however, indirectly address one of the central questions posed by Stobbe and Roscher, to wit, the extent to which Jewish occupational and demographic distribution had been the result of external pressure. The great Jewish diaspora of pagan antiquity, writes Herzfeld, was born of the pull of commercial opportunity, not the push of the persecution of Palestinian Jewry by its pagan overlords:

The dispersion of the Jews, already extraordinary by the end of the first century C.E., put into motion such a great number of subsequent migrations, that the conventionally given explanation alone does not suffice. And I have found in the search for a further cause nothing more feasible and simultaneously forceful than the awakened commercial spirit. . . . On this point I would like to repeat that this great dispersion of Israel and its increasingly diverse commercial activity exerted mutual influence upon each other. . . . After several centuries, and in general without any visible oppression from without, Jews [were] present—with the exception of isolated Spain—in all regions from Medea to Rome, from Pontus to the Persian Gulf, from Macedonia unto Ethiopia. . . . [I]n this enormous region lay no significant commercial city in which Jews were not represented[:] clearly the Jews outside of Palestine had already become a primarily commercial people.[116]

Despite this interesting observation, Herzfeld's book does not engage fundamental questions about the essence of Jewish civilization and the role of economic factors in its formation. A more substantial and substantive economic scholarship by Jews would come only after the turn of the century and would represent, in one form or another, a response to the most influential and popular German writer on Jewish economic life, Werner Sombart.

Sombart was perhaps the most volatile member of that distinguished body of German academics known in the late nineteenth century as *Kathedersozialisten,* or socialists of the (academic) chair. This community of professors of law and social science produced a vast body of publications that were intended to serve as the basis for systematic, practical, and, above all, peaceful resolutions to the burning social problems of the era. In his youth, Sombart was pushed toward socialism by idealism and rebelliousness against his *Kathedersozialist* father, but during his doctoral studies a blend of visceral nationalism, careerism, and haughty individualism pushed him toward a glorification of capitalism. As a young lecturer, Sombart flirted once again with socialism; the result was a book of 1901, *Socialism and Social Movements* (which had the rare distinction of having been translated into Hebrew a decade later by David Ben-Gurion).[117] Sombart's socialism was far removed from sober, rational Social Democracy. He was in search of heroes, bearers of the vital spirit that would break through the detritus of the vulgar, small-minded, and instrumental culture of capitalism. Within a couple of years, the mercurial Sombart had been disillusioned by the proletariat, and he returned to capitalism's embrace. But he worked out an intellectual justification for his latest intellectual turn by positing a distinction between a heroic, entrepreneurial capitalism, embodied in German trade and industry from the days of the Hanseatic League, and the base commercialism of everyday capitalist life, exemplified by the Jews.[118] By 1909 he had become a model of the protofascist (or, to use the scholar Zeev Sternhell's term, "nationalist socialist") intelligentsia of the era: viscerally nationalist yet revolutionary, elitist yet communitarian, drawn to socialism not out of compassion for the downtrodden masses so much as an aesthetic yearning to both lead and meld into the mobilized, collective human will.[119]

Jews appeared briefly in Sombart's popular book of 1903, *The German Political Economy in the Nineteenth Century,* and by 1909 they were figuring prominently in his writings and public lectures. Sombart was intrigued and troubled by Weber's investigations into the origins of capitalism, for example, his celebrated 1905 book, *The Protestant Ethic and the Spirit of Capitalism*. Weber denied that classical Judaism nurtured "worldly asceticism," a combination, which he attributed to Puritanism, of self-denial and a compulsion to accumulate wealth that typifies a capitalist cultural system. Moreover, Weber claimed that Jews, who had historically been closely tied to state power and had cautiously done their patrons' bidding in providing credit on demand, did not display an innovative, risk-taking spirit during capitalism's formative centuries. Sombart challenged Weber's argument not only out of reluctance to attribute capitalism to a cultural force in Christendom but also because he had come to believe that cultural difference was ultimately rooted in racial essences. This murky palette of economics, culture, and race was applied, with broad and powerful strokes, in Sombart's notorious book of 1911, *The Jews and Economic Life*.[120]

The book constructs a series of conceptual concentric circles; the internal ones focusing on the Jews' economic profile throughout history and the outer ones engaging cultural and at times racial theories to account for Jewish economic distinctiveness. Sombart documents (and considerably exaggerates) the role of Jews in the financing of European colonial trade during the early modern period and in banking in his own. He attributes the Jews' alleged financial and commercial preponderance in part to externally imposed factors, for example, centuries of exclusion from the bureaucracy, historically the primary source of high-status employment. But his main interest is the allegedly capitalist ethos of biblical and Rabbinic Judaism, which, he claimed, esteems "riches . . . as a valuable good." As against Weber, Sombart attributes to Jewish culture a worldly asceticism, not self-abnegating or monastic as in medieval Christianity, but an ethos that filtered all sensual pleasure and natural experience through a prism of sanctification. The result was an ideal-typical protocapitalist: hardworking, purposeful, sober, and continent.

Sombart goes on to argue that Jews are immune to sentimentality and that their gifts for calculation, coolheaded analysis, and rapid judgment predispose them to success in many modern professions, including medicine as well as finance and commerce. These qualities, he claims, have been present from the Jews' very beginnings, as their origins as a people of nomadic shepherds accustomed them to the concept of mobile capital and to its rational husbandry. They invented the bearer bond during the Hellenistic period. (Sombart derives this dubious claim from the fifth chapter of the apocryphal book of Tobit, which describes a signed note redeemable for a supply of silver.) Despite the Jews' commercial ingenuity and precocity, Sombart concludes, their talents were only fully realized in early modernity, when commerce changed from an offshoot of pirating to a somber, rational enterprise.

The book's principal claims are at best inaccurate and at worst breathtakingly silly. It is filled with strident assertions and self-contradictions. Yet few of its arguments are intrinsically antisemitic. Jewish sources adumbrated or replicated most of Sombart's themes. Indeed, Sombart drew heavily on Jewish scholarly sources, although he distorted them. Sombart's depiction of the Jew as calculating nomad, however troubling, lacked the overtly hateful elements of antisemitic literature, like the Viennese professor Adolf Wahrmund's screed of 1886, *The Law of the Nomad and Contemporary Jewish Domination*.[121] Indeed, Sombart's book did not sit well with antisemites. Theodor Fritsch, Germany's most virulent Jew hater of the era, angrily accused Sombart of placing Jews at the center of history and of attributing economic growth to their presence alone.[122]

Assessing Jewish reactions to Sombart requires an appreciation of the Protean nature of his work and of the self-contradictions it contained. Sombart's writings could easily serve as a mirror in which Jews saw those aspects of themselves that they most admired or feared. Moreover, Sombart was what we would call in current parlance a media phenomenon. His books sold well and were widely reviewed. He was a charismatic speaker and had a prepossessing appearance that served him well on the public lecture circuit, on which he, like his fellow political economists in universities throughout Germany, became increasingly dependent to supplement his professorial salary. Sombart had a knack for public relations; he would send out advance men to paste placards onto kiosks to advertise his lectures. Jews could not help but take notice of him. In part motivated by genuine interest in the "Jewish question," but perhaps also sensing that a large audience would pay well to hear him speak and read his work on Jewish themes, in the year after the publication of *The Jews and Economic Life* he published a book on the position of Jews in contemporary society, *The Future of the Jews,* and he edited a collection of essays, by Gentile and Jewish notables alike, on this theme.[123] Since these latter two books focused less on Jewish economic life than on Jewish distinctiveness as such, they touched the heart of an escalating conflict between Zionists and Liberal Jews in Germany. Thus we need to be careful to note the text or themes to which Sombart's Jewish interlocutors were responding, and whether they wished or were able to separate economic from existential questions.

In 1909 Sombart delivered a four-part lecture series on Jews and capitalism in Berlin. The hall was packed for the first two lectures, many people were turned away, and the subsequent lectures were held in a larger auditorium. The audience, according to the *Israelitische Familienblatt* (a sober and politically neutral newspaper) contained "the elite of Berlin Jewry," including Hirsch Hildesheimer. When Sombart proclaimed that the idea of maximizing turnover and minimizing profit "is a specifically Jewish contribution, for the Jews are the fathers of the idea of free trade," he was greeted with lively and sustained applause.[124]

Three years later Sombart was a more controversial, albeit still popular, figure. Lecturing on antisemitism, he claimed that he was indeed an antisemite if that term described one who believes that Jews comprise a unity "in the national sense," that there are specifically Jewish particularities, for good and for ill, and that the "Jewish problem" is, in fact, a real problem. The Berlin leadership of the Centralverein urged its Munich branch to boycott Sombart's lectures there, while Zionists defended him, feeling that Sombart substantiated their claim that Jews comprised a distinct nationality. Zionists were attracted particularly to Sombart's depiction of Jewish economic life because it demonstrated Jewish distinctiveness and celebrated Jewish greatness while, at the same time, pointing out the arrested state of Jewish cultural and psychic development, which the return to Palestine and to a life of productive manual labor would revive. Sombart's writings became a casus belli; at a meeting of Jewish students in Berlin at which Sombart's work was discussed, a fistfight broke out between Zionist and non-Zionist youth, and thirty people were wounded.[125]

Such altercations generated much heat but little light. Yet Sombart's work, particularly that of the period before 1911, also stimulated thoughtful reflection among some Jewish writers about the motive forces of Jewish history and the relationship between economics and culture. On one level, this new genre of literature was purely explanatory; it sought to establish whether the Jews of antiquity and the Middle Ages were, as the earlier Gentile historiography had assumed, economically exceptional and constituted the lifeblood of the early European commercial economy. On a deeper level, this literature probed the very essence of Jewish civilization by assessing the virtue of essentialist versus contextualist, as well as idealist versus materialist, approaches to the study of the Jews.

The first shot was fired by Lasar Felix Pinkus, a Zionist journalist who wrote extensively on economic issues. Pinkus's *Studies in the Economic Position of the Jews* (1905) agreed with Sombart that Jews, even in antiquity, had engaged in protocapitalist behavior and that these behavioral patterns served the Jews well in the primitive economic conditions of the early Middle Ages. Pinkus denied, however, the existence of a Jewish "commercial spirit" (*Handelsgeist*) and attributed Jewish economic distinctiveness to environmental pressures alone.[126] A more wide-ranging and better-substantiated challenge to Sombart came from the historian Georg Caro, whose *Social and Economic History of the Jews in the Middle Ages and Modern Times,* the first volume of which appeared in 1908, was the most thorough work of its kind by a Jewish author in the period up to 1918. Caro rejected the main arguments of not only Sombart but also Roscher. Ancient Jews, Caro wrote, had no distinguishing economic features, and although medieval Jewry developed certain economic specializations, the nature of those trades varied widely from place to place: fabric dyeing in southern Italy, silk weaving in Greece, moneylending in Norman England, and so on. Moreover, the exclusive association of Jews with one economic field is atypical, for it occurred only in lands whose economic structures differed radically from those of pagan antiquity, and only where Jews were a minuscule and highly scattered minority. The doctoral dissertations of Moses Hoffman and Bruno Hahn (1910 and 1911, respectively) argued even more strenuously that the scope of Jewish trading activity in pre-Crusader Europe had been exaggerated by earlier scholarship.[127]

That these latter two works, along with Caro's, were produced within an academic framework indicates the growing acceptance of Jewish topics in the historical discipline in universities in the German-speaking realm, although discrimination against the Jews who wrote on these subjects often kept them out of teaching posts in Germany. (Caro, for example, found his academic home in Zurich.) Yet the growing interest by Jews, often from traditional backgrounds, in the relationship between Jewish economic life and that of their host societies represents at least a partial realization of Philippson's vision, dating to the 1840s, of a Jewish political economy that simultaneously considered the Jews a distinct economic unit and explored their symbiosis with their host societies.

Hoffman, an Orthodox rabbi who had a pulpit in Baden and would follow in his father's footsteps as rector of the Orthodox rabbinical seminary in Berlin, studied history and national economy at university. In addition to a doctoral dissertation in medieval economic history, he wrote a book-length critique of Werner Sombart's writings on the relationship between the Jews and capitalism.[128] Similarly, a brief yet powerful contribution to Jewish economic history came from the pen of the twenty-seven-year-old Julius Guttmann, recently ordained by the Conservative rabbinical seminary in Breslau. Guttmann, who would in later life become a major scholar of Jewish philosophy, sets out to uncover in his essay *The Economic and Social Significance of the Jews in the Middle Ages* (1907) the very foundations of Jewish existence.

Guttmann establishes from the start that "Judaism stands at the central point of the history of human faith, and faith stands at the central point in the history of the Jews." Having said that, he goes on to argue for the importance of understanding how economic factors have affected the historical development of Judaism. "One wonders," he writes, "how a people so specifically religious as the Jews simultaneously could become so eminent an economic people, and surely it is the greatest testimony for the universalism of Jewish gifts that the people of faith are, at the same time, the people of the economy." Guttmann sees an apparent contradiction between Jewish social and religious life (the "weekday" and the "Sabbath" Jew), and he considers it a desideratum to solve this contradiction through group-psychological study. Guttmann therefore calls — four years before Sombart's *Jews and Economic Life* — for a study of the internal sources within Jewish culture that have made possible the Jews' economic success: "The powerful economic sensibility of the Jew can be correctly understood only if one does not ignore the ethical commitment to the practice of a career; it originates from this and is an essential element of the ethic of religious Judaism."[129]

Like Guttmann, Caro stressed the primacy of religion as the central constitutive force in Jewish civilization. Jewish history, he wrote, is divided into internal and external realms; the former, the realm of faith and religious observance, "comprises the true content of Jewish history," but the ability to fulfill religious obligations has depended on the Jews' socioeconomic status. Thus a prime reason for studying Jewish history is to determine the material conditions for spiritual flowering. In general, Caro argued, material prosperity and spiritual creativity worked together symbiotically. (This view was very different from that of nationalist historians like Yitzhak Baer, who would associate wealth with assimilation, e.g., in Christian Spain.) An additional and even more important issue for Caro is that Jewish economic uniqueness, originally a product of discrimination, has reinforced Jewish separatism from general society, and the Jews' economic activity has helped account for their survival over time. "In some lands, Jews have, in their entirety, formed a significant component in the organism of the national economy." Caro's masterwork provides eloquent proof that the development of

Jewish economic history depended on neither nationalist nor socialist ideology.[130]

Ironically, *The Jews and Economic Life* did more to hinder than promote this promising new line of inquiry, because its forceful arguments caused many Jews to feel compelled to issue apologetic, defensive responses.[131] The provenance of the reviewers is of no less interest than the content of their critiques. Rabbis, attorneys, and scholars, often with university training in economics, engaged the work both as a reflection on contemporary Jewry and as a contribution to economic historical scholarship as such. Caro had an academic post, Hoffman had written a doctoral dissertation in economic history, Guttmann had studied economics at Breslau with Sombart, and another reviewer, Ludwig Feuchtwanger, had written extensively in his youth on economic issues before going on to manage the affairs of one of Munich's largest publishing firms.

Feuchtwanger, along with a number of discomfited reviewers, dismissed the book in its entirety. Others, however, were rather pleased with its depiction of Jewish essentiality to the modern economy and rejected only the cultural and racial arguments for an eternal Jewish capitalist ethos enshrined in the textual sources of the faith.[132] Georg Caro, however, true to the spirit of his own work, warmed to Sombart's presentation of a Jewish religious tradition that promoted capitalist activity.[133] Similarly, Julius Guttmann agreed with Sombart that there is a fascinating contradiction between "the aggressively purposeful and instrumental economic practices" of the Jews and the guild mentality of a traditional economy. Guttmann suggests that there was indeed a Jewish commercial spirit, embodied in "the rationalization of life management. The attitude produced thereby also accounts for the adaptation of the Jewish economic ethic to the capitalist form, which was originally foreign to it. It made it, as can be easily seen, possible to overcome the considerations that originally were opposed to an economy based on acquisition."[134]

One of the most fascinating and revealing reactions to Sombart's book came from Moses Hoffmann. Although Hoffmann was not free of bias—he championed Jewish agricultural renewal, especially in Palestine—his lengthy critique of Sombart demonstrates the full range of effects that Sombart's book could have on a thoughtful Jewish reader. The critique took the form of a run of thirty articles, serialized over almost a year in *Der jüdische Presse,* in which Hoffmann registered admiration, irritation, and exasperation about a "brilliantly written book" setting forth an "odious and incorrect . . . thesis." Hoffmann's first impression of the book was that it was "an encyclopedia of Judaism," possessed of "rare objectivity": "It will be not merely the book of the season," Hoffmann wrote in the first installment of his critique, "but rather the standard work on Jews and Judaism for the entire epoch."[135]

In subsequent articles, Hoffmann fundamentally accepts Sombart's depiction of the Jews' role in the development of modern colonial trade, retailing, and advertising. As pariahs in the medieval Christian and feudal order, "in the interests of their own survival they had to unleash the storm against the walls of the medieval economic order. Through this they contributed to the opening of the path to the modern capitalist economy."[136] Although he disputes Sombart's claim that Jews invented the bearer bond or bill of exchange, Hoffmann claims that medieval Jews made particularly good use of commercial paper because it allowed them to move and hide their capital (if need be, under the name of a straw man) "without leaving behind the slightest trace of their former property."

Hoffmann bridles, however, at Sombart's claim to prove the existence of an eternal Jewish capitalist ethos by comparing Old and New Testament dicta on wealth. The Hebrew Bible, writes Hoffmann, was the work of a mature, stratified people consisting of many classes and interests, whereas the Gospels were social-revolutionary works, directed at the poor. Besides, even if Judaism does instill a certain receptive attitude toward the consumption of material goods, it has nothing to say about production, which is the key to the capitalist order. More than anything else, Hoffmann argued, traditional Jewish economic ideals were theocratic, demanding the fulfillment of charitable and ritual obligations that constituted the total opposite of economic freedom.

Gentile critics perceived that overzealous Jewish scholars were at least in part responsible for Sombart's excesses. Hermann Waetjen, a lecturer at the University of Heidelberg and a serious scholar of European economic history, wrote a careful refutation of Sombart's book that was as much a critique of Heinrich Graetz and other Jewish historians as of Sombart himself. For example, Sombart's description of Jewish economic prominence in the financing of the Dutch colonial empire came from his reading of Graetz. Waetjen and another critic, Felix Rachfahl, dismissed Graetz's writings on this subject as "boasting, stemming from ignorance, to which no one today would subscribe."[137] Similarly, Waetjen attacked Sombart's assertions that Marrano capital provided the funding for Christopher Columbus's voyages of discovery and that Co-

lumbus was of Jewish origin by impugning the Jewish source on which
Sombart relied: Mayer Kayserling's work of 1894, *Christopher Columbus
and the Participation of Jews in the Spanish and Portuguese Discoveries.*[138]

Kayserling, a German rabbi with a pulpit in Budapest, wrote this
book at the behest of the newly formed American Jewish Historical
Society, which wished to celebrate the four hundredth anniversary of
Columbus's discovery of America by publishing material on the role of
Jews "in the discovery, settlement, and development of our land." The
president of the society, Oscar Straus, believed that a book on "the
extent to which our race had direct part and share with Columbus in
the discovery of our continent" would "be an answer for all time to
come to anti-Semitic tendencies in this country."[139] Straus had every
reason to believe at the time that the economic triumphalism of German
Jewish scholars like Kayserling would be a popular import in the United
States, the capitalist land par excellence. Indeed, this learned bragga-
docio, so in tune with the self-congratulatory and boosterist spirit of
American culture, was zealously exported from Germany by Kaufmann
Kohler, the leader of American Reform Judaism.

In 1883 Kohler proclaimed in the pages of a German Jewish journal
that "Jewish commercial spirit and Jewish capital essentially built almost
all the great commercial cities of Europe."[140] Twenty-five years later,
Kohler brought the full force of this message home to an audience in
Cincinnati, where he delivered a thundering address on the "world-
historical significance of Jewish trade." His remarks went far beyond
Sombart's most vivid fantasies about Jewish financial power. Kohler
argued that the Jewish commercial spirit, which spread Jews throughout
the ancient world in search of profit, enabled them to disseminate their
civilizing mission to all humanity. Solomon's empire absorbed the best
of Phoenician mercantile culture, and the later biblical prophets displayed a "lively interest" in commerce. During the Greco-Roman period, Jews were the backbone of Mediterranean trade and the key commercial link between the Roman and Parthian Empires. They were the
principal "civilizing force" in pre-Crusader Europe and had continued
in this vein up to Kohler's own time: "Russia needs the Jews much more
than the Jews need Russia, and the German kaiser knows better than
the tsar or the Prussian Junkers what this [Jewish] trade has accomplished for the ascent and flowering of nations."[141]

German Jewish economic triumphalism, let loose on American soil,
resembled flora and fauna removed from their indigenous environment
and set down in a new home free of natural predators. To be sure,

antisemitism figured prominently in the United States in Kohler's day, and even more so in the 1920s, when Jewish apologists like George Cohen protested immigration restrictions by documenting the alleged dependence of the American dream on Jewish commercial genius.[142] Moreover, as we shall see in chapter 6, American Jewish philanthropies were just as enamored as their European counterparts with the dream of transforming poor immigrant Jewish peddlers and craftsmen into sturdy farmers.

Pre-1914 German Jewish historiography accomplished far more than nourish vulgar apologetics. The pioneering economic-historical investigations of the prewar period provided the basis for the systematic historical research carried out in the 1920s by the Academy for the Science of Judaism, founded by the distinguished historian Eugen Täubler in Berlin and directed by Täubler along with Julius Guttman. Before the war Täubler had called for the integration of economics into the study of the Jewish past. Under his influence economic and sociological inquiry became central to Jewish scholarship in Weimar Germany.[143] Moreover, the questions posed by Sombart and his interlocutors intrigued the young Salo Baron, as evidenced in his three-volume *Social and Religious History of the Jews* (1937). Although Baron pointed out that none of the instruments of capitalist technology, such as paper currency, the bill of exchange, and the stock exchange, was invented by Jews, there was nonetheless a "metaphysical sympathy" between the Jews and capitalism. Its origins lay in "their detachment from the soil, the bourgeois spirit of their urban life, the artificiality of all Jewish existence, the consequent prevalence of speculative thinking, as against peasant concreteness. . . . Capitalism, in essence 'artificial,' based upon an exchange of abstract values, represented by the most abstract and irrational of values, viz., money, found the Jews ready to carry its implications to the logical extreme."[144]

The writing of Jewish economic history informed and enriched the nascent Jewish social sciences of the early twentieth century and, even more, the interwar period. Sombart's speculations on Jewish economic activity, and Jewish reactions thereto, were contemporaneous with the birth of Jewish statistics and sociology. The historical and social sciences formed a seamless web of knowledge that simultaneously purported to be objective, born of scholarly rigor, and practical, a source of data necessary for the healing of the Jews' social and cultural ills. The economist Arthur Cohen, professor of finance at the Munich Technical University and cofounder and director of Munich's Jewish Statistical Society, valued Sombart's research not only because it demonstrated the Jewish paternity of capitalism but also because it restored to the Jews a sense of historical agency. Capitalism was the accomplishment not of a handful of court factors or bankers but of the Jewish people as a whole. In this spirit, in 1914 Cohen challenged the validity of a culturally centered conception of Jewish civilization and of its concomitant, the "great man" theory of historical development: "A people like the Jews, a people without a country, must carefully preserve its human capital. A culture whose bearers are only a few exceptional individuals is built on quicksand. It lacks the source from which it preserves and rejuvenates itself: the masses."[145]

For a historian, economist, or sociologist in the early twentieth century, the "masses" could be seen as a constructive, dynamic force, but they could also be objects of pity and fear — a mob of paupers, a degenerate horde assaulting the bourgeois moral order, a socialist army threatening revolution against capitalist society. The *Homo economicus judaicus* who was glorified by middle-class Jews in western Europe was one of their own kind or a heroic progenitor of bourgeois Jewish society. When bourgeois Jews turned their attention from themselves to eastern Europe, their visages darkened. Impoverished eastern European Jews, particularly the millions who traveled westward, became the site of a different kind of Jewish social knowledge and the object of a new academic language: the language of scientific philanthropy. The relationship among the Jewish immigrant poor, social policy, and social knowledge is the subject of the next chapter.

CHAPTER 5

Solving the "Jewish Problem"

Jewish Social Policy, 1860–1933

Thus there is a social question, not only for the workers but also for the Jews.

Adolph Jellinek, 1891

The journey to synagogue three times yearly, piety, certain family traditions—[these] are of no account in comparison with the significance of the question whether the Jew should, in the future, assume a particular position in his occupational, everyday, activity— whether he even can assume it or not.

Alfred Marcus, 1931.

A melding of state and civil society took place in much of the Western world in the latter part of the nineteenth century. According to Jürgen Habermas's classic formulation, the liberal-constitutional state that had developed over the previous two centuries had not intervened in economic and family life, that is, the spheres of commodity production and social reproduction. But by the fin de siècle, the state was a powerful presence in the spheres of economics, education, and social and family welfare.[1]

Habermas's characterization of the liberal society of the early nineteenth century is idealized and has provoked considerable criticism.[2] But his depiction of the fusion of state and civil society nicely illustrates the origins of modern social policy, that is, the mobilization of public resources and administrative expertise for the material benefit of the populace as a whole. Scholars of European history have fruitfully applied the Habermasian paradigm to the study of social welfare.[3] Here, I would like to apply it to structural changes in Jewish communal life at the fin de siècle. Just as the melding of state and civil society—the realms of public administration and economic life—engendered modern social policy, simultaneous intertwining of the institutional-administrative and socioeconomic aspects of Jewish society produced a particularly Jewish social policy.

Even where and when liberalism enjoyed its greatest hegemony in Europe, the nineteenth-century Jewish community as a legal entity had never dissolved, and the provision of charity had remained one of the community's most important functions in the eyes of the host society. From the 1860s collective social action on the communal and eventually on the national and even international levels assumed an ever greater scope. At the same time, Jewish philanthropy began to evolve into a comprehensive Jewish social policy, administered by experts and affecting all areas of Jewish life, from economic to intimate relations.

Before the 1860s the philanthropic gaze was directed inward, toward the Jewish poor in the lands in which the benefactors dwelled. Even where, as in England, the poor were often recent immigrants, Jewish philanthropy limited its purview to alleviating the distress of Jews wherever they happened to be at the moment; it did not have the power to project itself onto and intervene in the lands from which the poor came. Jewish philanthropy did not attempt to regulate immigration, siphon it to the New World, or engage in planned colonization therein.

The purview of Jewish philanthropy widened considerably in the late 1860s. A fresh wave of crises galvanized Jewish public opinion, stimulated wide-ranging philanthropic activity, and promoted international Jewish solidarity through concerted action on behalf of one's oppressed brethren. This time, however, the problem was not at home but to the east, in Romania and Russia, where famine, cholera, and endemic poverty sent thousands of Jews to the West. The plight of eastern European Jewry became the cynosure of Jewish institutional life in western and central Europe. As expenditures for poor care by individual communities skyrocketed, Jewish philanthropy began to organize on the national and international levels. The process of international Jewish organization accelerated after 1881, when pogroms in southern Russia and the anti-Jewish legislation that followed exacerbated the long-standing economic crises of the Jews, greatly increasing the volume of the immigrant stream. Ironically, the increasing prosperity of the Jews in the West, and the completion of their emancipation, empowered Jewish leaders financially and politically just as the burden of the greatest economic crisis in modern Jewish history was being placed on their shoulders.

The Communal Arena:
From Philanthropy to Social Welfare

Emancipated Jews retained a sense of communal identity, an identity expressed largely through the distribution of charity to their needy brethren. Although by the mid-1800s no Jewish community in Europe retained formal legal autonomy, a separate Jewish organizational life flourished with the approval of the state and at times in response to state decree. The modern state did not abolish intermediary structures separating the Jew from the center of authority but rather reshaped, rationalized, and regulated those intermediary bodies as best suited its own interests.

In Britain the very struggle for political emancipation helped to catalyze the unification of Anglo-Jewish religious institutions. In 1835 the British government recognized the Board of Deputies of British Jews as the representative body for Anglo-Jewry. In Napoleonic France the religious affairs of religious minorities (Protestants and Jews) came under the authority of the French Ministry of Cults, but the French state delegated much authority to the minorities themselves via a consistorial system, in which a central consistory in Paris supervised the religious, educational, and philanthropic activity of the subaltern consistories in the administrative units (*départments*) of the hexagon. In Germany, in contrast, throughout most of the nineteenth century the authorities did not look favorably on the establishment of Jewish organizations on the state level, but they maintained the existence of the organized community (*Kultusgemeinde*) as a legal entity, to which, with certain exceptions, all Jewish citizens in a particular locality were required to belong.[4] Well into the twentieth century, members of Germany's Jewish communities were obliged to pay taxes for the upkeep of their religious institutions and the welfare of their coreligionists.

Even in the era after emancipation had been successfully realized, Jews in western and central Europe for the most part continued to care for their own poor. In Germany and Austria it remained difficult for Jews to receive charity from Gentile sources. The emancipation of Frankfurt Jewry in 1864 came with the expectation that the Jewish community would continue to educate and succor its poor and ill members. Although the 1869 Industrial Ordinance of the North German Confederation permitted German Jews and foreign Jews on German soil to receive aid from non-Jewish charities, these sources were not forthcoming. The 1909 statutes of the Berlin poor care commission, for example, explicitly required charities to send Jewish applicants to Jewish institutions.[5]

In Vienna, although by law anyone resident in the city for ten years was empowered to claim residency (*Heimatsrecht*) and thus public charity, the Jewish poor were clearly underrepresented in the city's relief programs. In 1895 less than 1 percent of the total number of individuals cared for in the municipal poorhouse were Jews, although they constituted some 8.5 percent of the city's population. In that same year, Jewish sources claimed, only 250 Jews figured among the 56,000 individuals aided by the Vienna Poor Council.[6] These were, at least technically, nonconfessional institutions; one must assume that the number of Jews receiving benefits from the myriad church-sponsored charities in the city was even smaller. Officers of the Viennese Jewish community complained bitterly about this state of affairs, wherein, they argued, confessional charities served no Jews at all and nonconfessional ones excluded them through various means, thus placing on middle-class Viennese Jews a vastly disproportionate poor care burden.[7]

In Britain the pressures on Jews to care for their own were less formal but just as powerful. Following a pattern established even before the spike in immigration of the late 1860s, the Anglo-Jewish leadership preferred to keep the Jewish poor out of the public eye lest Jewish paupers stimulate antisemitism and endanger the social acceptance that the Anglo-Jewish middle class had come to enjoy. Anglo-Jewry, no less than its continental counterparts, lived in a quid pro quo arrangement with Gentile society, but whereas for the latter the exchange was one of rights for regeneration, for the former, who already enjoyed civil rights and were not expected to undergo fundamental change, it was more a matter of social acceptance in return for a display of financial responsibility.[8] Gentiles' favorable opinions of Jews frequently invoked their practice of being, as one friendly Gentile observer remarked in 1871, "singularly charitable, not merely to their brethren, but to members of other churches when in want or in affliction." This observer continued, "A Jew scarcely ever needs parish relief; the wealthy of his people make it unnecessary. They give marriage portions to their poor maidens; they bury such as die in poverty."[9]

The quid pro quo was acknowledged and accepted by Anglo-Jewish leaders. The prominent rabbi and scholar Israel Abrahams noted in a sermon, "We must deal effectively with our own problem of the poor, because our Christian friends expect it of us."[10] Michael Henry, editor of the *Jewish Chronicle* between 1868 and 1875 and a tireless philanthropic activist, wrote that "the charge of maintaining their poor falls very heavily on the Jews—especially on the Jews of this country." The philanthropist Lionel Van Oven acknowledged, "It is true that the Jews pay the poor rates, and derive but little benefit therefrom, since they consider it their duty to educate and provide for their own poor."[11]

After 1905 the nascent British welfare state began to take on many of the Jewish community's most expensive philanthropic functions, such as the provision of health care; but the community still was a highly visible provider of social services, and the image of the Anglo-Jewish leadership elite as the proprietors of communal largesse continued to be held by both Gentiles and the immigrant Jewish poor. Moreover, most of this transformation occurred after World War I; as of 1914 what has been called the British "social service state" still relied heavily on voluntary agencies.[12]

In Germany, although Chancellor Otto von Bismarck is well known to have pioneered modern social policy in the form of workers' insurance, state governments made little provision for the unemployed or unemployable. Traditionally, the churches and municipalities were the pillars of philanthropic activity. In the second half of the 1800s, both became increasingly visible agents of social reform, the former out of concern about the spiraling "social problem" and the latter due to state legislation requiring communities to care for paupers in the jurisdiction in which they became indigent.[13] Theoretically, then, Jews should have had access to municipal poor care. Yet even in situations in which Jews were granted access to municipal charity, the communal leadership desired to keep philanthropic services within its purview. In an unusually blunt admission, the journalist Gustav Tuch, longtime president of the Hamburg B'nai B'rith, stated, "Insofar as America's and western Europe's Jews engage in rescue work for their eastern European brothers and sisters, they also work for the benefit of their own reputation; indeed, they protect themselves from injuries whose implications perhaps cannot now be realized."[14] Added to these forces working from above, from the Jewish leadership elite, were the desires of the poor themselves. In Germany itinerant Jews from eastern Europe preferred Jewish to Gentile charities, partly out of fear of Gentile authority and partly because Jewish charities provided higher levels of aid.[15]

Besides, certain kinds of aid involved the fulfillment of religious commandments that only a Jewish charity could provide. Thus, whereas a Jewish pauper might conceivably turn to a Gentile charity for clothing or a cash handout, if that pauper died there was no realistic alternative to a free Jewish burial ("They bury such as die in poverty"). This service was readily used, and it nicely indicates the levels of poverty in a Jewish community at a particular time. In Paris until the 1860s, more than half the Jewish burials were subsidized. In Vienna in 1909, 62 percent were free.[16]

Scholars concur that Jewish philanthropy in Germany tended to be more generous than its non-Jewish counterparts.[17] There is reason to believe that this was the case in other lands as well. There was an exponential increase in the quantity of and funding for Jewish philanthropic services throughout western and central Europe after 1870. These services took the form of both "indoor," that is, institutional, relief, and "outdoor" relief, in the form of cash (handouts and loans), in-kind benefits (such as firewood and Passover matzoh), and assistance programs (e.g., vocational education, aid to new mothers, subsidized burials).

From the mid-nineteenth century onward, we see a steady pattern of a rate of increase of philanthropic expenditures far in excess of the rate of population growth or of inflation (if any). In London Jewish charities spent some £30,000 in 1856 and £271,000 in 1905—a ninefold increase—while the population increased five times, from 30,000 to 150,000.[18] In Paris outlays by the Comité de bienfaisance increased from Fr 153,000 in 1878 to Fr 693,000 in 1910—a more than fourfold increase—while the Jewish population of the city grew by at most half, from 40,000 to 60,000.[19] Hamburg's Poor Care Commission expenditures leaped from RM 49,000 to RM 67,000—almost 40 percent—between 1888 and 1893 alone.[20] In Berlin poor care outlays over the period 1893–1911 ranged between RM 115,000 and RM 228,000, with the amount increasing steadily over time.[21] These sums do not include the activities of the national league of German Jewish communities, the Deutsch-Israelitischer Gemeindebund (hereafter DIGB), which, between 1901 and 1908, founded schools for wayward boys and girls and a home for retarded children in Berlin. Expenditures on these institutions climbed from RM 28,000 in 1907 to RM 91,000 in 1912.[22]

Perhaps the most spectacular evidence comes from Vienna, where the communal poor care budget leaped from k. 158,000 in 1886 to k. 420,000 a decade later, to k. 683,000 in 1904 and k. 1,100,000 in 1910.[23] This sevenfold increase came while the city's Jewish population grew by

250 percent, from some 70,000 to 175,000. Poor care took up one-third
of the Viennese community's budget; it was its largest single component. Before the turn of the century, Viennese Jewish charities were not
necessarily more generous than Gentile ones. In 1895 poor care expenditures by the Jewish community were 6 percent of those of the municipality, and Jews made up 8.5 percent of the population. But by 1910 the
Jewish hospital in Vienna was spending almost as much on care for the
indigent as the other seventeen hospitals in Vienna combined. Moreover, in the same year expenditures per child in the Viennese Jewish
orphanages were somewhere between 60 and 100 percent higher than
those maintained by the municipality and the state.[24] And Vienna's Jewish community featured a full array of philanthropic institutions, including a hospital, orphanages, sanitoriums, and summer camps.

A similar landscape existed throughout Germany. In 1889 there were
20 Jewish hospitals and sanitoriums, 10 retirement homes, and 25 orphanages. By 1913 there were 109 institutions for children, 71 hospitals
and sanitoriums, 56 retirement homes, 34 institutions for women's education, and 22 labor exchanges and workhouses.[25]

Even in England, where the Jewish Board of Guardians (JBG) had
traditionally favored outdoor relief because of the formidable costs of
building institutions, a workhouse (actually, in the words of its director,
"an asylum for our aged and decrepit poor") was established in 1871;
and "industrial schools," reformatories for wayward boys and girls, were
founded in 1901 and 1906, respectively.[26] These institutions responded
more to perceptions of crisis and of a desire to keep dysfunctional Jews
away from Gentile eyes than to overwhelming need. True, the Jewish
workhouse offered a welcome alternative to the parish facilities, where
observing the Sabbath and Jewish dietary laws was often impossible,
and to which Jewish paupers and *agunot* (grass widows) were occasionally sent. A year after its opening, however, the workhouse held only
twenty inmates, plucked from parish facilities throughout England.
Moreover, at the turn of the century there were not enough criminal
Jewish youth to justify so expensive an enterprise as a reform school,
but Jewish philanthropists wished to make public gestures of their intent
and ability to corral the allegedly dangerous impulses of the immigrant
Jewish youth.[27]

These institutions were maintained by a handful of the wealthiest
members of the community. In the 1850s James de Rothschild had donated three-fourths of the building costs of the Jewish hospital in Paris,
and the banker Salomon Heine underwrote the costs of the Hamburg

Jewish hospital.[28] In London in the early 1870s, Nathan Meyer Rothschild provided half the funds for the boys' industrial school. A decade later forty families provided most of London Jewry's charitable funds.[29] In Paris in 1898, only 900 Jews out of a population of some 50,000 were subscribed patrons of the Comité de bienfaisance.[30] Although in England and France the immigrants made valiant efforts to care for their own, those initiatives that succeeded depended on funding by established Jews. And there were limits to the resources and charitable impulses of the communities and the Jewish magnates in them. In the early 1900s even in London, perhaps the most prosperous Jewish community in Europe and certainly the one with the greatest amount of Jewish philanthropic spending per capita, a lack of funds stymied plans for a Jewish Toynbee Hall in the East End and sharply restricted the number of tuition scholarships available for the religious education of London's burgeoning Jewish youth.[31]

The financial demands that were placed on the Jewish leaders of England, France, Germany, and Austria, and that these leaders placed on themselves, were too much to bear. In addition to providing for the native poor, they were called on to succor many of the 2.75 million Jews who, between 1881 and 1914, emigrated from the Russian Empire, Romania, and the eastern Hapsburg Empire. Almost 90 percent of the immigrants went on to the New World, departing from northern European ports, but en route to the port they passed through Germany or, being impoverished and in need of health care, lodging, and transportation, sought refuge, for the short or long term, in Jewish communities anywhere between Budapest and London.

Even during the far smaller, but still, at the time, ominous, immigration wave of the early 1870s, the Anglo-Jewish press was filled with dire warnings about the rapid depletion of the poor chests and the need to rationalize and conserve expenditures. After 1881 the feeling of being overwhelmed became more pervasive and universal. Another quantum leap occurred after the turn of the century, when political unrest and pogroms augmented the stream of emigration from Russia and with it the sense of helplessness on the part of Jewish philanthropists in western Europe.[32]

A few examples illustrate the extent of Jewish poverty in the communities and the overwhelming demands placed on them. Over the period 1861–80, before the immigration crisis ushered in by the events of 1881, some one-fifth of London Jewry received aid from the JBG. In 1891 a surge of immigration sent the JBG into debt, and it had to borrow funds to continue its operations. In Paris in 1884, a Jewish labor exchange that had been founded three years before was forced to shut its doors, overwhelmed by the rush of immigrants.[33] In 1909 some nine thousand Jews in Paris—one-seventh of the community—received Jewish charity. In Vienna a member of the community's supervisory board noted in 1911 that the Jewish population of the city increased annually by five thousand, nearly all of them poor, and that the poor care budget could not meet their needs: "And thereby we touch upon the most painful point and one of the worst problems of our communal life, namely, the painful fact that we stand powerless in the face of the growing misery of the Jews, that we are no longer in a position to keep in step with the increase of the population and also with the increase in earlier guaranteed levels of support because of the growing expense of necessities."[34]

Jewish activists in major metropolises, where the immigrants congregated, hoped to disperse the immigrant poor into smaller communities. The philanthropists' motives combined humanitarianism and self-interest. Trepidation about antisemitic reactions to the presence of vast pools of impoverished and unmistakably foreign Jews combined with a sincere concern for the welfare of Jews struggling to make ends meet and crowded into filthy and unsanitary slums. Attempts to disperse the immigrants out of London and Paris rarely succeeded, in part because the newcomers preferred the relative security of a large community of people like themselves and in part because outlying communities feared overtaxing their limited charitable resources.[35] The case of Germany shows that these fears were rational; in this land, through which as many as two million transmigrants passed between 1870 and 1914, few communities could avoid caring for the itinerant Jewish poor. In the two thousand-member community of Würzburg in 1913, 1,500 Jews, most of them itinerants, received charity.[36] In the same year a Jewish activist in Darmstadt wrote piteously:

There are now about 85 Russian and Galician families here, of which fifty must be permanently supported; the resources of our relatively small community [2,000] are thereby overcommitted, especially since a large number of poor German Jews still live here, and the rural Jews in Hesse must be increasingly supported by us, for their occupational opportunities become steadily more difficult. The foreigners cannot support themselves here, because there is no work. Except for a few machine, boiler, and furniture factories there is almost no industry here; it lies almost entirely in Christian hands, and because the Russian [Jews] do not work on Saturday, employment is closed to them.[37]

Unable to slow immigration or redirect it from the major centers, Jewish philanthropists concentrated their efforts on centralizing the distribution of aid. From the late 1860s through World War I, the call for philanthropic centralization was a constant refrain in England, Germany, and Austria. In 1859 the London JBG was founded to eliminate the inefficiency and waste caused by applicants submitting multiple claims to scores of Jewish charitable associations. Following suit, England's second-largest Jewish community, Manchester, founded a board of guardians in 1868. But in neither city did the Board of Guardians take all philanthropic activity under its purview. In London in 1900, only 40 percent of Jewish poor care outlays came from the JBG.[38] The London Jewish workhouse was founded and run independently of the JBG.[39] Resistance to the centralization of charity was fierce; a proposal in 1871 by Lionel Van Oven to place more charitable services under the aegis of the JBG set off months of debate in the pages of the *Jewish Chronicle*. Many of the letters protested that centralization would suppress the individuality of the giver and throttle spontaneous expressions of the philanthropic spirit. It would harm both the beneficiary, by impeding people from giving freely, and the benefactor, whose charitable impulses would be smothered. In the wake of this debate, the chair of the JBG, Lionel Cohen, enunciated that the goal of the JBG was merely to provide information to the various charitable associations of each other's doings in the hope of thereby reducing inefficiency and fraud.[40] The proliferation of charities continued into the twentieth century, despite the professionalization of the philanthropic enterprise as the older generation of notables was replaced by a staff of salaried social workers.[41]

The case of London was not one of Anglo-Saxon eccentricity and abhorrence of central power. An identical scenario played out in the German lands at the fin de siècle. In Hamburg the League of Jewish Welfare Associations was founded in 1893 as a central clearinghouse that would investigate every applicant for public assistance, refer the needy to the appropriate agency, and provide employment counseling. But the body lacked authority and became mired in conflict with the charitable associations that it was supposed to both regulate and serve. Another attempt was made in 1911, but a true centralization of philanthropic services only came after World War I.[42]

In Vienna a great deal of poor care was undertaken by autonomous charitable organizations, not the organized community. In about 1900 there were at least 180 Jewish welfare organizations there: fourteen just for the care of new mothers and seventeen that distributed winter clothing to needy children. The battle for the centralization of charity began in 1891, with the establishment of the Central Office for Poor Care to offer the poor referral services. Six years later a committee appointed by the board of the community recommended a more substantive centralization of philanthropy. There followed fifteen years of struggle, in which the advocates of change pleaded for the adoption in Vienna of the celebrated Eberfelde system, which was implemented in that Westphalian town in 1853 and soon became a model for charitable practices throughout Germany. In this system a central supervisory body delegated authority to district commissions, who employed a fleet of volunteer caseworkers who visited all applicants for aid and crafted an individualized aid program. The caseworkers zealously separated the able-bodied and employable poor from the invalid, providing an allowance for the latter and sending as many of the former as possible into the workforce. The rationalization of charitable services allegedly lowered total expenses while allowing an increase in benefits per recipient.[43]

Some Viennese Jewish champions of philanthropic centralization, including Rudolf Kraus, a physician and director of the Jewish community's Poor Care Office, favored going beyond the Eberfelde system and creating a unified social welfare system, consolidating the sundry associations and replacing volunteers with salaried officials. Most advocates of reform were less radical, preferring that charitable associations retain their autonomy and that the work continue to be carried out by volunteers. In 1908 a central information bureau and register was created, with an agreement to share information with the municipal police, who would be on the lookout for professional beggars and confidence men. A mixed staff of volunteers and salaried employees managed the bureau, which, all the way up to World War I, encountered considerable resistance from local charities, suspicious that registering with it would impede their freedom of action.[44]

In France centralization was less of an issue, because after 1871 and the loss of Alsace-Lorraine to Germany, two-thirds of French Jewry were concentrated in Paris, whose Comité de bienfaisance had controlled most philanthropic services since its founding in 1809. The clustering of Jewish philanthropic institutions in Paris, overcrowding, and jurisdictional preferences for Seine *départment* Jews led to the denial of essential services to Jews in the provinces. In 1892 Chief Rabbi Zadoc Kahn recommended setting up a provincial Jewish orphanage, but almost twenty years later it had not been built.[45]

There was general agreement among all parties in the debate over centralization that reform of the distribution of charity was necessary.

Virtually no one advocated the indiscriminate giving of alms to itinerants, lavish handouts to door-to-door beggars, or indefinite maintenance of the able-bodied poor. In Germany even Orthodox Jews, who in the early nineteenth century tended to be less invasive and controlling in their charitable practices than *maskilim,* by the end of the century had generally accepted the wisdom of closing their doors to the migrant poor and replacing traditional charity with rationalized philanthropy.[46] Moreover, virtually all agreed that rationalization was to take place outside the parameters of the state, which Jewish philanthropists, like their Gentile counterparts, rarely saw as a source of funding or guidance.

The clash was, rather, between different views of what rationalization meant and how it was to be attained. For some, it meant organization at the grass roots in order to assert ethnic identity and stimulate the greatest possible expression of the charitable impulse. Others were captivated by the mobilized liberalism of the Eberfelde system, in which cadres of volunteers simultaneously maintained total autonomy and shared a common purpose that united them invisibly, like gas contained within a magnetic bottle. And then, finally, there were the champions of scientific social work, possessed of a postliberal vision of a Jewish philanthropy practiced only by credentialed professionals, who would be empowered not merely to funnel the poor into the private sphere of the market economy but also to create a vast infrastructure linking the spheres of economics and administration—the sphere of social welfare.

Jewish Social Policy and Bourgeois Social Reform

To what extent did the evolution of Jewish communal social policy parallel general trends in European society? To answer this question, we must first establish the types of institutions and professional cohorts with which Jewish communities should be compared. Do we compare Jewish philanthropy with that of churches, municipalities, or voluntary associations, and Jewish philanthropists with clerics, bureaucrats, or bourgeois notables? All must be examined, given the anomalous status of the Jewish community as both a religious body and a legal corporation, empowered to tax and provide educational and charitable services, and within which flourished myriad voluntary associations.

Throughout the late nineteenth and early twentieth century, the churches presented themselves as the natural source of a solution to the social problem. In Germany in 1864, the Catholic bishop Wilhelm Ketteler claimed that Christ was the "savior of the working class"; and the academically oriented Evangelical Social Congress, founded in 1890, produced what the historian Rüdiger vom Bruch has described as an "alignment of theology and political economy."[47] Like their Christian counterparts, German Jewish activists looked to the powers of organized religion to solve the social question. Editorials in the *Allgemeine Zeitung des Judentums* attest to this sentiment, be it in Ludwig Philippson's statement of 1867 that "the *social* question is the religious idea of our time" or Gustav Karpeles's proclamation in 1905 of the existence of a "social Judaism" akin to "social Christianity."[48] The general prescriptions offered by Jewish activists differed little from those coming from the churches. One encounters the same assault against traditional charitable practices and the same striving for efficiency. For example, the Bohemian rabbi Adolf Kurrein's pamphlet of 1890, "The Social Question in Judaism," concludes a sixty-page survey of the history of Jewish social ideals and legislation with a bland call for social involvement by the well-to-do, honest labor from the poor, and rationalized philanthropy.[49]

Just as the churches proclaimed that Christian ethics provided the answer to the social question, and interpreted Christian doctrine to support their views, so did Jews state that theirs was an inherently social-activist faith whose biblical and Talmudic texts foreshadowed advanced policies of social welfare. The idea of a "Jewish mission" to embody rational religion in its purest form originated in the late eighteenth century; and during the decades before 1848, the mission assumed a specifically political connotation, calling on Jews to fulfill their religious obligations by being exemplary citizens. From the 1870s, particularly in Germany, Jewish activists expressly associated their creed with an imperative to resolve social tensions. Statements to this effect abounded in the periodical and pamphlet literature of the time. No speech on "social Judaism" could refrain from piously invoking Moses Maimonides' celebrated medieval compilation of Talmudic dicta on charity.[50] In keeping with general trends of modern Jewish secularization, Maimonides' statements about charity, which represent only the smallest fragment of his vast code of Jewish Law, were wrenched out of context and placed in the center of a new form of Jewish identity centering around social action.

To the extent that there were parallels between Jewish and Gentile philanthropic theory and praxis, did Jews anticipate Gentile practices or copy them? Or, rather, did Jews and Gentiles operate within a similar mental universe, thus producing similar forms of social praxis? At times Jewish philanthropy was indeed more innovative than that of Gentiles; certain aspects of the Eberfelde system were adumbrated in the poor care practices of the Berlin Jewish community fifteen years before the former was founded. More often, Jews and Gentiles simply shared a common conceptual framework and acted accordingly. For example, the ethos and methods of the London JBG were similar to those of British Gentile philanthropists who labored throughout the nineteenth century to rationalize the operations of London's seven hundred charitable societies. The London Charity Organisation Society, founded in 1869, operated within the same voluntarist and liberal framework as the JBG: its striving for efficiency was tempered by an inability and unwillingness to compel inclusion under its purview or acceptance of its directives.[51] Likewise, German Jewish philanthropic discourse was often indistinguishable from that of bodies like the German Association for Poor Care and Philanthropy, founded in 1880 as an attempt to coordinate charitable activity on the national level and to put an end to unreflective alms giving, which was said to relieve only the symptoms of poverty and not its causes.[52]

Toward the end of the 1800s, European philanthropic discourse and praxis underwent a paradigm shift. Poverty came to be seen less as a sign of moral weakness than as the inevitable result of the structural flaws of capitalist society. This perception, combined with fears of social upheaval (due to class tension) and demographic catastrophe (due to low birthrates) stimulated the formation of modern eugenics—the attempted improvement of the physical and psychic health of the populace through public policy. A comprehensive body of preventive and social-maintenance programs, including health services, subsidized housing, and child care, was envisioned to meet the goals of the eugenic project. This bundle of policies came to be known as "social welfare," distinguished from the older "philanthropy," which was associated with piecemeal reformism. The scope of the eugenic project and its centrality in maintaining the social fabric caused welfare work to become incorporated into the purview of public administration. There was an infusion into municipal administration of "experts," that is, paid officials possessed of a discrete form of technical expertise. Social work thus shed its purely voluntarist quality and assumed the status of a profession.[53]

Many of these experts were doctors, and this, combined with the

general hegemony of the natural sciences in late-nineteenth-century social thought, brought about a shift in emphasis in philanthropic discourse from economics and morality to nature, gender, and race. As
George Steinmetz has written, "[T]he privileged sites for social-work
interventions were the family, sexuality, and the body."[54] Earlier forms
of poor relief had striven to get people to work, to create a "Homo
laborans," but social work aspired to mold the bodies of the poor, to
create a "Homo hygienicus." Prophylaxis, in all its manifold meanings,
became the goal of the new social policy, which was inextricably linked
with population policy. Paradoxically, social activists in France and Germany feared both a social revolution by the masses and a demographic
catastrophe caused by a falling birthrate, which would in time cause
those masses to dwindle away. In the earlier 1800s the nightmare of
overpopulation had driven the movement to make charity as sparing as
possible; now a fear of underpopulation promoted an explosion of public health activity: home help for new mothers and clinics for their ba-
bies, day care centers, and summer camps for at-risk children.

Many of the leading philanthropic activists among German and Austrian Jewry were doctors, and the biological metaphors that pervaded
middle-class sensibility of the fin de siècle peppered discussions on the
national and international mobilization of Jewish capital and expertise
to confront the crisis of eastern European Jewry. Before World War I
the Jewish doctor-philanthropists were unsalaried officials or freelance
publicists, not paid professionals as was the case in municipal adminis-
trations, but their worldviews were similar nonetheless. The biologization of social policy hardly put an end to the discourse on Jewish economic dysfunction and the need for occupational change: quite the
contrary. The combination of virulent antisemitism, with its economic
component, and the dire poverty of masses of Jews in eastern Europe
ensured that the economic moment in Jewish social thought would not
be marginalized.

A melding of philanthropy, biology, and political economy was apparent in the rhetoric of the B'nai B'rith in Germany. B'nai B'rith had
been founded in the United States in 1843 as a fraternal order with a
strong philanthropic mission. The German order was founded in 1882,
and at the turn of the century its membership was about 3,300. Membership increased significantly thereafter, reaching 8,600 by 1912 and
14,000 by the early 1920s. At first the order contented itself with the
promotion of good fellowship, solidarity, and mutual aid among the
brethren. In about 1890, however, a group of activists started to push

the order away from its original philanthropic mission toward national social work. This group was led by Louis Maretzki, a physician from Berlin who was president of the German Grand Lodge between 1887 and 1897. Other members included Benjamin Auerbach, a doctor from Cologne, Julius Plotke, an attorney from Frankfurt am Main, and Gustav Tuch, whom we have already encountered. The writings of these activists defined social work as the very essence of the order.[55]

Maretzki's writings betray a brooding cultural pessimism girded by Social Darwinism. The Jews have been left on their own, he wrote, to fight the "struggle for existence" that modern capitalism and urban life have engendered. Trying to keep the Jews' heads above water, the B'nai B'rith strives "to equip our coreligionists physically, economicaly, spiritually, and ethically so that a socially healthy ethnic body [*Volkskörper*] is mobilized, which will be capable of combating opposing powers, hostile influences, internal social ills and dangers which threaten human society."[56] The military metaphors are obvious; of interest as well is the use of the word *Volkskörper*. I translate the word as "ethnic" and not "national" because there is nothing in Maretzki's thought to suggest that he was a Jewish nationalist in any conventionally understood sense of the term. But Maretzki undoubtedly conceived of the Jews as a separate entity within German society, an entity that required an independent social policy.[57]

Other Jewish philanthropists in the German *Kulturbereich* employed Darwinist language. In May 1895 some five hundred philanthropic activists gathered in Hamburg, at the invitation of Gustav Tuch, to discuss the Jews' sundry social and cultural problems. Tuch called this gathering the Free Israelite Association.[58] When some of its members met a year later, their remarks were steeped in cultural pessimism. Commenting on the speeches, Georg Minden, an attorney and activist in the Berlin Reform congregation, said, "We are going through tough times, and we need a generation of steel and iron" to endure.[59] At around the same time, an article in the Viennese Jewish press framed a discussion of Jewish poverty in terms of the eternal and inevitable *Kampf ums Dasein* (struggle for existence), which some were incapable of waging and others shirked, but which some virtuous individuals could gamely fight if given temporary assistance. It is thus the goal of scientific philanthropy to help people so they can reenter the arena of struggle.[60]

According to the article, although philanthropy should be primarily a male activity, the services of women are essential due to their tenderness, compassion, perseverance, and intuitive discernment. This article nicely demonstrates that the biologization of European social policy in the late nineteenth century strengthened long-standing associations between charity and motherly nurturing and accentuated the gendered inflection of modern philanthropic discourse.

Until the final decades of the nineteenth century, philanthropies in western Europe were administered largely by men, and rationalized philanthropy's harsh rhetoric of discipline, surveillance, classification, and hard labor were signifiers of masculine power. At the same time, the ideal of the *mère-éducatrice* accorded women a vital role in the philanthropic sphere. That role expanded with the exacerbation of the nineteenth-century "social problem" and the growing need for competent volunteers to visit, classify, and succor the industrial poor. Such volunteers were abundantly available in the form of educated, middle-class women. In England already by midcentury, women had overcome male hostility and had assumed important roles as visitors and fund-raisers for philanthropic institutions. In Germany, as part of the reactionary politics of the post-1848 era, women were excluded from positions of responsibility in philanthropic life, but by the turn of the century women were increasingly allowed to work as public relief guardians.[61]

The combination of the need for a fleet of unpaid social workers and the thickening bonds between political economy and eugenics caused male philanthropic activists to lavish praise on women as uniquely qualified to nurture the youth of the nation. This praise simultaneously elevated women and constrained them. In Germany, where women had traditionally enjoyed fewer legal freedoms than in France or England, women tended to remain the helpmates in male-directed philanthropies, and their activities were limited to what men defined as the feminine sphere of home economics and child care. Yet in general, although female philanthropic activists demanded responsibility, they did not object to the notion of the feminine sphere itself, for they had internalized bourgeois ideals of the female as endowed with discrete yet invaluable powers to moralize the nation and bridge the chasm between classes through altruistic *caritas*. The feminine, or more accurately, "maternal," sphere encompassed both domestic and public space. Philanthropic activity comprised a liminal zone between intimacy and publicity, between home economics and political economy. Middle-class women inhabited overlapping and amorphous spheres that could embrace municipal and even national government so long as their activity could be seen as an extension of maternalist nurturing of the family.[62]

In Jewish communities as well, women projected the image of the maternal caregiver out from the home onto society as a whole.[63] Like their Gentile counterparts, middle-class Jewish women visited the homes of the poor and established philanthropic institutions, particularly those responsible for infants, children, and women. In Manchester the Jewish Ladies' Visiting Association, founded in 1884, functioned along the lines of the general ladies' charitable association founded in that city twenty years previously. The Hamburg Jewish Women's Association, founded in 1893 and directed from 1909 by Sidonie Werner, sought to overcome male hostility to women's participation in the philanthropic arena, not out of any broader desire for political emancipation in either the Jewish or Gentile public sphere, but to realize what the association's activists believed was the unique potential of Jewish women to preserve the Jewish community.[64] In many localities in Germany, Jewish charitable organizations were run entirely by and for women. This pattern of Jewish women's philanthropic activism replicated itself in Austria, where in 1905, at a conference of major Jewish philanthropies, six of the eighteen associations were represented by women. By 1914 Vienna Jewry featured the Female Welfare League with twenty-eight member charities.[65]

The philanthropic activities of Jewish women aroused mixed feelings among male Jewish activists, who, like Gentile philanthropists, accorded women a vital but circumscribed role in the solution of the social problem. Maretzki attributed to Jewish women vast caritative powers; he saw women as the glue that binds families together and mends a shattered social order. It is the task of well-to-do women, he argued, to inculcate domestic skills into their poorer sisters and to provide them with household services after childbirth. Thereby, working women will take their rightful place in the home, and thanks to the interaction between women of different classes, "oppressive reserve disappears, the icy crust of envy melts, trust develops between them, they approach one another without restraint. This does more to bridge the social chasm than all arguments, regulations, and [expressions of] sympathy."[66]

Despite this gushing praise, men in the B'nai B'rith leadership offered women only limited operational independence. The order's philanthropic activities on behalf of women were often initiated by men, and men held the highest positions. Such was the case for the women's vocational school in Breslau, founded in 1891; a similar institution in Hamburg, founded in 1897, was directed by the prominent philanthropist Gustav Tuch. In 1889 a group of Jewish men in Frankfurt founded the first association to train Jewish nurses; the Munich B'nai B'rith's association for the training of Jewish nurses was run entirely by men.[67] The women's auxiliary of the B'nai B'rith pioneered the development of social services for Jewish women and children, but ultimately its activities were controlled by the male leadership.

Dissatisfaction with male domination over the B'nai B'rith women's auxiliary led the Jewish social activist Bertha Pappenheim to found the League of Jewish Women, whose membership of some thirty-two thousand by 1913 was four times greater than that of the B'nai B'rith's men's lodges. Working on equal terms with the B'nai B'rith and other male-dominated organizations, the League of Jewish Women founded and linked together employment exchanges throughout Germany, and it took the lead in the fight against the international white slave trade, in which Jewish procurers and prostitutes were heavily represented.[68] The case of Pappenheim and the League of Jewish Women demonstrates that in Jewish society, as in western and central Europe as a whole, the membrane dividing the feminine and public spheres was porous. A women's philanthropic organization, designed to provide for the needs of women and children, could become national in scope, draw on a mass membership, and command the attention of public opinion.

Regardless of gender, when Jewish philanthropists spoke of preserving the Jewish community, they thought in terms of improving the Jews' physical health, increasing their material well-being through vocational training, and impeding defection and drift through educational activity. That is, the philanthropists conceived of themselves as acting on a dysfunctional and disunited mass, which they would shape into a stable and aesthetically pleasing form. The philanthropists rarely evidenced awareness that *they* were the ones who were being molded and whose collective identity was strengthened through their charitable activity. In this sense, Jewish philanthropists in western Europe at the fin de siècle were little different from their Christian counterparts, for whom social activism as such provided an important source of identity where religious faith was crumbling and "Christianity" was increasingly defined in terms of associational life.[69] Like the *Vereinscatholicismus,* or associational Catholicism, analyzed by the historian Thomas Nipperdey, there developed an "associational Judaism," that is, a Jewish identity expressed through activity in sub- or extracommunal voluntary social organizations.

European historians have long emphasized the importance of associational life as the expression of a maturing bourgeois consciousness, and Jewish historians have applied this paradigm to Jews throughout nineteenth-century western Europe.[70] The attraction of associational Judaism in the decades before World War I is revealed by a study of Berlin Jewry carried out in 1909. It found that out of a population of 122,000, 20,141 belonged to at least one Jewish association, 1,090 to three associations, and 250 to six or more. Similarly, in Paris at the turn of the century, it was estimated that 5 percent of the city's Jews maintained its philanthropies. These figures, particularly the ones indicating multiassociational involvement, nicely point to the existence of an activist elite, members of which grounded their Jewish identity at least in part in associational life.[71] Throughout the 1800s philanthropy figured prominently among the activities of middle-class associations, and toward the end of the century their engagement with philanthropy deepened considerably.

To be sure, in the Jewish case the synchronic adoption of the bourgeois association coexisted with the diachronic retention of traditional notions of the holy society (*hevrah kadishah*), an integral component of the premodern Jewish community. Associational Judaism represented in part a secularized expression of group solidarity, wherein, for example, involvement in a local hospital association created a sense of communal sympathy akin to that gained by practicing the rabbinic commandments of ministering unto the sick and dead. Such associational identity was common enough in Christian society, but it was of particular importance to the leaders of Germany's small Jewish minority. For Maretzki, only social work, salutary both for the empathy its practice instills into the agent and its healing effects on the social body, could revive the Jewish spirit.[72]

Antisemitism strengthened the Jewish need for association as a vehicle of defense and a source of solace.[73] It provoked Jews to engage in collective self-criticism, to contemplate what Maretzki called "the defects which have nested within our ethnic body."[74] These "defects" were in part imagined, an internalization of a host of Gentile stereotypes about the alleged physical, mental, and moral degeneracy of the Jews. At the same time, Jewish philanthropists faced a very real problem, that of millions of impoverished people, unassimilated and unassimilable in their lands of residence, and who collectively comprised a Jewish variant of the "social problem" that so worried the bourgeosie at the fin de siècle. Like bourgeois Gentiles, Jewish philanthropists were motivated by a mixture of fear and humanitarianism; their rhetoric was a brew of heartfelt compassion, paternalism, and scorn.[75] It was a common assumption among Jewish philanthropists that, until proven otherwise, all applicants for aid were schnorrers who aspired to live indefinitely off communal largesse. B'nai B'rith literature described eastern European Jews as wretched human material whose regeneration would require Herculean efforts and constant surveillance.[76] The problem, according to Michael Henry of the *Jewish Chronicle,* was that "we necessarily do not exercise the moral control over the foreign poor that we exert over our own."[77] An article in the Viennese Jewish periodical *Die Neuzeit* compared the Jewish vagrant poor to a plague of locusts.[78]

Gentile and Jewish philanthropists did not differ in their perception of the moral incapacity of the poor. But the image of the poor and the primary object of anxiety did vary, for whereas the Gentile was wary of the proletarian, the Jew feared the dominant Gentiles who controlled the social order. To Jewish philanthropists, the ideal-typical immigrant was something untamed, filthy, and chaotic, resembling the "Pöbel," the rabble, of the European imagination of the 1830s and 1840s rather than the fin-de-siècle organized industrial proletarian, whose socialist political activities, ostensibly aimed at social revolution, struck terror in the hearts of the middle classes and inspired much of their philanthropic work.

The Jews, so claimed a German Jewish newspaper in 1873, have no revolutionary proletariat. There were poor masses, to be sure, but no threatening element that sought to destroy the "educated upper classes."[79] Throughout the Imperial period, Jewish philanthropists were not wont to express fear of their charges, or to describe their work as a way of diffusing revolutionary tensions. In France Isidore Cahan, editor of the *Archives Israélites,* wrote in 1885 that the Jewish masses are neither violent nor destructive but rather comprise an element of "order and stability."[80] Such statements can be read as apologetics, attempts to combat antisemitism by claiming the Jewish poor to be more virtuous — and less threatening — than their Gentile counterparts. After all, immigrant Jews in fin-de-siècle France were active in the labor movement, engaged in strikes and other radical activity, and did not hesitate to complain publicly about exploitation by Jewish factory owners.[81] In some ways, moreover, it actually served the interests of the Jewish elites to acknowledge the extent of Jewish poverty, as it challenged stereotypes about Jewish wealth. Yet not only its public discourse, but also its operational methods, suggest that Jewish philanthropy in Germany, France, and England regarded the Jewish poor more as a vast social problem than as the shock troops of socialism. Unlike Gentile philanthropy, which often aspired to mold an eternal and docile working class, Jewish philanthropy aimed at the creation of an entrepreneurial, socially mobile Jewish bourgeoisie.[82]

To be sure, one encounters references to class strife in the western

European Jewish press. Editorials in the *Jewish Chronicle* called for social harmony between the Jews of London's affluent West End and grimy East End so as to prevent a "war of classes": "In proportion as the higher orders are brought into sympathetic contact with the lower, are the dangers of social revolt minimized."[83] In Germany Maretzki claimed that, thanks to the social work of the B'nai B'rith, "the gap between the propertied and the propertyless, between the educated and the uneducated, is gradually filled in. . . . Delicate threads are spun from the low to the high, from the well-off to the poor. The spirit of the weary is elevated and strengthened, when they see that a feeling of community manifests itself in goodwill and humanity."[84] And wherever western and eastern Jews, benefactors and beneficiaries, came into direct contact, there were certainly unpleasant and anxiety-ridden confrontations. When some twelve thousand Russian Jewish refugees concentrated in Brody in spring 1881, Charles Netter, the Alliance Israélite's representative on the scene, and his colleagues were sickened with fear at the sight of the hordes and the prospect of this sight becoming a permanent occurrence. A representative of the Israelitische Allianz zu Wien (hereafter IAzW) in Brody dreamed that refugees forced their way into his bedroom and threatened him: "These delusions were so vivid that I leaped out of bed and examined every corner of the room, to assure myself that not a single one of the unfortunate Russians was hiding out in any of them."[85] A bourgeois nightmare, to be sure, but our dreamer's palpitations were induced by an unruly mob, not a disciplined revolutionary army. And the great terror was brought on at least as much by the magnitude of the crisis and a sense of powerlessness before it as by a specific dread lest the mob wreak havoc on the social order.

The "Jewish social problem" was vast, too vast to be solved through piecemeal activity on the communal level. National and international solutions were called for, along with new ways of thinking about Jewish society so as to provide the theoretical underpinnings necessary for effective philanthropic praxis. It is to this organizational and conceptual revolution that we now turn.

The National Arena: Jewish Immigration Policy

Jewish social policy on the national plane was carried out by three types of organizations. First, there were those that served the needs of Jews in one particular country or represented the interests of that country's Jewish population to state authorities. The Board of Deputies of British Jews and France's Central Consistory are examples of this type of institution, as was the DIGB, a federation of communities founded in Leipzig in 1869.[86] Second, there were purely philanthropic bodies such as the B'nai B'rith. A third type of organization, common throughout the lands of emancipation, intervened with the international community on behalf of oppressed and impoverished Jewish communities in eastern Europe and the Middle East. Functioning as both diplomatic intercessors and international relief agencies, such organizations transmitted funds to victims of pogroms and natural disasters, sought to regulate emigration from east to west, and founded schools in distressed and impoverished communities. The Alliance Israélite Universelle (f. 1860), the Anglo-Jewish Association (f. 1873), and the Hilfsverein der deutschen Juden (f. 1901, hereafter Hilfsverein) all fall into this category. In Austria the IAzW [f. 1871] functioned as both a national and an international agency, as most of its efforts focused on Galicia, a part of the Hapsburg Empire, although it did lobby on behalf of Romanian Jewry as well. In the next chapter I analyze the activities of these international organizations outside of their lands of origin; here my concern is their domestic activity, which, paradoxically, centered on citizens of foreign lands, that is, Jewish immigrants from eastern Europe.

In any given state, national Jewish institutions cooperated closely with organizations with an exclusively international purview. In 1878 the Board of Deputies of British Jews and the Anglo-Jewish Association established the Conjoint Foreign Committee to coordinate Anglo-Jewish foreign policy. The DIGB worked hand in glove with the Hilfsverein and the German B'nai B'rith, which was itself part of an international network. Although organizations in various lands collaborated with each other, the strongest levels of contact were between national and international agencies in a single country.

Philanthropic organization on the national level was more intense in Germany than in its neighbors to the west. So was the conceptualization of social policy as a national task. There were many reasons for this phenomenon, only one of which was the stimulative effect of antisemitism or fear of Gentile disapproval of the philanthropic spirit. Germany was the main passageway between east and west; between 1880 and 1914 some two million Jews traveled this route. Moreover, the decentralized demographic structure of German Jewry, which, unlike its English or

French counterparts, was divided into several large communities, along with the relatively high rates of prosperity and acculturation in those communities, supported the formation of multiple cohorts of activists, empowered to form and in need of overarching philanthropic networks. The Jews of the Hapsburg Empire, in contrast, were too diffuse and fissured, economically and culturally, to build effective philanthropic structures on the supracommunal level. Thus the Hilfsverein, at its height, boasted 21,000 members, whereas membership in the IAzW, which had branches throughout Austria, Bohemia, Hungary, and Galicia, never surpassed 4,500. The comparison is all the more impressive given that there were more than three times as many Jews in the Hapsburg Empire than in Germany.[87]

Finally, Wilhelmine German society as a whole was mobilized into nationally based interest groups. In a state with limited parliamentary powers, large-scale organization by extraparliamentary groups was an accepted and expected response to challenges to one's political agenda or economic welfare.[88] Thus Jews encountered a conducive atmosphere to the formation of national philanthropies, whose leaders, conversant with political-economic thinking of the era, acted in ways that, they believed, would simultaneously maximize the economic welfare of the Jews and of the state in which they lived.

From the start, the highest priority of national Jewish social policy in western and central Europe was to speed eastern European immigrants through the countries, to the ports, onto steamships, and off to the New World as quickly and circumspectly as possible. This goal was to be accomplished by reducing, if possible, the number of immigrant Jews allowed into the country to begin with and then ensuring that those who were permitted entry not tarry and become public charges. In England from the early 1870s, the Anglo-Jewish press regularly and nervously chronicled the entry of Jewish immigrants and noted with satisfaction the work of the JBG in repatriating unemployable or invalid Jews back to their points of origin.[89] The founding of the DIGB gladdened the heart of Asher Myers, editor of the *Jewish Chronicle* and a former officer of the JBG, because of its stated goal of promoting the "elimination of reigning abuses in the system of aid for foreign [Jews]." The DIGB, Myers hoped, would "obviate the mischief arising from these professional mendicants, the chief nursery of whom is Poland and Russia."[90]

Indeed, the DIGB quickly went to work transmitting information between communities so that methods of itinerant poor care in one region could be implemented elsewhere.[91] Model proposals distributed by the DIGB in the early 1870s stipulated that the itinerant poor in a given locality be directed to a central office, certified, and given cash and/or a rail ticket, all in order to ensure a rapid departure from the area. All applicants were to be checked against "black lists" of inveterate schnorrers. No aid was to be given to certain types of people who, it was feared, played on the sympathies of gullible and well-meaning donors: sellers of sacred books, self-professed *shelihim* (emissaries from Palestine), or Jews claiming, "out of 'pious' impulses," to be en route to the Holy Land.[92]

Between 1869 and 1881 four international conferences were sponsored by Jewish organizations seeking to resolve the crisis of eastern European Jewry through planned, selective emigration to the United States. Two of the four were hosted in Berlin, and Ludwig Philippson envisioned German Jewry taking the lead in the formation of a coordinated international Jewish social policy on the immigration question. The grand talk of concerted action produced less than impressive results. In 1868 an aid committee was founded in the port city of Memel, and branches soon followed in other German cities. But in the early 1870s all that had been accomplished was the adoption of eighty-four Polish orphans by German Jewish communities and the distribution of food and clothing to some six hundred immigrants by an aid committee in Königsberg.[93]

In historical hindsight, the immigration crisis of the late 1860s and early 1870s was a minor affair. In London in 1869, 226 new applications for aid from the JBG came from recent immigrants; in 1875 the figure was 527. Over the period 1864–75, the number of applicants for assistance from the JBG rose only modestly, from 1,707 to a peak of 2,106.[94] The real turning point in the history of Jewish immigration was spring 1881, when 12,000 Jewish refugees, mostly from the Russian Empire, congregated in Brody, on the border between the Russian Ukraine and Austrian Galicia. These destitute souls believed that western Jewish philanthropies had the power and will to spirit them to lives of safety and comfort.[95] The number of Jews congregated in Brody pales in comparison with the immigration waves after 1900, when more than 100,000 Jews were arriving in America annually, yet the agglomeration in Brody in fact constituted a tremendous shock to the international Jewish philanthropic network. A central aid committee was established in Berlin, and it, along with London's Mansion House Relief Fund, the Alliance Israélite, the IAzW, and New York's Hebrew Emigrant Aid Society, pondered how best to respond to the crisis.

They agreed on a two-pronged strategy of sending the invalid and unemployable back to Russia and assisting the able-bodied to emigrate, mostly to the United States. Charles Netter, the Alliance's man in Brody and the leading figure among the philanthropic activists on the scene, managed by the end of 1881 to dispatch 1,600 refugees to America and provide funds for 460 individuals with a marketable craft to settle somewhere in the New World. At least 800 refugees, whose family heads had no craft, were sent back to the East.[96] A resolution to the crisis would come only in the following year, when the Austrian authorities closed the border to immigrants without enough money for their passage abroad, and when the Jewish philanthropies, mainly the Mansion House Relief Fund, mobilized sufficient resources to forward the remaining refugees from Brody to the United States.[97]

Additional criteria for assistance were that the supplicant be a Russian, as opposed to a Galician or Romanian Jew, and a bona fide political refugee, that is, a victim of a pogrom or someone who fled out of fear for his physical safety, not an economic refugee escaping grinding poverty and underemployment. The crisis of eastern European Jewry was more economic than political, for during the late 1800s Jews in the economically troubled northern portions of the Pale of Settlement were more heavily represented in immigration figures to the United States than those in the relatively prosperous south, although the pogroms were concentrated in the latter. The proportion of Jews emigrating from Austrian Galicia was not less than that of Russian Jewish emigrants, although the former had been emancipated and did not endure pogroms.[98] The Jewish philanthropic elite understood this situation quite well at the time. In its 1881 annual report, the Alliance Israélite complained about many thousands of would-be emigrants who hailed from locations such as Russian Poland or Austrian Galicia that were far from the sites of violence. The Alliance, the report stated, will only help victims of pogroms; poverty by itself does not justify assisted emigration.[99] According to Netter, "We have no intention of establishing here a place of refuge for every beggar."[100]

Why did the Jewish philanthropies draw this line? Surely a starveling Russian Jew, packed into the Pale of Settlement, limited to a handful of livelihoods, and thrown into desperate, futile competition with his fellow Jews, was as deserving of pity as one who had been beaten or whose property had been ransacked by an angry Gentile mob. Perhaps the answer lies in debates in recent years over immigration policy in America and western Europe, where governments, fearing an overtaxing of public resources and a rise of nativist sentiment, have made similar distinctions, partly because political persecution is more sensational than grinding poverty, but also because political refugees are by far the smaller of the two categories. Thus in 1881–82 public representations by western Jews of the crisis in the east dwelled on its political nature. The *Jewish Chronicle*'s editorials mentioned the poverty of Russian Jewry only to point out the need of western Jewish philanthropy to help their brethren to emigrate. The emphasis was on persecution and pogroms.[101] In the years to come, the *Jewish Chronicle* would draw a distinction between true refugees and "chronic incurable paupers"; the former could be allowed to stay in England if they proved self-sufficient and amenable to anglicization, while the latter must be repatriated to their eastern European homes.[102] One historian has suggested that a reading of the problem as inherently political strengthened belief that emancipation, which had brought security and prosperity to the Jews of the West, could have the same therapeutic effects if granted to the teeming masses of eastern European Jewry.[103] Thus the former's faith in the efficacy of emancipation was strengthened by prescribing it to the latter, who also, if emancipated, would remain in situ and not trouble the sleep of their western brethren.

In Germany the debate was not over the classification of refugees in Brody so much as the care for eastern European Jews on German soil. In 1881 aid committees were established throughout Germany; in the first ten months of 1882 the Hamburg committee assisted 10,000 transmigrants (an impressive number, given that total Jewish migration to the United States in that year was some 32,000, with an additional several thousand moving to Palestine). As the crisis eased, the committees were dissolved, but when, in the wake of expulsions of Jews from Moscow and elsewhere in the interior of Russia, immigration spiked in 1891, the committees were reactivated in the form of a national confederation, known as the German Central Committee for Russian Jews. By March 1892 the seventy-seven local committees had fully paid for the transport of 25,000 immigrants to the New World; 25,000 more were given train tickets to get them through Germany and to the ports of Bremen or Hamburg, and scores of thousands received food and lodging en route. Despite infusions of money from the Alliance Israélite and the Mansion House Relief Fund, the German committees were overwhelmed by the number of petitions for assistance, and in 1892 the Central Committee decided, as had the Alliance Israélite ten years before, to assist only Russian Jews, as opposed to those from Romania, Galicia, or even Congress Poland.[104]

A further kind of selection came in response to American legislation of the early 1890s prohibiting entry to paupers and invalids. The German Jewish aid committees responded by denying financial assistance to the elderly, ill, and unemployed, as well as to families with more than six children. Responding to the wishes of their western European brethren, the German Jewish activists did nothing to promote immigration to the United Kingdom, France, or the Low Countries. The aid committees' policies dovetailed with those of the major German shipping companies, HAPAG of Hamburg and the Norddeutscher Lloyd of Bremen, which maintained their own border stations for the medical and financial examination of immigrants. The companies allowed passage only to Jews with a railway ticket and sufficient funds for return passage if denied entry by the the U.S. government. By requiring Jews at the border stations to buy passage on a HAPAG or Norddeutscher Lloyd vessel, the companies precluded the possibility of Jewish emigration to Great Britain from which they might travel to the New World on the rival Cunard Line.[105] In 1905 the German government made admission into the country dependent on display at the border of tickets for transportation to a port city and for passage abroad. The latter was required to be with one of the official concessionaires.[106]

The shipping companies, with at least the tacit approval of the Jewish border committees, also required the immigrants to undergo medical examinations and submit their baggage for disinfection. The association between immigrant Jews and disease was strengthened by the 1892 Hamburg cholera epidemic, which distinguished doctors, including the celebrated Robert Koch, blamed on the new arrivals; thus trains bearing Jews were required to bypass central Hamburg and proceed straight to the harbor, where clothes and possessions were subject to yet another disinfection.[107] The Jewish aid committees agreed with the authorities that transportation should take place, whenever possible, in special trains.[108]

With the founding in 1901 of the Hilfsverein, the drive for a coordinated national social policy gained momentum. In the wake of the 1903 pogrom in Kishinev, Bessarabia, and the acceleration of emigration from strife-ridden Russia, western Europe's various Jewish philanthropies met in Frankfurt to try to stanch the immigration hemorrhage in order to allow recent arrivals in the United States to establish themselves and ease the burden on the American Jewish philanthropies. The result was the Central Office for Jewish Emigration Affairs, directed by the Hilfsverein's general secretary, Bernard Kahn, an attorney of Swedish origin who would go on, during and after World War I, to become the most prominent administrator of philanthropic services in Europe. The office continued the practice of cooperation between Jewish aid committees and the shipping companies. It obtained discounts for Jewish passengers and provided guarantees that the immigrants would be accepted in the United States lest they be shipped back at the companies' expense.[109]

How dependent was Jewish immigration on the national efforts of the aid committees and, after 1904, the Hilfsverein? How many individuals emigrated to the New World who might, without assistance, not have been able to do so? It appears that in the early years of the great immigration, the Jewish philanthropies affected a sizable percentage of the immigrant pool. As we saw above, the German Jewish aid committees, consolidating contributions from a number of European Jewish philanthropies, offered substantial assistance to some 50,000 Russian Jewish immigrants in 1891 and early 1892. Over this period total Russian Jewish emigration to the United States was about 69,000, with approximately 20,000 more Jewish immigrants from elsewhere in Europe. Over the years 1904–7, when some 540,000 Jews emigrated from Europe to the United States, the Hilfsverein subsidized or paid in full for the transportation of 54,500 individuals to the New World. Total distributions in 1891 and early 1892 equaled RM 1.5 million, whereas those between 1904 and 1907 were RM 1.3 million.[110]

What conclusions can we draw from the data? It appears that the financial and administrative capacities of the Jewish philanthropies were stretched to the maximum by the crisis of the early 1890s and that despite the administrative changes and endless deliberations that took place in the following years, those capacities did not change significantly. Thus as immigration swelled exponentially after 1900, philanthropy administered by German Jewish sources reached an ever-decreasing percentage of the pool. During the first decade of the 1900s, perhaps 10 percent of the immigrants received substantial German Jewish philanthropic aid. A larger fraction, however, received meals and lodging en route to or at the harbor. And countless thousands of immigrants received information and counseling about employment and housing in the New World.

German Jewish philanthropy was utterly incapable of slowing down the torrent of immigration. The next line of defense was to ensure that those Jews entering Germany not become public charges, that vagrancy and door-to-door begging not disturb the social fabric of the Jewish communities, and that those immigrants wishing to stay in Germany who had job skills be directed to appropriate employment. This latter goal is noteworthy, because by 1914 some 70,000 Jewish immigrants from eastern Europe were living in Germany as residents, not transients. Care for the itinerant poor became the purview of the Central Welfare Office for the Jewish Vagrant Poor (hereafter CWOJVP), established in Berlin in 1910 under the aegis of the DIGB, Hilfsverein, Alliance Israél-ite, and B'nai B'rith.[111] All of the CWOJVP's officers were members of the B'nai B'rith, whose fifty-seven employment exchanges, scattered throughout the Reich, were essential to the agency's operation. The CWOJVP's purview extended beyond immigrants to include all of Ger-many's Jewish vagrant poor, regardless of provenance. (This group, es-timated at 3,000 in 1913, included Jews returning to eastern Europe after unsuccessful forays in the West.) Immigrants judged by a local com-mittee to be able-bodied and honest were given nontransferrable rail tickets, for uninterrupted journeys, to the nearest labor exchange or workers' colony. Although Russian and Galician Jews predominated, many applicants to the CWOJVP's local offices were German citizens (*Reichsdeutsche*) and Jews from Hungary and Bohemia.

The CWOJVP reached across the Reich, with at least thirteen offices in major cities. Its structure provided an impressive model for Austrian Jews. In 1911 the Österreichisch-Israelitisches Union, an organization that combated antisemitism in Austria, announced the establishment of a philanthropic body that would unite Jewish communities scattered throughout the Austrian half of the Hapsburg Empire. As in Germany, communal poor boards were expected to spend a fixed percentage of their annual budgets specifically on the vagrant poor and to transfer four-fifths of this sum to the central office in Vienna. Thus itinerant beggars would be channeled into productive labor or returned to their cities or lands of origin.[112]

The campaign against vagrancy (*Kampf gegen Wanderbettlerei*) in Germany and Austria was redolent with the language of surveillance and regulation. The IAzW strengthened its network of border stations that selected those immigrants worthy of aid and attempted to prevent the unfit from entering Galicia in the first place.[113] In Germany border sta-tions and local poor care committees flooded the CWOJVP with black-lists of vagrants, schnorrers, and hardened criminals; the lists were then distributed throughout the country in the hope that these unsavory fig-ures would be denied aid and, if need be, reported to the authorities should they turn up in a Jewish community. The lists were issued daily; there were more than 1,700 entries in 1911 and 1,500 in 1912.[114] The entries describe people as crooked, work-shy, and "cheeky" (*fraich*); they receive rail tickets from one location and try to resell them elsewhere; they refuse to follow the CWOJVP's directions and wander off the itinerary or never show up at the jobs assigned to them. Particularly irritating were confidence men bearing fake letters of recommendation; one applicant had the chutzpah to forge a reference letter on Hilfsverein stationery.[115] The lists urge careful surveillance and cautious treatment of individuals who evidently, in the eyes of the lists' writers, were of a dangerous sort. It is not surprising that such individuals, who were widely perceived by middle-class society as disruptive and even threatening, would provoke anxiety among Jews who felt that they were being held responsible for the misdeeds of the Jewish underclass.

The problem of the vagrant poor was, of course, not unique to the Jews. The late nineteenth and early twentieth century was a period of global dislocation and population movement, due to the combination of rapid population growth and economic stagnation in eastern and southern Europe, faster and cheaper transatlantic transportation, and the New World's open borders. Over the period 1899–1920, some fourteen million Europeans emigrated to the United States. Even within Europe, the outpouring of two million Jewish transmigrants into Germany was not totally without parallel. Under the Kaiserreich, freedom of movement and an easing of residency requirements for the receipt of communal charity promoted an explosion of internal migration. By 1914 some two million people, mostly Gentile, had migrated from the eastern provinces to Berlin, the Ruhr area, and central Germany.[116] The noted economist Gustav Schmoller claimed in 1889 that contemporary Germany was witnessing "a vagabondage of the whole laboring population of an order which even the nomadic peoples have not known."[117]

At the turn of the century the DIGB's poor care commission was aware of the common elements shared by the Jewish and the general "social problem." The commission studied church and communal philanthropic practices and called in a prominent Lutheran pastor for expert advice.[118] In 1899, the year that work began near Berlin on a work colony for Jewish vagrants, there were twenty-eight interconfessional workhouses in Germany, similar in structure and program to the Jewish colony.[119] Yet although Jewish philanthropists were aware that their efforts against begging by vagrants were part of a concerted German social policy toward internal migration as a whole, in the correspondence and literature of the Jewish organizations this context is missing. Instead, one sees that antisemitic obsessions with the eastern Jew instilled in Jewish activists a tendency to see the problem of the poor, wandering

Jew as sui generis. Jews eager to speed their immigrant brethren out of Germany, or to root some of them quietly therein, did not take into consideration Imperial Germany's need for foreign workers (more than 732,000 in 1907). Internalizing German hostility to Slavic peoples, Jews did not seek common ground with the hundreds of thousands of Poles, most of them German citizens, living in the Reich.[120] Nonetheless, even if Jewish philanthropists exaggerated the uniqueness of the immigration, its vast size and the government's expectation that the Jewish community would handle it alone do support the philanthropists' self-image as the bearers of a unique burden.

There were significant operational, structural, and, ultimately, philosophical differences between philanthropies like the Hilfsverein and its predecessors, on the one hand, and the CWOJVP, on the other. Whereas the former worked primarily to dispatch Jews out of Germany, the latter, despite its aid to transients who eventually left the Reich in one direction or another, also stabilized and secured the existence of Jews within the country. For the former, whose gaze was directed entirely outward, toward the lands from which immigrants came or to which they were heading, the "Jewish problem" was defined as external to Germany. There was neither the inclination nor the impetus to think seriously about the economic fabric of German Jewry, to place the crisis of the Jews of eastern Europe into a broader sociological framework including the Jewish poor, regardless of origin. All the more so were the immigration-oriented philanthropies unlikely to cast a reflective, critical glance and ponder the economic problems of the Jewish bourgeoisie. A more introspective and inclusive approach characterized the activists in the CWOJVP and other philanthropies striving to alter the occupational profile of Jews in Germany, regardless of geographic origin or social class.

"Productivization": Apologetic, Romantic, or Realistic?

In chapter 1 I analyzed two paradigms of modern antisemitism: one associating Jews with paupers and savages and the other conceiving of Jews as plutocratic conspirators. The new wave of antisemitism of the 1870s featured both paradigms, with the requisite roles played by impoverished eastern European Jews and prosperous western

European Jewish merchants, bankers, and professionals. In chapter 4 I discussed the prosperity and political advances enjoyed by Jews after midcentury that dampened self-critical economic rhetoric and encouraged the formation of a triumphalist vision of "Jewish economic man." But after 1870 this triumphalism coexisted with a much darker view of Jewish economic behavior. Whereas the early proponents of Jewish vocational training in the early to mid-1800s had looked only upon poor youth as in need of occupational restructuring, their fin-de-siècle counterparts unleashed a harsh critique against the economic behavior of the middle as well as the lower class. For at least some prominent activists in the field of Jewish social politics, the Jews as a whole suffered economic dysfunction and required a drastic alteration of their occupational profile.

Jewish vocational activity picked up throughout western and central Europe in about 1870. In London in 1872, the JBG and its Manchester counterpart established an industrial department that provided Jewish craftsmen with tools and funded apprenticeships to master artisans.[121] The goal was to remove poor immigrant youth from not only petty commerce but also certain crafts, such as tailoring and cigar making, in which eastern European Jews had long congregated. The Anglo-Jewish press called for poor Jews to be trained to become not only craftsmen but also clerks, copyists, and bookkeepers.[122] In France horticultural education was central to the activity of the École professionnelle et horticole du Plessis-Piquet. At first a home for wayward Jewish girls, in 1888 it began to take in boys and expanded into a professional school with emphasis on gardening. Chief Rabbi Zadoc Kahn praised the school's "oeuvre moralisatrice."[123]

In the Hapsburg Empire crafts associations founded in the 1840s were still functioning more than a half century later, now assisting several hundred poor children yearly.[124] More important, the activities of the Israelitische Allianz zu Wien in Galicia accorded, at least ideally, equal weight to elementary, artisanal, and agricultural education. In fact, agriculture received little attention save for one spectacular, but unrepeated, effort to apprentice out hundreds of children to Jewish estate owners and leaseholders.[125] But handicrafts were treated far more seriously. By 1890 half of the IAzW's Galician budget was devoted to crafts education, largely in the form of a vocational school in Cracow.[126]

There was no equivalent, however, to the national organization of Jewish vocational education in Germany, or to the extensive political-economic reflection produced by enthusiasts of *Berufsumschichtung* in the Second Reich. One finds the seeds of both in the DIGB, whose Central Committee met in March 1880 to prepare a circular urging member communities to promote handicrafts.[127] Two years later the DIGB went beyond its established purview and added "encouraging educating youth in crafts, agriculture, and technical occupations" to its official list of responsibilities. And in 1884 the DIGB established a department that sponsored apprentices and publicized the virtues of crafts and agriculture.[128] From the early 1890s, the subject of Jewish artisanal education began to be regularly discussed at the B'nai B'rith's annual conferences, and both the national organization and individual lodges contributed to vocational projects.[129] In 1902 the DIGB established a workers' colony at Weissensee, near Berlin. The colony housed Jewish vagrants and ex-convicts for three-month stays, during which, according to DIGB literature, they received vocational training and acquired a taste for hard work and clean living.[130] In 1903 the DIGB sponsored the formation of a national league of Jewish vocational educational associations.

These projects, the initiative of a handful of activists in the DIGB and B'nai B'rith, enjoyed support from middle-class German Jews. In the 1880s Germany's oldest extant society for Jewish vocational training, the Berlin-based Society for the Propagation of Handicrafts and Agriculture among the Jews in Prussia, experienced a sharp rise in membership after decades of stagnation.[131] A new crop of societies and trusts promoting Jewish vocational training sprang up; there were 31 such enterprises in 1889, 65 in 1898, and 129 in 1913. One of the most popular began in Düsseldorf in 1880 with a handful of Jewish members; ten years later it boasted 1,464 members (both corporate and individual) from 185 communities throughout the Ruhr and the Reich as a whole.[132] Jews who were already working as artisans received aid from prosperous well-wishers. In 1911 Berlin's Jewish artisans' sick fund listed, in addition to 201 regular members, 50 life and more than 300 extraordinary members, many of whom bore professional and honorific titles.[133] Perhaps the most spectacular evidence of popular endorsement of the productivization project was the national Association for the Promotion of Agriculture among the Jews of Germany (hereafter APA); established in Berlin in 1897, seven years later it claimed some 2,000 members.[134]

Although German Jewish philanthropy in general expended much of its energy on Jews in and from eastern Europe, the discourse of Jewish productivization often failed to specify the provenance of its subjects and instead depicted them simply as Jews in Germany. The Weissensee workers' colony featured a largely foreign clientele, but the colony's publicists did not make anything of this fact and instead presented the institution as a source of aid for Jews on German soil.[135] Moreover, as far as one can tell from the sources, the scores of societies in Imperial Germany that promoted handicrafts and agriculture among Jewish youth did not depict themselves as specifically serving Jews of eastern European origin. If they targeted any group, most Jewish philanthropies addressed the poor as such. When the Central Committee of the DIGB met in March 1880 to prepare a circular urging member communities to promote handicrafts, the Dresden lawyer Emil Lehmann complained that the circular demeaned the merchant class and did not specify that only poor Jews were to undergo vocational training. The authors of the circular assured Lehmann that they were critical only of impoverished peddlers and hawkers; "the educated merchant," they said, "is entirely out of the picture."[136]

The APA and Ahlem, a Jewish agricultural school near Hannover, explicitly directed their efforts at German Jewry, claiming that incoming eastern European Jews merely aggravated what an APA report described as a preexisting "Jewish social problem."[137] Nor did activists in these organizations limit their purview to the poor. In these and other organizations one finds a body of Jewish activists for whom the "Jewish social problem" afflicted German Jews no less than the masses to the east, and the bourgeois no less than the *Luftmensch*. Jewish philanthropic rhetoric was like a point on a Möbius strip, switching surfaces without rupture: Jews in the Pale of Settlement, transients and immigrants in Germany, the Reich's own "eastern" Jews from Posen, and finally Jews in Germany regardless of origin became the subjects of criticism that always had the potential to become self-criticism.

Leaders of the DIGB, the B'nai B'rith, and other organizations responded to the antisemitic movement of 1879–80 by indulging in trenchant economic self-criticism. Indictments of Jewish economic behavior saturated the Jewish press and appeared in scores of pamphlets and philanthropic reports. Its producers were the B'nai B'rith leaders mentioned earlier and some two dozen others. Despite their bulk, the arguments can be easily summarized, as they repeated themselves time and time again.

The Jews' occupational concentration in commerce and the professions was said to be both economically and psychically toxic. Commerce was overcrowded, hence overly competitive, offering little financial security and encouraging unethical business behavior. The professions, the argument continued, were no better; Germany teemed with unemployed doctors, lawyers, and scholars. Clerical and other salaried middle-class occupations offered low pay, high expenses, and boring work, and antisemitism in large enterprises kept Jews out of managerial positions. These purely economic criticisms virtually always overlapped with psychological and medical ones: Jews lacked manual dexterity and self-reliance; they were too highstrung, and rates of suicide and mental illness were disproportionately high. German Jewry was said to be overly acquisitive and materialistic. It suffered from unnatural hungers; it was "given over to Mammon."[138] Finally, the medical indictment ran, Jews are soft and pampered, reluctant to engage in healthy exercise like swimming or gymnastics.[139]

These arguments were not the rantings of individuals tormented by their Jewishness and yearning to shed it and assimilate fully into German society.[140] Nor did they come from Jewish social critics with Zionist leanings. Rather, they came from Jewish critics intensely committed to the Jewish community, and who expressed that commitment through labor to improve and strengthen German Jewry within the German fatherland. These non-Zionist social critics worked in organizations such as the DIGB and the B'nai B'rith, organizations that Jehuda Reinharz has identified as the province of a "highly acculturated, upper-class" elite.[141] Indeed, the B'nai B'rith's high educational requirements and entrance fees assured that only members of the Jewish professional and mercantile elite would be admitted.[142] Maretzki and Samuel Kristeller, a learned but nonobservant Jew who served as president of the DIGB between 1882 and 1896, are typical examples of the Jewish notable corps.[143] Yet terms such as *notable* and *elite* do not capture the complexity and radical tendencies of the figures being analyzed here. Marcus Adler, a wealthy factory owner, had spent his youth as a mason and foreman, and his advocacy of Jewish vocational education was based on profound personal experience.[144] Arthur Kahn, a physician from Hesse, was a savage critic of Jewish economic behavior, yet considered himself Orthodox and labored tirelessly on behalf of consciousness-raising youth groups in the B'nai B'rith.[145]

Perhaps the most fascinating figure is Julius Moses, a physician best known as a Socialist Reichstag member and proponent of public health programs under the Weimar Republic.[146] Before World War I, however, Moses, who had a traditional Jewish upbringing in his native Posen and wrote essays on Hebrew poetry, was intensely involved in Jewish politics and philanthropy. A political firebrand, Moses published the *General-Anzeiger für die gesamten Interessen des Judentums,* a socialist-oriented newspaper that was unsparing in its criticism of the German Progressive Party and the leadership of German Jewry's leading defense organization, the Centralverein deutscher Staatsbürger jüdischen Glaubens for supporting it. As an activist in the Berlin B'nai B'rith lodge, Moses presented himself as the enemy of the Jewish *haute bourgeoisie* and champion of the Jewish artisanate.[147]

By and large, enthusiasts for Jewish vocational education in Germany limited their purview to crafts. Agriculture was considered too difficult, unrewarding, and alien to Jewish urban sensibilities to be feasible. But one faction of Jewish philanthropists saw in agriculture alone the salvation of German Jewry. In 1884 Alexander Simon, a wealthy Hannover merchant, decided to establish a Jewish agricultural school. The result was the Ahlem school, founded in 1893. Four years later, Kahn, Gustav Tuch, and his son Ernst founded the APA in Berlin. The association sponsored agricultural education projects throughout the Reich and collaborated with the Simon Foundation, set up after the philanthropist's death in 1905, in the establishment of a training farm near Hannover in 1909.[148]

These undertakings embodied the Jewish ideology of productivization in its most extreme form. Their publications combined autarkic economic nationalism, *völkisch* romanticism, and profound self-criticism. They argued that a massive Jewish return to the soil would simultaneously provide a guaranteed livelihood, heal moral defects, and strengthen the German economy in its struggle with the nations of the world.[149] Moreover, German Jewish agrarians made the sentimental association between country life and spirituality that was so widespread among Wilhelmine German cultural critics. Ravaged by flight from the land, the rural Jewish communities were seen as the bedrock of traditional Judaism, wherein piety and fertility were inextricably linked. One APA enthusiast proposed that incoming eastern European Jews be forcibly directed into the countryside where they could serve as spiritual ballast for the tottering rural Jewish communities.[150]

This last suggestion enjoyed considerable support. In 1913 leading activists in the Centralverein, alarmed by the outflow of Jews from Prussia's eastern provinces, called for an economic association to reverse the movement and repopulate Posen with Jews. Commenting on this proposal, the attorney Jakob Segall, a researcher for the Centralverein and director of Berlin's Bureau for Jewish Statistics, claimed that strong and stable Jewish communities in the east had long been the bulwark of German Jewry.[151] With the emigration of Posen Jews westward, he wrote, "the Jewish organism" loses "precious forces." Posen Jews, once in the cities of the west, enter into competition with resident Jews and the increasing numbers of Christians in traditionally Jewish occupations. As the Jews' general economic situation worsens, marriage rates and birthrates decline. The solution to the problem is twofold: a population policy designed to increase the number of births and the promotion of Jewish colonization in what was for centuries the nursery of German Jewish civilization.[152]

Talk of a return to the soil, population transfer, and national rebirth, when expressed by late-nineteenth-century central European Jews, is normally associated with Zionist yearnings for an autonomous Jewish national economy and a regenerated Jewish culture. But German Jewish agrarianism developed separately from and alongside the Zionist movement. Its ethos, like that of the idealization by some German Jews during the late Imperial and Weimar eras of the Ostjude, was introspective and nostalgic, a search by acculturated city dwellers for authenticity in the folkways of the rural Jew.[153]

The Jewish agrarians' attitude toward Zionism was complex. None was overtly sympathetic to Jewish nationalism, which contradicted the agrarians' goal of maximizing Jewish integration into the fatherland. On the operational level, in contrast, a certain measure of collaboration existed between the World Zionist Organization (ZO) and the agrarian groups. Most of the 214 gardeners trained at the Ahlem school by 1913 went to work in central Europe or the United States, but eight wound up in Palestine.[154] Arthur Ruppin, director of the ZO's Palestine office, corresponded frequently with the Ahlem school and similar German Jewish philanthropies, although the correspondence suggests that the Zionists sought a closer relationship with the philanthropies than the latter desired. Nonetheless, the Simon Foundation donated money to a number of Zionist enterprises in Palestine.[155]

Some of German Zionism's greatest luminaries encountered Germanocentric Jewish agrarianism either before or while professing Zionist sentiments. Max Bodenheimer, founder of the German Zionist Federation and director of the ZO's Jewish National Fund, became familiar with international Jewish settlement operations while serving in 1895–96 on the colonization committee of Tuch's Free Israelite Association.[156] Franz Oppenheimer, a utopian socialist economist who began in 1903 to agitate on behalf of cooperative settlement in Palestine, was a member of the APA's board of directors, as was the botanist Otto Warburg, who initiated the ZO's first colonization ventures. In 1908

Warburg became the APA's director. Finally, although Ruppin, the ZO's reigning technocrat up to World War I, did not participate directly in any of the agrarian philanthropies, his own turn to Zionism was preceded by more than a decade of longing to witness a massive Jewish occupational restructuring in his native Germany.[157]

Like Zionists, the German Jewish agrarians refused to consider their enterprise utopian or unfeasible. The Jewish agrarians provide an especially clear example of a tendency, running through all Jewish vocational projects, to present themselves as extending logical and successful German social policies to the Jewish minority. For the agrarians, popular German antiurban sentiment, the Garden City movement, and state-sponsored colonization projects in Prussian Poland seemed to justify their actions.[158] For Jewish crafts enthusiasts, two different sets of models presented themselves for use. First, there was Germany's network of industrial continuation schools (*Fortbildungsschule*), established by liberal social reformers seeking to preserve the artisanate and save laboring youth from the snares of socialism.[159] Second, pedagogic reformers at the fin de siècle placed arts and crafts within the framework of universal primary education. The "art education movement" (*Kunsterziehungsbewegung*) championed the education of the "whole child," whose motor skills, creative powers, and self-confidence would be heightened through exposure to the industrial arts.[160] The DIGB leadership discussed both of these developments in detail.[161] The latter was especially important to the founders of a Jewish student workshop in Cologne, which taught children to work with wood and papier mâché in order to promote "a harmonious development of all the spiritual and bodily powers slumbering inside the child."[162]

The vocational societies and Jewish arts-and-crafts programs accomplished little. The Düsseldorf society aided at most 100 apprentices annually; its Berlin-based counterpart reached 845 young men between 1889 and 1898.[163] The few youths who turned to the societies received small subventions for room and board, a referral to a master willing to take Jewish apprentices, and periodic supervision of their progress. The reason most often given for this narrow range of operations was a chronic lack of funds, about which the societies complained bitterly. The DIGB itself, despite the publicity it lavished on vocational projects, spent far less on them than on religious education, institutions of indoor relief, and cultural projects.[164] Vocational training was promoted by a fixed group of activists, and when, after the turn of the century, they began to die off or withdraw from the organization, the DIGB's vocational activity ebbed, although its propaganda continued unabated.

There is little doubt why such programs remained unsuccessful. Throughout the nineteenth century German Jews remained in the commercial sector of the economy because it was familiar and promised substantial rewards. Neither handicrafts nor agriculture, both in decline throughout the period, was particularly enticing. Philanthropists who labored on behalf of Jewish vocational education complained constantly that the Jewish public had little respect for manual labor and that only mental defectives and other misfits were pushed into artisanal careers. Moreover, those few hardy souls who did try to make it in handicrafts aroused antisemitism from their Christian workmates. Indeed, throughout the period 1880–1914, opponents of the vocational education drive pointed to these obstacles.[165] Even enthusiasts for vocational education acknowledged that a massive shift of Jews into crafts would only arouse antisemitism among the artisanate.[166]

Why, then, did the concept of occupational restructuring win so much support in German Jewish philanthropic circles? The most obvious reason is that Jewish social critics internalized economic antisemitism. Respectable Jews engaged in self-criticism precisely because they wanted so dearly to be respected. Sometimes this desire for acceptance resulted in bizarre actions, such as Kattowitz Jewry's attempt in 1912 to import six thousand Polish Jews into Silesia, put them to work in the mines, and prove thereby that Jews were capable of hard labor.[167] More often, projects that served genuinely useful goals were burdened with apologetic intentions. For example, between 1901 and 1911 the B'nai B'rith sponsored the training of more than two hundred nurses, who staffed Germany's growing network of Jewish hospitals. For Maretzki, what mattered most about this venture was that Jewish nurses would raise the image of Jews in Gentile eyes by countering the accusation that Jewish women were spoiled and indolent.[168]

A Jew did not have to suffer, however, from internalized antisemitism to accept wholeheartedly mainstream German social and economic ideologies, many of which were nostalgic for the preindustrial order. Beginning in the 1870s numerous studies by members of Germany's prestigious Association for Social Policy (Verein für Sozialpolitik) anxiously took the pulse of the country's master craftsmen, symbols of the preindustrial order. In the Wilhelmine period, public policy sought to strengthen the artisanate through financial aid and the empowerment of the guilds.[169] Ironically, these guilds, bastions of political reaction and antisemitism, were cited by the DIGB as proof that the artisanate was holding its own and that crafts rested on "golden ground." There was nothing out of the ordinary about a Jewish activist's complaint that "we must return from the surfeit of culture and from the evils it has created to natural and simple relationships—that very concept that has been spread throughout the world by the Rousseauian school."[170]

The Jewish economic self-critique, then, was not anomalous. Nor was it totally without substance. Self-employed Jewish merchants were but a part of the vast pool of German shopkeepers who faced cutthroat competition from each other, department stores, and consumer cooperatives.[171] It was in this spirit that Ernst Tuch characterized the B'nai B'rith's labor exchanges as seedlings of an "economic union" of German Jews, pressed to locate alternative employment for Jews pushed out of trade by the concentration of production and the streamlining of the distributive sector.[172] As to the professions, law and medicine in Imperial Germany were indeed overcrowded; the term "educated proletariat," which Jewish critics so readily applied to their own kind, enjoyed wide currency in the late 1800s.[173] And because Jews found access to the civil service and academia extremely difficult, the plight of the Jewish educated proletariat was especially acute. Finally, although many craftsmen lost their livelihood during the economic crises of the 1870s and 1880s, others actually profited from the new economic order. Industrialization created more, not less, need for butchers and bakers, and bourgeois affluence sustained demand for handmade furniture and other luxury crafts.

Aware of these developments in handicrafts, Jewish philanthropists routinely claimed that vocational training sought to create technically advanced Jewish artisans whose products would be assured of a market. Jewish agrarians also took a technophilic approach; it was assumed that agriculture would have little appeal to Jews were it not for recent technological advances that reduced the need for menial labor and increased yields.[174] Such arguments, combined with those raised above, suggest that the Jewish vocational training project was not quite as naive and unfeasible as historians have made it out to be. Nonetheless, we must keep in mind that most Jewish artisans aided by vocational societies were traditional craftsmen, and there is no sign that their production techniques were any more advanced than those of non-Jews. Moreover, given the especially large number of tailors, cobblers, and locksmiths churned out by these societies, it is hard to see how the artisans stood on the firm foundation that Jewish philanthropists often attributed to handicrafts.[175]

Finally, the most damning and unmistakable evidence for the unworkability of the Jewish vocational program came from the fact that eastern European Jews were already largely concentrated in crafts and that this concentration was one of the chief sources of economic woe. If anything, crafts attracted poorer Jews than commerce, because the latter required the purchase of some inventory. At the turn of the century at least one-third of employed Russian Jews were artisans; in some districts the figure was over 40 percent.[176] More than half of the Russian Jewish poor were craftsmen, who were most seriously affected by Russia's rapid industrialization.[177] The records of Germany's CWOJVP show that craftsmen vied with peddlers and merchants as the single largest vocational category among those requesting financial assistance.[178] An occupational profile heavily oriented to crafts also characterized Germany's own eastern Jews, in Posen and Silesia. In 1907, 24 percent of Prussia's employed Jews were artisans.[179] During the Second Reich, thousands of Jewish craftsmen migrated to Germany's western regions and, once there, encountered significant problems trying to make a living. They aroused antisemitism from German craftsmen, who considered them a threat.[180] In addition, the Jewish artisans' relations with their own communities were tense. In Berlin and other cities, professional associations representing Jewish artisans waged a propaganda war against community leaders over the latter's alleged unwillingness to hire Jews for public works projects.[181] The artisans also accused Jewish consumers of being loath to patronize Jewish producers.

Clearly, then, the Jewish vocational project in Imperial Germany was fatally flawed. The project does have great historical significance, however, not for its paltry accomplishments, but as an expression of the sensibilities of a segment of the German Jewish leadership elite. As mentioned above, for a certain type of Jewish activist, social work in and of itself both created and affirmed Jewish identity. The sense of crisis created by antisemitism and the plight of eastern Jewry intensified this associational identity. But more than anything else, it was the corrective enterprise itself, the project of Jewish socioeconomic regeneration, that nourished the Jewish identity of the activists described here. It was not merely a case of collective action instilling a sense of esprit de corps into a group of actors. Rather, as Alphonse Blum, a leader of the B'nai B'rith in Baden and a proponent of occupational restructuring, explained:

Our task is the true and final emancipation of the Jews in the ethical and social realms. . . . This goal becomes clearer and the prospects for its attainment more promising the more the awareness spreads that Jewry as a whole must be treated because of its common social structure. The singular occupational and professional limitations, which held into the 1860s, have naturally separated us from the rest of society, and we appear today as a special social body.[182]

Jewish social critics perceived of Jewry as a political-economic entity that had to act collectively, through communally generated social policy, to solve its ostensibly unique economic problems. Paradoxically, then, the expression of belief in a "Jewish social problem" was not only an exercise in self-criticism but also a confession of identity.

Social Policy and Jewish Social Science

In the 1870s Jewish scholars and activists, particularly in Germany, began to produce works of economic history, frequently out of purely apologetic motivations, but also as a reflection of the historicist approach, dominant in Germany at the time, to the study of political economy. This interest in the material as opposed to the spiritual or literary aspects of Jewish civilization represented a first step away from the philological and textual emphasis of the early-nineteenth-century "Science of Judaism" and toward a sociologically oriented "Science of the Jews." But the essential push in this direction came from the sense, expressed by Jewish philanthropic activists, that Jews lived in a state of socioeconomic crisis. Just as modern academic sociology originated as a response to the "social problem" of industrial Europe and as a reform-ist alternative to Marxist diagnoses of and prescriptions for the problem, so too did Jewish philanthropic activists feel compelled to search for new forms of knowledge that could produce successful responses. This new knowledge took the form of Jewish social science.

The fin-de-siècle origins of Jewish social science, long obscure, have been nicely illuminated in recent works by John Efron and Mitch Hart.[183] Efron's work points to the hegemony of biological motifs in Jewish social science, for it was, he argues, a discourse created largely by doctors and undergirded by racialist taxonomy. Hart presents Jewish social science as principally a Zionist project, a "cultural undertaking" that, via the use of empirical methods and statistical data, would indu-bitably demonstrate the unity and distinctiveness of the Jewish peo-ple.[184]

Both scholars are largely right. Jewish social science had strong bio-logical and racial underpinnings, and discussions of economic dysfunction were often couched in the language of social pathology. (To give one striking example, for the physician Hermann L. Eisenstadt, the terms "social policy," "public hygiene," and "population policy" [*Bevölkerungspolitik*] were interchangeable, and the prescribed remedies for the Jews' ills included not only the promotion of handicrafts and agriculture but also sport, vegetarianism, and a regimen of bloodletting and laxative cures.)[185] Fin-de-siècle cultural Zionists such as Martin Buber and Chaim Weizmann were ardent proponents of Jewish statistical inquiry. In turn, the impetus for the establishment of the Association for Jewish Statistics in Berlin in 1902 came largely from Zionists.

I would note, however, that supporters of Jewish social science came from outside Zionist circles and that the concept of social science as a vehicle for the establishment and assertion of collective identity was more a sign of a heightened ethnic identity than of a specifically nationalist one. Moreover, although the producers of social-scientific knowledge often thought in biological terms, the consumers of that knowledge, that is, philanthropic activists, displayed the greatest interest in its economic components and prescriptions.

The earliest manifestation of Jewish social science was statistical inquiry. A rabbinical synod held in Augsburg in 1871 formed a commission to undertake statistical studies of the Jews in German-speaking lands. A decade later the secretary of London's United Synagogue began research on morbidity and emigration among Anglo-Jewry. Asher Myers of the *Jewish Chronicle* noted this approvingly and called for statistical studies of Anglo-Jewry's population and income so that its leaders may know "the exact claims they have upon the government."[186] In the mid-1880s Joseph Jacobs in England and Cyrus Adler in the United States began producing statistical studies of their respective communities and the DIGB issued its first statistical yearbook.[187] The Society for Jewish Statistics, founded in London in 1904 and sponsored by the most powerful members of the Anglo-Jewish leadership, initiated comprehensive studies in order to formulate effective educational and hygienic policies.[188]

In Germany the pragmatic spirit of statistical inquiry was maintained by Alfred Nossig, founder of the Association for Jewish Statistics. Despite his Zionist sympathies, Nossig claimed that statistical inquiry was both a purely scholarly enterprise and a source of practical information for Jewish communities to use in the construction of their social policies.[189] A similar line of thought came from Julius Moses, a physician and Zionist activist from Mannheim (not to be confused with the Julius Moses from Berlin). The Mannheim Moses, who spoke on the "economic Jewish question" at the 1903 Zionist Congress, wrote shortly afterward that despite the uncertain future of the Zionist project, its stated goal of promoting planned, rational colonization should be applied to any form of Jewish social policy: "German Jewry must successfully transform its understanding of Jewish economic relationships into a social praxis and bring forth, from its own powers, social self-help— may it only seriously want this!"[190]

These statements reflected the common conception in fin-de-siècle Germany of social reform as praxis, that is, purposeful action resting on solid theoretical underpinnings and accompanied by constant empirical investigation. The exhaustive statistical studies of the German Association for Social Policy and the publications of the two-million-member Society for Social Reform were not meant to be purely academic exercises but rather the building blocks of a rational social policy.[191]

Operating in this spirit, Maretzki claimed that Jewish social science was the handmaid of his programs for social reform.[192] Sure enough, German Jewry's statistical enterprise depended heavily on the B'nai B'rith and other philanthropic organizations. The statistical association may have been Nossig's brainchild, but it was Maretzki who mobilized funds from various Jewish communities and organizations to bring it to life. Throughout the period before World War I, Maretzki was the association's chairman, and its directorial board included representatives of the B'nai B'rith, DIGB, Hilfsverein, Alliance Isralélite Universelle, and Centralverein. The statistical association's working arm, the Bureau for Jewish Statistics, received funding from these and other organizations to undertake statistical inquiries.[193] Before the statistical office began operations in 1904, the B'nai B'rith sponsored its own demographic and occupational investigations of the Jews of Hesse, Baden, and Posen. In these investigations there was no clear dividing line between scholarship and social activism; the Baden study was prepared by Alphonse Blum and the Mannheim Julius Moses.[194]

When seen as a source of Jewish social policy, statistical data appeared as manifestations of Jewish particularism and the statistical enterprise as an exercise in consciousness-raising.[195] This sentiment was forcefully expressed in a 1911 article by the economist Arthur Cohen, cofounder and director of Munich's Jewish Statistical Society:

We see a statistical organization arise everywhere states exist, where the state's life is felt, a living state flourishes, in every sociologically distinct people or portion of a people. Jewish statistics arose with the strengthening of Jewish self-consciousness. The Bureau for Jewish Statistics and the *Zeitschrift für Demographie und Statistik der Juden* are its aids. Statistics are Jewish in that they restrict themselves to Jewish society and the numerical recording of those social data by which Jews are differentiated from the rest of society.[196]

Cohen ends this article by reproducing, with underscoring, a comment on the manuscript by his mentor, the celebrated statistician Georg von Mayr: "Only peoples on the descent scorn statistics. Those on the ascent love them."

Despite the nationalist tone of his remarks, Cohen does not appear to have had a Zionist orientation or affiliation.[197] And although statements of this type appeared in the statistical office's publications, and Zionists like Ruppin and Theilhaber contributed heavily to them, the office itself, as Efron notes, "was never truly a Zionist organization."[198] The office was hired to engage in several projects for Jewish communities and organizations that craved statistical knowledge for its practical benefit alone. The economic ideology of the Jewish social critics strongly resembled Zionist thought, but the former worked within the framework of a Jewish *Volkskörper*, which, despite its unique features and needs, would remain integrally attached to the German fatherland.

The Birth of Sociological Judaism

A sociological, as opposed to nationalist or religious, Jewish identity, a sense of belonging to a collectivity defined in part by the social forces that threaten to destroy it, reached its pinnacle after World War I, in Weimar Germany. Although ideological differences continued to block the formation of a political organization uniting German Jewry, the centralization of social welfare was made possible by supportive government policies and made necessary by the communities' massive economic needs, aggravated by war, revolution, and hyperinflation. The B'nai B'rith, DIGB, and League of Jewish Women combined forces to create the Central Welfare Office of German Jews (Zentralwohlfahrtsstelle der deutschen Juden; hereafter CWOGJ), in 1917. The German Zionist Federation joined soon thereafter.[199]

The Zionists' participation in this enterprise is significant; they saw in a united Jewish social policy a vehicle of national solidarity.[200] In general, there was a strong link during the 1920s between social-welfare activism and a nationalist, or, to use a more accurate term, ethnicist, Jewish self-awareness. The Jüdische Volkspartei, which from the mid-1920s played a major role in Jewish communal politics in Germany, championed, far more than the Liberals, the extension of the Jewish social-welfare network.[201] Despite its benign attitude to the Zionist project, however, the Jüdische Volkspartei did not share the Palestinocentric worldview of the German Zionist Federation; its underlying sensibility was Diaspora-nationalist. All the more so was the CWOGJ a manifestation of ethnicism rather than explicit Zionism. Its first president, Berthold Timendorfer, was president of the German B'nai B'rith; its executive director, Eugen Caspary, had devoted much of his life to the welfare services of the Berlin Jewish community; and its secretary, Jakob Segall, had worked before the war for the Liberal Centralverein.[202]

Ironically, in Weimar's "social republic," where public welfare was now entirely available to Jews, particularist Jewish social policy flourished as never before. Government subsidies to Jewish welfare agencies, and the organization of umbrella organizations linking these agencies with their Catholic and Protestant counterparts, raised the status of Jewish welfare work and improved its financial footing.[203] At the same time, tensions between Social Democratic, Progressive, and church-sponsored welfare organizations projected into the welfare sphere the cleavages dividing the Weimar Republic as a whole, thus accentuating, rather than attenuating, the long-standing corporatist nature of German society, split as it was along confessional and class lines.[204]

Aggressive antisemitism, high unemployment, and declining birthrates raised the alarm of Jewish activists and fueled their view of social welfare as a form of rescue. Even before the onset of international depression in 1929, the economic circumstances of many German Jews were bleak. In 1927, almost a decade after the war's end and a relatively stable time for the rocky Weimar economy, there were some twenty-two thousand itinerant Jews in Germany, a third of them *Reichsdeutsche,* the rest from eastern Europe.[205] Antisemitism in large corporations limited access for Jewish white-collar workers; protective legislation stymied foreign Jewish laborers seeking to enter the industrial workforce. Although increasing numbers of Jews were employed by large concerns, and despite the vertical concentration of wholesale and retail trade in the German economy, German Jews remained attached to independent employment in small-scale commerce.[206] German Jewry appeared to be moving back toward its early-nineteenth-century social pyramid: a minuscule, privileged upper class; a small bourgeoisie, this time as much professional (doctors and lawyers) as mercantile; and a mass of unemployed and underemployed merchants, craftsmen, and laborers.

This atmosphere stimulated the rapid extension of the Jewish statistical endeavors that had begun before World War I. Many of the Jewish social scientists working in Germany during the 1920s were from eastern Europe and influenced by Zionist ideology. Statistical publications began to appear in Yiddish as well as German.[207] Yet a strong sense of a specifically German Jewish identity characterized much of the social-scientific writing of the era. One Jewish social-welfare journal claimed in its statement of purpose that "there can be no underlying doubt that the welfare and social-political measures which the Jews of Germany are obligated to provide very often carry and must carry a character which differs from the forms of general welfare and social policy. The peculiar realities of the Jewish situation force [the use of] peculiar methods."[208] An article in the same journal sounded a direr note; German Jewry's very existence will depend on an "economic rearrangement, an economic reformation," and "an independent Jewish economic and social policy."[209] Another contributor claimed that Jews are justified "to speak of an economic special situation for the Jews of Germany, and at the same time to recognize the need for a separate Jewish social policy. And this policy is needed to preserve the very existence of the Jews."[210]

The solutions offered by Weimar Germany's Jewish social-welfare activists were little different from those suggested in earlier periods: employment referral services, railway tickets to return itinerants to their homes or dispatch them to new jobs, communally funded projects, and vocational training. One notable change was that proponents of Jewish occupational restructuring finally accepted the unworkability of massive Jewish movement into crafts and agriculture. Glumly, with a sense of having their backs against the wall, they saw no alternative to what they called "proletarianization," a movement from white- to blue-collar occupations, from the front office to the shop floor. One such reluctant advocate, Alfred Marcus, worried that proletarianization, although economically necessary, would cause German Jewry to lose its collective identity, because the culture of the factory imposes uniformity and conformity. Echoing the inventors of a distinct Jewish economic identity, Marcus wrote that economic abnormality combined with extraordinary effort and success in one's livelihood are inextricably linked with cultural particularity.[211]

After 1918 the tone of social-welfare discourse was different: it was less harsh and judgmental, reflecting both the professionalization of social welfare and the sense that, as the Jews' economic crisis became universal, the distinction between German and foreign Jew dwindled to a mere technicality. Bernard Kahn, director of European operations for the American Jewish Joint Distribution Committee, expressed regret that German Jews, formerly prosperous and munificent in their donations to Jews abroad, were now in need of outside assistance themselves.[212] Today's reader perusing the German Jewish social-welfare literature of 1933 and thereafter cannot help but feel the deepest compassion for the activists, who reacted to the Nazi seizure of power and its subsequent horrors by marshaling rapidly dwindling manpower and resources in a heroic attempt to provide for an increasingly persecuted and impoverished community.[213]

Such were the limits of Jewish social policy in Germany. Even in less hostile environments, Jewish social policy could not alter the occupational pyramid of the Jews or eliminate their poverty, although, as we have seen, the accomplishments of communally and nationally based Jewish philanthropies were impressive, both in terms of the benefits they offered and the collective spirit they inspired.

The "Jewish problem" weighed heavily on the minds of the architects of Jewish social policy. Conceptions of the problem and solutions to it did vary, but there is a sufficient family resemblance between the various individuals discussed above to claim the existence of a community of Jewish activists united by a sense of political and economic crisis. The activists agreed that Jews would have to solve the problem alone and that they would do so through a mobilization of Jewish capital and expertise. According to this activist worldview, Jewish leadership could no longer be limited to spiritual or communal affairs alone; the socioeconomic fabric of Jewish life was in tatters, and the Jews' public responsibilities perforce extended into the private sphere of the family and economy.

The sense of common fate (*Shicksalgemeinschaft*) transcended national boundaries. Despite rivalries between states, and between Jews living in those states, expressions of international Jewish brotherhood were frequent and sincere. Thus in 1869, on the eve of the Franco-Prussian War, at a meeting of the leadership of the Alliance and German Jewish communities, Alliance president Adolphe Crémieux embraced Morritz Lazarus, the German Jewish scholar and activist, and exclaimed, "At this moment we are not French or Germans—we are Jews!"[214] In the last chapter we will see to what extent Crémieux's vision was realized among Jews in the arenas of international rescue and colonization activity.

CHAPTER 6

From Social Policy to Social Engineering, 1870–1933

Colonization is education writ large, and education ... is colonization writ small.

Georg Minden, 1895

The most spectacular attempts by Jews to solve their socioeconomic problems took the form of social engineering, that is, planned, large-scale agricultural colonization in a chosen territory. The most familiar example of Jewish social engineering was the Zionist project that, among its many aims, sought to establish a productive national economy based in agriculture and manufacture. The Zionist dream of transforming the Jews' occupational structure and economic behavior was hardly new, for it represented a continuation of a discourse that dated to the late eighteenth century. Moreover, Zionist ideology featured a prominent economic self-critique that shared many points in common with fin-de-siècle Jewish social policy. Finally, as we shall see in this chapter, Zionism's association of Jewish economic health with planned colonization was shared by a variety of Jewish international relief agencies that experimented, from the 1870s through the 1930s, with social engineering in South America, eastern Europe, and the Middle East. Zionism was the only one of these experiments to succeed. The others have been forgotten, in part because of the natural consequences of failure and in part because of intentional neglect by writers influenced by Zionist ideology, which regarded these experiments as a foolish and even destructive diversion of precious resources from nation-building efforts in Palestine.

One of the major themes of this book has been that the nineteenth-century "Jewish problem," as perceived by Jews as well as Gentiles, contained economic as well as political components. Thus in the late nineteenth and early twentieth century, Jews who believed that social engineering was an effective response to the problem saw no contradiction between simultaneous engagement in economic reconstruction and political action, for example, lobbying world leaders and appealing to international public opinion. Therefore, in the realms of international politics and social policy, the Zionist movement was embedded in a larger project of Jewish rescue and renewal.

Until now I have focused largely on the German lands, where Jewish economic ideologies were more fully developed and clearly represented than in the westernmost parts of Europe, and where, correspondingly, philanthropic praxis, on both the communal and national levels, stood on a rich and intriguing theoretical base. In the realm of international social politics, however, and in particular in the field of transcontinental Jewish social engineering, the philanthropies of German and Austrian Jews were junior partners in a pantheon dominated before 1918 by the Jewish communities of the world's great colonial empires, England and France, and thereafter by the Jews of the United States. Before World War I much of the settlement activity of the World Zionist Organization was directed by German Jews, who, like the non-Zionist, German Jewish philanthropists, were influenced by contemporary developments in political economy and social welfare in their native land. After the war, however, the construction of the Jewish National Home became the purview of eastern European Jews, most often in Palestine. Moreover, during the interwar period there was a second major form of Jewish social engineering — mass agricultural colonization of Jews in the Soviet Union — and this was an American product, the work of the Jewish Joint Distribution Committee. Zionism and what was known as the "Crimean project" each realized, albeit in radically different forms, the ideal of Jewish productivization that dated back to the Enlightenment and the radical German Haskalah.

Zionism as a Form
of International Jewish Politics

The term "Jewish politics" can mean many things. From the late nineteenth century to the Holocaust, Jewish political organizations and parties flourished in central and eastern Europe. Jewish political life took form within a dense, three-dimensional space defined by the axes of religious, national, and economic identification. The extremes of these axes were, respectively, ultra-Orthodoxy and secularism, Zionism and assimilationism, and revolutionary socialism and bourgeois liberalism. There were Jewish political organizations representing virtually every conceivable permutation of loci along the three axes. For example, the Centralverein was religiously "Liberal" (reformist but not secular), officially antinationalist (but at times sympathetic to Zionism), and staunchly liberal on socioeconomic issues. On the other hand, the Jewish workers' party in Russia and Poland, the Bund, was secularist and socialist and over time became Diaspora-nationalist, although it remained staunchly anti-Zionist. And the Zionist movement featured a dizzying array of parties spanning the spectrum of religious and socioeconomic ideologies. Regardless of ideological stance, these expressions of Jewish political interest shared the common goal of advancing the position of Jews in the lands in which these organizations operated.

In western Europe and the United States, Jewish politics at times took the form that I have just described. Immigrant, working-class Jews supported socialist political parties and trade unions that had an exclusively or explicitly Jewish character. These organizations strove to improve the working conditions and promote the cultural interests of Jews in major centers such as New York, Paris, and London. Middle-class Jews in the West engaged in extensive philanthropic activity on behalf of their immigrant brethren, but they were also committed to improving the lot of unemancipated and persecuted Jews living outside the West, mainly in the Russian and Ottoman Empires. Between 1860 and the turn of the century, leaders of the major Jewish communities in the West founded a variety of bodies with a primarily international purview. These organizations included the Anglo-Jewish Association, Alliance Israélite Universelle, Hilfsverein der deutschen Juden, and Israelitische Allianz zu Wien, headquartered in London, Paris, Berlin, and Vienna, respectively. These organizations represented a major departure from the tradition of responding to persecution through intercession

(*shtadlanut*), quiet, direct dealings between the minuscule Jewish plutocratic elite and territorial rulers. The new international organizations,
following a pattern established as early as the Damascus Affair of 1840,
presented their cause before the Western world's educated public, via
publications, assemblies, and open appeals to world leaders.[1]

Clearly, the two types of Jewish politics, domestic and international,
have much in common. Both are, like modern politics as a whole, manifestations of notions of inalienable human rights and a public sphere in
which private individuals assemble to mold the forces that govern them
and their fellows. The difference between the two is that in domestic
Jewish politics the subject and the object of ameliorative activity were
one and the same, whereas in international Jewish politics they were
separate. Moreover, the former tended to be more democratic than the
latter, although, as we shall see, even plutocratic international aid agencies were in some ways responsible to Jewish public opinion.

In which framework does Zionism belong? There is good reason to
place it in the first type of political organization. Zionism was a Diaspora
political movement that, in certain circumstances and geographic
regions, was able to appeal to the hearts and minds of the Jewish masses
more successfully than its rivals such as the socialist Bund, the Diaspora-
nationalist, nonsocialist Folkists, or the anti-Zionist, ultra-Orthodox
Agudat Yisra'el.[2] But although the Zionist movement consisted of a
welter of nationally based parties and pioneering organizations, its institutional underpinning was an international body, the World Zionist
Organization. Although the ZO's constituent federations (e.g., the Orthodox Mizrachi and the socialist Po'alei Tsiyon) engaged in political
activity in the Diaspora, in the eyes of the ZO leadership, "politics" was,
first and foremost, an international affair, consisting of diplomacy, in-
fluencing Great Power policies, and establishing a foothold in territory
separate from the ZO's European base. My concern in this chapter,
therefore, is international rather than domestic Jewish politics; the politics of the ZO and not of Zionist parties in various lands; and the
relationship between international Jewish politics and social policy—the
latter being a fundamental component of the former.

All agents of international Jewish politics, the ZO included, envisioned a mutually beneficial relationship with the government of the
state that housed the organization in question. The Alliance and the
Hilfsverein, for example, claimed a consonance of interests between
themselves and those of France and Germany, respectively. The Alliance
appealed to the *mission civilisatrice* of French imperialism, but it did so

to carry out a *mission civilisatrice israélite* of its own design.[3] Similarly, the journalist and politician Paul Nathan, director of the Hilfsverein, saw in the Ottoman Empire a site of German economic and cultural influence as well as the home of hundreds of thousands of Jews in need of philanthropic assistance. By founding Jewish schools that instilled a knowledge of German and German culture, the Hilfsverein was striking a dual blow for the German fatherland and Jews the world over.[4] Agents of international Jewish politics were not, as Zionist propagandists put it, merely currying favor with their host governments to enhance their status in the eyes of the Gentiles; rather, they were following a stratagem, displayed most clearly by the ZO itself, of claiming a symbiotic relationship between the political interests of the Jews and those of a certain Great Power or concert of them. There is little substantive difference between the approach of the Alliance or Hilfsverein and claims by Theodor Herzl, founder of the ZO, that the Zionists would, in return for a charter to Palestine, manage the Ottoman Empire's finances, or Chaim Weizmann's depiction, during the negotiations leading up to the Balfour Declaration, of the Yishuv as Britain's Cerberus, zealously guarding the eastern approach to the Suez Canal.[5]

Herzl carried out diplomatic activity largely on his own initiative, as did Weizmann during World War I. Nonetheless, these individuals claimed to speak for a well-organized international movement with a mass membership base. With some 217,000 members by 1913 and 844,000 by 1933, the ZO was the world's largest Jewish political organization.[6] Yet these numbers should not obscure the admittedly smaller, but still significant, membership base and international appeal of other agents of international Jewish politics. In 1885 the Alliance claimed more than 30,000 members, and some 20,000 individuals voted in its 1911 central committee elections. Hilfsverein literature claimed a membership of 21,000 in 1909.[7]

The IAzW, the Anglo-Jewish Association (AJA), and the Hilfsverein all owed their existence in part to a desire by Jewish activists of various nationalities to free themselves of the hegemony of the Alliance. At the same time, the Alliance retained an international appeal (in the 1880s, 60 percent of the Alliance membership was not French), and close administrative and institutional ties linked it with its ostensible rivals. For example, the Deutsche Conferenz Gemeinschaft, formed in 1906, comprised the German membership of the Alliance central committee. Berthold Timendorfer, president of the German B'nai B'rith, also served as both vice president of the Hilfsverein and president of the Conferenz

Gemeinschaft.[8] Moreover, most of the agents of Jewish politics sought to work in concert when addressing social-political issues such as the plight of eastern European Jewry and its mass movement westward. Thus despite the obvious discontinuities between them, there are important semantic connections between the Alliance's Hebrew name, Kol Yisrael Haverim (All Israel Are Comrades), and Herzl's celebrated proclamation in *The Jewish State*, "We are a people—one people."[9]

True, large memberships and international cooperation did not necessarily translate into democratic management. Agencies of international Jewish politics were by and large oligarchic and plutocratic, and in this sense the ZO was something of an exception. The management style of organizations that devoted themselves purely to Jewish social policy was particularly oligarchic. The Jewish Colonization Association (JCA), the wealthiest Jewish philanthropy in Europe, was managed by a board of directors and a salaried bureaucracy and drew its funds entirely from the estate of the railway magnate Maurice de Hirsch.[10] According to longtime JCA official Emil Meyerson, "[H]is board was not sensitive to public opinion. . . . [I]t enjoyed perfect immunity from any and all attacks by the Jewish press . . . [and it] was not only autocratic and bureaucratic, but also plutocratic."[11] A similar managerial style characterized the American Jewish Joint Distribution Committee (known as the Joint), the most prominent Jewish philanthropy in interwar America and second only to the JCA in wealth among Jewish philanthropies worldwide.

The Joint was founded in 1915 as an amalgam of American Jewish agencies for the relief of millions of Jews trapped in the eastern theater of World War I. Palestine's beleaguered Jewish population received considerable assistance as well. After the war, it contributed to and participated directly in the work of the American Relief Administration in eastern Europe and the Soviet Union. In 1923 the American Jewish Joint Reconstruction Foundation was founded to combine the resources of the Joint and the JCA in systematic programs of medical care, education, and financial assistance in the successor states in eastern Europe. At first glance, it would appear that the financing and molding of these programs were democratic affairs; the Joint featured a complex organizational structure that reached down to local communities, and during the 1920s it ran the United Jewish Campaign, whose assemblies provided grassroots Jewish activists with the opportunity to state their views on Joint policies.[12]

In fact, however, policy was made and most of the funds were provided by a narrowly circumscribed community of plutocrats: the bankers Felix Warburg and Paul Baerwald, Sears-Roebuck magnate Julius Rosenwald, and the attorney James Rosenberg. Louis Marshall, president of the august American Jewish Committee and a founder of the Joint, said, "The work was so conducted that we would dispose of millions of dollars without a vote being taken."[13] The leaders of the Joint delegated administrative responsibility to technocrats like Bernard Kahn, the director of its European activities.

A somewhat different path was taken by the Russian Society for Craft and Agricultural Labor, known by its initials, ORT. ORT began as a committee of Jewish notables, mostly from Saint Petersburg, who agreed in 1880 to propagate crafts and agriculture among Russian Jewry. The committee's organizational structure resembled that of its Western counterparts; it was controlled by a handful of Russia's wealthiest Jews, including Samuel Poliakov and Horace Gunzberg, and management duties fell to the journalist and educator Nikolai Bakst. In the 1890s, however, young Jewish professionals began to demand that the committee adopt both a more democratic structure and a reformist political posture. By World War I a new generation of leaders assumed control over ORT, which now connected economic reform with radical political change. After the 1917 revolution, ORT continued to function for some time in the Soviet Union, while the ORT World Union, headquartered in Berlin, provided assistance to Jewish technical schools, craftsmen, and farmers in eastern Europe. The World Union was directed by professional men, not plutocrats, with a democratic ethos and Bundist, Zionist, and Laborite affiliations.[14]

ORT's leaders saw theirs as a grassroots organization and looked upon the JCA, which worked extensively in interwar eastern Europe, as a form of paternalistic *shtadlanut*. Indeed, both the JCA and the Joint looked with suspicion on eastern European Jews in general and the socialists among them in particular. In correspondence between the JCA and the Joint Distribution Committee, the words *worker* and *democrat* were used interchangeably, and both had negative connotations.[15] The JCA's colonization projects in Argentina and Palestine, as well as those sponsored by the Maurice de Hirsch Fund in the United States, were riven with strife between settlers and administrators, who accused each other of authoritarianism and insolence, respectively.[16]

The Joint and the JCA also disliked Orthodoxy and strove to ward off rabbinic influence over their actions. Kahn wanted to shoulder the Orthodox away from any leadership role in the Joint's post–World

War I activities for economic reconstruction. He claimed that Orthodox Jews could never support its innovative credit cooperative schemes because of Mosaic prohibitions against the lending of money at interest.[17] Kahn's hostile and uninformed comment (Orthodox Jews had for centuries lent to one another at interest) nicely illustrates that modern Jewish politics and social politics were, by and large, a secular affair. (The Agudat Yisra'el constitutes, of course, a vital exception.) Jewish political leaders were frequently, like Herzl or Nathan, assimilated Jews who sought to accomplish in the sphere of Jewish politics what they could not in the Gentile world.

As is well known, many Orthodox Jews opposed Zionism on theological grounds; the creation of a Jewish homeland appeared to embody the sin of "forcing the end," that is, attempting in the present an action that should only be undertaken during the Messianic era. But Orthodoxy's hostility to Zionism stemmed from other sources as well, sources that link Zionism with the Palestinian activity of philanthropic agencies like the Alliance and the Hilfsverein. All were feared as vehicles of assimilation, largely because of the agencies' common agenda to submit the Yishuv to a socioeconomic sea change involving dismantling the *halukkah* system, introducing Western education, and occupationally restructuring the Yishuv population. This view affected even the German neo-Orthodox, who had been deeply influenced by the Haskalah. In the 1870s Sampson Raphael Hirsch claimed that Yishuv society did not need to be reformed, that productivization projects were impracticable, and that control over *halukkah* should stay in the hands of the Yishuv's rabbinic leadership. *Der Israelit,* the newspaper of the Frankfurt neo-Orthodox, remained hostile to groups like the Hilfsverein well into the twentieth century.

Those Orthodox Jews who became involved in organizations like the ZO, the Hilfsverein, and the Alliance were able to compartmentalize their religious sensibilities and justify their involvement in secular affairs in humanitarian terms. This way of thinking characterized the founders of the religious-Zionist organization Mizrachi and also appears to account for Orthodox involvement in Jewish social politics, for example, the Berlin rabbi Esriel Hildesheimer's support for the Alliance and various German Jewish secular philanthropies, or the leadership role of France's chief rabbi, Zadoc Kahn, in the Alliance. Both men accepted as valid the Haskalah's critique of Jewish economic dysfunction, particularly in Palestine, although Hildesheimer, in keeping with traditional Jewish attitudes toward charity, shunned the harsh, Social Darwinist language of the secular Jewish organizations and took a more generous stand on offering aid to the infirm and unproductive.[18]

Orthodox unease about international Jewish politics tells us that it involved far more than diplomatic intercession or humanitarian distribution of charity. Rather, diplomacy and systematic social work were inseparable; the former sought to improve the political and economic environment in which Middle Eastern or eastern European Jews lived, but the latter aimed at improving the Jews themselves. The mission statements of the IAzW and the Anglo-Jewish Association gave equal weight to diplomatic and educational work. In the mid-1890s the AJA Council claimed that although it prized its political activity, it had, "as far as possible, concentrated [its] energies on education as the most powerful factor in the intellectual, moral, and social advancement of Jews in the East." Virtually all the AJA's funds were used to subsidize schools, about thirty in all, throughout the Balkans, the Middle East, and India.[19] A similar emphasis on education characterized the work of the Alliance and the Hilfsverein, which maintained networks of schools in the Balkans and the Middle East.

The Alliance's concept of Jewish regeneration was holistic; it incorporated not only instruction in the arts and sciences but also moral enlightenment and physical well-being. Thus economic change, the transformation of Jews from peddlers into respectable tradesmen and farmers, was no less important to the Alliance's educational staff than the instilling of French language and culture or the assault against obscurantist religious practices.[20] Vocational training was a major component of the Alliance's educational project. In the early 1870s two Alliance school directors in the Middle East independently proposed the establishment of apprenticeship programs for pupils who had finished their course of study; the program was accepted with alacrity by the Central Committee. By the eve of World War I, there were apprenticeship programs in thirty-three locations, involving more than one thousand youths. In Salonica there were trade schools for girls, whom the Alliance did not wish to see placed in private workshops lest they be harassed or seduced. And in Algeria there were three "écoles d'apprenticeage," where vocational and general education were combined.[21]

Significantly, the first proposal for vocational training included provisions for relocating young Jewish journeymen, if necessary, to anywhere within the Alliance's sphere of operations as well as France and the United States. This was part of the Alliance's grand vision, enunciated by its president, Narcisse Leven, "to transplant them to a different soil, in a different atmosphere, in more hospitable regions where they could finally lead a normal life, worthy of their history and their abilities."[22] The Alliance's efforts to assist young tradesmen to reach this goal were rather modest, taking the form of provision of referrals and loans. But the Alliance took further steps toward social engineering when it established an agricultural school, Djedeida, in Tunisia in 1895. The economic straits of Tunisian Jewry, combined with the French protectorate over the region and its relative stability, induced the Alliance to purchase an estate; the need to place the *ferme école*'s graduates then led to the establishment of a colony near Algiers in 1908.[23] Yet another source of agriculturally trained manpower was Or Yehuda, a *ferme école* near Smyrna, established in 1900 via close collaboration between the Alliance and the JCA.[24]

The developmental dynamic inherent in organizations such as the Alliance and the JCA, the yearning to bring about a change in the Jews' occupational structure and economic behavior, was realized most fully in Palestine. This statement might sound odd, given the celebrated history of conflict between the ZO and Jewish political and philanthropic organizations that shunned Zionist ideology. Yet numerous areas of concord, cooperation, and overlap existed between the ZO and its ostensible rivals in the field of *social* policy, for example, education and agricultural settlement. Assimilationist political organizations may have considered Zionism illegitimate, a bar sinister to be kept off their patriotic coats of arms, but nonetheless they maintained a deep, if not always clearly articulated, attachment to Eretz Israel, their natural parent.

Jewish Social Policy in Palestine

From its inception the Alliance Israélite Universelle exhibited a particular passion to, as its own literature put it, "regenerate the indigenous population, demoralized by misery and servitude, to preserve in Palestine a center of Jewish civilization." There were two keys to the production of a new Zion, exuding enlightenment as the Zion of old radiated Torah. The first was Mikveh Israel, the Yishuv's first agricultural school, founded by the Alliance leader Charles Netter in 1870. The second was a vocational school in Jerusalem. The two institutions enjoyed a place of pride in the Alliance's publications, which not only devoted more attention to them than to other educational institutions but also frequently claimed their right to "a special position among the schools of the Alliance."[25] The Jerusalem school was unique in the Alliance's educational network in that it was the only purely vocational school for boys. It featured the most elaborate workshops, and, depending on the year, it had the second- or third-highest budget of any Alliance school. More important, its costs per pupil far exceeded those of all other schools, and it had to draw on the resources of London's Montagu Fund and the Paris Rothschilds as well as the Alliance.[26]

Similar patterns characterize Jerusalem's Evelina de Rothschild girls' school, supported by the London Rothschilds and the Anglo-Jewish Association. In 1901 one-third of the AJA's entire educational budget was dedicated to the school; by 1914 the fraction had climbed to two-thirds. (The school enrolled about 10 percent of the pupils assisted by the AJA worldwide.) The Rothschilds' annual contribution did not change over this time, but the AJA's own infusions increased markedly.[27] Claude Montefiore, the AJA's president, justified the high expenses by invoking Jerusalem Jewry's dire poverty, which made for a large number of pupils on scholarship.[28] Similar arguments came from Albert Antébi, who from 1897 directed the Alliance Jerusalem school's vocational programs. But Antébi acknowledged other forces that "designated this city as the seat of its only professional school": "[t]he traditions and memories that Jerusalem evokes in the Jewish heart, the attention that it exercises on the imaginations of some, the [widespread] interest to give its population a taste for useful work and the desire for learning."[29]

Surely, the latter arguments, rooted in modern Jewish sensibility and culture, were more decisive than the economic condition of the Yishuv. Jerusalem was a magnet, attracting the attention of world Jewry and European public opinion. The poverty of Jerusalem's Jews was not necessarily greater than that of Jews in the far-flung corners of the earth where institutions like the Alliance and the AJA maintained schools, but it was more visible, hence a source of pathos and embarrassment. The AJA's schools in Bombay and Mogador (Morocco) also had large numbers of nonpaying students, but in 1910 these children received average subventions of only £ 1, 4 s. and £ 1, 5 s., respectively, whereas allocations per scholarship pupil in Jerusalem were £ 4, 10 s.[30]

Jewish philanthropy did not require Zionist or traditional Pietist motivations to invest heavily in Palestine. In fact, quite the opposite was the case. An Orthodox Jew or Zionist could find fulfillment in dreams of messianic eras or the future glories of sovereignty and thus adopt a passive attitude toward the economic situation of the Holy Land. But for philanthropists whose Jewish identity was forged and sustained by constructive action, the current, degenerated state of the Yishuv was intolerable and required immediate intervention. Moreover, cultural goals dear to Zionists, such as the revival of Hebrew, could be pursued by non-Zionist philanthropies for ostensibly pragmatic reasons.

Thus, after a visit to Palestine in 1907, the Hilfsverein's director, Paul Nathan, responded to what he believed was the Yishuv's cultural backwardness by throwing himself heart and soul into the construction of a network of schools for Palestine's Jewish youth. Reasoning that the polyglot Yishuv could be united only by Hebrew, Nathan approved of the sole use of Hebrew in twenty-two of the twenty-eight Hilfsverein schools, which included the Yishuv's first Hebrew-language kindergartens. Nathan rejected Zionist conceptions of a distinct Jewish nationhood, but he invested enormous amounts of time, energy, and money (both the Hilfsverein's and his own) in the Yishuv. Jewish philanthropic causes in general and developmental work in Palestine in particular gave Nathan a sense of purpose and accomplishment when he had failed to obtain either from earlier sallies into German journalism and politics.[31]

The dynamic spirit of the Alliance, the AJA, and the Hilfsverein was dampened somewhat by resistance from Jerusalem's ultra-Orthodox, and even more so by the very limited economic opportunities for the graduates of their schools. Antébi admitted that "from an industrial point of view," the choice of Jerusalem "was not particularly fortunate," given the small number of workshops and commercial enterprises in the city. Thus Jerusalem was now saturated with Jewish craftsmen — an observation made also by Nathan of the Hilsverein, which also trained children for careers in industry and commerce even through the Yishuv had little of either.[32] About one-third of the graduates of the Alliance's Jerusalem vocational school over the years 1882–1902 found employment in Palestine. Yet the philanthropies made a virtue of necessity and proudly documented their successful placement of graduates abroad. Alliance literature boasted, "Formerly, the fathers of our apprentices were excommunicated; no Jew dared leave the Holy City; today, many workers ask to leave." In addition to Palestine, "Constantinople, Smyrna, Adrianople, Beirut, Damascus also have craftsmen who are former students from Jerusalem. For ten years, we have counted them in the principal factories in Egypt, at the Suez Canal, in the railways."[33]

The Alliance's movement of Jerusalem school graduates to other

points in the Middle East reminds us of its relocation services for apprentices trained throughout its school network and for graduates of
the *ferme école* Djedeida. It was part of the grand project for planned
immigration, for an orderly solution to the "Jewish problem." Throughout the region, the JCA assisted the Alliance in its project of transplan-
tation, and in Palestine the JCA paid particular attention to unsuccessful
farmers, who were sent back to Europe or to the New World. These
practices by the Alliance and the JCA infuriated Zionists, who saw them
as a betrayal of the Jewish national project. But for non-Zionist philanthropists, there was no contradiction between attachment to Palestine
and the belief that the Yishuv's population should be limited to the land's
economic capacity. As we shall see, Zionists themselves voiced similar
views, although they wanted to be the ones controlling the flow and
direction of immigration. Moreover, the non-Zionists philanthropies'
developmental activism frequently led them to make enormous financial
and personal commitments to the Yishuv, commitments that could not
possibly be justified from an economic or even humanitarian perspective
alone.

The Yishuv's rural sector owed its very existence to non-Zionist
sources. Close connections developed between the Alliance, the administration established by Edmond de Rothchild over the fledging Jewish
colonies established in the 1880s, and the JCA. In 1896 the JCA became
involved in Palestine, and in 1900 a separate section of the JCA, the
Commission Palestinienne (CP), took over the administration of the
Rothschild colonies. In 1913 the CP became a more autonomous agency,
and in 1924, under the presidency of Edmond's son, James, it broke
away from the JCA altogether and became the Palestine Jewish Colonisation Association, or PICA. In 1914 the JCA and the CP held more
than half of the Yishuv's rural real estate; in 1936 JCA/PICA holdings
amounted to one-third of the rural Yishuv.[34]

At the turn of the century, the JCA's managerial board contained
both opponents and zealous enthusiasts for colonization in Palestine.
During the decade after 1896, the enthusiasts, led by Zadoc Kahn and
Narcisse Leven, the JCA's president, won the day.[35] Leven and Kahn
were explicitly Zionist; they had been leaders of the Paris Choveve Tsiyon, in which the director of the CP, Emil Meyerson, was also active
during the 1890s. Leven and Meyerson drew up plans for Jewish colonization and instructed the JCA's man in Palestine, Joseph Niégo, to
purchase large tracts in the Galilee. Meyerson hoped to demonstrate the
superiority of Palestine over Argentina as a site for colonization, and he,

like Niégo, favored the gradual development of a sizable Jewish presence in the Palestinian countryside.[36] After World War I Meyerson and Louis Oungré, director-general of the JCA, expressed smug satisfaction with the JCA's accomplishments; they observed ironically that because of the constraints of political Zionism, the ZO "took no interest for many years" in colonization and that it was the colonies set up or administered by the JCA that had enabled political Zionism to achieve its greatest triumph, the Balfour Declaration.[37]

There were close links between Zionism and the major agents of international Jewish social policy. Armand Kaminka, a rabbi and Orientalist who became secretary of the IAzW in 1901, was an early Zionist enthusiast. At the first Zionist Congress he delivered a speech on the Jewish bond with Eretz Israel and the status of the Zionist colonies therein. This was a most unusual rabbi, who studied political economy in Berlin and Paris and translated the *Iliad* into Hebrew.[38]

An even more interesting case is that of Bernard Kahn. Before the war he worked as secretary of the Hilfsverein, where, among other things, he was involved with the construction of the Haifa Technikum, an institute for higher technical education. The Technikum became notorious because of the conflict between the Hilfsverein and the ZO over which language, German or Hebrew, would be used for technical instruction. At the time of the so-called language struggle, Zionists portrayed the Hilfsverein as a vehicle of assimilation and a lackey of German imperialism. But as we have seen from Paul Nathan, the Hilfsverein actually promoted Zionist goals such as Hebrew education. Moreover, before going to work for the Hilfsverein, Kahn had been an avowed Zionist and a delegate to the Fifth and Sixth Zionist Congresses. A series of lectures that he delivered in Munich between 1901 and 1903 expressed a deep attachment to cultural Zionism. "Not the need, not the poverty of the Jewish people," he declaimed, "are the impulsive force of Zionism, but the riches of the Jewish people accumulated in thousands of years. Instead of fleeing to the Jewish state out of need and misery, we want to go down to the pits of our inner life, to unearth the treasures which are concealed there in sufficient quantities to make us strong and powerful." Kahn believing that striving for a Jewish state was important. But, he said, "[if] it gets the upper hand in the Zionist movement . . . then it kills the soul of Zionism, or let me rather say, the soul of Judaism because Zionism in its pure form is the soul of Judaism."[39]

Although Kahn's youthful Zionist fire cooled markedly as he matured, he remained devoted to the Yishuv, even if he did choose to build his career outside of a formal Zionist framework. While employed at the Joint Distribution Committee, Kahn sat on the board of directors of the Palestine Economic Corporation (PEC), which invested in a wide variety of business enterprises and public works in the Yishuv. He also sat on the board of Keren Hayesod (Foundation Fund, the ZO's principal fund-raising instrument) and, after 1929, of the non-Zionist portion of the Jewish Agency Executive.[40] It is difficult to determine precisely why Kahn chose to devote much of his life to the Joint, although high levels of responsibility, the opportunity to work in a professional, apolitical atmosphere, and a handsome salary may have had much to do with his decision.[41]

The Joint paid considerable attention to Palestine, both in the form of reconstruction activity and support for the PEC. The Yishuv received more than 10 percent of its worldwide distributions to Jews over the period 1914–28.[42] Much of this aid came during World War I, when the Yishuv, some eighty-five thousand strong in 1914, was in desperate straits. Still, the amount of aid is notable, given that the number of destitute eastern European Jews during and after the war ran into the millions. Despite the Joint's largesse, relations between it and the ZO were often tense. Chaim Weizmann's efforts throughout the 1920s to attract the Joint's plutocratic leaders into an enlarged Jewish agency, which would marshal non-Zionist, philanthropic support for the Yishuv, aroused considerable opposition in Zionist circles. Zionists were enraged by the Joint's heavy investments in a Jewish colonization venture in the Crimea and the Ukraine. This venture, known as the Agro-Joint, as well as the JCA's Argentinean colonies, appeared to Zionists as a sign of equivocation toward or outright rejection of the only authentic and feasible solution to the "Jewish problem." Zionism demanded exclusivity and total commitment.

Unlike other recipients of the Joint's assistance, members of the Yishuv, according to David da Sola Pool, director of the Joint's reconstruction activity in postwar Palestine, believed that "it is the *duty* of outside Jewry to send them money for them to distribute and used [*sic*] as they see fit."[43] No matter how strong the commitment of agencies like the JCA or the Joint to the Yishuv, there were essential differences between the philanthropies, which were hierarchical, oligarchic, and plutocratic, and the anti-authoritarian, egalitarian, and politicized factions that made up the Yishuv. As da Sola Pool complained, not only was the Yishuv wretchedly poor, it contained no reliable persons in whose hands Joint funds could be left, because no one, from the ultra-Orthodox to the barefoot pioneer laborer, stands "above party and narrower interests." Epitomizing the Brahmin spirit of the Joint, da Sola Pool observed mournfully that the Yishuv had no class of "leisured and disinterested men needed to constitute the directors of public institutions."[44]

Clearly, there were significant differences between the Zionists and the other agents of Jewish social policy in the conception and envisioned solution of the "Jewish problem." The interesting case of the young Bernard Kahn aside, non-Zionist philanthropists rarely articulated the existence of a "problem of Judaism," that is, a cultural or spiritual crisis among the Jews. This notion was, of course, central to cultural Zionism. And while both Zionists and non-Zionists agreed that there was a political "problem of the Jews," non-Zionists, no matter how attached and committed to the development of the Yishuv, balked at the proclaimed goal of the attainment of Jewish sovereignty over Palestine. Finally, just as the ZO's politics was a more public affair than that of other international Jewish organizations, so did Zionist social policy breathe an unusually democratic, even radical spirit.[45] Yet despite all these differences, Zionists and activists in non-Zionist international Jewish organizations shared many common assumptions about the "Jewish problem": not merely the idea of Palestine as a solution to the problem but also an entire array of social and economic sensibilities.

Colonization as Social Engineering

We have seen throughout this book how bourgeois society stigmatized poverty as a sign of moral degeneration. The indiscriminate giving of alms was seen as a stimulus to profligacy. Jewish social policy's careful selection of those worthy of aid, strict supervision, and unceasing moral education of its beneficiaries clearly reflected current bourgeois conceptions of the relationship between industry and morality and of the need for a tutelary relationship between benefactor and beneficiary. From 1870 these concepts motivated Jewish social policy in Palestine, which western European Jewish activists viewed as both the Holy Land and a sink of poverty, to be reformed, like the European Jewish *Lumpenproletariat,* through education, vocational training, and close supervision.[46]

Agencies of Jewish social policy concurred that only the young, fit, and employable should make the trek from the Old World to the New.

Joseph Ritter von Wertheimer, founder of the Israelitische Allianz zu Wien, compared those deemed unfit for the journey to the generation of the desert, intractable and ineducable.[47] The Darwinistic culling of humanity that was practiced by the emigration assistance programs was even more apparent in the Argentinean and Palestinian colonies of the JCA, which invested great effort in locating what Emil Meyerson called "selected human material": sturdy, resourceful, and independent.[48]

Zionism fits well into this cultural matrix. Mainstream Zionist thinking contained much of general Jewish social policy's sense of embarrassment and shame, its internalization of economic antisemitism and desire to demonstrate to the Gentiles that Jews are not inveterate schnorrers. This point may be nicely illustrated by comparing Arthur Ruppin, the ZO's chief technocrat through the 1920s, and James Rosenberg, a leader of the Joint whose pet project was the Agro-Joint. As youths, both men endured antisemitic taunts and in large measure accepted as true claims that Jews tended to be crass, venal, and parasitic. Both were confirmed believers in racial science and in Jewish racial distinctiveness, yet they thought that environmental changes would bring about an aesthetic as well as economic improvement of the Jews. As a youth, Ruppin's yearning for self-denial and social acceptance led him to attempt to join an antisemitic German political party. The mature Rosenberg deliberately purchased Ford tractors for the Joint's Russian work to prove to Henry Ford, America's most influential antisemite, that Jews could successfully work the soil.[49]

Rosenberg's yearning to escape from the Jewish urban and mercantile tradition and steep himself in the agrarian mystique is apparent from the title of his 1925 booklet about the early work of the Agro-Joint, "Two Years of Blazing the New Jewish 'Covered Wagon' Trail across the Russian Prairies."[50] Rosenberg, like other Joint officials, expressed pride in the Soviet Jewish peasants similar to the veneration by Zionists of heroic Hebrew laborers draining swamps and paving roads. For Rosenberg, as for Zionists, the return to the soil meant more than economic or psychic renewal, but an actual rescue of the Jewish people from extinction caused by falling birthrates. "No race suicide here," Rosenberg observed of a Soviet Jewish colony chock full of children.[51]

On a more pleasant note, Zionist social policies, like those of the non-Zionist philanthropies, had little to do with any concept of an imminent Red Peril. Even before World War I, the ZO established close relations with the Yishuv's Labor movement; an organization supported almost entirely by middle-class central European Jews funded collectivist colonization experiments and, shortly after the war, subsidized the newly formed national trade union, the Histadrut.[52] To be sure, the ZO-Labor alliance always had its opponents, first among the planter class in the Rothschild colonies and officers of the ZO bank. During the inter-war period, these attacks became more intense, as the Revisionist movement accused the Labor-dominated Yishuv economy of squelching individual initiative, hampering economic growth, and fomenting class separatism. Yet even Labor's staunchest enemies rarely spoke of a forthcoming massacre of the Yishuv's middle class.[53]

Further, intriguing lines of commonality between Zionism and other forms of Jewish social policy are the concepts "selective immigration" and "human material." Until the 1930s the Zionist labor movement and its bureaucratic allies in the ZO agreed that emigration, although a matter to be left entirely in the hands of the Zionists rather than any external authority, must be selective, with careful consideration of the quality of the "human material" (*homer enushi; Menschenmaterial*) seeking entrance into the Jewish National Home. (The term *human material* was pervasive and appeared early on, in the writings of both Herzl and Hirsch, not to mention in those of the leaders of the Yishuv's labor movement.[54]) For the Zionists, as for the other agents of Jewish social policy, the phrase "human material" had numerous conceptual echoes, evoking notions of human meliorability and malleability, yet also of the power of degenerate material to destroy a fragile and precious undertaking; of the essentiality of a Pygmalion to mold the material into its proper shape and the ambiguity of the "material's" freedom of agency.[55] For the Zionists and their counterparts, immigration was not necessarily a universal right; it needed to be regulated, adjusted to the absorptive capacity of the destination (be it Palestine during the Ottoman or early Mandate period or the United States at the fin de siècle), and suited to the long-term economic interests of the new homeland.[56]

International Jewish social policy attempted to create a blueprint for a new type of Jew, both in the Diaspora and in Palestine. Throughout the Western world, the makers of Jewish social policy strove for rationality, planning, and centralization. Between 1869 and 1882 six international assemblies of Jewish political and philanthropic organizations were held to organize eastern European Jewish emigration to the West. The 1903 Kishinev pogrom spurred another round of internationally coordinated relief activity and emigration assistance.[57] Within a few years of being authorized in 1892 to operate within the Russian Empire, the JCA undertook systematic statistical studies of rural Russian Jewry;

these studies formed the basis of an extensive program of vocational education and technology transfer, including trade schools, model farms, and assistance to the Jewish farm colonies in the Crimea and the Ukraine.[58]

For Maurice de Hirsch, the JCA's creator, "planning" entailed not merely the rationalization of aid distribution but rather a full-blown program for mass colonization in Argentina. In 1891 Hirsch formulated a vision of Jewish social engineering no less audacious than Herzl's celebrated manifesto, *The Jewish State*, written four years later. Hirsch called for the movement of 3.5 million Jews out of Russia over twenty-five years. Like Herzl, Hirsch argued that the migration, settlement, and vocational training of these millions of Jews was to be carefully orchestrated and carried out with full and public approval from the suzerain. "One cannot," said Hirsch, "start colonizing haphazardly, and the movement should be preceded by a preliminary serious and careful investigation." These lines, which could easily have come from Herzl, were penned by Hirsch with reference to Palestine, which he believed to be unsuitable for mass colonization.[59]

Social engineering demands direction — not charismatic leadership or military command so much as technical administration. From its inception, the Zionist movement was steeped in a cult of technical expertise. Herzl's writings abound with Jules Verne–like technological wonders and paeans to their makers. From the turn of the century, the ZO developed a technocratic elite with considerable policy-making powers, and during the Mandate period the technical expert was absorbed into the Yishuv's pantheon of heroes, alongside the farmer, laborer, and warrior.[60]

Other forms of Jewish social policy were, if anything, even more in thrall to technocracy because they lacked the democratic structure of the ZO and the anti-authoritarian ethos of the Yishuv's Labor movement. Hirsch relied heavily on commissions of experts before approving the Argentinean project, and his principal objection to the Russian Choveve Tsiyon's Palestinian activity was their failure to employ experts to perform a feasibility study.[61] Similarly, the Joint Distribution Committee, its official history boasted, assembled a fleet of "efficient social engineers, experts in welfare work and relief, men and women trained in medical sanitation, migration, child care, cultural and economic affairs."[62] Bernard Kahn and Joseph Rosen (1876–1949), director of the Agro-Joint in Russia, wielded wide-ranging policy-making powers. Rosen, a distinguished Russian agronomist with a revolutionary background,

enchanted Felix Warburg and the Joint's other Croesuses with his scientific knowledge, good relations with the Soviet authorities, and inten-
sity, even severity, of character. During a 1927 visit to the Russian colonies, Warburg jotted in his dairy, "It's all Rosen and he is the genius
and genial soul of it all." A similarly entranced Hyman gushed that "the
influence of the man everywhere is far-reaching"; the Soviet leadership
and simple farmers alike heeded his council.[63]

In one of the great ironies of Zionist history, the Joint's adoration of
technical expertise both helped to set off a major crisis in the ZO's relations with non-Zionist Jewish philanthropists and provided a solution
to that crisis. The Agro-Joint's activities in the Crimea and the Ukraine
provoked outrage among Zionist activists who despaired at seeing millions of dollars poured into the Soviet Union when that money, they
felt, should be going to support the Zionist project. While the ZO's
president Chaim Weizmann labored to win over the likes of Marshall
and Warburg to an enlarged Jewish Agency, American Zionist leaders
deeply offended these pillars of the Joint by denouncing them as anti-
Jewish, anti-British, and even pro-Bolshevik. Seeking a solution to the
crisis, Weizmann suggested that Rosen be sent to Palestine to inspect
the land and prepare recommendations for its rational development. The
proposal was the balm of Gilead; Marshall accepted it immediately. Rosen did not serve on the commission, but other noted authorities did,
and Marshall agreed to accept the expansion of the Jewish Agency on
submission of the committee report (few of whose recommendations
were, in fact, followed).[64]

For the founders of the Zionist movement, as for other exponents of
Jewish social engineering, expertise was closely identified with efficiency,
which in turn was associated with profitability. In Herzl's *Der Judenstaat,* the entity that will carry out the colonization process, the Jewish
Company, is an *Erwerbswesen* (business enterprise). Despite enormous
responsibilities involving the transport, employment, and maintenance
of masses of Jewish proletarians, the Jewish Company will remain financially sound and a source of profit to its stockholders. Similarly,
Maurice de Hirsch saw the JCA as a businesslike operation, like a railroad, whose adherence to sound business principles would ensure success.[65] Shortly after its founding in 1881, America's Hebrew Emigration
Aid Society proposed settling ten thousand Russian Jews as farmers on
American soil; the project was to be implemented "strictly on business
principles."[66] In Palestine the JCA's operations fetishized the balance
sheet. The JCA's most promising project in Palestine, the Sejera training
farm, was dismantled because of its deficits.[67]

Although Herzl was bitterly critical of the JCA and other forms of "philanthropic" settlement, which he accused of inefficiency and merciless parsimony, the ZO's first settlement ventures, like Herzl's vision itself, adopted a businesslike approach that sought minimal, short-term deficits, a profit on investment, and long-term economic independence for the philanthropies' beneficiaries. In the decade before 1914, the ZO's settlement experts labored, with little success, to establish in Palestine profitable plantation and land-development societies.[68] This approach was kept alive during the interwar period by apolitical Zionists associated with the American Supreme Court justice Louis Brandeis. Brandeis called for businesslike and efficient colonization to be carried out by independent agencies run by expert managers.

Brandeis and his followers had a stronger appreciation for expertise and attributed a greater decision-making role to the expert than the workers' movement and its sympathizers. The Brandeisian notion of the expert was technocratic in the classic sense of the word—empowered, apolitical, and businesslike, along the lines of the efficiency-minded "production engineers" of the American sociological imagination of the early twentieth century.[69] This vision was shared by Brandeis's peers, the directors of the Joint Distribution Committee. The Joint was a pillar of the Palestine Economic Corporation, founded, largely due to Brandeis's initiative, in 1926. Unlike the heavily bureaucratized and politicized projects sponsored by the Jewish Agency and the Histadrut, the PEC strove for sound business methods, economies of scale, competitive bidding, and careful accounting.[70]

Ideally, Jewish social policy—planned, centralized, well funded, and guided by competent experts—was to solve the "Jewish problem" through one of three ways: improvement of the social and political position of eastern European Jews in situ; limited, assisted emigration of skilled workers to economically advanced regions like the eastern United States; and mass agricultural colonization in thinly populated territories such as Argentina, the western United States, or Palestine (if one accepts conventional Zionist views of the land as an empty land, a *Raum ohne Volk*). In fact, none of these three scenarios worked out as planned, not for lack of will or vision, but rather for a lack of resources in the face of the unstoppable sea of refugees that overwhelmed the relatively prosperous Jewish communities of western and central Europe.

The flood of refugees created a sense of deep crisis and impending catastrophe. The ominous tone that characterized Zionist discourse on the future of the Diaspora was part and parcel of modern Jewish social policy as a whole. It is a staple of Zionist historiography that the founding fathers of Zionism understood, and Jewish assimilationists did not, that antisemitism was indelible and that there was no alternative to mass emigration of Jews from Europe. But this view is not accurate.

It is true that most agencies of Jewish social politics began work with the aim of improving the conditions of Jewish life in situ. When it was founded in 1871, the Israelitische Allianz zu Wien aimed to bring enlightenment to what were believed to be the benighted Jews of Romania and the Balkans. But the 1881–82 pogroms altered the IAzW's scope and mission, as educational programs gave way before the immense needs of Russian Jewry. During the 1880s, the IAzW did establish a school network in Galicia, but the expulsions of foreign Jews from Russia in 1890 once again taxed the organization's resources to the breaking point, and so educational matters were entrusted to the newly established Baron Hirsch Stiftung.[71] Similarly, the Hilfsverein was founded with the intention of aiding poor Jews in eastern Europe so as to reduce the need for migration abroad. During its first couple of years, the Hilfsverein worked intensively to promote cottage industries among the Jews of Galicia. It was only after the Kishinev pogrom that the Hilfsverein's activities moved increasingly to immigration assistance.[72]

The Jewish philanthropies, however, were anything but euphoric about the future of Jewish life throughout much of the Diaspora. In 1869 Narcisse Leven spoke of the grave threat to continued Jewish life in Russia: the railroads were destroying the Jewish commercial network based on small-scale peddling; there were too many Jewish laborers and craftsmen in the Pale; and agriculture was forbidden to them. Emigration to the Russian interior was a possible solution, but it was fraught with risk: passports were hard to obtain and could be confiscated in the wink of an eye; the local populations and authorities were primitive and prone to violence. Large-scale emigration to the United States was a welcome solution to this pressing problem.[73] In the early 1880s the flood of eastern European Jewish refugees in Brody led Charles Netter, the Alliance's man on the scene, to write that antisemitism was unstoppable, that mass emigration had only begun, and that it was the responsibility of Western Jewry to organize and rationalize this great wave of humanity.[74]

At the same time that Netter penned these lines, the leaders of the IAzW were sadly observing the limited ability of Jewish politics to improve the situation of the Jews of Romania, whose government blithely ignored the commitments that, thanks to Jewish lobbying, had been imposed on it by the Congress of Berlin. By 1910 the IAzW had despaired altogether of the power of Jewish politics to secure the future of eastern European Jewry; its annual report observed darkly that just as Russia's "rape of Finland" had failed to provoke substantial opposition from international public opinion, neither would Russia's oppression of the Jews.[75] To be sure, some philanthropists, like Montefiore of the AJA, continued to claim that Russia could, given time and diplomatic pressure, reform itself and provide its Jews a hospitable environment.[76]

The pressure of events, combined with lack of funds, meant that there was neither the time nor the money to plan and implement a comprehensive Jewish social policy; instead, Jewish aid agencies jumped from one stopgap measure to the next: immigration assistance, relief efforts, and reconstruction activities in areas ravaged by war, disease, and pogroms. The sense of urgency, and the amounts expended, increased greatly after World War I, when the Joint and the JCA shouldered the burden of reconstructing shattered Jewish communities in eastern Europe.[77] Most emigration, both before and after the war, took place spontaneously and without philanthropic guidance or assistance. In Argentina most Jewish emigration from the 1890s through the 1930s took place outside the framework of the JCA's colonization program. Similarly, during the Ottoman and Mandate periods, the bulk of Jewish emigration to Palestine took place without significant support from the ZO, whose shoestring immigration and settlement budget was committed largely to rural cooperative settlements, home to only 5 percent of the Yishuv's population.[78] Even during the 1930s, the ZO's heroic rescue operations on behalf of German Jewry reached only half of those who left Germany for Palestine.[79] Much as the officers of the ZO strove to formulate grand plans for the development of the country, little could be done in the face of the worsening crisis of eastern European Jewry, strife with the Palestinian Arabs, painfully slow fund-raising efforts, and the fickleness of Palestine's suzerain, be it Turkey or Britain.

Better prospects for planned colonization reigned in projects sponsored by non-Zionist philanthropies that had more money than the ZO and operated in less flammable environments. The JCA managed by 1911 to settle 19,000 Jews on the Argentinean pampas, 50 percent more than the number of Jews in agricultural colonies in Palestine at the time.[80] But the Argentinean project eventually failed because of the attraction of Argentina's booming cities and the lack of a social or political ideal that could compensate Jewish immigrants for the enormous difficulties of agricultural life. Even greater obstacles stood in the way of the sundry agricultural projects attempted by and on behalf of Jewish immigrants in the United States. If a non-Zionist colonization project was to work, it required not only a favorable attitude from the territorial suzerain but also a large pool of potential colonists already in situ and without any attractive options to life as farmers. The one case in the history of Jewish social policy where this constellation of factors appeared to operate was the work of the Agro-Joint in the USSR.

The Agro-Joint, active between 1924 and 1938, spent in excess of $16 million, more than the entire ZO immigration and colonization budget for the period. The project enjoyed many other advantages over its Zionist counterpart: whereas the Zionists had to pay dearly for the land they bought in the USSR, vast tracts—over one million acres in the Ukraine and the Crimea—were leased out to Jewish settlers at no or nominal charge. The settlers had access to copious and free supplies of lumber, reduced rates for the transportation of agricultural produce and machinery, and exemption from conscription.[81] What is more, in the mid-1920s the USSR was home to some 800,000 déclassé (*lishentsy*) Jewish petty tradesmen who, being neither workers nor peasants, had been deprived of civil rights by the Bolshevik government and were desperate for a livelihood that would return them to full citizenship. Conveniently, the *lishentsy* Jews were not entirely bereft of funds, and the Agro-Joint expected four hundred to five hundred rubles from every new settler. (The ZO, in contrast, frequently had to settle immigrants without a kopeck to their names.) Finally, the Soviet government appeared to welcome the Agro-Joint's involvement as a source of hard currency and a means of increasing agricultural production and solving the problem of the *lishentsy* Jews.[82]

The Agro-Joint operated in a wholly depoliticized and hierarchical atmosphere. True, some of the colonies had been founded by Zionists. Tel Chai, a collective settlement founded in 1922 by Hehalutz, was, according to Bernard Kahn, "in a certain sense the mother colony of all the Jewish colonies in the Crimea." There were other Zionist colonies, such as nearby Mishmar (a split-off from Tel Chai), run as a moshav rather than as a kibbutz, and another collective, Haklaj [*sic*].[83] But these Zionist colonies account for only a few hundred souls, whereas the Agro-Joint actively assisted the settlement of some sixty thousand Jews on the soil. Unlike the Yishuv, whose agricultural population made considerable demands on the ZO, the Agro-Joint's colonists had no say in the management of the operation or the disbursement of resources. Policy was made by Rosen and his staff of some three thousand technicians of various sorts.[84] Rosen was a strict manager, disciplining or rewarding settlers as he saw fit.

Rosen was a fascinating figure, a fully Russified Jew, who was bereft of Jewish nationalist or religious consciousness yet devoted the better part of his life to Sisyphian labor on behalf of Soviet Jewry. Born in Moscow, Rosen was exiled to Siberia at age seventeen for revolutionary activities. He escaped and reached Germany, where he attended the University of Heidelberg. In 1903 he emigrated to the United States, where he obtained a doctorate in agronomy, won fame as the discoverer of a new variety of winter rye, and established a career introducing American grains and fodder crops into Russia. In 1921 he joined the staff of the American Relief Administration in the USSR as the Joint's representative.[85] Here, he deeply impressed both the Joint leadership and the American Relief Administration's director, Herbert Hoover, who, shortly before his election to the American presidency, praised the Joint's agricultural activity in the USSR as "one of the outstanding pieces of human engineering in the world today."[86]

The Agro-Joint's very existence was, in fact, largely due to Rosen's initiative. It was Rosen who, in 1924, presented the Joint leadership with an offer from the Ukrainian government of two hundred thousand acres of free land for Jewish colonization and asked for $400,000 to begin the settlement work. Warburg and Rosenberg were enthusiastic about the project, but Louis Marshall expressed reservations about the stability of the Soviet regime and the likelihood of raising the $5 million that, Rosen claimed, would be needed over the long run. Even Rosenberg, who had strong agrarian yearnings, fretted that in a society without private landownership, Jewish colonies could find their lands confiscated without cause and on a moment's notice.[87] Moreover, the JCA, a far wealthier philanthropy than the Joint and one with a long history of involvement in Russia, was reluctant to take part in this venture, partly out of inveterate conservatism and partly out of rivalry with its upstart American cousin.[88]

But Marshall's doubts found little echo. Rosen calmly assured his employers that Jewish peasants, like all tillers of the soil in the USSR, would enjoy perpetual use of the land.[89] Ezekiel Grower, the Agro-Joint's legal adviser, made much of the Soviet authorities' opposition to antisemitism and claimed that should there be another revolution in Russia, Jews would be much safer in the countryside than in the cities.[90] Wishing to be convinced, the Joint forged ahead without JCA cosponsorship.

In 1928 the Joint's financial involvement intensified considerably. At Rosen's initiative, it established the American Society for Jewish Farm Settlements in Russia (ASJFSR), a body separate from the Agro-Joint. The ASJFSR was a financial instrument that sought to raise $10 million in order to receive a matching amount from the Soviet government.[91] Although it did not reach this lofty goal, within five years it had raised almost $5 million, most of which came from Rosenwald and Warburg.[92]

The ironies of the Joint's behavior are striking. Wealthy American capitalists voluntarily transferred millions of dollars to a communist government. The Ukraine, whose soil was still soaked with the blood of scores of thousands of Jews slain during the period of the Russian civil war, was now touted as the location of a Jewish agricultural utopia. Scholars of Israeli history have noted the unusual alliance between bourgeois capital and organized labor in which the ZO and its financial instruments heavily subsidized the economic enterprises, rural and urban, of the Zionist labor movement. Such scholars assume that the appeal of the Zionist project, and by implication the Zionist project alone, crossed class lines: middle-class Jews acknowledged that the Jewish National Home could be built only by the labor movement, and the Zionist labor movement, in turn, sacrificed socialist commitment on the altar of nation building.[93] The case of the Agro-Joint is even more striking; it testifies to the deep yearnings by bourgeois Jews to engineer a massive transformation of Jews into a new, and what was considered normal, economic profile, and to the eagerness of a former revolutionary like Rosen to devote himself heart and soul to this endeavor.

For the leaders of the Joint, the Agro-Joint and the enlarged Jewish Agency were part of a greater whole, a vast solution to the eastern European "Jewish problem."[94] Clearly, Zionism broke with the Joint leadership's fundamental assumption—an assumption central to Jewish political economy dating back to the Haskalah—that Jewish self-improvement would take place within the framework and for the benefit of the Jews' host society. At the same time, the Zionist economic critique of eastern European Jewry was in many ways congenial to the views of the plutocratic directors of the Joint. It was difficult for any early-twentieth-century philanthropist interested in addressing the issues of Jewish poverty and economic dysfunction not to be at least partially supportive of Zionist endeavors.

Thus the rapprochement between the ZO and the Croesuses of American Jewry occurred precisely as the latter were intensifying their involvement in the Soviet Union. The 1929 agreement of the Joint's leaders to support an enlarged Jewish Agency for Palestine came on the heels of the founding of ASJFSR in the previous year. Zionists considered this action an act of folly and a sign of craven assimilationism. But it was endorsed enthusiastically by the likes of Bernard Kahn, no enemy of Zionism, who, when the Agro-Joint was starting up, cabled his superiors that "Jewish settling on land Russia [*sic*] is most important [*sic*] reconstructive work we can do. . . . This new agricultural movement among Russian Jews has in my opinion no equal in Jewish history and cannot be measured by any other colonization experience."[95]

The work of the Agro-Joint did not enjoy wide popularity among the Jewish public. In the United States the project was bitterly criticized by the American Jewish Congress and, of course, the Zionist Organization of America. Some communal activists retained an open mind, such as a well-meaning Jewish businessman from Calgary, who in 1928 proposed a public debate on the merits of Palestine versus Russia, with proceeds from the debate to go to either Keren Hayesod or the Joint, depending on which side won.[96] Far more significant—and scandalous, in the eyes of Zionists—was the conversion to the Soviet project of the Hebrew writer and Zionist activist Reuben Brainin.

Brainin, a gifted essayist who was born in Belarus and made his career in Vienna, was a major force in fin-de-siècle Hebrew journalism. In 1909 he moved to North America. He spent five years in Montreal, whose community of recent Jewish immigrants was, compared with eastern Europe, indifferent to Hebrew letters. Out of conviction or necessity, Brainin vigorously promoted Yiddish journalism and education while in Montreal. On moving to New York during World War I, Brainin became active in Zionist affairs, serving as vice president of the Zionist Organization of America. In 1926 he took a tour of the Crimean colonies, began to question absolute faith in Zionism, and became a tireless fund-raiser for Jewish farm settlements in the Soviet Union.[97] Brainin's refusal in his publicistic writings about the Soviet Union to condemn the communists' suppression of Jewish culture provoked outraged from Zionist activists, including the poet Haim Nahman Bialik, whose venomous published attacks caused Brainin to demand a formal apology from the famed Hebrew writer and a hearing before the World Zionist Organization's "Court of Honor" in Berlin.

The court, presided over by the genial Zionist humorist Sammy Gronemann, heard Brainin claim that he saw no contradiction between devotion to the Zionist and the Soviet projects. Unlike Bialik, he claimed, "I wish the survival of the body of the Jewish people for the perpetuation of the Jewish spirit." And nowhere, said Brainin, were Jews more physically secure than in the Soviet Union. Although sharply critical of the communists' suppression of Hebrew culture, Brainin drew discomfiting parallels between these practices and the war against Yiddish conducted by Zionist zealots in Palestine. Not surprisingly, Brainin lost his case.[98]

As things turned out, the Zionists were quite right in accusing Brainin and his newfound allies in the Joint Distribution Committee of placing too much faith in the goodwill of the Soviet government. Surely Rosen erred when he claimed in 1937 that "after a short period of fifteen years of reconstructive work there is no more specifically economic and social Jewish problem in Russia. . . . There is absolutely no discrimination against Jews as Jews in any walk of life."[99] Soviet policy toward the Agro-Joint was in fact informed by antisemitism, suspicion, and exaggerated notions of American Jewish wealth. It is true that the official policy of the Soviet Union was, especially during the 1920s, "antiantisemitic," that is, opposed in principle to antisemitism, which was thought to be an expression of frustration by economically threatened individuals in a capitalist system. Antisemitism, "the stupid man's socialism," in the words of August Bebel, had no place in a communist society. During the 1920s, Soviet ideologues sought to attenuate centuries of hostility between Jews and Slavs by drawing a rather dubious distinction between autochtonous Russian Jews, descendants from the ancient Crimean Khazar kingdom and hence a Tatar nationality, like the many central Asian peoples of the Soviet Union, and allochtonous Polish Jews, an unfortunate by-product of the acquisition of Polish territory in the eighteenth century. The settlement of Jews in the Crimea would return them to their ancestral soil and, in Lamarckian fashion, restore their Tatar nobility of character.[100]

Although the Soviet leadership in Moscow looked favorably, albeit warily, on the Agro-Joint's activities, administrators in the republics involved were far less sanguine. At first, Ukrainian authorities were willing to accept a limited number of Jewish colonists, mainly in the hope that the settlements would pull Jews out of the Ukraine's cities, thereby fostering the creation of a Ukrainian urban bourgeoisie. But by 1926 Ukrainian attitudes toward the Agro-Joint had become solidly adversarial. It was at this time and for this reason that Soviet authorities switched the Agro-Joint's focus to the Crimea, only to encounter stiff opposition from Crimean Communist Party officials as well as the indigenous Crimean Tatars, who felt that their land was being overrun by foreigners, first Russians and now Jews.[101] In sum, the bureaucrats on the ground who were ultimately responsible for the success or failure of the Agro-Joint reacted with the same combination of suspicion and recalcitrance that characterized the attitude of Russian officialdom during the agricultural projects of the early 1800s. The difference was that in the later case nationalistic sentiment reinforced long-standing xenophobia toward and feelings of economic competition with the Jews.

Like nineteenth-century *maskilim,* the leaders of the Agro-Joint claimed that the state looked benevolently on their project of Jewish renewal and that expressions of antisemitism were isolated and ephemeral. From the beginning of the Agro-Joint's activity, its leaders claimed that the Tatars vigorously supported the entry of Jews, along with other ethnic minorities, as a source of increased wealth.[102] There is no sign that this assumption was ever questioned. Champions of the Agro-Joint were wont to claim that their project was superior to that of the Zionists because the Russian territories, unlike Palestine, were thinly populated and lacked a hostile indigenous population. But this was not the case. The Agro-Joint featured the same combination of misunderstanding and denial of native resistance to Jewish colonization that characterized Zionist discourse on the Arab question. They shared the notion that the natives longed for the material improvement that would inevitably accompany a Jewish presence, that expressions of hostility, even violent ones, were spontaneous, disorganized, and, most of all, reactionary, destined to fade with time and the full implementation of the Jewish program of social engineering.

The Zionist project did succeed, whereas a combination of fierce antisemitism and massive economic change in the Soviet Union ensured that the path blazed by the Agro-Joint would lead to oblivion. In 1927 Rosen and his colleagues predicted confidentially that Stalin's influence was waning and that advocates of collectivized agriculture and rapid industrialization would not have their way in Moscow. The launching of the first Five-Year Plan in 1928 proved them wrong. As it turned out, many of the Jewish colonies already practiced high levels of collectivization, and the collectivization process per se did not contribute significantly to Jewish emigration from the colonies. Famine, a result of both natural and man-made factors, played a more prominent role in weakening the attractiveness of farming to Jews. Most of all, though, it was the successful industrialization of the country, the creation of demand for technicians, scientists, and administrators in factory life, that enticed many colonists to leave in the early 1930s and prevented young, able-bodied Soviet Jews from choosing an agricultural life.

The Agro-Joint's end, however, would be neither happy nor peaceful. In the mid-1930s Stalin's purges wiped out most of the Agro-Joint staff; in 1941 the German army annihilated the agricultural colonies themselves.[103] Soviet assistance for Jewish colonization would henceforth be limited to a remote and inhospitable region in the Far East, near the Manchurian border. Synecdochically, the region is usually given the name of its capital city, Birobidzhan.

In 1928 the Soviet government began to promote Jewish immigration to this territory, and in 1934 the Soviet authorities officially proclaimed it the "Jewish Autonomous Region." Birobidzhan had supporters worldwide among anti-Zionist leftist Jews, who were given a framework in which to espouse a secular, Yiddishist Jewish identity while remaining loyal to the Soviet Union. Leaders of the Joint, in contrast, displayed tepid support for the project, which they saw more as last-ditch refugee assistance than a well-structured program of social engineering. Besides, by the end of the 1930s, Rosen, many of whose friends and colleagues had been liquidated or sent off to the gulag, had decided that the Soviet Union was, as he put it, "a rotten country," and he wanted nothing more to do with it.[104] As it turned out, Birobidzhan failed as both a Jewish national home and a site for Jewish social engineering; by the outbreak of World War II, the Jewish population of the region was barely twenty thousand, most of it urban. And Stalin's purges were no less savage in Birobidzhan than in western Russia.[105]

Too late, Rosen became a territorialist; he realized that control over Jewish immigration to and settlement in any territory must be entirely in the hands of Jews. He toyed with the idea of transferring Palestine's Arabs to British Guiana and making Palestine into a purely Jewish territory "in spite of the fact that Palestine could never be expected to be a peaceful country, being as it is located in a pivotal position and at the crossroads of the three religions."[106] But this thoroughly assimilated Jew, who, in a life of ceaseless labor to solve the "Jewish problem," had studiously avoided any involvement in or even mention of Palestine, did not turn his gaze toward the Middle East. Instead he tried to develop a Jewish colony in British Guiana and then in the Dominican Republic, where he hoped to settle one hundred thousand Jews. But Rosen's new career as a planner of banana plantations was cut short; in 1940 he suffered a stroke, after which he lingered in agony until his death in 1949.[107]

Rosen remains an enigma. During his final tortured decade of life, he referred occasionally in correspondence to his Jewish ancestry, but only to account for his sardonic sense of humor.[108] Even in his last years

Rosen continued to evoke admiration, even veneration, among those whom he met. One man in the Dominican Republic with whom Rosen had worked gushed that he was "the grandest person living," "created in the image of God."[109] Rosen embodied the virtues and flaws of the engineer, of the unpolitical man who sees life as a technical problem to be solved through inquiry, experiment, and innovation. The relentless optimism that Rosen manifested up through the late 1930s derived not from a sanguine view of human nature but rather from a desperate faith in science when all political ideologies had failed. Rosen represented, in an exaggerated form, the spirit of the Joint, in all its strength and weakness: its humanitarianism, efficiency, and pragmatism; yet, at the same time, its inability to consider the political dimensions and ramifications of its activities.

Despite its marshaling of funds and expertise, the Agro-Joint did not solve the problem of Jewish persecution, poverty, and economic marginalization. To be fair, however, neither did any other form of Jewish social policy active in the Diaspora. Nor was it clear in the 1930s that the Zionist movement would necessarily reach a better result. The Yishuv could not feed or sustain itself; it depended heavily on Arab labor, and it was politically dependent on Britain, whose intentions concerning the Jewish National Home were unclear. All forms of Jewish social engineering in the interwar era shared certain fundamental weaknesses. Despite its relative wealth in comparison to the World Zionist Organization, the Joint did not command the resources to reconstruct the shattered lives of eastern European Jews. Although the Joint was plutocratic and the ZO democratic, both lacked guaranteed revenue but relied on donations that could vary drastically from year to year. Pledges always exceeded actual collections; for example, by July 1928, although more than $7 million had been pledged to the ASJFSR, only $311,000 had actually been paid in.[110]

Jewish social engineering, divorced from the politics of state building, was at best a palliative. The construction of a new Jewish society could take place only in an autonomous Jewish polity. At the same time, it would be inappropriate to dismiss all other forms of Jewish social policy or social engineering as ill conceived or as merely stepping-stones toward the realization of the Zionist ideal. Jewish social policy did not portend the Zionist project, just as there was no neat, linear progression, in either an institutional or an ideational sense, from national or international to nationalist Jewish politics. The relationship between Zionism and other forms of Jewish social policy should be conceived not in mathematical terms of unidirectional vectors but rather in biological terms of lateral evolution from a common ancestor. Zionism was not the child of Diaspora-oriented Jewish politics; rather, the two were cousins, sharing a common ancestor in the very conception of a "Jewish problem" and the contradictory senses of crisis and competence that stimulated the formation of modern Jewish social policy.

Epilogue

The "Jewish question," first posed during the Enlightenment, remained in the forefront of European consciousness through the 1930s, when the Nazi regime undertook to answer the question definitively — first through deemancipation and ultimately, during World War II, through annihilation. Developments since 1945 have restructured the economic components of the Jewish question and have, accordingly, transformed Jewish economic discourse and philanthropic practice.

The massacre of two-thirds of European Jewry in the Holocaust, combined with the economic modernization of postwar Europe, have eliminated the Jews from their previous position as a prominent urban elite in what had been the largely agrarian societies of east central and eastern Europe. Even before the war, German and Austrian Jewry had been pauperized by the expropriation of Jewish businesses, property, and capital. Once the Nazis invaded eastern Europe, this process took place throughout the region at lightning pace. The postwar regimes in eastern Europe exacerbated Jewish pauperization by nationalizing the economy, thus depriving many surviving Jews of their livelihoods as independent merchants and craftsmen and pushing the latter into the industrial labor force. Meanwhile, an elite of educated Jews became functionaries in the hypertrophied communist state governments and technocrats in state-owned enterprises. Thus eastern European Jewry underwent simultaneous pauperization, proletarianization, and, at least for some, bureaucratization. All of these changes, above and beyond the Nazi decimation of eastern European Jewry, ensured the destruction of the centuries-old Jewish economic base of independent trade and crafts as well as the Ashkenazic Jewish civilization that that economic base had nurtured.[1]

Postwar Germany became a magnet for the destitute and traumatized Jewish survivors of the Holocaust. In summer 1945 there were some 70,000 Jews within the borders of the Reich; most were concentration camp survivors or slave laborers. Within two years that figure swelled to 200,000, as Jews in eastern Europe reacted to postwar persecutions, like the Kielce pogrom of 1946, with mass flight to Germany's Displaced Persons camps, managed by the United Nations and the Allied military authorities. Although the number of Jews in Germany declined sharply in 1948, thanks to mass immigration to Israel and the New World, still in 1949, 40 percent of the Jews in Germany were dependent on relief. Financial assistance came primarily from the Joint Distribution Committee, which poured more than $230 million into Europe in the three years after the war's end.[2]

By contrast, economic recovery came quickly to the Jews of western Europe, and in the 1950s and 1960s in lands not touched directly by the Holocaust—England and especially the United States—Jews experienced unprecedented economic mobility. In these countries, home to more than half of contemporary Jewry, Jews have, over the past fifty years, gradually shed many of their classic economic characteristics. Whereas in eastern Europe the traditional Jewish economic profile was the object of deliberate assault, in the West it was altered by the lifting of social barriers and the freeing of market forces. Thus, although political persecution and economic want still afflict Jews in certain parts of the globe, in the West the notion of Jewish economic dysfunction has almost entirely faded away.

Before World War II there were many areas of similarity between Jews and other middleman minorities living in diaspora, such as ethnic Chinese in Southeast Asia. These minorities engage in low-status but essential commercial occupations, experience considerable social hostility, and concentrate in small, independent enterprises. Each of these qualities reinforces the others, and all three, taken together, create bonds of ethnic solidarity.[3] But the mobility, prosperity, and prestige enjoyed by contemporary North American and western European Jews have removed them from the category of a middleman minority. One could argue that the Jews' disproportionate affluence is itself a sign of ongoing economic distinctiveness, as is their continued overrepresentation in certain occupations, ranging from financial services to the professions of medicine, psychotherapy, law, and university teaching. But the socio-economic situation of contemporary Jews in the West cannot be compared with that of, say, Indonesia's ethnic Chinese, who are pillars of the country's distributive sector and serve as lightning rods for social discontent. Despite the vast wealth that some of them enjoy, their position more closely resembles the condition of pre-Holocaust eastern European Jewry than that of Jews anywhere today.[4]

Both of the antisemitic paradigms that I analyzed in chapter 1 — the notion of the Jew as parasitical pauper and as conspiratorial banker — flourished in the dank atmosphere of occupied Europe in the immediate postwar era. Jewish displaced persons (DPs) were the object of considerable prejudice by the occupying British authorities, who regarded them as conniving, immoral, and dangerous. Wary of Jewish pressure to allow mass immigration to Palestine, British officials expressed fears of collusion among the DPs, Zionist groups, and the Joint Distribution Committee. By the 1950s, however, this conspiratorial worldview had faded, not only in Britain, but in western Europe as a whole, and antisemitism was no longer a major part of the cultural landscape. Eastern Europe, however, was fertile ground for conspiratorial fantasies of Jewish world domination. Both the Prague show trials of 1951–52 and the so-called doctors' plot in the Soviet Union in 1953 invoked the Joint as an agent of international Jewish power, which, along with Zionists and other political deviants, was accused of plotting to overthrow the communist regime.[5] The visceral and virulent antisemitism that has swelled in post–cold war Russia is but a continuation of this long-established conspiratorial worldview.

I am writing these lines in the autumn of 2000. Over the past year, there have been in North America and western Europe alarming bursts of anti-Jewish hate crime, ranging from synagogue and cemetery vandalism to shootings of Jewish children. In the United States, a Judeophobic worldview, prominently featuring fantasies of a global Jewish economic conspiracy, may be found, ironically, among both white supremacist groups and the African American Nation of Islam. And just in the past month, a massive escalation of the Israeli-Palestinian conflict has catalyzed acts of violence and vandalism against Jews and Jewish targets throughout the western world. But whereas in the West before 1945 antisemitism was pervasive, socially acceptable, and widely institutionalized, the antisemitic cognitive framework that conceived of Jews as constituting a specific sociopolitical problem is no longer a part of mainstream sensibility. Most Jews today do not live in daily confrontation with antisemitism as part of a cultural code, a telegraphic expression of discontent with the hegemonic social order.[6] In the United States, although in 1964 as many as 29 percent of Americans believed that Jews "hold too much power," that figure dropped to 12 percent in 1998. In 2000 the Democratic candidate for the presidency, Al Gore, considered antisemitism so inconsequential that he saw only benefit in the pathbreaking choice of a Jew, Joseph Lieberman, as his running mate.[7] To be sure, antisemitism has not disappeared, but in the western world it has become but one form of hate crime, directed most often against foreigners (e.g., in Germany and Austria), gays, and members of visible minorities.

In view of the ongoing Arab-Israeli conflict, and especially its recent intensification, it is tempting but mistaken to equate the worst excesses of conspiratorial European antisemitism with Arab antisemitism, which alleges, among other things, that Jewish economic power dictates American foreign policy and that Israel yearns to dominate the Middle Eastern economy. The difference between the two is that in the Middle East, antisemitism, however irrational and indefensible, is a by-product of a political and economic struggle against authentic opponents, Israel and Western colonialism, respectively. This situation is quite different from that which nurtured classic European antisemitism, whose image of the Jew was nothing but a reflection and reification of European society itself.

As to the Jews themselves, the horrors perpetrated on them in the Holocaust have done much to block the internalization of economic antisemitism. Moreover, the idealization of physical labor and primary production, central to earlier forms of Jewish social thought, have not been able to survive in a world where smallholding farming has given way to impersonal agribusiness and where services in high-technology industry have supplanted heavy industrial production as the leading economic sectors. Israel's robust productive sector and the meritocratic and dynamic nature of North American society have blunted the stimulus to apologize for Jewish economic practice.

In the state of Israel, the economic ideologies that were so central to the Zionist movement have become increasingly irrelevant. Israel represents both a realization and a failure of classic Zionist ideals. On the one hand, Israel has become a prosperous state, whose per capita gross domestic product is greater than that of southern European states and approaches that of the United Kingdom. On the other hand, despite the bucolic dreams of many of the country's founders, Israel is one of the world's most urbanized countries, manual labor is performed largely by Arabs and foreign workers, and Israelis display classic Diaspora-Jewish talents for entrepreneurship in new economic fields, such as computer technology. Ironically, Israel has normalized the Jewish people by replicating Diaspora Jewry's occupational profile and proclivities, which mesh well with the needs of the global economy. Although Israelis may grumble about the dark side of their country's prosperity, for example, the growing income gap between rich and poor, contemporary Israeli economic discourse is cut off from the heritage of European Jewish political economy and is instead dependent on the vagaries of economic thinking in the Western world.

In the Diaspora, Jewish financial and commercial genius is no longer a major source of Jewish self-pride. This may be so because of residual embarrassment about the historic ties between Jews and trade, or perhaps simply because of the great variety of professions in which North American Jews have, of late, excelled. A popular American book of 1994 listing the one hundred most influential Jews of all time mentioned only one financier or entrepreneur, Meyer Amschel Rothschild.[8] And although the Rothschilds continue to draw the attention of scholars and amateur historians, they are no longer powerful cultural symbols. The 1970 musical comedy *The Rothschilds,* with music and lyrics by Jerry Bock and Sheldon Harnick, was notably less successful than the duo's previous effort, the blockbuster *Fiddler on the Roof.* Perhaps it was simply a bad musical, but part of its weakness lay in its attempt to embed a melodramatic tale about Jewish familial solidarity—a forceful myth in modern Jewish consciousness—in a context of nineteenth-century financial machinations unlikely to quicken the pulse of a contemporary audience. The most powerful and glamorous economic sector today, computing and information services, is not strongly associated with Jews, and, as Nicholas de Rothschild of the family's British branch recently remarked, "None of us is Bill Gates. He has done it in this century."[9]

The fading of the Jewish question from public consciousness, and the ensuing decline of interest on the part of Diaspora Jews in their political economy, has altered the nature and scope of Jewish philanthropy. This process has been gradual and has only become easily visible in the last two decades. Throughout most of the postwar period, the associational Judaism described in chapter 5 typified North American Jewish life. Jewish identity was expressed less through synagogue attendance or religious study than through social activity, often of a philanthropic nature. Jewish philanthropies, although dedicated to the provision of social services to the aged and infirm, concentrated, as in Europe before World War II, on the mobilization of resources for the relief of the Jewish poor and oppressed in distant lands. Similarly, the inextricable link between providing financial aid to the fledgling state of Israel and lobbying on its behalf embodied the spirit of the fin-de-siècle international Jewish politics that was analyzed in chapter 6.

Jewish activists in the postwar period, like the subjects of this book, have operated in a mental universe of constant crisis. Of late, however, the nature of that crisis has changed considerably. Although Israel's security remains a constant concern, threats to Jewish survival are seen to emanate as least as much from domestic, demographic sources, namely, assimilation and intermarriage, as from economic want or physical danger. Over the past decade Jewish philanthropies have increasingly targeted domestic rather than overseas projects, and among domestic issues education has assumed priority over social welfare. In addition to these changes in the allocation of resources, the quantity of funds available and the willingness of Jews to invest time and effort on behalf of Jewish philanthropic causes appear to be in decline. Between 1971 and 1991 total giving to Jewish causes in the United States—what we could call the Jewish gross national product—declined in real terms by 28 percent. Similarly, since 1989 total donations to the Council of Jewish Federations–United Jewish Appeal have, when adjusted for inflation, generally decreased. Given the vast increase in personal wealth during this period, the downward curve suggests not that Jews have less to give but rather that they are giving elsewhere, or not at all. Universities, museums, and other institutions that previously did not welcome Jewish gifts now aggressively solicit them. At the same time, associational Judaism is at risk of breaking apart as younger Jews turn away from service organizations such as the B'nai B'rith and Hadassah.[10]

The ascent of associational Judaism in the nineteenth century and its decline in our time are part of a broader social phenomenon: the rise and fall of the bourgeois public sphere, that zone between the intimate realm of the family and the administrative realm of the state. Modern associations were voluntary and free; their membership cut across old estate lines, and, unlike all-encompassing guilds, they had specific purposes. The association thus embodied the spirit of modern individualism, in which the free man or woman chooses to associate for purposes of his or her own design. At the same time, the activities of associations favored public service over private cultivation. The philanthropic institutions of modern Jewry embodied a sphere of empowerment in which freely acting individuals, operating beyond both traditional communal structures and the purview of the state, devoted themselves to the simultaneous realization of a social vision shared by middle-class society as a whole and an assertion of Jewish ethnic identity. The specificity of the Jewish philanthropic project, like the defined purviews of Catholic or women's philanthropy in early-twentieth-century Europe, does not contradict its universalist qualities.

All forms of collective identity have been affected by the decline of the public sphere. The enlargement of the intimate realm (now devoted at least as much to consumption as to its traditional function of social reproduction) and the omnipresence of the administrative sphere (increasingly molded by corporate as opposed to state power) have catalyzed massive resentment but have constricted the space in which that antagonism can be constructively expressed. The result is the clash, particularly in the developing world, between what the political scientist Benjamin Barber has called "McWorld" and "Jihad": transnational corporate culture, on the one hand, and, on the other, communities that define themselves primarily in terms of opposition to that culture.[11] Whereas the confrontation between Jihad and McWorld has been violent in Third World countries, in the industrialized West ethnoreligious identities have become increasingly privatized, eclectic, and syncretic, realized through a personal search for spiritual fulfillment or grounding in one's ethnic roots. This process is quietist and accommodating of society rather than antagonistic to it. (The overwhelming popularity in recent years of genealogical research among middle-class North Americans, including Jews, is a manifestation of this development.)

The blurring of contemporary North American Jewry's economic distinctiveness, the diminution of its philanthropic involvement, and the privatization of Jewish identity may be causally linked. An intriguing sociological study of first-generation Japanese Americans observed that ethnic solidarity, manifested in, among other things, religious observance and philanthropic activity, was both engendered and reinforced by a concentration in certain commercial occupations. The study concludes from changes in the occupational and organizational patterns of second- and third-generation Japanese Americans that "when minorities become like the majority economically, it is difficult to preserve their distinctiveness."[12]

It is not clear if and how fully this statement applies to the Jews. Clearly, ethnic solidarity cannot be reduced to economic factors alone; contemporary Jewish collective identity is woven out of a complex and supple fabric. Besides, the economic changes in recent Jewish life are irreversible and, for the most part, beneficial. It is neither feasible nor desirable to re-create the associational Judaism whose raison d'être was a vision of imminent economic catastrophe. Still, anyone concerned with the question of the future of the Jews will need to take into account structural economic changes when crafting strategies for a revival of Jewish organizational life.

Jewish identity is molded by ambient cultural frameworks. In the nineteenth and early twentieth century, when capitalism's transfiguration of Europe was the guiding star of social thought, speculation about the position of the Jews in Europe—the Jewish question—could not be separated from anxiety about the new industrial order—the social question. The inextricable linkage of the two characterized Jewish thinking on the subject as much as that of Gentiles. The Jewish peddler, merchant, and banker were powerful cultural symbols, signifiers of momentous, revolutionary social transformation. The Jews were, metaphorically speaking, Shylock's children, and they felt compelled to come to terms, in one form or another, with their parentage. Although today's Jews are still haunted by many specters from the past, Shylock's ghost is not among them. Jews continue to have grave, even existential problems, but for the vast majority of world Jewry, the "Jewish question" as it was understood throughout modern European history has ceased to exist.

Notes

UOBB   Unabhängiger Orden Bnei Briss
ZDSJ   *Zeitschrift für die Demographie und Statistik der Juden*
ZGJD   *Zeitschrift für die Geschichte der Juden in Deutschland*

Introduction

1. See the call for a direct examination of the relationship between socioeconomic factors and modern Jewish identity formation in Arnold M. Eisen, "Rethinking Jewish Modernity," *Jewish Social Studies,* n.s.1, no. 1 (1994): 1–21.

2. E.g., Jonathan Frankel's classic study, *Prophecy and Politics: Socialism, Nationalism, and the Russian Jews, 1862–1917* (Cambridge, 1981).

3. The notion that not only earning but also spending patterns of Jews are unusual and that philanthropic expenditure is a prime area of difference between Jews and Gentiles in modern times is one of the few contributions of Gerald Krefetz's journalistic work, *Jews and Money: The Myths and the Reality* (New Haven, 1982).

4. See the discussions of this problem in Jacob Katz, ed., *Toward Modernity: The European Jewish Model* (New Brunswick, N.J., 1987).

5. The Jewish economic elite in modern Europe is the subject of numerous, exhaustive studies, e.g., Fritz Stern, *Gold and Iron: Bismarck, Bleichröder, and the Building of the German Empire* (New York, 1977); Werner Mosse, *Jews in the German Economy: The German-Jewish Economic Elite, 1820–1935* (Oxford, 1987); idem, *The German-Jewish Economic Elite: A Socio-Cultural Profile* (Oxford, 1989); and Daniel Gutwein, *A Divided Elite: Economics, Politics, and Anglo-Jewry, 1882–1917* (Leiden, 1992). Historiography on the Rothschilds is a cottage industry unto itself. See, inter alia, Egon Corti, *The Rise of the House of Rothschild* (London: 1928); idem, *The Reign of the House of Rothschild* (London, 1928); Bertrand Gille, *Histoire de la Maison Rothschild,* 2 vols. (Geneva, 1965–67); Amos Elon, *Founder: A Portrait of the First Rothschild and His Time* (New York, 1996); and Niall Ferguson, *The House of Rothschild: Money's Prophets, 1798–1848* (New York, 1998).

6. Pierre Bourdieu, *Distinction: A Social Critique of the Judgment of Taste* (Cambridge, Mass., 1984), 176.

7. In 1850 the German Jewish newspapers *Der Orient* and *Die Allgemeine Zeitung des Judentums* had 550 and 700 subscribers, respectively; the French *Archives Israélites* had about 400 in 1841 and perhaps as many as 1,000 two years later; subscriptions to London's *Jewish Chronicle* reached 2,000 in the early 1860s. In the 1920s the circulation of the Hamburg *Israelitische Familienblatt* reached 26,000, and the organs of the Berlin Jewish community and the Central Association of German Citizens of the Jewish Faith distributed at least 50,000. Baruch Mevorah, " 'Ikvoteihah shel 'alilat Damasek be-hitpathutah shel ha-'itonut ha-yehudit ba-shanim 1840–46," *Zion* 23–24 (1958–59): 46–65; Arie Bar, ed., *The Jewish Press That Was: Accounts, Evaluations and Memories of Jewish Papers in Pre-Holocaust Europe* (Tel Aviv, 1980), 353; David Cesarani, *The "Jewish Chronicle" and Anglo-Jewry, 1841–1991* (Cambridge, 1994), 33; David Vital, *A People Apart: The Jews in Europe, 1789–1939* (New York, 1999), 235; Jonathan Frankel, "Jewish

Politics and the Press: The 'Reception' of the Alliance Israélite Universelle," *Jewish History,* forthcoming.

8. Jürgen Habermas, *The Structural Transformation of the Public Sphere* (Cambridge, Mass., 1989). A number of historians of modern Europe and the United States have made use of Habermas's paradigm, although it has also come under considerable criticism. Two important overviews of the literature, which offer powerful critiques of their own, are Geoff Eley, "Nations, Publics, and Political Cultures: Placing Habermas in the Nineteenth Century," in *Culture/Power/History: A Reader in Contemporary Social Theory,* ed. Nicholas B. Dirks, Geoff Eley, and Sherry B. Ortner (Princeton, N.J., 1994), 297–335; and Harold Mah, "Phantasies of the Public Sphere: Rethinking the Habermas of Historians," *Journal of Modern History* 72 (2000): 153–82.

9. On the relationship between the Jewish press and the emergence of the Jewish public sphere, see Eli Lederhendler, *The Road to Modern Jewish Politics: Political Tradition and Political Reconstruction in the Jewish Community of Tsarist Russia* (Oxford, 1988), esp. 119–33; and Frankel, "Jewish Politics and the Press."

10. Jacob Toury, "The Jewish Question: A Semantic Approach," *LBIYB* 11 (1966): 85–106; Peter Pulzer, *Jews and the German State: The Political History of a Minority, 1848–1933* (London, 1992), 28–43.

Chapter One. Jews, Paupers, and Other Savages: The Economic Image of the Jew in Western Europe, 1648–1848

1. Léon Poliakov, *The History of Antisemitism* (New York, 1975), 3:397.

2. Poliakov's universal history is a good example of the indiscriminate use of the term; Jacob Katz's *From Prejudice to Destruction: Antisemitism, 1700–1933* (Cambridge, Mass., 1980), offers a more limited chronological and conceptual framework. The word *antisemitism* gained currency in the late 1870s.

3. See Gavin Langmuir, *Toward a Definition of Antisemitism* (Berkeley, 1990); Robert Chazan, *Medieval Stereotypes and Modern Antisemitism* (Berkeley, 1997).

4. According to Weber's classic analysis, in Protestantism, magic and superstition, like many Catholic practices, were thought to give the individual false senses of human agency and autonomy and distracted him from the necessity of a constant and total encounter with God. Thus in Protestantism, rationalization promoted soteriological goals, whereas the modern state sought utility and efficiency to maximize power and promote the common weal. Compare Max Weber, *The Protestant Ethic and the Spirit of Capitalism* (New York, 1958), 105, 117, with R. Po-Chi Hsia, *The Myth of Ritual Murder* (New Haven, 1988), 84, 147–48, 217.

5. R. Po-Chia Hsia, "The Usurious Jew: Economic Structure and Religious Representations in an Anti-Semitic Discourse," in *In and Out of the Ghetto: Jewish-Gentile Relations in Late Medieval and Early Modern Germany,* ed. R. Po-Chia Hsia and Hatmur Lehmann (Washington, D.C., 1995), 161–76.

6. *The Republic of Plato,* trans. and ed. Francis MacDonald Cornford (New York, 1941), 57–58, 102–11.

7. *Politics,* bk. 1, chap. 10. See also M. I. Finley, "Aristotle and Economic

Analysis," in *Articles on Aristotle 2: Ethics and Politics,* ed. Jonathan Barnes, Malcom Schofield, and Richard Sorabji (London, 1977), 140–58, esp. 151–52.

8. *Oeconomica,* trans. E. S. Forster (Oxford, 1920), 1:2.

9. J. Gilchrist, *The Church and Economic Activity in the Middle Ages* (New York, 1969), 51–52.

10. Salo Baron, "The Economic Views of Maimonides," in *Essays on Maimonides,* ed. Salo Baron (New York, 1941), 170–71.

11. Raymond de Roover, "The Scholastic Attitude toward Trade and Entrepreneurship," in de Roover's collected essays, *Business, Banking, and Economic Thought in Late Medieval and Early Modern Europe* (Chicago, 1974), 336.

12. Thomas Aquinas, "On the Ethics of Trading," in *Main Currents in Western Thought: Readings in Western European Intellectual History from the Middle Ages to the Present,* ed. Franklin Baumer (New York, 1952), 88–89.

13. Jeremy Cohen, *The Friars and the Jews: The Evolution of Medieval Anti-Judaism* (Ithaca, 1983), 41; Raymond de Roover, *San Bernardino of Siena and Sant' Antonio of Florence: Two Great Economic Thinkers of the Middle Ages* (Boston, 1967), 29. See also Gilchrist, *Church and Economic Activity,* 53–58; Joseph Shatzmiller, *Shylock Reconsidered: Jews, Moneylending, and Medieval Society* (Berkeley, 1990), 45–46; Robert Bonfil, *Jewish Life in Renaissance Italy* (Berkeley, 1994), 29; Bronislaw Geremek, *Poverty: A History* (Oxford, 1994), 22, 35.

14. Lester Little, *Religious Poverty and the Profit Economy in Medieval Europe* (Ithaca, 1978); Jacques Le Goff, *Your Money or Your Life: Economy and Religion in the Middle Ages* (New York, 1988).

15. William Bouwsma, "Anxiety and the Formation of Early Modern Culture," in *After the Reformation,* ed. Barbara Malament (Philadelphia, 1980), 215–46.

16. Early utopian fantasies possessed an agrarian orientation; as products of a society on the threshold of modernity, these texts demonstrate discomfort with the commercial forces on which modernity itself depended. For example, Thomas More's *Utopia* (1516) features a society based on agriculture and handicrafts. The island of Utopia is economically self-sufficient; it imports nothing, and whatever agricultural surplus it produces is given to the poor of other lands or sold abroad on such generous terms that the sale amounts to charity as much as commerce. There is no description in the book of a merchant class. Similarly, the anonymous Italian utopian work *Settennario* (ca. 1570) calls for reducing the number of shops and tradesmen to a minimum. Compare Thomas More, *Utopia* (New York, 1974), 56–69, 76–79, with Carlo Ginzburg, *The Cheese and the Worms* (Baltimore, 1980), 113–15.

17. Kenneth R. Stow, *Alienated Minority: The Jews of Medieval Latin Europe* (Cambridge, Mass, 1992), 210–17.

18. Stow, *Alienated Minority,* 218–20; Léon Poliakov, *Jewish Bankers and the Holy See* (London, 1977), 59, 94, 102; Shatzmiller, *Shylock Reconsidered,* 53–54.

19. On the ecclesiastical debates about usury, see Benjamin Nelson, *The Idea of Usury,* 2d ed. (Chicago, 1969), 3–28. For cases of Christians lending at interest to Jews, see David Niremberg, *Communities of Violence: Persecution of Minorities in the Middle Ages* (Princeton, 1997), 40, 174, 27.

20. Bonfil, *Jewish Life in Renaissance Italy,* 43–48; also Poliakov, *Jewish Bankers and the Holy See,* 88–89; and Shatzmiller, *Shylock Reconsidered,* 71–79.

21. Poliakov, *Jewish Bankers and the Holy See,* 38–43; Kurt Grunwald, "Lombards, Cahorsins, and Jews," *Journal of European Economic History* 4, no. 1 (1975): 393–98.

22. Gilchrist, *Church and Economic Activity,* 70; see also Bonfil, *Jewish Life in Renaissance Italy,* 29.

23. Poliakov, *Jewish Bankers and the Holy See,* 141–43; Haim Hillel Ben-Sasson, "The Middle Ages," in *A History of the Jewish People,* ed. Shmuel Ettinger (Cambridge, Mass., 1976), 578–79.

24. Hsia, "The Usurious Jew," 170n, 172.

25. Martin Luther, "On the Jews and Their Lies," in *Works,* vol. 47, ed. Franklin Sherman (Philadelphia, 1971), 292. Most analyses of this text attribute its venomous tone to Luther's disappointment at not having won the Jews to his reformed version of Christianity. But the work also needs to be placed in the context of Luther's intense and protracted struggle with the problem of usury. Nelson, *The Idea of Usury,* 42–56.

26. Nelson, *The Idea of Usury,* 73–108.

27. Azriel Shohat, *'Im hilufei ha-tekufot* (Jerusalem, 1960), 22; David Sorkin, "The Impact of Emancipation on German Jewry: A Reconsideration," in *Assimilation and Community: The Jews in Nineteenth-Century Europe,* ed. Jonathan Frankel and Steven Zipperstein (Cambridge, 1992), 179.

28. Yacov Guggenheim, "Meeting on the Road: Encounters between German Jews and Christians on the Margins of Society," in Hsia and Lehmann, *In and Out of the Ghetto,* 125–36.

29. Moses A. Shulvass, *From East to West: The Westward Migration of Jews from Eastern Europe during the Seventeenth and Eighteenth Centuries* (Detroit, 1971), passim; Menachem Friedman, "Mikhtavei hamlatsah le-kabtsanim—'ketavim'; Le-ba'yat ha-navadim be-Germaniyah ba-meah ha-yod-het," *Mikhael* 2 (1973): 34–51.

30. Jacob Toury, "Der Eintritt der Juden ins deutsche Bürgertum," in *Das Judentum in der Deutschen Umwelt, 1800–1850,* ed. Hans Liebesschütz and Arnold Paucker (Tübingen, 1977), 149–50.

31. The pioneering study of Jewish criminality in Germany is Rudolf Glanz, *Geschichte des niederen jüdischen Volkes in Deutschland* (New York, 1968). See also Otto Ulbricht, "Criminality and Punishment of the Jews in the Early Modern Period," in Hsia and Lehmann, *In and Out of the Ghetto,* 49–70. For the development of a similar discourse on Jewish banditry and financial crime in early-eighteenth-century England, see Frank Felsenstein, *Anti-Semitic Stereotypes: A Paradigm of Otherness in English Popular Culture, 1660–1830* (Baltimore, 1995), esp. 62–78.

32. The most exhaustive scholarly work on the Court Jews is Heinrich Schnee, *Die Hoffinanz und der moderne Staat,* 6 vols. (Berlin, 1953–67). The work is tainted, however, by antisemitic overtones and questionable conclusions; see in particular vol. 3 (1955), 171–266. Selma Stern, *The Court Jew* (Philadelphia, 1950), provides an effective overview. Recent analyses of the Court Jews include Jonathan Israel, *European Jewry in the Age of Mercantilism, 1550–1750,* 2d ed.

(Oxford, 1989), esp. 123–43; William McCagg, "Jewish Wealth in Vienna, 1670–1918," in *Jews in the Hungarian Economy, 1760–1945,* ed. Michael Silber (Jerusalem, 1992), 54–91; and Mordechai Breuer's contribution to *German-Jewish History in Modern Times,* ed. Michael Meyer (New York, 1966), 1:104–26.

33. Moreover, although France under the ancien régime did not feature a corps of Court Jews, during the Revolution it relied heavily on Jewish army suppliers. See Michael Graetz, " 'Aliyato u-shkia'to shel sapak ha-tsava ha-yehudi: Kalkalah yehudit be-'itot milhemah," *Tsiyon* 56, no. 3 (1991):255–74.

34. Schnee, *Hoffinanz,* 3:250.

35. Barbara Gerber, *Jud Süss. Aufstieg und Fall im frühen 18. Jahrhundert* (Hamburg, 1990), 59–64. A similar image of the Jew developed in England; mid-eighteenth-century engravings by William Hogarth depicted Jews as either fabulously wealthy Sephardim or poor peddlers. Felsenstein, *Anti-Semitic Stereotypes,* 52–57.

36. Poliakov, *The History of Antisemitism,* 1:233.

37. Benjamin Braude, "The Myth of the Sephardi Economic Superman," unpublished ms. Thanks to Dr. Braude for sharing this manuscript with me.

38. Thanks to John Efron for bringing this book to my attention.

39. Bernardino Ramazzini, *Diseases of Workers* (New York, 1964), 287, 291. When the book was translated into French by Antoine-François de Fourcroy, the chapter title was changed to "Des maladies des fripiers, des cardeurs de matelas, et des chiffoniers" (On the illnesses of old clothes dealers, carders of mattresses, and rag men), because, according to the translator's note, the occupations discussed by Ramazzini, although commonly practiced by Jews in Modena, Padua, and indeed all Italy, are not practiced by Jews in France. See the *Essai sur les maladies des artisans, traduit du Latin de Ramazzini, avec des notes et des additions* (Paris, 1777), 378.

40. Yosef Hayim Yerushalmi, "Assimilation and Racial Antisemitism: The Iberian and the German Models," *Leo Baeck Memorial Lecture 26* (1982); Jonathan Elukin, "The Eternal Jew in Medieval Europe: Christian Perceptions of Jewish Anachronism and Racial Identity" (Ph.D. dissertation, Princeton University, 1994); Hsia, "The Usurious Jew"; James Shapiro, *Shakespeare and the Jews* (New York, 1996).

41. Arthur Kuhn, "Hugo Grotius and the Emancipation of the Jews in Holland," *Publications of the American Jewish Historical Society* 31 (1928): 173–80; Shmuel Ettinger, "The Beginnings of the Change in the Attitude of European Society towards the Jews," *Scripta Hierosolymitana* 7 (1961): 193–219; Israel, *European Jewry in the Age of Mercantilism,* 35–52.

42. Marc Raeff, "The Well-Ordered Police State and the Development of Modernity in Seventeenth- and Eighteenth-Century Europe," *American Historical Review* 80 (1975): 1221–43; Rainer Erb, "Warum ist der Jude zum Ackerbürger nicht tauglich? Zur Geschichte eines antisemitischen Stereotyps," in *Antisemitismus and Jüdische Geschichte. Studien zu Ehren von Herbert A. Strauss,* ed. Rainer Erb and Michael Schmidt (Berlin, 1987), 116–17; James van Horn Melton, *Absolutism and the Eighteenth-Century Origins of Compulsory Schooling in Prussia and Austria* (Cambridge, 1988), 140–44; Thomas McStay Adams, *Bureaucrats and Beggars: French Social Policy in the Age of the Enlightenment* (New

York, 1990), 255; Joan Campbell, *Joy in Work, German Work: The National Debate, 1800–1945* (Princeton, 1993), 7–9.

43. Chris Clark, *The Politics of Conversion: Missionary Protestantism and the Jews in Prussia, 1728–1945* (Oxford, 1995), 27–29, 40–43.

44. Arthur Hertzberg, *The French Enlightenment and the Jews* (Philadelphia, 1968), 41–43.

45. Ruth Necheles, *The Abbé Grégoire, 1787–1831* (Westport, Conn., 1971), 10–19.

46. John Toland, *Reasons for Naturalizing the Jews in Great Britain and Ireland, On the same foot with all other Nations. Containing also, A Defence of the Jews against all Vulgar Prejudices in all Countries* (London, 1714), 6–7, 12–17.

47. Eli F. Hekscher, *Mercantilism* (London, 1934).

48. See the excellent study by Keith Tribe, *Governing Economy: The Reformation of German Economic Discourse, 1750–1840* (Cambridge, 1988). See also Rudolf Vierhaus, *Germany in the Age of Absolutism* (Cambridge, 1988), 28–29.

49. Hertzberg, *French Enlightenment and the Jews*, 71–77.

50. Jacob Toury, "Emanzipation und Judenkolonien in der öffentlichen Meinung Deutschlands (1775–1819)," *TAJDG* 11 (1982): 17–53; Joseph Karniel, *Die Toleranzpolitik Kaiser Joseph II.* (Gerlingen, 1985), 449; Shmuel Almog, "Produktivizatsiyah, proletarizatsiyah, ve-ʿavodah ʿivrit," in *Temurot ba-historiyah ha-yehudit ha-hadashah: Kovets ma'amarim shai li-Shmuel Ettinger* (Jerusalem, 1985), 41, 43.

51. Physiocratic thinking may have influenced Polish and Russian thinking about the Jewish question. In 1800 the Russian imperial senator Gavriil Romanovich Derzhavin included in a memorandum on the Jews of the newly acquired Polish territories detailed calculations of the ideal ratio of townsmen to agriculturalists reminiscent of the elaborate mathematical calculations of a classic physiocratic text, the *Tableau* of François Quesnay. Matityahu Mintz, "Heʿerah arukah be-shulei havat-daʿato shel Derzhavin mi-shnat 1800," in *Ben Yisra'el le-umot: Kovets ma'amarim shai li-Shmuel Ettinger* (Jerusalem, 1987), 103–12; see also Israel Bartal, " 'Ha-model ha-mishni'—Tsorfat ke-makor hashpaʿah be-tahalikhei ha-modernizatsiah shel yehudei mizrah Eyropah (1772–1863)," in *Ha-mahpekhah ha-tsorfatit ve-rishumah*, ed. Yerahmiel Cohen (Jerusalem, 1991), esp. 273, 277. But I suspect that in these lands Physiocracy provided little more than a theoretical embellishment for a ruler or reformer seeking to maximize wealth, power, and efficiency in a predominantly agricultural society.

52. Elizabeth Fox-Genovese, *The Origins of Physiocracy: Economic Revolution and Social Order in Eighteenth-Century France* (Ithaca, 1976); David McNally, *Political Economy and the Rise of Capitalism: A Re-interpretation* (Berkeley, 1989), 85–151; Tribe, *Governing Economy*, chap. 6; and the following essays from H. M. Scott, ed., *Enlightened Absolutism: Reform and Reformers in Later Eighteenth-Century Europe* (Ann Arbor, 1990): H. M. Scott, "The Problem of Enlightened Absolutism," 31–32; Derek Beales, "Social Forces and Enlightened Policies," 50; M. S. Anderson, "The Italian Reformers," 65–67; and Charles Ingrao, "The Smaller German States," 228, 233.

53. David F. Lindenfeld, *The Practical Imagination: The German Sciences of State in the Nineteenth Century* (Chicago, 1997), 27–28.

54. Marion Gray, "From the Household Economy to 'Rational Agriculture': The Establishment of Liberal Ideals in German Agricultural Thought," in *In Search of Liberal Germany: Studies in the History of German Liberalism from 1789 to the Present,* ed. Konrad H. Jarausch and Larry Eugene Jones (New York, 1990), 25–54. An agrarian and manufacturing orientation lay behind classical political economy as well. See the discussion of Adam Smith in Laurence Dickey, "Historicizing the 'Adam Smith Problem': Conceptual, Historiographical, and Textual Issues," *Journal of Modern History* 58 (1986):579–609; and McNally, *Political Economy and the Rise of Capitalism.*

55. Vierhaus, *Germany in the Age of Absolutism,* 19–20, 28–29, 45–48.

56. Christian K. Wilhelm von Dohm, *Über die bürgerliche Verbesserung der Juden* (Berlin, 1781; rpt. Hildesheim, 1973). Recent analyses of Dohm include Ilsegret Dambacher, *Christian Wilhelm von Dohm* (Frankfurt am Main, 1974); Horst Moeller, "Aufklärung, Judenemanzipation und Staat. Ursprung und Wirkung von Dohms Schrift Über die bürgerliche Verbesserung der Juden," *Deutsche Aufklärung und Judenemanzipation (TAJDG,* Beiheft 3) (Tel Aviv, 1979), 119–54; and Robert Liberles, "The Historical Context of Dohm's Treatise on the Jews," in *Das deutsche Judentum und der Liberalismus — German Jewry and Liberalism* (St. Augustin, 1986), 44–69. Grégoire's *Essai sur la régénération physique, morale, et politique des juifs,* originally published in Metz in 1789, was reprinted in facsimile form in Paris in 1988. For biographical material on Grégoire, see Necheles, *The Abbé Grégoire.*

57. Tribe, *Governing Economy,* 99–100; Vierhaus, *Germany in the Age of Absolutism,* 73–75.

58. Hertzberg, *French Enlightenment and the Jews,* 329.

59. Dohm, *Bürgerliche Verbesserung,* 26, 34, 95, 106.

60. Ibid., 111–14.

61. Ibid., 114–16.

62. Mordeché Rappaport, *Christian Wilhelm von Dohm. Der Gegner der Physiokratie und seine Thesen* (Berlin, 1908), 96–118.

63. Dohm, *Bürgerliche Verbesserung,* 92.

64. Grégoire, *Essai,* 54–64, 71–99, 112–20, 142–46.

65. Compare Necheles, *The Abbé Grégoire,* 29, with the discussion of Grégoire in Lynn Hunt, *Politics, Culture, and Class in the French Revolution* (Berkeley, 1984), 2. The Prussian Pietists displayed a similar passion for the integration of ethnic minorities as part of the nation-building process. See Clark, *The Politics of Conversion,* 39.

66. q.v. "Regeneration," in *A Critical Dictionary of the French Revolution,* ed. François Furet (Cambridge, Mass., 1989), 782.

67. Dieter Langewiesche, "Liberalismus und Judenemanzipation im 19. Jahrhundert," in *Juden in Deutschland. Emanzipation, Integration, Verfolgung, und Vernichtung. 25 Jahre Institut für die Geschichte der deutschen Juden,* ed. Peter Freimark, Alice Jankowski, and Ina Lorenz (Hamburg, 1991), 148–63.

68. See the English edition of Hippel's book, *On Improving the Status of Women,* trans. and ed. Timothy Sellner (Detroit, 1979).

69. See Ute Frevert, *Women in German History: From Bourgeois Emancipation to Sexual Liberation* (New York, 1988), 19–20; and Lynn Hunt, *The Family Romance of the French Revolution* (Berkeley, 1992), passim.

70. Van Horn Melton, *Absolutism and the Eighteenth-Century Origins of Compulsory Schooling in Prussia and Austria*, 91–105, 109–44, 209–30.

71. For biographical information about Winkopp, see the *Allgemeine deutsche Biographie* (Leipzig, 1898), 43:456–57.

72. Peter Adolph Winkopp (1759–1813), *Über die bürgerliche und geistliche Verbesserung des Mönchwesens* (Gera, 1783), 123; see also 76, 88.

73. Ibid., 9, 108–9, 115. Associations between idleness and immorality, on the one hand, and separation from the body politic, on the other, are common tropes in Enlightenment discourse. Compare Winkopp with Emmanuel Joseph Sieyès's famous pamphlet of 1789, "What Is the Third Estate?" in which the nobility is portrayed as an *imperium in imperio,* not merely because of its separate legal status, but because of its failure to contribute to the common weal. The relevant selections are reproduced in Omar Dahbour and Micheline R. Ishay, eds., *The Nationalism Reader* (Atlantic Highlands, N.J., 1995), 35–37.

74. Winkopp, *Verbesserung,* 96.

75. Ibid., 147–48.

76. Ibid., 164, 170, 172, 175–77.

77. Johann August Schlettwein, "Bitte an die Grossen wegen der Juden: Zu Verhütung trauriger Folgen in den Staaten," *Ephemeriden der Menschheit. Vierter Band 1776. Erster Theil 1778* [*sic*], 41–47.

78. E.g., the Bible scholar Johann David Michaelis, whose critique of Dohm is reprinted in *Bürgerliche Verbesserung,* 2:31–71; and the Prussian historians Anton Balthasar König (1753–1814) and Friedrich Albert Zimmerman (1745–1815), whose views are analyzed in Arno Herzig, "Die Anfänge der deutsch-jüdischer Geschichtsschreibung in der Spätaufklärung," *TAJDG* 20 (1991):59–76.

79. "Jewish trade, *even if conducted with thorough honesty, can never mean anything but harm to civic society....* Jewish commerce does not advance this circulation [of wealth]. The Hebrew always returns less than he receives. He is a swamp that absorbs a great part of the water that passes through it." Cited in Katz, *From Prejudice to Destruction,* 61–62 (emphasis in Kortum's original).

80. Israel, *European Jewry in the Age of Mercantilism,* 56. For more examples of this reasoning from the later seventeenth century, see Ettinger, "The Beginnings of the Change in the Attitude of European Society towards the Jews," 215.

81. E.g., the protests of 1672, presented by the estates to the Great Elector of Brandenburg-Prussia, and of ca. 1700 from the merchants of Landsberg an der Warthe (in the Mark Brandenburg), discussed in Stefi Jersh-Wenzel, "Jewish Economic Activity in Early Modern Times," in Hsia and Lehmann, *In and Out of the Ghetto,* 92, 97. See also Miriam Bodian, "Ha-yazamim ha-yehudim be-Berlin, hamedinah ha-absolutistit, ve-'shipur matsavam shel ha-yehudim' be-mahatsit ha-shniyah shel ha-me'ah ha-yod-tet," *Tsiyon* 49 (1984):162. On mercantile antisemitism in France at this time, see Ettinger, "The Beginnings of Change," 214; for England, see Todd M. Endelman, *The Jews of Georgian England, 1714–1830* (Philadelphia, 1979), 28; Katz, *From Prejudice to Destruction,* 32; and Felstenstein, *Anti-Semitic Stereotypes,* 187–214.

82. Ettinger, "The Beginnings of Change," 214; Hertzberg, *French Enlightenment and the Jews,* 20–24, 64–71; Bodian, "Yazamim."

83. Hertzberg, *French Enlightenment and the Jews,* 63, 320.

84. Several of the decree's provisions that did not directly concern

commercial or moneylending activity had an economic component nonetheless. Demands that Jews take surnames and no longer keep business records in Hebrew were made, in large part, to impede fraud, tax evasion, and other acts of economic crime. Robert Anchel, *Napoléon et les juifs* (Paris, 1928), 353–67; Simon Schwartzfuchs, *Napoléon, the Jews, and the Sanhedrin* (London, 1979), 124–30, esp. 127.

85. William O. McCagg, Jr., *A History of Habsburg Jews, 1670–1918* (Bloomington, Ind., 1989), 54–55; Robert S. Wistrich, *The Jews of Vienna in the Age of Franz Joseph* (Oxford, 1990), 15–22, 25–26.

86. This contradiction stemmed from a simultaneous desire to change the occupational structure of the Jewish masses while preventing them from competing with the middling Christian mercantile and artisanal bourgeoisie. Raphael Mahler, *A History of Modern Jewry, 1780–1815* (London, 1971), 230; Wolfgang Häusler, "Toleranz, Emanzipation, und Antisemitismus. Das österreichische Judentum des bürgerlichen Zeitalters (1782–1918)," in *Das österreichische Judentum,* ed. Anna Drabeck et al. (Vienna, 1974), 83–86.

87. Cited in Mahler, *A History of European Jewry,* 318.

88. Cited in Gerson Wolf, *Studien zur Jubelfeier der Wiener Universität* (Vienna, 1865), 120.

89. Albert A. Bruer, *Geschichte der Juden in Preussen (1750–1820)* (Frankfurt am Main, 1991), 76.

90. Selma Stern, *Der preussische Staat und die Juden* (Tubingen, 1971), 3/1: 134–53.

91. Ismar Elbogen and Eleonore Sterling, *Die Geschichte der Juden in Deutschland* (Frankfurt am Main, 1988), 143–48; Steven M. Lowenstein, *The Berlin Jewish Community: Enlightenment, Family and Crisis, 1770–1830* (New York, 1994), 11–12; Toury, "Eintritt," 218.

92. Stuart Woolf, *The Poor in Western Europe in the Eighteenth and Nineteenth Centuries* (London, 1986), 7; S. Posener, "The Social Life of the Jewish Communities in France in the 18th Century," *Jewish Social Studies* 7 (1945): 223; Vierhaus, *Germany in the Age of Absolutism,* 45–48; Rolf Landwehr and Rüdiger Baron, eds., *Geschichte der Sozialarbeit. Hauptlinien ihrer Entwicklung im 19. und 20. Jahrhundert* (Weinheim, 1983), 11–13.

93. The scholarly literature on the *Begriffsgeschichte* of poverty and of poor care is immense. Historians tend to find in their period of specialty the transition from views of poverty as a spiritual blessing (for both those who suffer it and those who give alms to alleviate it) to a result of misfortune or moral turpitude. For an assignment of the turning point to the High Middle Ages, see Gilchrist, *Church and Economic Activity,* 80; for an early modern emphasis, see Woolf, *The Poor of Western Europe,* 18, 20, 24, 28–29; Nicholas Terpstra, "Apprenticeship in Social Welfare: From Confraternal Charity to Municipal Poor Relief in Early Modern Italy," *Sixteenth-Century Journal* 25, no. 1 (1994): 101–20, and the important book by Bronsilaw Geremek, *Poverty: A History* (Oxford, 1994). For concentrations on the eighteenth century, see Adams, *Bureaucrats and Beggars;* William J. Callahan, *Honor, Commerce, and Industry in Eighteenth-Century Spain* (Boston, 1972); Clark, *Politics of Conversion;* Christoph Sachsse and Florian Tennstedt, *Geschichte der Armenfürsorge in Deutschland* (Stuttgart, 1980); and Cathe-

rine Duprat, *"Pour l'amour de l'humanité"*: *Le temps des philanthropes; La philanthropie parisienne des Lumières à la monarchie de juillet* (Paris, 1993).

94. Haans Daalder, "Dutch Jews in a Segmented Society," in *Paths of Emancipation: Jews, States, and Citizenship,* ed. Pierre Birnbaum and Ira Katznelson (Princeton, 1995), 46; Florike Egmond, "Countours of Identity: Poor Ashkenazim in the Dutch Republic," *Dutch Jewish History* 3 (1993):205–25. In 1850, 55 percent of Ashkenazic and 63 percent of the Sephardic Jews in Amsterdam were receiving support from Jewish welfare institutions, whereas only 17 percent of Christians were counted among the poor. Stefi Hersch-Wenzel, "Minderheiten in der bürgerlichen Gesellschaft: Juden in Amsterdam, Frankfurt a.M. und Posen," in *Bürgertum im 19. Jahrhundert. Deutschland im europäischen Vergleich,* ed. Jürgen Kocka (Munich, 1988), 404.

95. Endelman, *The Jews of Georgian England,* 31–32.

96. Posener, "Social Life," 223; Zosa Szajkowski, *Poverty and Social Welfare among French Jews (1800–1880)* (New York, 1954), esp. 41–47; Paula Hyman, *The Emancipation of the Jews of Alsace* (New Haven, 1991), 40.

97. Glanz, *Geschichte des niederen jüdischen Volkes in Deutschland,* 138–40; Gerber, *Jud Süss,* 71.

98. For biographical information about Bundsschuh, see the *Lexikon verstorbener baierischer Schriftsteller des 18. und 19. Jahrhunderts* (Augsburg, 1825), 2/1: 19; and the *Allgemeine Deutsche Biographie* (Leipzig, 1876), 538–39.

99. Joseph Isaak, "Authentische Berechnung, was eine Judengemeinde von 26 Haushaltungen (im Reichsdorf Gochsheim) jährlich zum Unterhalt ihrer bettelnden Glaubensgenossen beytragen muss," *Journal von und für Franken,* 1. Band (Nürnberg, 1790), 435–46; idem, "Fortgesetzte Betrachtungen über die Betteljuden, mit einigen dahin abzweckenden Vorschlägen in vorzüglicher Hinsicht auf das Hochstift Wirzburg und die in demselbigen liegenden ritterschaftlichen Orte," *Journal von und für Franken,* 2. Band (Nürnberg, 1791), 606–19; idem, *Unmassgebliche Gedanken über Betteljuden und ihre bessere und zweckmässigere Versorgung* (Nürnberg, 1791).

100. Hermann Beck, "The Social Policies of Prussian Officials: The Bureaucracy in a New Light," *Journal of Modern History* 64 (June 1992): 275–77.

101. Rainer Erb and Werner Bergmann, *Die Nachtseite der Judenemanzipation* (Berlin, 1989), 67–68, 70–73, 80–86.

102. See the discussion in Erb, n. 25 supra; and Reinhard Rürup, "Die Emanzipation der Juden in Baden," in his *Emanzipation und Antisemitismus* (Göttingen, 1975), 58.

103. In both cases, the recipient, State Chancellor Karl August von Hardenburg, did not heed the petitions. Salo Baron, "Zur ostjüdischen Einwanderung in Preussen," *ZGJD* 3 (1931): 193–202.

104. Erb and Bergmann, *Nachtseite,* 108.

105. The evolution of this concept is traced in Gertrude Himmelfarb, *The Idea of Poverty: England in the Early Industrial Age* (New York, 1983), 492–93.

106. For Dohm, see Robert Liberles, "The Historical Context of Dohm's Treatise on the Jews," in *Das deutsche Judentum und der Liberalismus — German Jewry and Liberalism* (St. Augustin, 1986), 55. For Grégoire, see Necheles, *The*

Abbé Grégoire; and his *Enquiry Concerning the Intellectual and Moral Faculties, and Literature of Negroes* (Brooklyn, N.Y., 1810).

107. In his provocative book *The Savage in Judaism* (Bloomington, Ind., 1990), Howard Eilbert Schwartz compares seventeenth- and eighteenth-century discourse on "savage" New World cultures and Jewish society, but his focus is on views of the religious beliefs and practices of Jews and savages, not their socioeconomic structure.

108. Ronald Meek, *Social Science and the Ignoble Savage* (London, 1976).

109. Ibid., 89.

110. Cited in Roy Harvey Pearce, *Savagism and Civilization: A Study of the Indian and the American Mind* (Berkeley, 1988).

111. Lindenfeld, *Practical Imagination,* 153.

112. Meek, *Social Science and the Ignoble Savage,* 146; Pearce, *Savagism and Civilization,* 109.

113. For the Jewish case, see the discussion in chapter 3 below. For the Native American case, see Bernard W. Sheehan, *Seeds of Extinction: Jeffersonian Philanthropy and the American Indian* (Chapel Hill, 1973), 119–47; Robert J. Berkhofer, Jr., *The White Man's Indian: Images of the American Indian from Columbus to the Present* (New York, 1978), 134–37, 149.

114. For Clermont-Tonnere, see Paul Mendes-Flohr and Jehuda Reinharz, eds., *The Jew in the Modern World: A Documentary History* (New York, 1980), 104; for American policy, see Sheehan, *Seeds of Extinction;* the quote from the missionary is from Berkhofer, *The White Man's Indian,* 151.

115. Benedict Anderson, *Imagined Communities: Reflections on the Origin and Spread of Nationalism* (London, 1983), 21.

116. Jacob Toury, "Emanzipation und Judenkolonien"; Joachim S. Hohmann, *Geschichte der Ziegeunerverfolgung in Deutschland* (Frankfurt am Main, 1988), 43, 52.

117. Berkhofer, *The White Man's Indian,* 157–66.

118. Yerushalmi, "Assimilation and Racial Antisemitism."

119. Compare Grégoire, *Enquiry Concerning the . . . Negroes,* 89–91, 114–15, 127, with his *Essai sur la régénération des juifs,* esp. 71–99.

120. Harry Liebersohn, "Discovering Indigenous Nobility: Tocqueville, Chamisso, and Romantic Travel Writing," *American Historical Review* 99 (June 1994): 746–66.

121. In sixteenth-century Spain and Italy, raw and rural European regions such as Calabria and Sicily were known as "the Indies." Antony Pagden, *The Fall of Natural Man* (Cambridge, 1982), 97–98. In his essay "On Cannibals," Montaigne considered the lower social orders of France more alien to him than the Indians of Brazil. Stephen Greenblatt, *Marvelous Possessions: The Wonder of the New World* (Chicago, 1991), 149.

122. Felsenstein, *Anti-Semitic Stereotypes,* 187–214, esp. 203, 206.

123. For an excellent recent overview of the emancipation of European Jewry, see Birnbaum and Katznelson, *Paths of Emancipation.* Other valuable studies on Jewish emancipation in the German *Kulturbereich* include Reinhard Rürup, "The Tortuous and Thorny Path to Legal Equality: 'Jew Laws' and Emancipatory Legislation in Germany from the Late Eighteenth Century," *LBIYB* 31

(1986): 3–33; and, for Austria, Häusler, "Toleranz, Emanzipation, und Antisemitismus."

124. Hymann, *Alsace*, 17, 40–49; Monika Richarz, "Jewish Social Mobility in Germany during the Time of Emancipation (1790–1871)," *LBIYB* 20 (1975): 75–77; Steven Lowenstein, "The Pace of Modernization of German Jewry in the 19th Century," *LBIYB* 21 (1976): 49; Avraham Barkai, "Temurot ba-kalkalat yehudei Germaniyah bi-tekufat ha-ti'us," in *Yehudim ba-kalkalah,* ed. Nachum Gross (Jerusalem, 1985), 271–72; Toury, "Der Eintritt der Juden ins deutsche Bürgertum," 169–71, 224–32.

125. Bruer, *Geschichte der Juden in Preussen,* 245.

126. Ibid., 247.

127. Dan Segre, "The Emancipation of the Jews in Italy," in Birnbaum and Katznelson, *Paths of Emancipation,* 217.

128. Michael Graetz, *The Jews in Nineteenth-Century France: From the French Revolution to the Alliance Israélite Universelle* (Stanford, 1996), 148.

129. Rainer Erb, "Warum ist der Jude zum Ackerbürger nicht tauglich? Zur Geschichte eines antisemitischen Stereotyps," in Erb and Schmidt, *Antisemitismus und Jüdische Geschichte,* 107–8.

130. Robert Byrnes, *Antisemitism in Modern France* (New Brunswick, N.J., 1950), 114–21; Poliakov, *History of Antisemitism,* 3:341–43, 367–79; Graetz, *Jews in Nineteenth-Century France,* 112–16.

131. Paul Rose, *Revolutionary Antisemitism in Germany from Kant to Wagner* (Princeton, 1990). I agree with Rose on this point, although I disagree with his assertions about the uniqueness of nineteenth-century German antisemitism. For a taste of Viennese radical antisemitic vitriol, see the discussion of Eduard von Müller-Tellering, the Vienna correspondent of Karl Marx's *Neue Rhenische Zeitung,* in Wistrich, *The Jews of Vienna in the Age of Franz Joseph,* 35–36.

132. Julius Carlebach, *Karl Marx and the Radical Critique of Judaism* (London, 1978).

133. As Marx matured, the focus of his economic ruminations switched from high finance to industrial production, an area in which Jews did not feature prominently, but he remained contemptuous of Jews nonetheless. He came to see them not as embodying capitalism but as standing outside of and against it, allies of the agrarian aristocracy and not the progressive industrial bourgeoisie. See Daniel Gutwein, "Kapitalism, pariyah-kapitalism, u-mi'ut: ha-temurot be-teyoriah ha-yehudit shel Marx 'al reka' ha-diyun be-me'afyenei ha-kalkalah ha-yehudit," in *Dat ve-kalkalah: yahasei gomlin,* ed. Menachem Ben-Sasson (Jerusalem, 1995), 65–76.

134. J. B. Graser, *Das Judenthum und seine Reform* (Bayreuth, 1828), 62.

135. The article was reprinted in its entirety in *Der Orient* 9, nos. 48–52 (25 November 1848): 9, 16; (23 December 1848): 379–80, 394–96, 402–4, 410–11.

136. Hendrikje Kilian, *Die Jüdische Gemeinde in München 1813–1871. Eine Grosstadtgemeinde im Zeitalter der Emanzipation* (Munich, 1989), 65; James Harris, *The People Speak! Anti-Semitism and Emancipation in Nineteenth-Century Bavaria* (Ann Arbor, 1994), 24–25.

137. Stefan Rohrbacher and Michael Schmidt, *Judenbilder. Kulturgeschichte antijüdischer Mythen und antisemitischer Vorurteile* (Hamburg, 1991), 90.

138. Ibid., 66.

139. See the discussion of the Munich *Handelstand*'s opposition to Jewish competition in Kilian, *Die Jüdische Gemeinde in München 1813–1871*, 65, 73, 76, 79–80. Similar fears of Jewish economic ability were expressed in antiemancipation petitions throughout Bavaria at midcentury. The situation in western Germany was different; Rhenisch entrepreneurs during the *Vormärz* period were often appreciative of Jewish economic activity and supportive of Jewish emancipation. Compare Harris, *The People Speak!* 132–34, 177, and Shulamit S. Magnus, *Jewish Emancipation in a German City: Cologne, 1798–1871* (Stanford, Calif., 1997), 103–43.

140. Hertzberg, *French Enlightenment and the Jews*, 123, 127, 350–51; Roland Marx, "La régéneration économique des juifs d'Alsace," in *Les juifs et la révolution française*, ed. Bernhard Blumenkranz and Albert Soboul (Paris, 1976), 117; Jacques Godechot, "La révolution française et les juifs," in Blumenkranz and Soboul, *Les juifs*, 61–62; and Jay Berkovitz, *The Shaping of Jewish Identity in Nineteenth-Century France* (Detroit, 1989), 41–44.

141. Rainer Erb, " 'Jüdische Güterschlächterei' im Vormärz: Vom Nutzen des Stereotyps für wirtschaftliche Machtstrukturen, dargestellt an einem Westfälishen Gesetz von 1836," *International Review of Social History* 30 (1985): 312–41.

142. Zosa Szjakowski, "Jewish Participation in the Sale of National Property during the French Revolution" (1952), reprinted in *Jews and the French Revolutions of 1789, 1830, and 1848* (New York, 1970), 483, 496–97; Marx, "Régéneration économique," 111–12, 115.

143. Harris, *The People Speak!* 37.

144. Erb, "Güterschlächterei," 338–39.

145. McCagg, *A History of Habsburg Jews*, 78.

146. Ibid., 336–37; Berthold Altmann, "Jews and the Rise of Capitalism," *Jewish Social Studies* 5 (1943): 174; Rohrbacher and Schmidt, *Judenbilder*, 74, 109–11, 120.

147. Poliakov, *History of Antisemitism*, 3:277–92. The citation is from 283–84. Associations between Jews and Freemasonry were first made in France and Germany in pamphlet literature produced during the Revolution of 1848. Jacob Katz, *Jews and Freemasons in Europe, 1723–1939* (Cambridge, Mass, 1970), 148–59.

148. This point has been made by a number of scholars, including Poliakov, *History of Antisemitism*, 3:345–49, and Pierre Birnbaum, "Antisemitism and Anticapitalism in Modern France," in *The Jews in Modern France*, ed. Francis Malino and Bernard Wasserstein (Hanover, 1985), 214–23. The economic activity of the Rothschilds has been exhaustively chronicled. The most important studies are Egon Corti, *The Rise of the House of Rothschild* (London, 1928); idem, *The Reign of the House of Rothschild* (London, 1928); Bertrand Gille, *Histoire de la Maison Rothschild*, 2 vols. (Geneva, 1965–67); and Niall Ferguson, *The House of Rothschild: Money's Prophets, 1798–1848* (New York, 1998).

149. Jonathan Frankel, *The Damascus Affair: Ritual Murder, Politics, and the Jews in 1840* (Cambridge, 1997), 198–99, 367.

150. Cited in Carlebach, *Karl Marx and the Radical Critique of Judaism*, 152.

151. Jacob Katz, "Pra'ot 'Hep-Hep' shel shnat 1819 be-Germaniyah 'al reka'n ha-histori," *Tsiyon* 38 (1973): 62–115.

152. See e.g., John Klier, *Russia Gathers Her Jews: The Origins of the Jewish Question in Russia, 1772–1825* (De Kalb, Ill., 1986); Heinz-Dietrich Loewe, *The Tsars and the Jews* (Chur, Switzerland, 1993). I am grateful to Professor Klier for his discussions with me on this point.

153. Birnbaum, "Between Social and Political Assimilation," 113.

Chapter Two. The Origins of Jewish Political Economy, 1648–1848

1. These two questions are raised in Ezra Mendelsohn's provocative article "Should We Take Notice of Berthe Weill? Reflections on the Domain of Jewish History," *Jewish Social Studies*, n.s. 1, no. 1 (1994): 22–39.

2. David Weatherall, *David Ricardo: A Biography* (The Hague, 1976), 12–13, 27.

3. On Sonnenfels, see Keith Tribe, *Governing Economy: The Reformation of German Economic Discourse, 1750–1840* (Cambridge, 1988), chap. 4; William O. McCagg, Jr., *A History of Habsburg Jews, 1670–1918* (Bloomington, Ind., 1989), 24–25.

4. Salo Baron, "The Economic Views of Maimonides," in *Essays on Maimonides*, ed. Salo Baron (New York, 1941), 129, 131.

5. Baron, "Maimonides," 142, 145–46, 170–71, 175–88; Jacob Katz, "Hirhurim ʿal ha-yahas ben dat le-kalkalah," *Tarbitz* 62 (1991): 111; Hillel Levine, *Economic Origins of Antisemitism* (New Haven, 1991), 107–35.

6. Katz, "Hirhurim," 102–4. A somewhat different scenario proposes that the shift from an agricultural to an artisanal economy among the Jews occurred earlier, by the end of the first century B.C.E., and in Palestine. Thus Hillel's celebrated *prosbul*, which circumvents the Torah's legislation commanding the periodic remission of debts, is explained as the product of an increasingly complex economy with a growing demand for capital and long-term credit. This view, first proposed by Ludwig Blau in 1930, has most recently been argued by David Novak, "Economics and Justice: The Jewish Example," in *Jewish Social Ethics* (New York, 1992), 206–24.

7. There is, however, a stream of rabbinic thinking that interprets Deuteronomy 23:20–21 as prohibiting Jews from paying interest to fellow Jews and allowing them to pay interest to Gentile creditors. See Rashi ad loc.

8. Moses Maimonides, *Sefer ha-mitzvot*, Positive Commandment No. 198; *Mishneh Torah: sefer mishpatim: hilkhot loveh u-malveh*, S. 5; Baron, "Maimonides," 212, 226–28; Siegfried Stein, "Interest Taken by Jews from Gentiles: An Evaluation of Source Material (14th to 17th Centuries)," *Journal of Semitic Studies* 1 (1956): 147.

9. Rabbenu Tam: "The Mishnah can refer only to interest-free loans, but moneylending at interest is to be permitted because the borrower suffers a good deal from it." Gersonides: "It is a commandment to lend money to an alien on interest if he needs it, . . . because one should not benefit an idolater . . . and one should cause him such damage as is possible without deviating from righteousness." Cited in Stein, "Interest Taken by Jews from Gentiles," 26, 143.

10. Benjamin Nelson, *The Idea of Usury*, 2d ed. (Chicago, 1969), 4; and

J. Gilchrist, *The Church and Economic Activity in the Middle Ages* (New York, 1969), 70.

11. Cited in Nelson, *The Idea of Usury,* xvi.

12. Siegried Stein, "The Development of the Jewish Law on Interest from the Biblical Period to the Expulsion of the Jews from England," *Historia Judaica* 17 (1955): 18–29; idem, "Interest Taken by Jews from Gentiles"; Jacob Katz, *Exclusiveness and Tolerance: Jewish-Gentile Relations in Medieval and Modern Times* (New York, 1961), 24–36.

13. Weber summarized his concept of capitalism nicely in the "Vorbemerkung" to his *Gesammelte Aufsätze zur Religionssoziologie* (Tübingen, 1920), 1: 4–9.

14. Jürgen Habeas, *The Structural Transformation of the Public Sphere* (Cambridge, Mass., 1991), 79–80; David McNally, *Political Economy and the Rise of Capitalism: A Re-interpretation* (Berkeley, 1989).

15. Baron, "Maimonides," 141, 249.

16. Yitzhak Baer, "Ha-historiyah ha-hevratit ve-ha-datit shel ha-yehudim," *Tsiyon* 3, no. 4 (1938): 295. This piece was a critical review of Salo Baron's recently published three-volume *Social and Religious History of the Jews* (New York, 1937).

17. Mordechai Levin, "De'ot ve-helikhot kalkaliyot ba-masoret: Behinat torato shel Sombart le-or sifrut ha-musar ve-ha-zikhronot," *Tsiyon* 46 (1978): 235–63; idem, *'Erkhei hevrah ve-kalkalah ba-ideologiyah shel tekufat ha-haskalah* (Jerusalem, 1975), 13–38. See also Imanuel Etkes, *Rabbi Israel Salanter and the Musar Movement* (Philadelphia, 1993), 153–62.

18. Levin, "De'ot ve-helikhot kalkaliyot," 260–62.

19. Jacob Katz, *Tradition and Crisis: Jewish Society at the End of the Middle Ages* (New York, 1993), 49–50. This conservative economic thinking continued in parts of Germany throughout the eighteenth century; see Berthold Altmann, "Jews and the Rise of Capitalism," *Jewish Social Studies* 5 (1943): 176–77.

20. Katz, *Tradition and Crisis,* 49.

21. David B. Ruderman, *Jewish Thought and Scientific Discovery in Early Modern Europe* (New Haven, 1995), 10.

22. Robert Bonfil, *Jewish Life in Renaissance Italy* (Berkeley, 1994), 225.

23. On Germany, see the contribution by Mordechai Breuer to Michael Meyer, ed., *German-Jewish History in Modern Times.* Vol. 1: *Tradition and Enlightenment: 1600–1780* (New York, 1996), 254. The most recent analysis of Napoleonic Jewish policy is Paula Hyman, *The Jews in Modern France* (Berkeley, 1998), 37–52, esp. 40–44.

24. Azriel Shohat, *'Im hilufei ha-tekufot* (Jerusalem, 1960).

25. Marvin Lowenthal, trans., *The Memoirs of Glückel of Hameln* (New York, 1977), 7, 10, 14–15, 94, 258.

26. Ibid., 64–65, 108.

27. Ibid., 20–21, 175, 236.

28. The most recent work to make this observation is Natalie Zemon Davis's section on Glückel in *Women on the Margins: Three Seventeenth-Century Lives* (Cambridge, Mass., 1995), 5–62. See also Davis's article, "Religion and Capitalism Once Again: Jewish Merchant Culture in the Seventeenth Century," *Representations* 59 (1997): 56–84.

29. Compare Glückel's memoirs with Gene Brucker, ed., *Two Memoirs of*

Renaissance Florence: The Diaries of Buonaccorso Pitti and Gregorio Dati (New York, 1967). The memoirs of the mid-eighteenth-century Polish Jewish wine merchant Ber of Bolechow also convey the insecurities of the life of a merchant, especially a Jewish one. See M. Wischnitzer, trans. and ed., *The Memoirs of Ber of Bolechow* (New York, 1973), 157–63.

30. The most recent account of the origins of one such community is Miriam Bodian's excellent monograph, *Hebrews of the Portuguese Nation: Conversos and Community in Early Modern Amsterdam* (Bloomington, Ind., 1997).

31. See Baron, *Social and Religious History of the Jews*, 2:207–12; Yizhak Baer, *Galut* (New York, 1947), 93–105; Haim Hillel Ben-Sasson, "The Middle Ages," in *A History of the Jewish People*, ed. Shmuel Ettinger (Cambridge, Mass., 1976), 718–23.

32. See the following articles by Yosef Kaplan: "The Jewish Profile of the Spanish-Portuguese Community of London during the 17th Century," *Judaism* 41, no. 3 (1992): 229–40; "The Portuguese Community of Amsterdam in the 17th Century: Between Tradition and Change," in *Society and Community*, ed. A. Haim (Jerusalem, 1991), 142–71; and "Netivah shel ha-yahadut ha-sefaradit ha-ma'aravit el ha-modernah," *Pe'amim* 48 (1991): 85–103.

33. Joseph de la Vega, *Confusion de Confusiones 1688: Portions Descriptive of the Amsterdam Stock Exchange*, trans. and ed. Hermann Kelenbenz (Boston, 1957).

34. See Yosef Yerushalmi, *From Spanish Court to Italian Ghetto: Isaac Cardoso, a Study in 17th-Century Marranism and Jewish Apologetics* (Seattle, 1971), 191.

35. Kaplan, "The Portuguese Community of Amsterdam," 167.

36. De la Vega, *Confusion de Confusiones*, 42. Emphasis in original.

37. Jacob Samuel Wigler, "Isaac de Pinto: Sa Vie est ses Oeuvres" (Ph.D. dissertation, University of Amsterdam, 1923), 62–88; Herbert Bloom, *The Economic Activities of the Jews of Amsterdam in the Seventeenth and Eighteenth Centuries* (Williamsport, Pa., 1937); Hertzberg, *The French Enlightenment and the Jews* (Philadelphia, 1968), 143–153.

38. The information about de Pinto's pamphlet and its content comes from the research-in-progress of Daniel Strum, a graduate student at the Hebrew University of Jerusalem.

39. Morris M. Faierstein, ed. and trans., *The Libes Briv of Isaac Wetzlar* (Atlanta, 1996), esp. 66–67, 81. I am grateful to David Sorkin for bringing this source to my attention.

40. Moses Wessely, *Hinterlassene Schriften* (Berlin, 1798), xviii–xx.

41. Ibid., 64. See Montesquieu: "As specie is the sign of the value of merchandizes, paper is the sign of the value of specie; and when it is of the right sort, it represents this value in such a manner, that as to the effects produced by it, there is not the least difference." *The Spirit of Laws* (Cincinnati, 1886), 2:54.

42. Ibid., 65–86.

43. Joseph Shatzmiller, *Shylock Reconsidered: Jews, Moneylending, and Medieval Society* (Berkeley, 1990), 80–84.

44. Yerushalmi, *Isaac Cardoso*, 361.

45. Yosef Kaplan, " 'Olamo ha-dati shel soher benle'umi yehudi bi-tekufat ha-merkantilism: Mevuhat ha-'osher shel Avraham Yisra'el Pereira," in *Dat ve-kalkalah: yahasei gomlin*, ed. Menachem Ben-Sasson (Jerusalem, 1995), 238.

46. See the critical edition of *The Hope of Israel* and the long introduction therein by Henry Méchoulan and Gérard Nahon, trans. Richenda George (Oxford, 1987). On the readmission debate, see David S. Katz, *Philo-Semitism and the Readmission of the Jews to England, 1603–1655* (Oxford, 1982), passim; idem, *The Jews in the History of England, 1485–1850* (Oxford, 1994), chap. 3; Benjamin Braude, "Les contes persans de Menasseh Ben Israël: Polémique, apologétique et dissimulation à Amsterdam au XVIIe siècle," *Annales* 49, no. 5 (1994): 1107–38.

47. Compare Benjamin Ravid's close analysis of Luzzatto's *Discorso, Economics and Toleration in 17th-Century Venice: The Background and Context of the Discorso of Simone Luzzato* (Jerusalem, 1978); with Menasseh Ben Israel, *To His Highnesse the Lord Protector of the Commonwealth of England, Scotland, and Ireland: The Humble Addresses of Menasseh ben Israel* (London, 1655). The argument that Jewish merchants remain economically active long after their Gentile equivalents have sunk their capital into real estate crops up periodically throughout the eighteenth century; see M. Zalkind-Hourwitz, *Apologie des Juifs en réponse à la question: Est-il des moyens de rendre les Juifs plus heureux et plus utiles en France?* (Paris, 1789; rpt. 1968), 43. These assertions have been confirmed in recent scholarship on Jewish economic practices in modern Europe. See B. W. De Vries, *From Pedlars to Textile Barons: The Economic Development of a Jewish Minority Group in the Netherlands* (Amsterdam, 1989), 98, 139; and Peter Hanak, "Jews and the Modernization of Commerce in Hungary, 1760–1848," in *Jews in the Hungarian Economy, 1760–1945*, ed. Michael Silber (Jerusalem, 1992), 23–39.

48. Ravid, *Economics and Toleration*, 39–40, 55, 72.

49. *Humble Addresses*, 3.

50. On this point, see Ravid, *Economics and Toleration*, 50; Ravid invokes here the judgment of Salo Baron in his 1953 review of A. Z. Aescholy's 1951 edition of the *Discorso* (*Jewish Social Studies* 15: 313–14).

51. Hertzberg, *French Enlightenment and the Jews*, 53; see also 54–64, 314–17.

52. Lois Dubin, *The Port Jews of Hapsburg Trieste* (Stanford, Calif., 1999), 34.

53. Bodian, "Yazamim," 162, 166.

54. *Beleuchtung der Petition welche (angeblich) der bürgerliche Handelstand der königliche Haupt- und Residenz-Stadt München, in Betreff des Verfalls des Handels, und der Abstellung der denselben untertragenden Missbräuche und Beeinträchtigungen, unterm 13. April 1810 an die erste Stände-Versammlung des Königreiches Baiern vergeben hat. Von den jüdischen Glaubens-Gemeinde zu München* (Munich, 1819), 25.

55. Cited in Bodian, "Yazamim," 176n.

56. Among the most famous opponents of the guilds were Anne-Robert-Jacques Turgot, Louis XVI's finance minister, who abolished the guilds in 1776, and the Prussian state councillor Christian Wilhelm von Dohm, who, in addition to favoring improvement of the Jews' civil status in Prussia, favored abolition of the guilds, although he judged the latter project to be unfeasible. Hertzberg, *French Enlightenment and the Jews*, 70; Horst Moeller, "Aufklärung, Judenemanzipation und Staat. Ursprung und Wirkung von Dohms Schrift 'Über die bürgliche Verbesserung der Juden,'" *Deutsche Aufklärung und Judenemanzipation (TAJDG, Beiheft 3)* (Tel Aviv, 1979), 134.

57. Bodian, "Yazamim," 168–70.

58. Ibid., 175.

59. David Sorkin, *The Transformation of German Jewry* (Oxford, 1987), 59; Steven M. Lowenstein, *The Berlin Jewish Community: Enlightenment, Family and Crisis, 1770–1830* (New York, 1994), 35–36. On the origins of the "public" and of "public opinion" in Germany, see Habermas, *Structural Transformation of the Public Sphere,* esp. 72.

60. Lowenstein, *The Berlin Jewish Community,* 89–95; see also idem, "Jewish Upper Crust and Berlin Jewish Enlightenment: The Family of Daniel Itzig," in *From East and West: Jews in a Changing Europe, 1750–1870,* ed. David Sorkin and Francis Malino (New York, 1990), 188–89.

61. The historian Shmuel Feiner has recently proposed an alternative classificatory schema for the German Haskalah, one that is typological rather than generational. Feiner divides the *maskilim* between a group writing in German and tending toward Deism and a group writing only in Hebrew and not interested in religious reform. Moreover, Feiner has argued that the Haskalah in the German *Kulturbereich* was a diffuse movement, existing in several geographic centers in addition to Berlin. But, I would argue, the more radical of the German *maskilim* tended to be younger than the traditional ones, and systematic thinking about political economy came primarily from *maskilim* who had been shaped intellectually in Berlin. Shmuel Feiner, "Mendelssohn and 'Mendelssohn's Disciples.' A Re-examination," *LBIYB* 40 (1995): 135–67.

62. Max Birnbaum, "Moses Mendelssohn, der Seidenfabrikant," *Jüdisches Gemeindeblatt der jüdischen Gemeinde zu Berlin* 19 (1929): 452–54.

63. Reproduced in Otto Hintze, *Acta Borussica: Die Preussische Seideindustrie im 18. Jahrhundert* (Berlin, 1892), 2:326–31.

64. Moses Mendelssohn, "Vorrede" to Menasseh Ben Israel's *Rettung der Juden, Gesammelte Schriften* (Leipzig, 1843), 3:187–93.

65. E.g., David Fränkel in *Sulamith,* Year 1, vol. 2, no. 6 (1807), 364; Ludwig Philippson, "Moses Mendelssohn über Volkswirtschaft," *AZdJ* 47, no. 35 (28 August 1883): 563–65.

66. Mendelssohn, "Vorrede," 3:187.

67. Alexander Altmann, *Moses Mendelssohn* (Philadelphia, 1973), 449–51; David Sorkin, *Moses Mendelssohn and the Religious Enlightenment* (Berkeley, 1996), 112.

68. Feiner, "Mendelssohn," 157–64; Sorkin, "Mendelssohn," 110–11.

69. Israel Zinberg, *A History of Jewish Literature* (Cleveland, 1976), 8:59–74.

70. Sorkin, *Transformation of German Jewry,* 54–57.

71. Naphtali Herz Wessely, *Divrei shalom ve-emet* (Warsaw, 1886), 35.

72. Ibid., 295.

73. Ibid., 24–31.

74. Mordechai Eliav, *Ha-hinuch ha-yehudi be-Germaniyah biymei ha-haskalah ve-ha-emantsipatsiah* (Jerusalem, 1961), 43–51.

75. For a general history of *Ha-Me'asef,* see Tsemah Tsamriyon, *Ha-Me'asef: K'tav ha-'et ha-rishon be-'ivrit* (Tel Aviv, 1988).

76. Eliyahu Morpurgo, "Mikhtav mi-Eliyahu," *Ha-Me'asef,* Shevet 5546 (1786): 62–78. On Morpurgo, see Dubin, *Port Jews,* 15.

77. There was an occasional exception, such as a report from a Jewish school in Mantua, where pupils were instructed in "studies of the polity and its management [*finanzwisenshaftn*] and the history of trading peoples [*geshichte der handelden velker*]." Ha-Me'asef, Iyar 5349 (1789): 255–56.

78. Michael Meyer, *The Origins of the Modern Jew* (Detroit, 1972), 64–70; Lowenstein, *Berlin Jewish Community*, 69–73, 82.

79. Lazarus Bendavid, "Selbstbiographie," in *Bildnisse jetzlebender Berliner Gelehrten mit ihren Selbstbiographien. Erste Sammlung*, ed. S. Lowe (Berlin, 1806), 5–9, 13–16, 27, 35, 42–44, 48–49, 54.

80. Ibid., 70.

81. Jakob Guttmann, "Lazarus Bendavid," *MGWJ* 61 (1917): 182.

82. Lazarus Bendavid, "Über Geld und Geldeswerth," in *Aufsätze verschiedenen Inhaltes* (Berlin, 1800), 80–104. On the debate over paper money and its impact on Western philosophy and literature from the late eighteenth through the mid-nineteenth century, see Marc Shell, *Money, Language, and Thought* (Baltimore, 1982), esp. 5–8, 99–105.

83. Lazarus Bendavid, *Etwas zur Characteristick der Juden* (Leipzig, 1793), 12–20.

84. Ibid., 20–21.

85. Ibid., 22.

86. Ernst Fränkel, "David Friedländer und seine Zeit," *ZGJD* 6 (1935): 65–77; Hugo Rachel and Paul Wallich, *Berliner Grosskaufleute und Kapitalisten* (Berlin, 1938), 2:378.

87. David Friedländer, *Akten-stücke, die Reform der jüdischen Kolonien in den Preussischen Staaten betreffend* (Berlin, 1793), 75–76, 105–6.

88. Meyer, *Origins of the Modern Jew*, 60–61; Sorkin, *Transformation of German Jewry*, 76–77.

89. David Friedländer, *Briefe über die Moral des Handels* (Berlin, 1817; orig. pub. 1785).

90. McNally, *Political Economy and the Rise of Capitalism*, esp. 209–57.

91. See also Friedländer's comments about the immoral behavior of petty traders, Jewish and Christian alike, in *Über die Verbeserung der Israeliten im Königreich Polen* (Berlin, 1819), xlvi.

92. Wessely, *Divrei shalom ve-emet*, 16.

93. Naphtali Herz Wessely, *Wörte der Wahrheit und des Friedens an die gesammten jüdischen Nation* (Vienna, 1782), 16.

94. Friedländer, *Akten-stücke*, 131.

95. Meyer, *Origins of the Modern Jew*, 68.

96. Friedländer, *Akten-stücke*, 172–74; cf. discussions on 136–83 passim and 167–68.

97. Ibid., 139, 156, 158–62, 167–78, 178–79.

98. Herz Homberg, "Igeret el ro'ei seh pezurah yisrael . . . ," *Ha-Me'asef*, Nisan 5548 (1788): 227–36.

99. Herz Homberg, *Imrei Shefer* (Vienna, 5566), 293–94.

100. Herz Homberg, *Ben Jakir. Über Glaubenswahrheiten und Sittenlehren für die israelitische Jugend* (Vienna, 1814).

101. Herz Homberg, *Benei Zion. Ein Religiös-moralisches Lehrbuch für die Ju-*

gend israelitischer Nation (Vienna, 1812), 128–31. Cf. *The Republic of Plato,* trans. and ed. Francis MacDonald Cornford (New York, 1941), 57–58.

102. Majer Balaban, "Herz Homberg in Galizien," *Jahrbuch für jüdische Geschichte und Literatur* 19 (1916): 215–17.

103. The suggestion was not implemented due to the onset of the revolutionary and Napoleonic wars, along with the Hapsburg emperor Franz's fear of any sort of radicalism, including radical reform of Jewish life. Indeed, Homberg was expelled from Galicia in 1806, suspected of revolutionary activity because of his interest in taking part in the Paris Sanhedrin. Ibid., 206–14.

104. The legend was retold by the Austrian Jewish writer Karl Emil Franzos, and Franzos's rendering is cited in Balaban, "Herz Homberg in Galizien," 198.

105. See Imanuel Etkes, "Immanent Factors and External Influences in the Development of the Haskalah Movement in Russia," in *Toward Modernity: The European Jewish Model,* ed. Jacob Katz (New Brunswick, N.J., 1987), 13–32; and the fascinating monograph of David E. Fishman, *Russia's First Modern Jews: The Jews of Shklov* (New York, 1995).

106. Fishman, *Russia's First Modern Jews,* 84–91.

107. The text, "Likutei kelalim," is reproduced as an appendix in N. M. Gelber, "Mendel Lefin-Satnover ve-hatsa'otav le-tikun oreh hayim shel yehudei Polin bifnei ha-seim ha-gadol (1788–1792)," in *Abraham Weiss Jubilee Volume* (New York, 1964), 296.

108. Raphael Mahler, *Hasidism and the Jewish Enlightenment* (Philadelphia, 1985), 59.

109. Ibid. See also Mordechai Levin, *Erkhei hevrah he-kalkalah,* 150–52.

110. Dan Miron, *Bein hazon le-emet: Nitzanei ha-roman ha-'ivri ve-ha-yidi bame'ah ha-19* (Jerusalem, 1979), 208–13; Levin, *Erkhei hevrah ve-kalkalah,* 154, 158; Steven J. Zipperstein, "Haskalah, Cultural Change, and Nineteenth-Century Russian Jewry: A Reassessment," *Journal of Jewish Studies* 34 (1983): 201–3; Magdalena Opalski and Israel Bartal, *Poles and Jews: A Failed Brotherhood* (Hanover, N.H., 1992), 31–33; Israel Bartal, "Le-an halakh tseror ha-kesef? Ha-bikoret hamaskilit 'al hebeteihah ha-kalkaliyim shel ha-hasidut," in Ben-Sasson, *Dat vekalkalah: Yahasei gomlin,* 378.

111. Etkes, "Immanent Factors"; Israel Bartal, "Mordechai Aaron Günzburg: A Lithuanian Maskil Faces Modernity," in Malino and Sorkin, *From East and West,* 144–46. For a thorough analysis of the economic thinking of the eastern European *maskilim,* see Levin, *Erkhei hevrah ve-kalkalah,* 129–86.

112. See Max Wiener, "The Concept of Mission in Traditional and Modern Judaism," *YIVO Annual of Jewish Social Science* 2–3 (1947–48):9–24; Sorkin, *Transformation of German Jewry,* 103–4.

113. Paula Hyman, *The Emancipation of the Jews of Alsace* (New Haven, 1991), 109–11; see also Jay Berkovitz, *The Shaping of Jewish Identity in Nineteenth-Century France* (Detroit, 1989), 146.

114. Homberg, *Ben Jakir,* 96–100.

115. Joseph Salvador, *Loi de Moïse ou Système religieux et politique des Hébreux* (Paris, 1822), 112–71 passim, esp. 129; see also idem, *Histoire des Institutions de Moïse et du peuple hébreu* (Paris, 1828), 227–356 passim, esp. 292–93. For biographical studies of Salvador, see Hanoch Reinhold, "Yosef Salvador: Hayyav

ve-de'otav," *Tsiyon* 9 (1941): 109–41; and Paula Hyman, "Joseph Salvador: Proto-Zionist or Apologist for Assimilation?" *Jewish Social Studies* 34 (1972): 1–22.

116. "Die sociale Frage und das Judenthum," *AZdJ*, 10 July 1877, 437–40.

117. Werner Conze, "Vom 'Pöbel' zum 'Proletariat,' " in *Moderne deutsche Sozialgeschichte,* ed. Hans-Ulrich Wehler (Cologne, 1966), 111–36; Gertrude Himmelfarb, *The Idea of Poverty: England in the Early Industrial Age* (New York, 1983).

118. Uriel Tal, "German-Jewish Social Thought in the Mid-Nineteenth Century," in *Revolution and Evolution: 1848 in German-Jewish History,* ed. Werner Mosse, Arnold Paucker, and Reinhard Rürup (Tübingen, 1981), 299–328.

119. See the series of articles by Dr. med. P. Philippson (most likely Phöbus, Ludwig's brother, and a physician) in the *Literarisches und homiletisches Beiblatt* of the *Allgemeine Zeitung* 2 (1838), nos. 1, 2, 4, 6, 7, 8, 9, 10, 14, 15, 17, 18, 19, from 6 January through 7 July.

120. Reproduced in M. Kayserling, *Ludwig Philippson. Eine Biographie* (Leipzig, 1898), 152–54.

121. Ibid., 156–60. For a more recent biography of Philippson, see Johanna Philippson, "Ludwig Philippson und die Allgemeine Zeitung des Judentums," in Liebeschütz and Paucker, *Das Judentum in der Deutschen Umwelt,* 243–91.

122. *AZdJ* 9, nos. 11 and 12 (10 and 17 March 1845): 145–48, 161–63. For a general discussion of Philippson's social thought, see Tal, "German-Jewish Social Thought," 303–7.

123. *AZdJ*, 10 and 17 July 1848, 409–10, 425–26. For the role of agrarianism in German social thought during the *Vormärz,* see the discussion at the end of the next chapter.

124. Yosef Haim Yerushalmi, *Zakhor* (New York, 1989), 88.

125. Isaak Marcus Jost, *Geschichte der Israeliten seit der Zeit der Maccabäer bis auf unsere Tage* (Berlin, 1820–47), 5:23–30, 6:65–76.

126. Zecharias Frankel, "Über manches Polizeiliche des talmudischen Rechts," *MGWJ* 1 (1851): 246.

127. Ibid., 246, 253, 255, 258.

Chapter Three. The Origins of Modern Jewish Philanthropy, 1789–1860

1. Ephraim Frisch, *An Historical Survey of Jewish Philanthropy from the Earliest Times to the Nineteenth Century* (New York, 1924), 118. For a similar tone, see the early chapters to Boris Bogen, *Jewish Philanthropy* (New York, 1917). For a more recent example of an essentialist and celebratory account of Jewish charity, see the entry "Charity" in the *Encyclopedia Judaica,* in particular the section on medieval and modern charity by Isaac Levitats.

2. E.g., Maimonides, *Mishneh Torah, Matanot 'Aniyim* 8, 10: "The redemption of captives has precedence over providing for and clothing the poor, and there is no commandment as great as that of redeeming captives, for the captive is among the hungry, thirsty, and naked, and stands in mortal danger." For a

general discussion of this concept and its application, see Salo Baron, *The Jewish Community* (Philadelphia, 1942), 2:333–39.

3. The distinction between contextualist and comparative approaches to the study of modern Jewish history has been made by David Sorkin, "The Case for Comparison: Moses Mendelssohn and the Religious Enlightenment," *Modern Judaism* 14 (1994): 121–38. Sorkin's analysis appears to indicate the beginning of a historiographical paradigm shift away from the highly contextual character of Jewish social history and toward a rethinking of the boundaries between Jewish and Gentile culture. See David Biale, "Confessions of a Historian of Jewish Culture," *Jewish Social Studies*, n.s. 1, 40–51 (1994); and Amos Funkenstein, "The Dialectics of Assimilation," *Jewish Social Studies*, n.s. 1, 2, 1–14 (1995).

4. Frisch, *Historical Survey*, 137–64; Bogen, *Jewish Philanthropy*, 25; "Hevra Kaddisha," *Encyclopedia Judaica*, 8:442–46.

5. This practice was common among Jews and Gentiles alike. On this subject see Baron, *The Jewish Community*, 2:321–22, 329, 344–45; and Elimelech Horowitz, " 'Ve-yihiyu 'aniyim (hagunim) bnei beytekhah': Tsedakah, 'aniyim, u-fikuah hevrati be-kehilot yehudei Eyropah bein yemei ha-beinayim le-reshit ha-'et ha-hadashah," in *Dat ve-kalkalah: Yahasei gomlin*, ed. Menachem Ben-Sasson (Jerusalem, 1995), 209–31.

6. Johannis Buxtorf, *Synagoga Judaica noviter restaurata: Das ist: Erneuerte jüdische Synagog, oder Juden-Schul* (Frankfurt am Main, 1738; 1st ed. 1603), 667.

7. "Am ersten Tag ein Gast, am andern Tag ein Last, am dritten Tag ein Flüchtiger oder Stinckender." Ibid., 668–69. Benjamin Franklin's famous aphorism about fish and visitors stinking after three days is apparently a universal concept.

8. Horowitz, " 'Ve-yihiyu 'aniyim (hagunim) bnei beytekhah,' " 229; Baron, *The Jewish Community*, 2:322–24; Frisch, *Jewish Philanthropy*, 127–28.

9. Israel Bartal and Yosef Kaplan, " 'Aliyat 'aniyim mi-amsterdam le-Eretz Yisra'el," *Shalem* 6 (1992):175–93.

10. Frisch, *Jewish Philanthropy*, 127–28; Jacob Katz, *Exclusiveness and Tolerance: Jewish-Gentile Relations in Medieval and Modern Times* (New York, 1961), 160–61.

11. Yosef Kaplan, "The Portuguese Community in Seventeenth-Century Amsterdam and the Ashkenazic World," *Dutch Jewish History* 2 (1989): 29–30, 37.

12. Moses A. Shulvass, *From East to West: The Westward Migration of Jews from Eastern Europe during the Seventeenth and Eighteenth Centuries* (Detroit, 1971); see also Menachem Friedman, "Mikhtavei hamlatsah le-kavtsamim— 'Ktavim': Le-ba'yat ha-navadim be-Germaniyah ba-meah ha-yod-het," *Mikhael* 2 (1973): 34–51. For examples of harsh treatments by Jewish communities of the vagrant poor in early-eighteenth-century Germany, see Sylvie-Anne Goldberg, *Crossing the Jabbok: Illness and Death in Ashkenazi Judaism in Sixteenth- through Nineteenth-Century Prague* (Berkeley, 1969), 184, 186.

13. Hertzberg, *The French Enlightenment and the Jews* (Philadelphia, 1968), 155–57.

14. The language is from a document of 1639, cited in Kaplan, "The Portuguese Community," 30.

15. Ibid., 32–33.

16. Miriam Bodian, *Hebrews of the Portuguese Nation: Conversos and Community in Early Modern Amsterdam* (Bloomington, Ind., 1997), 140.

17. Todd M. Endelman, *The Jews of Georgian England, 1714–1830* (Philadelphia, 1979), 227–42.

18. Eugene C. Black, *The Social Politics of Anglo-Jewry, 1880–1920* (New York, 1988), 71–74.

19. David Cesarani, *The "Jewish Chronicle" and Anglo-Jewry, 1841–1991* (Cambridge, 1994), 23–24.

20. *JC,* 27 October 1854, 81–82; also 11 February 1859, 6–7.

21. *JC,* 25 September and 2 October 1857, 1156–57, 1166–67. See also Cesarani, *"Jewish Chronicle" and Anglo-Jewry,* 34–35.

22. On the origins of the Jewish workhouse, the occasional admission of Jews to parish workhouses, and the attempts by the London JBG to win special conditions for these unfortunates, see *JC,* 24 November 1871, 11–12; 1 December 1871, 7–9; 19 April 1872, 35; 6 December 1872, 496.

23. This point is made cursorily by Geoffrey Alderman, "English Jews or Jews of the English Persuasion? Reflections on the Emancipation of Anglo-Jewry," in *Paths of Emancipation: Jews, States, and Citizenship,* ed. Pierre Birnbaum and Ira Katznelson (Princeton, 1995), 140. It serves as a pillar of Rainer Liedtke's important monograph, *Jewish Welfare in Hamburg and Manchester, c. 1850–1914* (Oxford, 1998).

24. Cited in Cesarani, *"Jewish Chronicle" and Anglo-Jewry,* 35.

25. *JC,* 17 December 1847, 349. See also 22 January 1847, 69–71; 10 December 1847, 342–43.

26. Christine Piette, *Les Juifs de Paris (1808–1840)* (Québec, 1983), 29–32, 105. At the same time, and operating from similar motivations, the Dutch High Consistory favored banning the admission of foreign Jews into Holland. Jozeph Michman, *Dutch Jewry during the Emancipation Period: Gothic Turrets on a Corinthian Building* (Amsterdam, 1995), 147–49.

27. Beer Isaac Berr, *Réfléxions sur la régénération complète des juifs en France* (Paris, 1806), 13–15.

28. Ibid., 48, 71.

29. David Friedländer, *Akten-stücke, die Reform der jüdischen Kolonien in den Preussischen Staaten bettrefend* (Berlin, 1793), 147.

30. Steven M. Lowenstein, *The Berlin Jewish Community: Enlightenment, Family and Crisis, 1770–1830* (New York, 1994), 111–19. There was a similar contrast between harsh reformers and lenient traditionalists in Amsterdam during the Napoleonic period. Faced with demands to supply the French army with recruits, members of the radical "New Community" favored impressing poor Jewish children into service, whereas the traditionalists resisted these demands. Marco H. D. van Leeuwen, "Arme Amsterdamse joden en de strijd om hun integratie aan het begin van de negentiende eeuw," in *De Gelykstaat der Joden. Inburgering van een minderheid,* ed. Hetty Berg et al. (Amsterdam, 1996), 63–64.

31. *Der Orient,* 7 May 1844, 150. For another example of this type of writing about the Jewish poor, see the series of articles titled "Jüdisch-soziale Fragen," by an anonymous author from Aachen, in *AZdJ,* 19 February, 26 February, 5 March 1849, 110–13, 118–20, 133–35.

32. *AZdJ*, 30 March 1840, 322–24; 1 August 1840, 465–67; 15 August 1840, 475–77.

33. Claudia Prestel, "Zwischen Tradition und Moderne—Die Armenpolitik der Gemeinde zu Fürth (1826–70)," *TAJDG* 20 (1991): 135–62.

34. Hermann Beck, "The Social Policies of Prussian Officials: The Bureaucracy in a New Light," *Journal of Modern History* 64 (June 1992): 279.

35. On the Vienna Armenverein (later Armenanstalt), see Gerson Wolf, *Geschichte der Juden in Wien (1156–1876)* (Vienna, 1876), 146. On the Amsterdam Nederlands-Israelitisch Armbestuur, see van Leeuwen, "Arme Amsterdamse joden en de strijd om hun integratie."

36. *AZdJ*, 31 May 1838, 261–63.

37. Cash and in-kind benefits did not go down, however, but steadily increased. Arno Herzig, "Die Juden in Hamburg 1780–1860," in *Die Juden in Hamburg 1590 bis 1990*, ed. Arno Herzig (Hamburg, 1991), 64–65; Anke Richter, "Das Jüdische Armenwesen in Hamburg in der 1. Hälfte des 19. Jahrhunderts," in *Die Hamburger Juden in der Emanzipationsphase (1780–1870)*, ed. Peter Freimark and Arno Herzig (Hamburg, 1990), 234–54.

38. *Statuten des Vorschuss-Institut der Israelitischen Armen-Anstalt zu Hamburg* (Altona, 1819); Report of the Vorschuss-Institut dated March 1853, SAH JG 485a.

39. Jacob Toury, "Der Eintritt der Juden ins deutsche Bürgertum," in *Das Judentum in der Deutschen Umwelt, 1800–1850*, ed. Hans Liebeschütz and Arnold Paucker (Tübingen, 1977), 224 ff.; Henry Wasserman, "Jews, 'Bürgertum,' and 'Bürgerliche Gesellschaft' in a Liberal Era (1840–1880)" (Ph.D. dissertation, Hebrew University, 1979), 85–87; David Sorkin, *The Transformation of German Jewry* (Oxford, 1987), 114.

40. Christoph Sachsse and Florian Tennstedt, *Geschichte der Armenfürsorge in Deutschland* (Stuttgart, 1980), 214–22; Rolf Landwehr and Rüdiger Baron, eds., *Geschichte der Sozialarbeit. Hauptlinien ihrer Entwicklung im 19. und 20. Jahrhundert* (Weinheim-Basel, 1983), 22–26.

41. W. O. Shanahan, *German Protestants Face the Social Question* (South Bend, Ind., 1954), 81.

42. Friedländer, *Akten-stücke*, 71.

43. Hendrikje Kilian, *Die Jüdische Gemeinde in München 1813–1871. Eine Grossstadtgemeinde im Zeitalter der Emanzipation* (Munich, 1989), 168–69; Dieter Langewiesche, "Liberalismus und Judenemanzipation im 19. Jahrhundert," in *Juden in Deutschland. Emanzipation, Integration, Verfolgung, und Vernichtung. 25 Jahre Institut für die Geschichte der deutschen Juden*, ed. Peter Freimark, Alice Jankowksi, and Ina Lorenz (Hamburg, 1991), 156. Similar phenomena occurred in Amsterdam a half century earlier, when Dutch Jewry was emancipated: the Burgomeister favored continued communal autonomy in philanthropic matters lest 18,000 indigent Jews be thrown into the lap of Amsterdam's municipal poor care system. Michman, *Dutch Jewry*, 44, 116–17.

44. *AZdJ*, 6 March 1854, 115–16, reported that Prussian Jews were currently allowed access to general poor care in Prussia and paid for its upkeep. In Magdeburg, for example, the Jewish poor received public charity, and the city hospital was open to all. A retrospective piece, "Die jüdische Armenpflege," in *AZdJ*, 9 November 1875, 739–40, noted that for decades Jews in some

communities had enjoyed access to general charity, but in others, for example, Berlin, they did not. In 1858 the Munich Armenpflegschaftsrat claimed that Jews were not excluded in principle from receiving general poor care but that they did not need it, as only one Jew was currently receiving a regular monthly allowance from the city. Kilian, *Die Jüdische Gemeinde in München*, 143.

45. For London, see "On the Necessity of Erecting a Hospital for the German and Polish Communities of London," *Hebrew Review and Magazine of Rabbinical Literature* 2 (1835–36): 368. Thanks to Dr. Kenneth Wyman for this reference. On concern about Christian proselytism as one force behind the founding of the Paris Jewish hospital in 1836, see Piette, *Les juifs de Paris*, 33. For Vienna, see *NZ*, 25 October 1861, 91, featuring two items about Jewish children being converted or proselytized in Christian charitable institutions.

46. Liedtke, *Jewish Welfare in Hamburg and Manchester*, chap. 3. See also Helga Krohn, *Die Juden in Hamburg, 1848–1918* (Hamburg, 1974), 58–60; Ina Lorenz, "Zehn Jahre Kampf um das Hamburger System (1864–1873)," in *Die Hamburger Juden in der Emanzipationsphase 1780–1870*, ed. Peter Freimark and Arno Herzig (Hamburg, 1989), 50–51; idem, "Die jüdische Gemeinde Hamburg 1860–1943," in Herzig, *Die Juden in Hamburg*, 78.

47. *AZdJ*, 9 November 1875, 739–40.

48. Jacob Kellner, *Le-ma 'an Tsiyon: Ha-hit 'arvut ha-klal-yehudit bi-metsukat ha-yishuv, 1869–1882* (Jerusalem, 1977), 12–13.

49. The best source of information on the pre-Zionist Yishuv is Israel Bartal's collection of essays, *Galut ba-aretz* (Jerusalem, 1994).

50. Israel Bartal, " 'Tokhnit ha-hityashvut' mimei masa'o ha-sheni shel Montefiori le-Eretz Yisra'el (1839)," in Bartal, *Galut ba-aretz*, 100–160.

51. See Frankel in *MGWJ* 5 (1856): 161–62; for background, see Mordechai Eliav, *Erets Yisra'el ve-yishuvah ba-meah ha-yod-tet, 1777–1917* (Jerusalem, 1978), 232–33; and David Ellenson, *Rabbi Esriel Hildesheimer and the Creation of a Modern Jewish Orthodoxy* (Tuscaloosa, Ala., 1990), 110–13.

52. Zecharias Frankel, "Die gegenwärtige Lage der Juden in Palästina," *MGWJ* 3 (1854): 291.

53. Ibid.

54. Michael Graetz, *The Jews in Nineteenth-Century France: From the French Revolution to the Alliance Israélite Universelle* (Stanford, Calif., 1996), chap. 10.

55. Kellner, *Le-ma'an Tsiyon*, 12–13.

56. *AZdJ*, 10 and 17 May 1847, 293–96, 309–11.

57. There are few sustained analyses of the theory and practice of Jewish occupational restructuring. The penultimate chapter of Jacob Katz's *Out of the Ghetto: The Social Background of Jewish Emancipation, 1770–1870* (New York, 1973), provides a nice summary, as does Shmuel Almog, "Produktivizatsiyah, proletarizatsiyah, ve-'avoda 'ivrit," in *Temurot ba-historiyah ha-yehudit ha-hadashah: Kovets ma'amarim shai li-Shmuel Ettinger* (Jerusalem, 1985), 41–70. There is useful information in (Sucher Dov) Bernard Weinryb, *Der Kampf um die Berufsumschichtung* (Berlin, 1936). Less useful is Tamar Bermann's *Produktivierungsmythen und Antisemitismus* (Vienna, 1973).

58. James van Horn Melton, *Absolutism and the Eighteenth-Century Origins of Compulsory Schooling in Prussia and Austria* (Cambridge, 1988), 91–105, 109–44, 209–30.

59. Hertzberg, *French Enlightenment*, 70.

60. Shmuel Feiner, "Yizhak Euchel: Ha-'yazam' shel tenua 't ha-haskalah be-germaniyah," *Tsiyon* 52, no. 4 (1987): 448.

61. *Ha-Me'asef* 1789, 255–56; 1794, 73.

62. *Jedidja: eine religiöse, moralische, und pädagogische Zeitschrift* 1, no. 1 (1817): 6; Siegfried Stein, "Die Zeitschrift 'Sulamith,'" *ZGJD* 7 (1937): 212; Mordechai Eliav, *Ha-hinuch ha-yehudi be-Germaniyah biymei ha-haskalah ve-ha-emantsipatsiah* (Jerusalem, 1961), 77, 116, 167, 210–12.

63. *Beleuchtung der Petition welche (angeblich) der bürgerliche Handelstand der königl. Haupt- und Residenz-Stadt München, in Betreff des Verfalls des Handels, und der Abstellung der denselben untergrabenden Missbräuche und Beeinträchtigungen, unterm 13. April 1810 an die erste Stände-Versammlung des Königreiches Baiern übergeben hat. Von den jüdischen Glaubens-Gemeinde zu München* (Munich, 1819), 25–26.

64. Toury, "Eintritt der Juden ins deutsche Bürgertum," 235.

65. Michael Benedict Lessing, *Die Juden und die öffentliche Meinung im preussischen Staat* (Altona, 1833), 68–72, 133–36.

66. Ibid., 134–35.

67. Although the following analysis focuses on western and central Europe, these patterns of thought also characterized the *maskilim* of eastern Europe. See Mordechai Levin, *'Erkhei hevrah ve-kalkalah ba-ideologiyah shel tekufat ha-haskalah* (Jerusalem, 1975), 144–60; Raphael Mahler, *Hasidism and the Jewish Enlightenment* (Philadelphia, 1985), 60–61.

68. This argument has been made for Germany most recently by David Sorkin, "Religious Reforms and Secular Trends in German-Jewish Life: An Agenda for Research," *LBIYB* 40 (1995): 179; and for Prague by Hillel J. Kieval, "Caution's Progress: The Modernization of Jewish Life in Prague, 1780–1830," in *Toward Modernity: The European Jewish Model,* ed. Jacob Katz (New Brunswick, N.J., 1987), 89–90.

69. *Sulamith,* Year 1, vol. 1, no. 6 (1807): 359–64.

70. *Sulamith,* Year 2, vol. 2, no. 6 (1809): 413–20.

71. M. Zalkind-Hourwitz, *Apologie des Juifs en réponse à la question: Est-il des moyens de rendre les Juifs plus heureux et plus utiles en France?* (Paris, 1789; rpt. 1968), 41.

72. For the Metz society, see *AI,* 1847, 483–87; for Paris, see Lee Shai Weissbach, "The Jewish Elite and the Children of the Poor: Jewish Apprenticeship Programs in Nineteenth-Century France," *Association for Jewish Studies Review* 12, no. 1 (1987): 123–42.

73. *UI* 9 (1854): 421.

74. The story is related by Isidore Cahen in *AI,* 1858, 262–70.

75. *AI,* 1847, 485; 1869, 25–26.

76. *Der Orient,* 22 February, 29 February, 7 March 1840, 61–66, 68–71, 76–79.

77. Mendel Hess's sermon is reproduced in Mayer Kayserling, ed., *Bibliothek jüdischer Kanzelredner* (Breslau, 1885), 2. The citations are from 156–57; emphasis in original. For Herxheimer, see his "Aufforderung, unsere armen israelitischen Knaben auf alle Weise zur Erlernnung der Erwerbe, der Wissenschaften und des Ackerbaues zu unterstützen," in *Predigten und Gelegenheitsreden,* 2d ed. (Leipzig,

1857), 239. For biographical material on Herxheimer, see the series of articles by S. Salfeld in *Adolf Brüll's Populär-wissenschaftliche Monatsblätter zur Belehrung über das Judentum* 5, 1 February, 1 March, 1 April 1885.

78. Isaak Noah Mannheimer, "Die Würdigung der Kunst und des Handwerkes in Israel" (1834), in Mannheimer, *Gottesdienstliche Vorträge über der Wochenabschnitte des Jahres* (Vienna, 1835), 409–28; and *Die Gewerbsscheu in Israel in ihren Ursachen and Folgen* (Vienna, 1841). Similar sentiments came as well from the influential reformer Abraham Geiger of Breslau; see his *Nachgelassene Schriften*, ed. Ludwig Geiger (Berlin, 1875), 1: 375–76.

79. The sermon is reproduced in Ignaz Reich, ed., *Beth Lechem. Jahrbuch zur Beförderung des Ackerbaues, Handwerk und der Industrie unter den Israelitien Ungarns* (Pest, 1871), 1: 93–98.

80. Eliav, *Ha-hinuch ha-yehudi be-Germaniyah,* 116, 167, 174, 210–12, 280–87.

81. *AI*, 1847, 48–87; *AI*, 1852, 205–8; Hyman, *The Emancipation of the Jews of Alsace* (New Haven, 1991), 80, 113, 115, 151.

82. *Sulamith,* Year 5, vol. 1, no. 1 (1817): 59–62; *AZdJ*, 24 April 1838, 193; Michman, *Dutch Jewry,* 147–49.

83. German communities featuring Handwerkvereine included Darmstadt, Dresden, Dessau, Frankfurt am Main, Frankfurt an der Oder, Fürth, Giessen, Hamburg, Hannover, Hechingen, Karlsruhe, Lübeck, Lyssa, Mainz, Minden, Munich, Münster, Offenbach, Ostrowo, Schwerin, and Wahrendorf. There were at least two associations that operated throughout an entire German state: the Verein zur Verbesserung der bürgerlichen Verhältnisse der Juden in Baden and the Berlin-based Gesellschaft zur Verbreitung der Handwerke und des Ackerbaues unter den Juden im Preussischen Staate.

84. On Vienna, see *NZ*, 12 November 1878, 67–69; for Bohemia, see *Der Orient*, 17 September 1847; for Pest, see *Beth Lechem* 1 (1871): 198–203.

85. *Statuten des Israelitischen Gewerbe Verein in Hechingen* (Hechingen, 1839), Central Archive for the History of the Jewish People (CAHJP) TD/92.

86. *Der Orient,* 2 April 1847, 109–10; 30 April 1847, 141–43.

87. *Bericht über den Verein zur Beförderung von Handwerken unter den israelitischen Glaubensgenossen in Mecklenburg vom Jahren 1846 bis 1849.*

88. "Deutsche Schulanstalten zur besseren Ausbildung der hierländischen Juden," in *Zweite Zugabe des zweiten Jahrgangs der hebräischen Monatsschrift Der Sammler* (October 1785): 28–34. For the total enrollment for the Prague Normalschule in 1784, see Kieval, "Caution's Progress," 95.

89. Eliav, *Hinuch yehudi be-Germaniyah,* 273–77.

90. *Sulamith,* Year 3, vol. 2, no. 4 (1811): 245.

91. On the relationship among class, education, and gender in early-nineteenth-century bourgeois culture, see Catherine Hall, "The Early Formation of Victorian Domestic Ideology" (1992), reprinted in Robert Shoemaker and Mary Vincent, eds., *Gender and History in Western Europe* (London, 1998), 193.

92. For France, compare Weissbach, "The Jewish Elite and the Children of the Poor," with his *"Oeuvre Industrielle, Oeuvre Morale*: The Sociétés de Patronage of Nineteenth-Century France," *French Historical Studies* 15 (1987): 99–120. For Germany, see Wolfgang Hardtwig, "Strukturmerkmale und Entwicklungstendenzen des Vereinswesens in Deutschland, 1789–1848," in *Vereinswesen und*

bürgerliche Gesellschaft in Deutschland, ed. Otto Dann (Munich, 1984), 21–22. (The German societies discussed by Hardtwig did not train apprentice craftsmen so much as develop savings banks, sick funds, and continuing education programs for established artisans.)

93. We must draw a distinction here between proposals for the agricultural colonization of Jews, which fit within the frameworks of cameralism and Jewish civil improvement, and calls made in late-eighteenth- and early-nineteenth-century Germany for "Jewish colonies." In the early 1780s calls for special Jewish colonies in isolated areas had cameralist and pedagogical goals in mind. But later in the decade, and over the next thirty years, the "Jewish colony" increasingly became an antisemitic fantasy, a vehicle for the expulsion of the Jews from their native lands. See Jacob Toury, "Emanzipation und Judenkolonien in der öffentlichen Meinung Deutschland (1775–1819)," *TAJDG* 11 (1982): 17–53.

94. Weinryb, *Der Kampf um die Berufsumschichtung,* 15.

95. Julius Landesberger, "Jüdische Ackerwirthe zu südpreussischer Zeit," *Historische Monatsblätter für die Provinz Posen* 1, no. 12 (December 1900): 177–83.

96. Joseph Karniel, *Die Toleranzpolitik Kaiser Joseph II* (Gerlingen, 1985), 469–72.

97. These attempts contrast unfavorably with the agricultural colonization of some sixty thousand Jews in Russia, both in the Pale of Settlement and in the recently acquired southern territories, between 1804 and 1860. Governmental attitudes toward the project were conflicted, and Jewish community leaders were critical of a program that was paid for by taxes imposed on the Jews themselves and that, by taking able-bodied men away from the community, decreased the tax base. But the desperate economic circumstances of Russian Jewry, suffering from severe residential and occupational restrictions, fueled the movement of a considerable number of Jews to the soil. Levin, *'Erkhei hevrah ve-kalkalah,* chap. 5 passim.

98. On Breslau, see *Der Orient,* 24 September 1847, 312. For Werth's biography, see the obituary in *AI,* 1877, 661–62. His efforts to found the school are reported in the *AI* of 1844, 399–403, and 1869, 49–54, 205–6.

99. Jacques Weill in *AI,* 1869, 25–28. See David H. Pinkney, *Napoléon III and the Rebuilding of Paris* (Princeton, 1958), 154; Rachel Fuchs, *Abandoned Children: Foundlings and Child Welfare in Nineteenth-Century France* (Albany, N.Y., 1984), 48, 256; Colin Heywood, *Childhood in Nineteenth-Century France* (Cambridge, 1988), passim.

100. Malcom Chase, *The People's Farm: English Radical Agrarianism, 1775–1840* (Oxford, 1988).

101. *AI,* 1844, 399–403; 1869, 1023–26; 1869, 25–28, 49–54, 87–90, 115–19, 205–6; 1870, 48.

102. *Der Orient,* 4 June 1846, 173–75; 11 June 1848, 185; 3 September 1846, 278–79; 24 September 1846, 304–5; 17 December 1846, 398–99.

103. Lessing, *Juden und die öffentliche Meinung,* 137.

104. *Sulamith,* Year 1, vol. 1, no. 2 (1807): 110–16.

105. *Sulamith,* Year 2, vol. 1, no. 5 (1808): 335–41.

106. *AZdJ,* 10 October 1837, 326–27.

107. Compare Julianna Puskas, "Jewish Leaseholders in the Course of Agricultural Development in Hungary, 1850–1930," in *Jews in the Hungarian Economy, 1760–1945,* ed. Michael Silber (Jerusalem, 1992), 106–23, with *Beth Lechem* 1 (1871): 118–31.

108. *Der Orient,* 23 and 30 July 1846; 6 August 1846, 235–36, 243–44, 251–52.

109. *Der Orient,* 29 July 1848, 246–47.

110. Berliner's Orthodox antagonist employed the language of economic antisemitism against the estate owner: "It is a tremendous error to believe that one can acquire knowledge and insight, like Mammon, through blind fortune or huckstering; all the less can Judaism, like an estate, be coolly dismembered, to gain thereby a nice piece of it [for oneself]." *Der Orient* 6 July 1845, 228–29.

111. *AZdJ,* 19 February 1849, 110–13.

112. M. Wischnitzer, trans. and ed., *The Memoirs of Ber of Bolechow* (New York, 1973), 33.

113. Jersch-Wenzel, "Minderheiten in der bürgerlichen Gesellschaft," 407. On Posen Jewry's long-standing crafts tradition, see Toury, "Eintritt der Juden ins deutsche Bürgertum," 145–46, 215–16.

114. *Statuten des Vereins zur Heranbildung jüdischer Handwerker in Ostrowo* (1855), ALBINY, Abraham Orlewicz Papers, AR-C 1228-/38; "Handwerk und Ackerbau unter den Juden in Preussen," *AZdJ,* 26 January 1900, 44–45; Jacob Toury, "Die jüdische Schneider Hamburgs, 1848–54," *TAJDG* 1 (1972): 101–18.

115. Bruer, *Geschichte der Juden in Preussen,* 354.

116. On the legislation connecting the right of residence with occupational change in Baden, see Reinhard Rürup, "Die Emanzipation der Juden in Baden," in *Emanzipation und Antisemitismus* (Göttingen, 1975), 46–49. For Bavaria, see Jacob Toury, "Manual Labour and Emigration — Records from Some Bavarian Districts, 1830–1854," *LBIYB* 16 (1971): 45–62.

117. Kilian, *Die Jüdische Gemeinde in München,* 8.

118. Reinhard Rürup, "Emancipation and Bourgeois Society," *LBIYB* 14 (1969): 81–82; Monika Richarz, "Jewish Social Mobility in Germany during the Time of Emancipation (1790–1871)," *LBIYB* 20 (1975): 69–77; James Harris, *The People Speak! Anti-Semitism and Emancipation in Nineteenth-Century Bavaria* (Ann Arbor, 1994), 33.

119. *Der Orient,* 19 February 1845, in the "Personalchronik und Miscellen" column.

120. Hamburg during the 1840s was an exception; see Toury, "Die jüdische Schneider Hamburgs," 101–4.

121. Toury, "Manual Labor and Emigration."

122. Michman, *Dutch Jewry,* 2–3, 32, 35.

123. Gerson Wolf, *Joseph Wertheimer. Ein Lebens- und Zeitbuch* (Vienna, 1868), 36, 106; Wolf, *Geschichte der Juden in Wien,* 143. Wertheimer was a remarkable figure whose philanthropic activity extended far beyond the Jewish community. A pioneer in early childhood education, he translated and composed original works on the subject and in 1828 founded the first kindergarten (Kinderbewahranstalt) in the Hapsburg Empire. He established one in Vienna in 1830 and a Jewish kindergarten in 1843. Wolf, *Wertheimer,* 30–36.

124. Wolf, *Wertheimer*, 105.

125. On agriculture, see John G. Gagliardo, *From Pariah to Patriot: The Changing Image of the German Peasant, 1770–1840* (Lexington, 1969), 210 ff.; on crafts, see Shulamit Volkov, *The Rise of Popular Antimodernism in Germany* (Princeton, 1978), 33–35.

126. On Alsace, see Roland Marx, "Régénération économique des juifs d'Alsace," in *Les juifs et la Révolution Française,* ed. Bernhard Blumenkranz and Albert Soboul (Paris, 1976), 112; and Hyman, *Emancipation of the Jews of Alsace,* 33, 37, 39–40, 135–36. On Germany, see Steven M. Lowenstein, "The Pace of Modernization of German Jewry in the 19th Century," *LBIYB* 21 (1976): 49, 51; Toury, "Eintritt der Juden ins deutsche Bürgertum," 224 ff.; Richarz, "Jewish Social Mobility"; and Sorkin, *Transformation of German Jewry,* 107–11.

127. *AZdJ* 13, no. 9 (26 February 1849): 118–20.

128. Harris, *The People Speak!* 36.

129. Richter, "Das jüdische Armenwesen in Hamburg," 245.

130. Kilian, *Die jüdische Gemeinde in München,* 8, 13.

131. Gagliardo, *From Pariah to Patriot.*

132. James Sheehan, *German Liberalism in the Nineteenth Century* (Chicago, 1978).

133. Sorkin, "Religious Reforms," 174.

134. Fritz Baer, "Der Ursprung der Chewra," *Zeitschrift für jüdische Wohlfahrtspflege* 1 (1929): 245.

Chapter Four. *Homo economicus judaicus* and the Spirit of Capitalism, 1848–1914

1. Hubert M. Blalock, Jr., *Toward a Theory of Minority-Group Relations* (New York, 1967), 210. See also Howard E. Aldrich and Roger Waldinger, "Ethnicity and Entrepreneurship," *Annual Review of Sociology* 16 (1990): 132.

2. Marsha Rozenblit, *The Jews of Vienna, 1867–1914: Assimilation and Identity* (Albany, N.Y., 1983); Calvin Goldscheider and Allan Zuckerman, *The Transformation of the Jews* (Chicago, 1984), esp. 95; Arthur Hertzberg, *The Jews in America* (New York, 1997), 125–26.

3. Good sources on the economic status of nineteenth-century Russian Jewry are Michael Stanislawski, *Tsar Nicholas I and the Jews, 1825–55* (Philadelphia, 1983); Heinz-Dietrich Loewe, *The Tsars and the Jews* (Chur, Switzerland, 1993); and John Klier, *Imperial Russia's Jewish Question, 1855–1881* (Cambridge, 1995).

4. William O. McCagg, Jr., *A History of Habsburg Jews, 1670–1918* (Bloomington, Ind., 1989), 105–39.

5. Paula Hyman, *The Emancipation of the Jews of Alsace* (New Haven, 1991), 37–40, 115–21; Monika Richarz, "Jewish Social Mobility in Germany during the Time of Emancipation (1790–1871)," *LBIYB* 20 (1975): 69–77; Steven M. Lowenstein, "The Pace of Modernization of German Jewry in the 19th Century," *LBIYB* 21 (1976): 41–56; idem, "The Rural Community and the Urbanization of German Jewry," *Central European History* 13, no. 3 (1980): 218–35. For the most recent survey of German Jewish economic life over the period 1848–71, see

Michael Brenner's contribution to *German-Jewish History in Modern Times,* ed. Michael Meyer (New York, 1997), 2: esp. 301–8.

6. David Landes, "The Jewish Merchant," *LBIYB* 19 (1974): 17.

7. In Germany over the period 1879–89, 17 percent of the holders of this honorific title were Jews, as were 31 percent of those who held the even more distinguished title Geheimkommerzienrat (privy counselor). Werner Mosse, *The German Jewish Economic Elite: A Socio-Cultural Profile* (Oxford, 1987), 84. In 1909 30 percent of the Kommerzienräte in Cologne were Jews; in Frankfurt am Main, the figure was 36 percent. Hansjoachim Hennig, "Soziales Verhalten jüdischer Unternehmer in Frankfurt und Köln zwischen 1860 und 1933," in *Jüdische Unternehmer in Deutschland im 19. und 20. Jahrhundert,* ed. Werner Mosse and Hans Pohl (Stuttgart, 1992), 260.

8. Pierre Birnbaum, "Le role limité des juifs dans l'industrialisation de la societé française," in *Les juifs et l'économique: Miroirs et mirages,* ed. Chantal Benayoun, Alain Medam, and Pierre-Jacques Rojtman (Paris, 1992), 163–77; Michael Graetz, *The Jews in Nineteenth-Century France: From the French Revolution to the Alliance Israélite Universelle* (Stanford, Calif., 1996), 156–62.

9. Information supplied by Hans Meyen, director of the Dresdner Bank, Frankfurt, via letter of 24 August 1992 to Frederick Rose of Toronto.

10. Werner Mosse, "Die Juden in Wirtschaft und Gesellschaft," in *Juden im Wilhelmischen Deutschland, 1890–1914,* ed. Werner Mosse and Arnold Paucker (Tübingen, 1976), 77; idem, *Jews in the German Economy: The German-Jewish Economic Elite, 1820–1935* (Oxford, 1987), 8; McCagg, *Habsburg Jews,* 196.

11. Stanley D. Chapman, "Merchants and Bankers," in *Second Chance: Two Centuries of German-speaking Jews in the United Kingdom,* ed. Werner Mosse et al. (Tübingen, 1991), 336–46; and Harold Pollins, "German Jews in British Industry," in Mosse et al., *Second Chance,* 362–77.

12. Paula Weiner-Odenheimer, "Die Berufe der Juden in München," *ZDSJ* 11 (1915): 92.

13. Avraham Barkai, "Temurot ba-kalkalat yehudei Germaniyah bi-tekufat ha-ti'us," in *Yehudim ba-kalkalah,* ed. Nachum Gross (Jerusalem, 1985), 267–81; idem, *Jüdische Minderheit und Industrialisierung. Demographic, Berufe, und Einkommen der Juden in Westdeutschland, 1850–1914* (Tübingen, 1988).

14. Barkai, *Jüdische Minderheit und Industrialisierung,* 4.

15. For Galicia, see Saul Laundau, "Die Juden als Gross-Landwirthe," *JP,* 11 January 1899, 17–18; and Moses Isler, *Rückkehr der Juden zur Landwirtschaft. Beitrag zu der Geschichte der landwirtschaftlichen Kolonisation der Juden in verschiedener Länder* (Basel, 1929), 52–56. For Hungary, see Julianna Puskas, "Jewish Leaseholders in the Course of Agricultural Development in Hungary, 1850–1930," in *Jews in the Hungarian Economy, 1760–1945,* ed. Michael Silber (Jerusalem, 1992), 112.

16. Silber, *Jews in the Hungarian Economy,* 19.

17. Jakob Segall, *Die beruflichen und soziale Verhältnisse der Juden in Deutschland* (Berlin, 1912), 30, 33; Simon Kuznets, "Economic Structure and Life of the Jews," in *The Jews: Their History, Culture, and Religion,* ed. Louis Finkelstein (New York, 1960), 2: 1606, 1609, 1628–30; Yehuda Don, "Patterns of Jewish Economic Behavior in Central Europe in the Twentieth Century," in Silber, *Jews in the Hungarian Economy,* 258.

18. Marsha Rozenblit, "Jewish Assimilation in Hapsburg Vienna," in *Assimilation and Community: The Jews in Nineteenth-Century Europe,* ed. Jonathan Frankel and Steven J. Zipperstein (Cambridge, 1992), 235.

19. This figure is abstracted from statistical tables in Weiner-Odenheimer, "Die Berufe der Juden in München," 93.

20. *IF,* 6 February 1908, 1–2; 13 February 1908, 4; 5 March 1908, 3–4; Segall, *Berufliche und soziale Verhältnisse,* 30.

21. Pierre Birnbaum, *The Jews of the Republic: A Political History of State Jews in France from Gambetta to Vichy* (Stanford, Calif., 1996); Ernest Hamburger, "Jews in Public Service under the German Monarchy," *LBIYB* 9 (1964): 206–38, esp. 234; idem, *Juden im öffentlichen Leben Deutschlands* (Tübingen, 1968), 63–65; Rozenblit, "Jewish Assimilation in Hapsburg Vienna."

22. Rozenblit, *Jews of Vienna,* 63–69.

23. *IF,* 5 March 1908, 3–4; 28 May 1908, 1–2; 7 March 1912, 9; 24 October 1912, 4; 7 November 1912, 6; 30 July 1914, 6.

24. Jakob Lestschinsky, *Das jüdische Volk im neuen Europa* (Prague, 1934), 93; idem, *Das wirtschaftliche Schicksal des deutschen Judentums* (Berlin, 1932), 103; Arthur Ruppin, *The Jew in the Modern World* (London, 1934), 183; Segal, *Berufliche und soziale Verhältnisse,* 27, 30, 44–57.

25. Norbert Kampe, "Jews and Antisemitism in Universities in Imperial Germany (I)," *LBIYB* 30 (1985): 368–73; Barkai, *Jüdische Minderheit und Industrialisierung,* 49–51; John Efron, *Defenders of the Race: Jewish Doctors and Race Science in Fin-de-Siècle Europe* (New Haven, 1994), 30–31.

26. Till van Rahden, "Mingling, Marrying, and Distancing: Jewish Integration in Wilhelmian Breslau and Its Erosian in Early Weimar Germany," in *Jüdisches Leben in der Weimarer Republik/Jews in the Weimar Republic,* ed. Wolfgang Benz, Arnold Paucker, and Peter Pulzer (Tübingen, 1998), 201–3; idem, "Die Grenze vor Ort—Einbürgerung und Ausweisung ausländischer Juden in Breslau 1860–1918," *TAJDG* 27 (1998): 50–51. See also Jack Wertheimer, *Unwelcome Strangers: East European Jews in Imperial Germany* (New York, 1987), 191.

27. Nancy L. Green, "The Modern Jewish Diaspora: East European Jews in New York, London, and Paris," in *Comparing Jewish Societies,* ed. Todd Endelman (Ann Arbor, 1997), table on 127. See also David Feldman, *Englishmen and Jews: Social Relations and Political Culture, 1840–1914* (New Haven, 1994), 164–65.

28. Segall, *Berufliche und soziale Verhältnisse,* 44; Jacob Toury, "Ostjüdische Handarbeiter in Deutschland in 1914," *BLBI* 6 (1963): 81–91.

29. Stefi Jersch-Wenzel, "Minderheiten in der bürgerlichen Gesellschaft: Juden in Amsterdam, Frankfurt und Posen," in *Bürgertum im 19. Jahrhundert. Deutschland im europäischen Vergleich,* ed. Jürgen Kocka (Munich, 1988), 406; Marie-Elisabeth Hilger, "Probleme Jüdischer Industriearbeiter in Deutschland," in *Juden in Deutschland. Emanzipation, Integration, Verfolugung und Vernichtung. 25 Jahre Institut für die Geschichte der deutschen Juden, Hamburg,* ed. Peter Freimark, Alice Jankowksi, and Ina Lorenz (Hamburg, 1991), 304–25.

30. Eugene C. Black, *The Social Politics of Anglo-Jewry, 1880–1920* (New York, 1988), 200–201; Feldman, *Englishmen and Jews,* 215–26, 245–47. On the difference between the German Jewish laboring classes and an industrial proletariat, see Hilger, "Probleme," 305.

31. *JC,* 21 February 1879, 6; see also *JC,* 24 March 1848, 473–75. David Feldman denies that cultural factors played a significant role in the immigrants' concentration in small-scale workshop production or their preference for individual advancement through independent entrepreneurship over workplace combination. He looks instead to antisemitism, which kept Jews out of heavily unionized workplaces such as dockyards and construction sites, and the nature of sweatshop textile production, whose small scale and low capital requirements encouraged laborers to engage in "penny capitalism" and strike out on their own. This may indeed be so. But there is nonetheless great significance in the power and pervasiveness of the notion that Jewish laborers were distinct from their Gentile counterparts and that they had unusually high ambition. This notion was popular among Jews no less than Gentiles, and although the latter frequently gave it an antisemitic twist, Jews employed the argument as a heuristic tool, a means of accounting for a great range of phenomena, from the rapid mobility of Jewish immigrants in western Europe or North America to the failure of the early Zionist movement to create a docile and productive Jewish peasantry.

32. Kuznets, "Economic Structure and Life of the Jews," 1600; D. Stanley Eitzen, "Two Minorities: The Jews of Poland and the Chinese of the Philippines," *Jewish Journal of Sociology* 10, no. 2 (December 1968): 221–40; Nachum Gross, "Entrepreneurship of Religious and Ethnic Minorities," in Mosse and Pohl, *Jüdische Unternehmer in Deutschland,* 11–23.

33. This point has been made most elegantly and powerfully by Shulamit Volkov; see "Jüdisches Assimilation und jüdisches Eigenart im Deutschen Kaiserreich," and "Soziale Ursachen des jüdischen Erfolgs in der Wissenschaft," in her collected essays, *Jüdisches Leben und Antisemitismus im 19. Jahrhundert* (Munich, 1990), 131–45, 146–65. See also the review of literature on this subject by Paula Hyman, "The Dynamics of Social History," *Studies in Contemporary Jewry* 10 (1994): 93–111.

34. Anthony Smith, *The Ethnic Origins of Nations* (Cambridge, Mass., 1986).

35. Adolph Jellinek, *Der jüdische Stamm: Ethnographische Studien* (Vienna, 1869), 5, 8, 46–47, 48–64, 194–98.

36. Elkar Weimann, sermon of 6 March 1871, reprinted in Meyer Kayserling, *Bibliothek Jüdischer Kanzelredner* (Breslau, 1885), 269; Friedrich Wachtel, *Das Judenthum und seine Aufgabe im neuen deutschen Reich* (Leipzig, 1871); Moritz Lazarus, "Was heisst National?" in *Treu und Frei: Gesammelte Reden und Vorträge über Juden und Judenthum* (Leipzig, 1887), 76–77. The organization referred to by Wachtel was the Deutsch-Israelitischer Gemeindebund, founded in 1869. For yet another statement relating the diversity of German Stämme to Jewish collective distinctiveness, see Marcus Hirsch, *Kulturdefizit am Ende des 19. Jahrhunderts* (Frankfurt am Main, 1893), 98–99.

37. Michael Brenner, *The Renaissance of Jewish Culture in Weimar Germany* (New Haven, 1996), 37, 39–42; Avraham Barkai, "Between Deutschtum and Judentum: Ideological Controversies inside the Centralverein," in *In Search of Jewish Community: Jewish Identities in Germany and Austria, 1918–1933,* ed. Michael Brenner and Derek J. Penslar (Bloomington, Ind., 1998), 78, 81; and Marsha Rozenblit, "Jewish Ethnicity in a New Nation-State: The Crisis of Identity in the Austrian Republic," in Brenner and Penslar, *In Search of Jewish Community,* 144.

38. Cited in Celia Applegate, "The Mediated Nation: Regions, Readers, and the German Past," discussion paper at the conference "Memory, Democracy, and the Mediated Nation: Political Culture and Regional Identities in Germany, 1848–1998," University of Toronto, 18–20 September 1998; conference volume, edited by James Retallack, forthcoming from the University of Michigan Press.

39. *NZ*, 1 December 1871, 567–69.

40. George Mosse, *German Jews beyond Judaism* (Bloomington, Ind., 1985).

41. For a lucid discussion of the first of these concepts, see Amos Funkenstein, "Zionism, Science, and History," in *Perceptions of Jewish History* (Berkeley, 1993), 344–47.

42. Judith R. Walkowitz, *City of Dreadful Delight: Narratives of Sexual Danger in Late-Victorian London* (Chicago, 1992), 203–4.

43. *Der Orient*, 16 April 1844, 123; 17 December 1845, 408; Lucien Wolf in *JC*, 16 April 1897; Toury, "Eintritt," 162.

44. On the period before 1848, see Stefi Jersch-Wenzel, *Jüdische Bürger und Kommunale Selbstverwaltung in Preussischen Städten 1808–1848* (Berlin, 1967). For the later period, see Mosse, *German-Jewish Economic Elite*, 215–26; Peter Pulzer, *Jews and the German State: The Political History of a Minority, 1848–1933* (Oxford, 1992), 75–77, 135–37; van Rahden, "Mingling, Marrying, and Distancing," 203–4; Silber, *Jews in the Hungarian Economy*, 17. A nice piece of anecdotal evidence on this subject comes from the memoirs of Samuel Spiro, who grew up in the 1890s in Schenklengsfeld, a rural community in Hesse. Jews made up 20 percent of the population, but because of the three-tiered voting system and the Jews' relative wealth vis-à-vis the Gentile farmers, one Jew composed the entire first tier, and most of the rest of the Jews voted in the second. Seven of twelve members of the village council were Jews. Monika Richarz, ed., *Jewish Life in Germany: Memoirs from Three Centuries* (Bloomington, Ind., 1991), 202.

45. James Sheehan, "Liberalism and the City in 19th-Century Germany," *Past and Present* 51 (May 1971): 116–37.

46. Shulamit S. Magnus, *Jewish Emancipation in a German City: Cologne, 1798–1871* (Stanford, Calif., 1967), 124; Henry Wasserman, "Jews and Judaism in the *Gartenlaube*," *LBIYB* 23 (1978): 47–60; Shlomo Na'aman, "Jewish Participation in the *Deutscher Nationalverein* (1859–1867)," *LBIYB* 24 (1989): 81–93; Stefanie Schüler-Springorum, "Assimilation and Community Reconsidered: The Jewish Community in Königsberg, 1871–1914," *Jewish Social Studies* (n.s.) 5, 3 (1999): 105–8.

47. Hyman, *Emancipation of the Jews of Alsace*, 27–29.

48. *JC*, 20 November 1874, 547; 10 July 1903, 22–23; *NZ*, 27 April 1888, 169–70; *GA*, 14 December 1903, 17 February 1907, 22 March 1908. For parallel (and more consistently positive) views in the United States, see Rudolf Glanz, "The Rothschild Myth in America," *JSS* 19 (1957): 3–28.

49. *NZ*, 28 November 1890, 472.

50. Cited in Heinrich Schnee, *Die Hoffinanz und der moderne Staat*, 6 vols. (Berlin, 1953–67), 3:171.

51. *AZdJ*, 18 March, 25 March, and 1 April 1849, 160–63, 175–78, 191–95. Quote is from 160. See also the remarks about the need to harness Jewish economic power made by a conservative member of the Saxon diet in the same year: *Der Orient*, 5 May 1849, 89–90.

52. *AI,* 1868, 1023–26. This piece evoked a strong reaction from the early Zionist ideologue Moses Hess; see *AI,* 1869, 46–49.

53. A journal need not have had a specifically antisemitic agenda to fix on the Jew as symbol of the crassness and pretension of the nouveau riche bourgeoisie. See Henry Wasserman, "The 'Fliegende Blätter' as a Source for the Social History of German Jewry," *LBIYB* 28 (1983): 93–138.

54. John Klier, *Imperial Russia's Jewish Question, 1855–1881* (Cambridge, 1995), 288–304, 328, 440–55.

55. On the simultaneous persistence and enervation of traditional, religious antisemitism at the fin de siècle, see Hillel Kieval, "Representation and Knowledge in Medieval and Modern Accounts of Jewish Ritual murder," *JSS* (n.s.) 1, no. 1 (1994): 52–72.

56. The literature on post-1870 antisemitism is vast. Jacob Katz, *From Prejudice to Destruction: Antisemitism, 1700–1933* (Cambridge, Mass., 1980), provides a useful overview. For England, see Feldman, *Englishmen and Jews.* For France, see Stephen Wilson, *Ideology and Experience* (East Rutherford, N.J., 1982); Zeev Sternhell, "The Roots of Popular Antisemitism in the Third Republic," in *The Jews in Modern France,* ed. François Malino and Bernard Wasserstein (Hanover, N.H., 1985), 103–34; Pierre Birnbaum, *Anti-Semitism in France: A Political History from Leon Blum to the Present* (Oxford, 1992). For Germany and Austria, the classic text remains Peter Pulzer, *The Rise of Political Antisemitism in Germany and Austria,* rev. ed. (Cambridge, Mass., 1988). On the social basis of antisemitism in these lands, see Shulamit Volkov, *The Rise of Popular Antimodernism in Germany* (Princeton, 1978).

57. Lloyd P. Gartner, *The Jewish Immigrant in England, 1870–1914* (London, 1960), 49. See also the chart on 283, which shows that Jewish immigration to England reached its peak in the 1880s and began to decline well before 1905.

58. Shulamit Volkov, "Antisemitism as a Cultural Code," *LBIYB* 23 (1978): 25–45; idem, "The Written Matter and the Spoken Word," in *Unanswered Questions: Nazi Germany and the Genocide of the Jews,* ed. François Furet (New York, 1989), 33–53; John Boyer, *Cultural and Political Crisis in Vienna: Christian Socialism in Power, 1897–1918* (Chicago, 1995), 63–64, 68–69, 82–83.

59. On this point, see the important book of Dolores L. Augustine, *Patricians and Parvenus: Wealth and High Society in Wilhelmine Germany* (Oxford, 1994). It is a useful corrective to the conventional view in older historiography of the German middle class as emasculated and beholden to the nobility (e.g., Fritz Stern, *Gold and Iron: Bismarck, Bleichröder, and the Building of the German Empire* [New York, 1977]).

60. Michael Marrus, *The Politics of Emancipation: A Study of the French-Jewish Community at the Time of the Dreyfus Affair* (Oxford, 1972); Ismar Schorsch, *Jewish Reactions to Antisemitism in Germany, 1871–1914* (New York, 1972).

61. Adolph Jellinek, *Der jüdische Stamm in nichtjüdischen Sprichwörtern* (Vienna, 1885), 3:42–43.

62. For an analysis of *Die Neuzeit's* position in the context of Austrian liberalism of the 1860s, see Jacob Toury, *Die jüdische Presse im Österreichischen Kaiserreich 1802–1918* (Tübingen, 1983), 39–42.

63. *NZ,* 4 October and 18 October 1861, 50–51, 76–77; 3 January 1873.

64. *AZdJ,* 20 May 1837, 34; 7 July 1838, *Beiblatt,* 73–74; 9 September 1862,

515–17; 16 December 1862, 738–40; 13 August, 20 August, 27 August, 3 September, 10 September 1872, 643–47, 663–66, 683–87, 703–5, 726–29; *JC,* 23 July, 30 July, 6 August 1886, 10–11.

65. M. J. Rosman, *The Lord's Jews: Magnate-Jewish Relations in the Polish-Lithuanian Commonwealth during the Eighteenth Century* (Cambridge, Mass., 1990), 120–21, 188–89.

66. On the orientation of German Jewish merchants toward free trade, see Toury, *Politische Orientierungen,* 168, 184; Mosse, *German-Jewish Economic Elite,* 257; Pulzer, *Jews and the German State,* 184–85, 187–90.

67. *NZ,* 12 November 1878, 367–69.

68. *AI,* 1869, 50–54.

69. *AI,* 1889, 189. See also Moritz Lazarus, "Was heisst National?"; Gustav Karpeles's editorial in *AZdJ,* 29 May 1908, 1–2; Ludwig Holländer, *Die sozialen Voraussetzungen der antisemitischen Bewegung in Deutschland* (Berlin, 1909), 18–20, and; for an expression of self-pride by an ordinary cattle trader, see the letter of Moritz Thalheimer, *IDR,* January 1898, 65–68.

70. *AZdJ,* 22 November 1852, 569–70; 21 February 1853, 103–5. Philippson dismissed as a waste of money plans by the Paris-based Alliance Israélite Universelle to establish an agricultural school (the future Mikveh Israel) for Jewish youth in Palestine. *AZdJ,* 2 February 1868, 92.

71. *AZdJ,* 23 July, 30 July, 6 August 1861, 423, 458. Also *AZdJ,* 21 January 1856, 41–43.

72. *AZdJ,* 10 December 1855, 633–34.

73. *AZdJ,* 3 August 1875, 505–7. The Latin monetary union included Belgium, Italy, France, and Switzerland. It kept its member countries' major currencies at par and equal to one French franc. *The Cambridge Economic History of Europe* 8, ed. Peter Mathias and Sidney Pollard (Cambridge, 1989), 267.

74. *JC,* 26 August 1870, 6. This same sort of sentiment would be expressed on occasion by the Jewish middle class in post-1861 Russia. In Lev Osipovich Levanda's novel of 1880, *Confessions of a Wheeler-Dealer,* the author writes: "While wheeler-dealers of other nationalities are more often than not people with human passions and desires, epicureans, easily distracted from business by music, or painting, or women, or horses, dogs, hunting, port, card games—we Jewish wheeler-dealers are neither fascinated nor distracted by anything not directly related to business." Cited in Ben Nathans, "Beyond the Pale: The Jewish Encounter with Russia, 1840–1900" (Ph.D. dissertation, University of California at Berkeley, 1995), 167.

75. *JC,* 24 March 1848, 473–75; 12 November 1852.

76. Cited in Birnbaum, "Le role limité des juifs dans l'industrialisation de la societé française," 168–69. The best account of the Jewish Saint-Simonians is in Graetz, *The Jews in Nineteenth-Century France.*

77. *AI,* 1912, 273–75; see also 1900, 89–90; 1911, 234–35; 1913, 50–51. Weill's piece first appeared in *REJ* 26 (1895): 261–73. This article was reproduced, in a condensed form and with an adulatory commentary, by Adeline Goldberg in *AZdJ,* 10 March 1899, 116–19.

78. *NZ,* 20 August 1864, 399; 8 November 1878, 353–54; 4 December 1891, 471.

79. *NZ,* 5 May 1899, 177.

80. *NZ,* 9 October 1896, 417–18. See similarly enthusiastic comments in a lecture printed as a three-part series of articles, "Aus der Handels- und Finanzwelt der Vergangenheit," *NZ,* 11, 18, and 25 November 1892, 450–51, 461, 468–69.

81. Sigmund Mayer, *Ein jüdischer Kaufmann* (Vienna, 1912); idem, *Die Wiener Juden. Kommerz, Kultur, Politik: 1700–1900* (Vienna, 1918).

82. E.g., the memoirs and family biographies by Louis Badt (1909–10), Morritz Austerliz (1913), Isidor Hirschfeld (1920), Hermann Hamburger (1920), and Lina Elsas (1924), ALBI-NY. Abridged versions of the writings by Hamburger and Hirschfeld may be found in Richarz, *Jewish Life in Germany.*

83. Holländer, *Die sozialen Voraussetzungen der antisemitischen Bewegung in Deutschland,* esp. 4, 13, 24–29. Similar arguments, albeit less developed and with a Zionist tinge, came from the Hamburg attorney Gotthelf Cohn: *IF,* 28 March 1912, 9.

84. E.g., a speech delivered in 1900 by Isaac Hirsch to the Jewish merchant's association: "If one removes the Sabbath from the Jewish merchant's life, so he falls prey, straight and helpless, to those dark powers, which so easily allow the merchant to deteriorate into the vulgar huckster." *JP,* 4 and 11 January 1900, 9–11, 13–15. Cite is from 15. On the gamut of Orthodox views, ranging from complacency to profound discomfort, of urban and commercial life, see Michael Brenner, "East and West in Orthodox German-Jewish Novels (1912–1934)," *LBIYB* 37 (1992): 309–23.

85. Compare S. R. Hirsch, *Commentary on the Pentateuch, v. II: Exodus* (New York, 1971), 379, with *AZdJ,* 22 December 1856.

86. *JP,* 28 July, 4 August, 11 August, 18 August 1887, 303–4, 311–13, 323–25, 331–34.

87. *IW,* 29 July and 5 August 1887.

88. Loeb was convicted under the German 1880 Usury Law, jailed for eighteen months, deprived of civil rights for five years, and forced to pay a 5,000 mark fine. This trial and one similar to it are related in dramatic form by Ph. Klausner, *Prozess gegen die jüdischen Wucherer Marcus Loeb von Mainz und Hirsch Süsser von Würzburg* (Mannheim, 1883). For a case from the Hapsburg Empire, see Ronald Klimkiewing, *Der Wucher und seine Folgen. Beleuchtungen der Vorgänge im Falle Samuel Horowitz aus Lemberg,* 2d ed. (Czernowitz, 1891).

89. *AZdJ,* 9 February 1846, 106–7; *Statuten des Vereins gegen die Wucher,* CAHJP Mi/14; see also the letters of the Hamburg Jewish activist Gustav Tuch to the association, 3 May and 3 June 1889, CAHJP Mi/14.

90. Deutsch-Israelitischer Gemeindebund, *Hat das Judenthum dem Wucher Vorschub geleistet?* (Leipzig, 1879); Wilhelm Roehrlich, *Wucher und Intoleranz. Zugleich eine Antwort auf die Schrift von W. Marr, "Der Sieg des Judenthums über das Germanenthum"* (Zurich, 1879); Mayer Kayserling, *Der Wucher und das Judenthum* (Budapest, 1893). See also the discussion of biblical and Rabbinic law on usury in chap. 1.

91. Philippson, cited in Toury, *Die politischen Orientierungen der Juden in Deutschland* (Tübingen, 1966), 161. Emphasis in original.

92. *AZdJ,* 30 May 1871, 429–33; 11, 18, 25 June and 2 July 1878, 369–71, 385–87, 401–3, 417–20.

93. Michael Graetz, "Jews in the Modern Period: The Role of the 'Rising Class' in the Politicization of Jews in Europe," in Frankel and Zipperstein, *Assimilation and Community*, 156–76; Daniel Gutwein, *The Divided Elite: Economics, Politics, and Anglo-Jewry, 1882–1917* (London, 1992), 5–50; Mosse, *German-Jewish Economic Elite*, 343; Stern, *Gold and Iron*, 473; McCagg, *Habsburg Jews*, 145–55.

94. Cited in S. S. Prawer, *Heine's Jewish Comedy: A Study of His Portraits of Jews and Judaism* (Oxford, 1983), 331, 359; *AZdJ*, 24 June 1837, 93; Shmuel Almog, "Judentum als Krankheit: antisemitisches Steretyp und Selbstdarstellung," *TAJDG*, 1991, 215–36.

95. *AI*, 1852, 203; *NZ*, 14 March 1873, 115–20.

96. Cited in Frankel, *Prophecy and Politics*, 82.

97. *NZ*, 30 July 1886, 290–92; 15 June 1888, 233–34.

98. *IF*, 8 February 1912, 3–4; 12 September 1912, 10; 22 November 1912, 2–4. This was not the first play about the Rothschilds; a play written by Adolph Oppenheim had been produced in Germany in the early 1870s.

99. Heinrich Graetz, "Correspondence on Judaism and Semitism," in *The Structure of Jewish History and Other Essays*, trans. and ed. Ismar Schorsch (New York, 1975), 215–19.

100. Anka Muhlstein, *Baron James: The Rise of the French Rothschilds* (New York, 1982), 145; see also 127; Stephen A. Shucker, "Origins of the 'Jewish Problem' in the Later Third Republic," in *The Jews in Modern France*, ed. Frances Malino and Bernard Wasserstein (Hanover, N.H., 1985), 149.

101. *AZdJ*, 15 January and 28 May 1867, 41–44, 429–32.

102. Amos Elon, *Founder: A Portrait of the First Rothschild and His Time* (New York, 1996), 158–62; Graetz, *Jews in France*, 86–100. Scholars disagree as to why the 1891 loan was canceled, but they concur that sympathy for Russian Jewry had little to do with the decision. Compare Matityahu Mintz, "Nesigat ha-Rotchildim mi-milvat April 1891 le-Russiyah min ha-hebet ha-yehudi," *Tsiyon* 54 (1989): 401–35; with Gutwein, *Divided Elite*, 310–35. On Schiff, see A. J. Sherman, "German-Jewish Bankers in World Politics: The Financing of the Russo-Japanese War," *LBIYB* 28 (1983): 59–73.

103. *GA*, 22 April 1906.

104. Mosse, *German-Jewish Economic Elite*, 345; McCagg, *Habsburg Jews*, 196.

105. Bernard (Sucher Dov) Weinryb, "Kalkalah yehudit," *Moznayim* 7 (1938): 336–44.

106. Leopold Zunz, "Grundlinien zu einer künftigen Statistik der Juden," *Zeitschrift für die Wissenschaft des Judenthums I* (1822; rpt. Hildesheim, 1976), 523–32. See also the perceptive essay by Ismar Schorsch, "Breakthrough into the Past: The Verein für Cultur und Wissenschaft der Juden," in idem, *From Text to Context: The Turn to History in Modern Judaism* (Hanover, N.H., 1994), 224.

107. Heinrich Graetz, *Geschichte der Juden*, 3d. ed. (Leipzig, 1894), 1: 323–28; 5: 206–8; 10: 2.

108. Baron coined the term in 1928. For discussions of different aspects of the term, see Ismar Schorsch, "The Lachrymose Conception of Jewish History," in idem, *From Text to Context*; and David Sorkin, *The Transformation of German Jewry* (Oxford, 1987), 93.

109. On Borochov, see Frankel, *Prophecy and Politics*, 329–63; and Matityahu

Mintz, *Ber Borochov: Ha-ma'gal ha-rishon, 1900–1906* (Tel Aviv, 1976). On Horowitz, see Ephraim Kleiman, "An Early Modern Hebrew Textbook of Economics," *History of Political Economy* 5 (1973): 339–58; and Daniel Gutwein, "Economics, Politics, and Historiography: Hayyim D. Horowitz and the Interrelationship of Jews and Capitalism," *JSS* (n.s.) 1, no. 1 (1994): 94–114.

110. Jacob Littman, *The Economic Role of Jews in Medieval Poland: The Contributions of Yitzhak Schipper* (Lanham, Md., 1984), 251.

111. Avraham Barkai, "Zur Wirtschaftsgeschichte der Juden in Deutschland," *TAJDG* 20 (1991): 195–214.

112. *AZdJ*, 20 June 1853, 316.

113. *AZdJ*, 23 July, 30 July, and 6 August 1861, 423, 458; see also Ludwig Philippson, *Über die Resultate in der Weltgeschichte. Sechs Vorlesungen* (Leipzig, 1860), 16–28.

114. David F. Lindenfeld, *The Practical Imagination: The German Sciences of State in the Nineteenth Century* (Chicago, 1997), 237. The citation describes the thought of Gustav Schmoller at the turn of the century, but it can be applied to many of the major German economists of the period 1840–1914. See also Erik Grimmer-Salem and Roberto Romani, "The Historical School, 1870–1900: A Cross-National Reassessment," *History of European Ideas* 24 (1998): 267–99.

115. A forthcoming doctoral dissertation by Jonathan Karp of Columbia University promises to throw new light on the origins of economic historiography by and about Jews. Until that is available, see Eugen Täubler, *Zur Handelsbedeutung der Juden in Deutschland vor Beginn des Städtewesens* (Breslau, 1916), 1–2; Solomon Grayzel, "The Jews' Function in the Evolution of Medieval Life," *Historia Judaica* 6 (1944): 3–26; Toni Oelsner, "The Place of the Jews in Economic History as Viewed by German Scholars," *LBIYB* 7 (1962): 183–212; idem, "Wilhelm Roscher's Theory of the Economic and Social Position of the Jews in the Middle Ages," *YIVO Annual of Jewish Social Science* 12 (1958–59): 176–95; Daniel Gutwein, "Beyn sotsiyologyah shel mi'ut le-etikah datit: Livehinat hate'oriyah shel ha-ilit ha-kalkalit ha-yehudit be-Germaniyah," *Tsiyon* 55 (1990): 419–47 (esp. 446); and Avraham Barkai, "Ha-yahadut, ha-yehudim, ve-hitpathut ha-kapitalism," in Ben-Sasson, *Dat ve-kalkalah*, 53–63.

116. Levi Herzfeld, *Handelsgeschichte der Juden des Alterthums* (Braunschweig, 1984), 273–74. See also Salo Baron, "Levi Herzfeld, the First Jewish Economic Historian," in *History and Jewish Historians* (Philadelphia, 1964), 322–44.

117. Shabtai Teveth, *Ben-Gurion: The Burning Ground, 1886–1948* (New York, 1987), 73.

118. For biographical information about Sombart, see Arthur Mitzman, *Sociology and Estrangement* (New Brunswick, N.J., 1973), 135–264. For specific analyses of Sombart's writings on Jews, see Paul Mendes-Flohr, "Werner Sombart's 'The Jews and Modern Capitalism,' " *LBIYB* 21 (1976): 87–107; Werner Mosse, "Judaism, Jews, and Capitalism: Weber, Sombart, and Beyond," *LBIYB* 24 (1979): 3–15.

119. Zeev Sternhell (with Mario Sznajder and Maia Asheri), *The Birth of Fascist Ideology: From Cultural Rebellion to Political Revolution* (Princeton, 1994). Surprisingly, Sternhell, whose 1998 book, *The Founding Myths of Israel,* leaves no stone unturned in his attempts to link Zionism with European "nationalist

socialism," missed the connection between Sombart (admittedly before his turn fully to the right) and Ben-Gurion.

120. On the relationship between Weber and Sombart, see Hans Liebes-schuetz, "Max Weber's Historical Interpretation of Judaism," *LBIYB* 9 (1964): 41–68; and Freddy Raphael, *Judaisme et capitalisme: Essai sur la controverse entre Max Weber et Werner Sombart* (Paris, 1982). *Die Juden und das Wirtschaftsleben* was published in English in 1982 (under the title *The Jews and Capitalism*) and features a long, useful introduction by Samuel Klausner.

121. Adolf Wahrmund, *Das Gesetz des Nomadenthum und die heutige Juden-herrschaft*, 2d ed. (Berlin, 1892). The sociologist Georg Simmel (who was of Jewish origin) would modify this stark view by positing a distinction between the nomad and the stranger. Whereas nomads never join society, strangers are fixed presences, although marginalized. Jews are archetypal strangers, not no-mads; thus they strive to excel in order to be welcomed from the periphery to the center. See Freddy Raphael's introduction to Chantal Benayoun, Alain Me-dam, and Pierre-Jacques Rojtman, eds., *Les juifs et l'économique: Miroirs et mirages* (Paris, 1992), 10.

122. Theodor Fritzsch [F. Roderich-Stoltheim], *Die Juden in Handel und das Geheimnis ihrer Erfolgen* (Steglitz, 1913); idem, *Geistige Unterjochung. Zugleich ein Antwort an Dr. G. Loner und Prof. Werner Sombart* (Leipzig, 1911). Similar crit-icisms of Sombart may be found in Heinrich Schnee's pioneering, but ultimately malevolent, study of the Court Jews: Jews in the Holy Roman Empire, writes Schnee, were at best the handmaidens of capitalism, but the most important contributions came from the states' rulers, bureaucrats, and self-sacrificing sub-jects. The Court Jews' main accomplishment, aside from providing a foot in the door for the establishment of Jewish communities, was serving as a sort of large-scale panderer, providing jewels, mistresses, and other luxuries to princes and prelates. Schnee, *Hoffinanz*, 3: 251–66.

123. Werner Sombart, *Judentaufen* (Munich, 1912).

124. *IF*, 19 and 25 November, 2 and 9 December 1911, 2, 2–3, 1–2, 3–4. But note the highly critical review of the lecture series in *JP*, 17 December and 24 December 1909, 3 January and 7 January 1910, 499–500, 507–8, 9–10, 14–15.

125. *IF*, 4 January 1912, 2–3; 15 February 1912, 1–3; 22 February 1912, 9; 29 February 1912, 4. See also Yehuda Eloni, "Die umkämpfte nationaljüdische Idee," in *Juden im Wilhelmischen Deutschland, 1890–1914*, ed. Werner Mosse and Arnold Paucker (Tübingen, 1976), 672–73.

126. Felix Pinkus, *Studien zur Wirtschaftsstellung der Juden* (Berlin, 1905).

127. Georg Caro, *Sozial- und Wirtschaftsgeschichte der Juden im Mittelalter und der Neuzeit*, 2 vols. (Hildesheim, 1964), 1: 9–11; Moses Hoffman, *Der Geldhandel der deutschen Juden während des Mittelalters bis zum Jahre 1350* (Altenberg, 1910); Bruno Hahn, *Die wirtschaftliche Tätigkeit der Juden im fränkischen und deutschen Reich bis zum zweiten Kreuzzug* (Freiburg, 1911). Interestingly, Hoffman also went against conventional wisdom by claiming that the Crusades did not mark the beginning of Jewish socioeconomic decline. Hoffman's argument would be made afresh in the 1980s by Robert Chazan in *European Jewry in the First Crusade* (Berkeley, 1987).

128. Hoffmann was an active member of Agudat Yisrael and emigrated to

Palestine in 1939. Werner Röder and Herbert A. Strauss, eds., *Biographisches Handbuch der deutschsprächigen Emigration nach 1933* (Munich, 1980), 1: 310.

129. Julius Guttmann, *Die wirtschaftliche und soziale Bedeutung der Juden im Mittelalter* (Breslau, 1907), 35. On Guttmann's scholarship in Jewish philosophy, which he also considered posterior and inferior to faith, see David N. Myers, *Re-inventing the Jewish Past: European Jewish Intellectuals and the Zionist Return to History* (New York, 1995), 101.

130. Caro, *Wirtschaftsgeschichte*, 1: 12.

131. Many of these critiques are analyzed in Alfred Philipp, *Die Juden und das Wirtschaftsleben. Eine Antikritisch-Bibliographische Studie zu Werner Sombart: "Die Juden und das Wirtschaftsleben"* (Strasbourg, 1929). As this book originated as a Ph.D. dissertation written under Sombart's guidance, it must be used as a bibliographic reference alone; it seriously underestimates the amount of negative publicity the book received. Not only Jews, but also prominent liberal German academics, categorically rejected its major aguments, e.g., Lujo Brentano, "Judentum und Kapitalismus," in *Der Wirtschaftende Mensch in der Geschichte. Gesammelte Reden und Aufsätze* (Leipzig, 1923), 426–90.

132. For expressions of unmitigated hostility by Jewish critics, see *IF*, 10 December 1910, 2–3, 4 January 1912, 2–3; *Jahrbuch der Jüdisch-Literarischen Gesellschaft* (Mainz) 8 (1910): 378–431; *IDR*, November 1911, 608–20; Ludwig Feuchtwanger in *Jahrbuch für Gesetzgebung, Verwaltung, und Rechtspflege des deutschen Reiches* 35 (1911): 1433–66; and M. Ekstein, "The Jews as an Economic Force," *Fortnightly Review* (n.s.) 95 (o.s.) 101 (1914): 694–704. M. Steckelmacher's *Randbemerkungen zu Werner Sombarts "Die Juden und das Wirtschaftsleben"* (Berlin, 1912) is in a similar vein. For favorable opinion of the book's purely economic arguments, see Max Eschelbacher, "Das jüngste Bild vom Judentum," *Ost und West* 11 (1911): 1042–52; and Raphael-Georges Lévy, "Le role des juifs dans la vie économique," *REJ* 62 (1911): 161–89.

133. *IDR*, 1911, 247–52.

134. Julius Guttmann, "Die Juden und das Wirtschaftsleben," *Archiv für Sozialwissenschaft und Sozialpolitik* 36 (1913): 149–212. Quotes are from 162–63 and 198.

135. Moses Hoffmann, *Judentum und Kapitalismus. Eine kritische Würdigung von Werner Sombarts "Die Juden und das Wirtschaftsleben"* (Berlin, 1912), 3.

136. Ibid., 191.

137. Felix Rachfahl, "Das Judentum und die Genesis des modernen Kapitalismus," *Preussischer Jahrbücher* 147 (1912): 52; Hermann Waetjen, *Das Judentum und die Anfänge der modernen Kolonisation. Kritische Bemerkungen zu Werner Sombarts "Die Juden und das Wirtshaftsleben"* (Berlin, 1914), 7.

138. Waetjen, *Judentum und die Anfänge der modernen Kolonisation*, 24–25.

139. Cited in Ismar Schorsch, "Jewish Studies from 1818 to 1819," in idem, *From Text to Context*, 354–55.

140. *Adolf Brüll's Populär-wissenschaftliche Monatsblätter zur Belehrung über das Judentum*, 1 May 1883, 101.

141. Kaufmann Kohler, "Die weltgeschichtliche Bedeutung des jüdischen Handels," delivered to the Deutsch-Literarisches Klub in Cincinnati, March 1907, printed in the *Jahrbuch für jüdische Geschichte und Literatur* (Berlin) 12 (1909): 90–109. Cite is from 109.

142. E.g., George Cohen, *The Jews in the Making of America* (Boston, 1924). Ironically, the writings of Kayserling, Cohen, and their sort about the extent of Jewish involvement in the European colonization of the Americas provided grist for the antisemitic mill of the Nation of Islam, whose book *The Secret Relationship between Blacks and Jews* (Chicago, 1991) is larded with references to publications by the American Jewish Historical Society. See the valuable corrective by Eli Faber, *Jews, Slaves, and the Slave Trade: Setting the Record Straight* (New York, 1998).

143. Eugen Täubler, "Die Entwicklung der Arbeit des 'Gesamtarchivs' und der Versuch einer methodologischen Gliederung und Systematisierung der jüdischen Geschichtsforschung" (1911), in *Aufsätze zur Problematik jüdischer Geschichtsschreibung 1908–1950* (Tübingen, 1977) 17–19; David N. Myers, "The Fall and Rise of Jewish Historicism: The Evolution of the Akademie für die Wissenschaft des Judentums (1919–1934)," *Hebrew Union College Annual* 63 (1992): 107–44.

144. Salo Baron, *A Social and Religious History of the Jews* (New York, 1937), 2:176–77.

145. Arthur Cohen, "Judenfrage und Statistik," *ZDSJ* 10 (1914): 147; S. Wininger, *Grösse jüdische National-Biographie* (Czernowitz, 1925–36), 1: 561.

Chapter Five. Solving the "Jewish Problem": Jewish Social Policy, 1860–1933

1. Jürgen Habermas, *The Structural Transformation of the Public Sphere* (Cambridge, Mass., 1991).

2. Geoff Eley offers a nice analysis of the reception of *The Structural Transformation of the Public Sphere* as well as a cogent critique of the work itself in "Nations, Publics, and Political Cultures: Placing Habermas in the Nineteenth Century," in *Culture/Power/History: A Reader in Contemporary Social Theory,* ed. Nicholas B. Dirks, Geoff Eley, and Sherry B. Ortner (Princeton, 1994), 297–335.

3. E.g., the essays in Elinor A. Accampo, Rachel G. Fuchs, and Mary Lynn Stewart, eds., *Gender and the Politics of Social Reform in France, 1870–1914* (Baltimore, 1995).

4. Robert Liberles, "Emancipation and the Structure of the Jewish Community in the Nineteenth Century," *LBIYB* 31 (1986): 51–67.

5. Ibid., 63; Aharon Bornstein, "Mi-kabtsanim le-dorshei 'avodah: navadim yehudim 'aniyim be-Germaniyah, 1869–1914" (Ph.D. dissertation, Tel Aviv University, 1987), 181, 192–93, 222. Bornstein's dissertation was published in abridged form as *Ha-kabtsanim: Perek be-toldot yehudei Germaniyah* (Jerusalem, 1992). In the notes to this chapter I refer to the original dissertation, which contains valuable material omitted from the published book.

6. *NZ,* 19 November 1897, 473–74; 24 December 1897, 524–25.

7. See speeches by Kultusgemeinde board member J. Samuel and vice president Rudolph Schorstein in *OW,* 5 March 1909, 169–70, 3 April 1914, 222–24.

8. This phenomenon is closely analyzed in Rainer Liedtke, *Jewish Welfare in Hamburg and Manchester, c. 1850–1914* (Oxford, 1998).

9. *JC,* 13 October 1871, 6.

10. *JC*, 27 November 1896, 17.

11. *JC*, 7 March 1873, 709; 21 March 1873, 743.

12. Eugene C. Black, *The Social Politics of Anglo-Jewry, 1880–1920* (New York, 1988), 94–99.

13. George Steinmetz, *Regulating the Social: The Welfare State and Local Politics in Imperial Germany* (Princeton, 1993), 65, 115, 119, 120–21.

14. From a speech by Tuch, reproduced in *UOBB. Das Logenheim in Hamburg. Festschrift zur Errinerung an die Einweihung. Sonntag, den 28.8.04*. SAH.

15. Bornstein, "Mi-kabtsanim le-dorshei 'avodah," 194, 275–76.

16. Zosa Szajkowski, *Poverty and Social Welfare among French Jews (1800–1880)* (New York, 1954), 41–47; *OW*, 25 August 1911, 559. The figure for Vienna no doubt reflects recent immigration from Russia and Romania. Allianz zu Wien, *XL. Jahresbericht der Israelitischen Allianz zu Wien erstattet an die XL. ordentliche Generalversammlung am 16. April 1913 nebst einem Rückblick auf die vierzigjährige Wirksamkeit des Vereines 1871–1912* (Vienna, 1913), 24–26, 26–30, 32–34; 1906 *Jahresbericht*, 17.

17. E.g., Giora Lotan, "The Zentralwohlfahrtstelle," *LBIYB* 4 (1959): 185–207; Bornstein, "Mi-kabtsanim le-dorshei 'avodah," chap. 6, passim; Stefi Jersch-Wenzel, "Minderheiten in der bürgerlichen Gesellschaft: Juden in Amsterdam, Frankfurt, und Posen," in *Burgertum im 19. Jahrhundert. Deutschland im europäischen Vergleich*, ed. Jürgen Kocka (Munich, 1988), 404–5, n. 22.

18. *JC*, 25 September 1857, 1156–57 [*sic*]; 19 October 1906, 22. Over this period, wholesale prices in the United Kingdom *fell* by almost one-third. My estimates for this and the following notes are taken from tables, divided by country and year, in B. R. Mitchell, *European Historical Statistics, 1750–1975* (New York, 1980), 771–84.

19. *AI*, 1 November 1878, 657–69; 1 September 1910, 275–76. Wholesale prices over this period experienced a slight deflation; the cost of living index showed little change.

20. See the annual reports of the Armenkommission in SAH, Jüdische Gemeinde, no. 462. The Jewish population of Hamburg in 1890 was 17,877. Felix Theilhaber, *Der Untergang der deutschen Juden* (Berlin, 1921), 51. The statistical tables show a paradoxical slight decrease in prices and increase in the cost of living over this period—but what matters is that the changes do not significantly alter the picture of a rapid climb in outlays for charity.

21. Jakob Segall, "Die Leistungen der Armenkommision der jüdische Gemeinde zu Berlin," *ZDSJ* 10 (1914): 104.

22. *Mitteilungen vom Deutsch-Israelitischen Gemeindebunde* (hereafter, *Mitteilungen vom DIGB*), no. 68 (1907): 13; no. 82 (1912): 83–85.

23. Prices rose approximately 20 percent over this period.

24. These figures are extrapolated from *NZ*, 19 November 1897, 473–74; 24 December 1897, 524–25; *OW*, 25 August 1911, 558–59.

25. *Statistisches Jahrbuch des Deutsch-Israelitischen Gemeindebundes* (Berlin, 1889), 90–91; 1913, 238–239.

26. *JC*, 9 December 1898, 11; 2 May 1902, 23; 9 March 1906, 26.

27. The necessity of the workhouse was heavily debated in the editorials and letters pages of the *Jewish Chronicle* in the early 1870s. On the industrial schools, see Black, *Social Politics*, 237–40.

28. *AI*, 1852, 203.

29. David Feldman, *Englishmen and Jews: Social Relations and Political Culture, 1840–1914* (New Haven, 1994), 322.

30. *AI*, 11 August 1898, 262.

31. Feldman, *Englishmen and Jews*, 348; Black, *Social Politics*, 128; Nancy L. Green, "To Give and to Receive: Philanthropy and Collective Responsibility among Jews in Paris, 1880–1914," in *The Uses of Charity: The Poor on Relief in the Nineteenth-Century Metropolis*, ed. Peter Mandler (Philadelphia, 1990), 211–15.

32. Between 1901 and 1914 the number of Jews leaving the Old World for the New was 1,630,00, more than twice the number (770,000) who had left over the period 1881–1900. *Encyclopedia Judaica*, "Migrations," 15, 1520.

33. V. D., Lipman, *A Century of Social Service, 1859–1959: The Jewish Board of Guardians* (London, 1959), 32; Feldman, *Englishmen and Jews*, 299, 306; Green, "To Give and Receive," 204; idem, *The Pletzl of Paris: Jewish Immigrant Workers in the Belle Epoque* (New York, 1986), 64.

34. Speech of Kultusgemeinde member Max Frank, printed in *OW*, 6 January 1911, 2.

35. Lloyd P. Gartner, *The Jewish Immigrant in England, 1870–1914* (London, 1960), 149–50; Green, *The Pletz of Paris*, 56–58.

36. Aharon Bornstein, "The Role of Social Institutions as Inhibitors of Assimilation: Jewish Poor Relief System in Germany, 1875–1925," *Jewish Social Studies* 50 (1988–93): 207.

37. SAH JG 483. Deutsche Zentralstelle für jüdische Wanderarmenfürsorge. Circular of 19 March 1913, reproducing memorandum from the Darmstadt Verein zur Beschränkung der jüdischen Wanderbettlerei.

38. *OW*, 11 May 1900, 350–53.

39. Compare *JC*, 1 December 1871, 7–9, with David Cesarani, *The "Jewish Chronicle" and Anglo-Jewry, 1841–1991* (Cambridge, 1994), 23–24. On Manchester, see Rainer Liedtke, *Jewish Welfare in Hamburg and Manchester, c. 1850–1914* (Oxford, 1998), chap. 3.

40. See the letters to the editor section of the *JC*, beginning 10 February 1871 and continuing for ten weeks or so. See also the supplement to the *JC* of 14 March 1873 featuring a report on the annual meeting of the contributors to the JBG.

41. Black, *Social Politics*, 75, 189–93.

42. "Das Wohlfahrtswesen der Deutsch-Israeliten Gemeinde und seine Organisation," ms. in SAH JG 464: Kommission für das Wohlfahrtswesen der jüdischen Gemeinde. See also the "Satzungen der Kommission für das Wohlfahrtswesen," dated 10 September and 9 October 1911, in the same file.

43. For a recent and cogent analysis of the Eberfelde system, see George Steinmetz, *Regulating the Social: The Welfare State and Local Politics in Imperial Germany* (Princeton, 1993).

44. This narrative is based on information from *NZ*, 19 November 1897, 473–74; 24 December 1897, 524–25; and *OW*, 3 February 1905, 68–71; 17 February 1905, 103–5; 4 January 1907, 19; 11 January 1907, 19; 27 September 1907, 637; 9 October 1908, 723; 5 March 1909, 169–70; 26 March 1909, 222–26; 4 June 1909, 402–5; 23 March 1910, 204–6; 31 March 1911, 204–6; 22 March 1912, 193–95. A similar central association, arousing similar debates, existed in Prague, although

it appears to have successfully reduced the number of applicants for aid while increasing individual benefits. *NZ,* 21 February 1896; *OW,* 5 March 1909, 169–70.

45. See the articles by Rabbi M. Schuhl of Epinal (Alsace) in *AI,* 1909, 19 August, 260–61; 26 August, 268–69.

46. Mordechai Breuer, *Jüdische Orthodoxie im deutschen Reich, 1871–1918: Die Sozialgeschichte einer religiöser Minderheit* (Frankfurt am Main, 1986), 210–11. *Die jüdische Presse,* the Berlin newspaper edited by the prominent Orthodox rabbi Esriel Hildesheimer, featured many articles on the rationalization of charity.

47. Rüdiger vom Bruch, "Bürgerliche Sozialreform im deutschen Kaiserreich," in *Weder Kommunismus noch Kapitalismus. Bürgerliche Sozialreform in Deutschland vom Vormärz bis zur Ära Adenauer,* ed. Rüdiger vom Bruch (Munich, 1985), 101, 109. Cf. E. I. Kouri, *Der deutsche Protestantismus und die soziale Frage 1870–1919* (Berlin, 1984), 104–11, 117–23.

48. Philippson, cited in Jacob Toury, *Die politischen Orientierungen der Juden in Deutschland* (Tübingen, 1966), 161 (emphasis in original); Karpeles's editorial in *AZdJ,* 13 October 1905.

49. Adolf Kurrein, *Die sociale Frage im Judenthume* (Mülheim am Rhein, 1890).

50. E.g., Friedrich Wachtel, *Das Judenthum und seine Aufgabe im neuen deutschen Reich* (Leipzig, 1871); Kurrein, *Die sociale Frage im Judenthume;* Benjamin Auerbach, "Die Aufgaben und Bestrebungen der Logen auf dem Gebiete der Wohlfahrtspflege und Fürsorgethätigkeit," in *Festschrift zur Feier des zwanzigjährigen Bestehens des U.O.B.B. Herausgegeben von der Gross-Loge für Deutschland. 20. März 1902. Redigiert von San.-Rath. Dr. Maretzki* (Berlin, 1902).

51. Gertrude Himmelfarb, *Poverty and Compassion: The Moral Imagination of the Late Victorians* (New York, 1991), 185–88.

52. Rolf Landwehr and Rüdiger Baron, *Geschichte der Sozialarbeit: Hauptlinien ihrer Entwicklung im 19. und 20. Jahrhundert* (Weinheim-Basel, 1983), 28–32, 145.

53. Ibid., 40, 67, 148; Christoph Sachsse and Florian Tennstedt, *Geschichte der Armenfürsorge in Deutschland* (Stuttgart, 1980), 220–21; Accampo, Fuchs, and Stewart, *Gender;* George Steinmetz, *Regulating the Social;* Anson Raniach, "Social Knowledge, Social Risk, and the Politics of Industrial Accidents in Germany and France," in *States, Social Knowledge, and the Origins of Modern Social Policies,* ed. Dietrich Rueschemeyer and Theda Skopcol (Princeton, 1996), 48–79.

54. Steinmetz, *Regulating the Social,* 199.

55. Louis Maretzki, *Geschichte des Ordens Bnei Briss in Deutschland, 1882–1907* (Berlin, 1907), 183–87. A similar development occurred simultaneously in the American B'nai B'rith. Leo Levi, the order's president from 1899 to 1904, formalized and gave an ideological base to this turn. Deborah Dash Moore, *B'nai B'rith and the Challenge of Ethnic Leadership,* (Albany, N.Y., 1981), 64.

56. Louis Maretzki, *Das Wesen und die Leistungen des Ordens U.O.B.B.* (Berlin, 1911), 28; also *Geschichte,* 183.

57. For applications of the concept of ethnicity to modern European Jewry, see Phyllis Cohen Albert, "Ethnicity and Jewish Solidarity in 19th-Century

France," in *Mystics, Philosophers, and Politicians: Essays in Jewish Intellectual History in Honor of Alexander Altmann*, ed. Jehuda Reinharz and Daniel Swetchinski (Durham, 1982); and idem, "L'intégration et la persistance de l'ethnicité chez les juifs dans la France moderne," in *Histoire politique des juifs de France*, ed. Pierre Birnbaum (Paris, 1990), 221–43.

58. Freie israelitische Vereinigung, *Bericht über die erste Tagung am Sontag, 5 Mai 1895*, CAHJP TD 860.

59. *Mitteilungen der Ausschüsse. Stenographischer Bericht über die Tagung vom Montag, den 22 Juni 1896*, CAHJP TD 860, 43. For biographical information on Minden, see S. Wininger, *Grösse jüdische National-Biographie* (Czernowitz, 1925–36), 4:390.

60. *NZ*, 15 December 1893, 501–2.

61. F. K. Prochaska, *Women and Philanthropy in Nineteenth-Century England* (Oxford, 1980), 138–44, 174; Catherine Prelinger, *Charity, Challenge, and Change: Religious Dimensions of the Mid-Nineteenth-Century Women's Movement in Germany* (New York, 1987), 160–72; Steinmetz, *Regulating the Social*, 166–67; Bonnie Smith, *Ladies of the Leisure Class: The Bourgeoisie of Northern France in the Nineteenth Century* (Princeton, 1981), 149–61.

62. See the useful review essays by Amanda Vickery, "Golden Age to Separate Spheres? A Review of the Categories and Chronology of English Women's History" (1993), and Seth Koven and Sonya Michel, "Womanly Duties: Maternalist Politics and the Origins of Welfare States in France, Germany, Great Britain, and the United States, 1880–1920" (1990), reproduced in *Gender and History in Western Europe*, ed. Robert Shoemaker and Mary Vincent (London, 1998), 197–225, 319–46.

63. For a general overview of the role and self-images of women in Jewish philanthropy, see Paula Hyman, *Gender and Assimilation in Modern Jewish History* (Seattle, 1995), 30–41. Marion Kaplan has produced a masterful survey of the German case in *The Making of the Jewish Middle Class: Women, Family, and Identity in Imperial Germany* (Oxford, 1991), 192–227.

64. Liedtke, *Jewish Welfare in Hamburg and Manchester*, chap. 7.

65. *OW*, 3 February 1905, 68–71; 15 May 1914, 347.

66. Louis Maretzki, "Die Frauen und der Orden," *Festschrift . . . des U.O.B.B.*, 89. Similarly, the physician Markus Hirsch called women "priestesses of the ideal" of humanitarianism when confronted with the vagrant poor. See his pamphlet, *"Betteln und Hausiren ist hier verboten," Eine Studie zur sozialen Frage* (Frankfurt am Main, 1890).

67. *OW*, 25 August 1893, 635–36; *NZ*, 16 August 1901, 334; Louis Maretzki, "Die Frauen und der Orden," 81–82, 86–87; *Satzungen der Israelitischen Haushaltungsschule in Hamburg*, Hamburg, 1900, CAHJP AHW/539.

68. Benjamin Auerbach, "Die Aufgaben und Bestrebungen der Logen auf dem Gebiete der Wohlfahrtspflege und Fürsorgethätigkeit," in *Festschrift zur Feier des zwanzigjährigen Bestehens des U.O.B.B.*, 59–63; Claudia Prestel, "Weibliche Rollenzuweisung in jüdischen Organisationen: Das Beispeil des Bnei Briss," *BLBI* 85 (1990): 51–80; Marion Kaplan, "Tradition and Transition: The Acculturation, Assimilation, and Integration of Jewish Women in Imperial Germany," *LBIYB* 27 (1982): 23; idem, *The Jewish Feminist Movement in Germany:*

The Campaigns of the Jüdischer Frauenbund, 1904–1938 (Westport, Conn., 1979), 154–56, 172–73, passim; idem, *The Making of the Jewish Middle Class*, 208–14.

69. Thomas Nipperdey, *Religion im Umbruch. Deutschland, 1870–1918* (Munich, 1988), 24–31.

70. On the relationship between associational life, in particular philanthropy, and modern Jewish identity, see Moore, *B'nai B'rith and the Challenge of Ethnic Leadership;* Albert, "Ethnicity and Jewish Solidarity," 266; Green, "To Give and to Receive"; Paula Hyman, *The Emancipation of the Jews of Alsace* (New Haven, 1991), 75–76; David Sorkin, *The Transformation of German Jewry* (Oxford, 1987), 112–23; Henry Wasserman, "Jews, 'Bürgertum,' and 'Bürgerliche Gesellschaft' in a Liberal Era (1840–1880)" (Hebrew) (Ph.D. dissertation, Hebrew University, 1979), 75–93; and Marsha Rozenblit, *The Jews of Vienna, 1867–1914: Assimilation and Identity* (Albany, N.Y., 1983), 148–50.

71. "Jüdische Wohlfahrtspflege in Berlin," *ZDSJ* 5 (1909): 75–78; Michael Marrus, *The Politics of Assimilation: A Study of the French-Jewish Community at the Time of the Dreyfus Affair* (Oxford, 1972), 80.

72. Maretzki, *Geschichte,* 186–87.

73. Jacob Toury, "Die bangen Jahren (1887–91). Juden in Deutschland zwischen Integrationshoffnung und Isolationsfurcht," in *Juden in Deutschland. Emanzipation, Integration, Verfolgung und Vernichtung,* ed. Peter Freimark, Alice Jankowski, and Ina S. Lorenz (Hamburg, 1991), 168–72; Shulamit Volkov, "Die Dynamik der Dissimilation: Deutsche Juden und die ostjüdischen Einwanderer," in *Jüdisches Leben und Antisemitismus im 19. Jahrhundert* (Munich, 1990), 168–70.

74. Maretzki, "Leistungen," 20.

75. Wertheimer, *Unwelcome Strangers,* esp. 144–51, 157–61.

76. Auerbach, "Die Aufgaben und Bestrebungen der Logen," 68–69.

77. *JC,* 1 December 1871, 7.

78. *NZ,* 23 August 1872, 381–82.

79. Cited in Toury, *Die politischen Orientierungen der Juden in Deutschland,* 169.

80. Cited in Marrus, *Politics of Assimilation,* 133. This way of thinking was voiced even in Russia. A proprietor of the journal *Russkii evrei* wrote in 1882, "Fortunately we do not have a *narod* in its fashionable sense, meaning the antipode and rival of the intelligentsia, although, unfortunately, and to our shame, among us are beginning to appear *narodniki* who would very much like to arouse in the people a distrust for the educated class. . . . [But] our masses are extremely sober and generally literate; therefore they are completely unsuitable material for various uprisings and disturbances." Cited in Jonathan Frankel, *Prophecy and Politics: Socialism, Nationalism, and the Russian Jews, 1862–1917* (Cambridge, 1981), 79.

81. Paula Hyman, *The Jews in Modern France* (Berkeley, 1998), 131.

82. For England, see Todd M. Endelman, "English Jewish History," *Modern Judaism* 11 (1991): 97. The goal of embourgeoisement, rather than stabilization of the status quo, was held by the Anglo-Jewish elite from the late eighteenth century onward; see Todd M. Endelman, *The Jews of Georgian England, 1714–1830* (Philadelphia, 1979), 246–47.

83. *JC,* 1 December 1871, 7–9 (Michael Henry); 12 March 1886, 11 (Asher Myers).

84. Louis Maretzki, "Die Leistungen des Ordens," in *Das Wesen and die Leistungen des Ordens U.O.B.B.* (Berlin, 1911), 37.

85. Jacob Kellner, *Immigration and Social Policy: The Jewish Experience in the U.S.A., 1881–1882* (Jerusalem, 1979), 1–3. Compare the case in the United States of the October 14, 1882, riot by immigrants at the shelter on Ward's Island, east of Manhattan. Emma Lazarus, the celebrated bard of free immigration, was badly shaken and, if only temporarily, adopted a frigidly Social Darwinist approach to the immigration problem. Ibid., 66–68.

86. For a general account of the DIGB, see Ismar Schorsch, *Jewish Reactions to Antisemitism in Germany, 1870–1914* (New York, 1972).

87. Hilfsverein der deutschen Juden, *Achter Bericht,* 1910, 9; Israelitischer Allianz zu Wien, *Jahresbericht,* 1887, xix.

88. This observation is a commonplace in German historiography. For a close analysis, see Dirk Stegmann, *Die Erben Bismarcks. Parteien und Verbände in der Spätphase des Wilhelminischen Deutschlands. Sammlungspolitik 1897–1918* (Cologne, 1970).

89. Between 1881 and 1906 the London JBG sent back some 24,000, and the Mansion House Relief Fund, which operated separately from the JBG, shipped out another 7,000. Feldman, *Englishmen and Jews,* 299–300. A different source provides a figure of 54,000 repatriated Jews for the period 1880–1914: V. D. Lipman, *A History of the Jews in Britain since 1858* (Leicester, 1990), 76.

90. *JC,* 25 May 1877, 8–10; Kellner, *Reshito shel tikhnun hevrati klal-yehudi: ha-hit'arvut ha-memusedet bi-metsukat yehudei Russiyah be-reshit shenot ha-shiv'im shel ha-me'ah ha-19* (Jerusalem, 1974), 11.

91. *Mitteilungen vom DIGB,* no. 1 (1873): 3–4, 15–17; no. 2 (1875): 27–43.

92. *Mitteilungen vom DIGB,* no. 2 (1875): 28–31.

93. Kellner, *Reshito shel tikhnun hevrati klal-yehudi,* 16–19.

94. *JC,* 29 September 1876, 406–7.

95. Jonathan Frankel, "Crisis as a Factor in Modern Jewish Politics, 1840 and 1881–82," in *Living with Antisemitism: Modern Jewish Responses,* ed. Jehuda Reinharz (Hanover, N.H., 1987), 49.

96. *NZ,* 3 February 1882, 80–81.

97. Between April and June 1882 the Mansion House Relief Fund selected and forwarded nearly 7,000 refugees from Brody. *JC,* 23 June 1882, 8. For a detailed, if partisan and critical, account of the Brody crisis, see Zosa Szajkowski, "The European Attitude to East European Jewish Immigration (1881–1893)," *Proceedings of the American Jewish Historical Society* 41 (1951–52): 127–62.

98. On Russia, see Shaul Stampfer, "The Geographic Background of East European Jewish Migration to the United States before World War I," in *Migration across Time and Nations: Population Mobility in Historical Contexts,* ed. Ira A. Glazier and Luigi de Rosa (New York, 1986), 220–30. On Galicia, see Gartner, *The Jewish Immigrant in England,* 41. A full 25 percent of the Jewish immigrants landing at New York over the period 1884–1903 were from the Hapsburg Empire; *Jewish Encyclopedia,* q.v. "Migration."

99. *NZ,* 3 February 1882, 80–81.

100. Kellner, *Immigration and Social Policy,* 4. This discourse survived under the torrent of Jewish immigration after 1905. In 1906 the Allianz zu Wien complained about the large numbers of Russian Jews, "in no way affected by the excesses [i.e., pogroms] which have occurred," pouring into Galicia. 1906 *Jahresbericht,* 17.

101. *JC,* 2 December 1881, 9; and 6 January 1882, 9–10.

102. *JC,* 3 February 1893, 15–16; 16 December 1904, 10. Many thanks to Sarah Amato for this reference.

103. Black, *Social Politics,* 243–44.

104. Deutsches Central-Komitee für die russischen Juden, *Dritter Bericht,* Berlin, March 1892; and "Instruction für die Beförderung," ms. dated January 1892, SAH IIE III P24: Auswanderungsamt. Comité für Russische Juden. See also Michael Just, *Ost- und südosteuropäische Amerikawanderung 1881–1914* (Stuttgart, 1988), 132–35.

105. "Instruction für die Beförderung"; also Jürgen Sielemann, "Eastern Jewish Immigration via the Port of Hamburg, 1880–1914," unpublished ms., SAH, 6–8.

106. Allianz zu Wien, 1906 *Jahresbericht,* 11–12, 17.

107. Ibid. The association between disease and immigrants, malnourished, ill clad, and forced while en route, by sea or land, into the most unhygienic conditions, was not limited to Germany, nor was it necessarily imagined. In February 1891 a ship from Constantinople, turned away by Turkish authorities from entering Palestine, was sent to New York; not surprisingly, after their arduous journey, many of the passengers fell victim to typhoid fever. The American government responded by temporarily quarantining all ships bearing immigrants. Deutsches Central-Komitee für die russischen Juden, *Dritter Bericht* (see n. 104 above).

108. "Instruction für die Beförderung" (see n. 104 above).

109. From an article in the *Israelitische Familienblatt,* n.d., attached to police report dated 16 December 1904, in SAH IIE III P24.

110. On the Hilfsverein's activity, compare *ZDSJ* 3 (1907): 60 with the Hilfsverein flyer of 1907, in SAH II E III P25 (Auswanderungsamt. Zentralbureau für Jüdische Auswanderungsangelegenheiten. Abteilung Hamburg). The figures on Jewish emigration to the United States over the years 1903–7 are taken from the *Encyclopedia Judaica,* q.v. "Migration." For 1891 and 1892 see the tables in Howard Markel, *Quarantine! East European Jewish Immigrants and the New York City Epidemics of 1892* (Baltimore, 1997), 140–41.

111. *Erster Rechenschaftsbericht der deutschen Zentralstelle für jüdische Wanderarmenfürsorge,* 28 January 1912, and accompanying mimeographed, typed ms., SAH JG 483. See also the Zentralstelle's circular, undated but certainly from the third quarter of 1910, and the offprint of Wilhelm Neuman's article, "Die Deutsche Zentralstelle für judische Wanderarmenfürsorge," dated January 1913, in the same file.

112. *OW,* 10 November 1911, 742–43.

113. Allianz zu Wien, 1910 *Jahresbericht,* 7; see also 1906, 17; and 1913, 20–22.

114. The lists are in SAH JG 483.

115. List of 14 June 1912.

116. Bornstein, "Mi-kabtsanim le-dorshei ʿavodah," 10–34; Ulrich Herbert, *A History of Foreign Labor in Germany, 1880–1980* (Ann Arbor, 1990), 73.

117. Cited in Steinmetz, *Regulating the Social*, 121.

118. *Mitteilungen vom DIGB*, no. 51 (1899): 20; see also the speech by Bernard Kahn, general secretary of the Hilfsverein der deutschen Juden, on German attempts to solve the problem of itinerant beggars, in *Mitteilungen vom DIGB*, no. 74 (1909): 109–30.

119. *Mitteilungen vom DIGB*, no. 51 (1899): 20; Bornstein, "Lidhot o-liklot? Piteronim le-baʿayat ha-ʿaniyim ha-yehudim ha-navadim be-Germaniyah 1900," in *Spiegel Lectures in European Jewish History*, no. 8 (Tel Aviv, 1988), 12–13. The first Christian Wanderarbeitsstätte had been founded in 1882. *Jüdische Arbeits und Wanderfürsorge* 1 (February 1928): 152.

120. By 1914, 400,000 Poles with German citizenship (Inlandspolen) were laboring in the Ruhr, and another 270,000 Poles with foreign citizenship were at work in Germany, mostly in agriculture in the eastern provinces. Ulrich Herbert, *A History of Foreign Labor in Germany, 1880–1980* (Ann Arbor, 1980), 54. See also Bornstein, *Mi-kabtsanim le-dorsheiʿavodah*, 58–59.

121. Black, *Social Politics*, 80–84.

122. In language reminiscent of Naphtali Herz Wessely, Michael Henry of the *Jewish Chronicle* called for a new type of Jewish school that would teach the "proper principles of social economy," that is, "the history and character of trades, productions, manufactures, useful arts and materials." *JC*, 27 June 1873, 216–17. See also 5 September 1873, 380–81; 5 April 1878, 9–10.

123. *UI*, 26 June 1903, 430–33. See also *AI*, 1 November 1888, 354.

124. On the association in Vienna, see *NZ*, 1 March 1872, 100–101, and 18 February 1881, 53–54; also *OW*, 9 June 1911, 382–83. For Budapest, see *NZ*, 9 June 1893, 228, and 1 June 1894, 223–25; also *OW*, 2 June 1911, 368.

125. About 140 children were actually selected for the program, and 80 made it through the first year of agricultural training. *Mitteilungen der Israelitischen Allianz zu Wien*, September 1885, 9; 1886 *Jahresbericht*, xii; 1887 *Jahresbericht*, x–xii.

126. Allianz zu Wien, 1890 *Jahresbericht*, ix, xvii; also 1891, vi.

127. *Mitteilungen vom DIGB*, no. 8 (1880): 63–64.

128. Ibid., no. 24 (1889): 7.

129. B'nai B'rith, *Verhandlungen der Grosse-Loge für Deutschland VIII (1886–1902):* 1893, 345, 357, 406; 1894, 418–19; 1895, 475–76; 1897, 569–70. See also the Düsseldorf Verein's *Bericht* for 1887, 2; *Mitteilungen vom DIGB*, no. 32 (1892): 6–7; Maretzki, *Geschichte*, 232, 237; Auerbach, "Aufgaben und Bestrebungen," 61.

130. The colony did, in fact, produce impressive results; by 1912 it had provided vocational training and job-placement services to some five thousand individuals, approximately three-fourths of whom were from Galicia or Russia. There were also Jewish *Arbeitsstätten* in Cologne and Breslau. *Mitteilungen vom DIGB*, no. 51 (1899): 21–22; no. 58 (1902): 91–94; no. 60 (1903): 11–12; no. 71 (1908): 19; no. 78 (1911): 48; no. 80 (1912): 39. A detailed study of the Weissensee colony may be found in Bornstein, "Lidhot o-liklot?"

131. Marcus Adler, *Chronik der Gesellschaft zur Verbreitung der Handwerke und des Ackerbaues unter den Juden im Preussischen Staate* (Berlin, 1898), 8.

132. *DIGB Statistisches Jahrbuch,* 1889, 90–91; 1898, 153–54; 1913, 238–39; *Bericht über die Wirksamkeit des Vereins zur Verbreitung und Förderung der Handwerke unter den Juden* (Düsseldorf, 1890).

133. *Namen-Verzeichnis der Mitglieder der Gesellschaft zur Unterstützung jüdischer Handwerker und Künstler in Krankheitsfällen* (Berlin, 1911), CAHJP TD114.

134. *Jahresbericht des Vereins zur Beförderung der Bodenkultur unter den Juden Deutschlands* 6 (1904).

135. Bornstein, "Lidhot o-liklot?" 18.

136. *Mitteilungen vom DIGB,* no. 8 (1880): 63–64.

137. *Jahresbericht des Vereins zur Förderung der Bodenkultur unter den Juden Deutschlands,* 3, 1901, 5, 1903; see also Eugen Katz, *Die Alexander und Fanny Simon'sche Stiftung zu Hannover. Ihre Ziele und ihre Arbeiten von 1907–1914* (Hannover, 1914), 5–6.

138. Arthur Kahn, "Klassengeist und Titelnarrheit. Eine Betrachtung zum Tode August Bebels," *JP,* Beilage to no. 36, 1913, 371–72. For an excellent analysis of the medical self-images of German Jews, see John Efron, *Defenders of the Race: Jewish Doctors and Race Science in Fin-de-Siècle Europe* (New Haven, 1994).

139. For an especially harsh example of this genre, see J. Loewenberg's speech at the 1896 meeting of the Freie israelitishe Vereinigung, 23–43.

140. E.g., the industrialist Walter Rathenau, the critic Otto Weininger, and the philosopher Theodor Lessing, before his return to a positive Jewish identity. On these figures, see Sander Gilman, *Jewish Self-Hatred* (Baltimore, 1986).

141. Jehuda Reinharz, *Fatherland or Promised Land: The Dilemma of the German Jew, 1893–1914* (Ann Arbor, 1975), 12, 28.

142. Prestel, "Weibliche Rollenzuweisung," 52.

143. Schorsch, *Jewish Reactions to German Antisemitism,* 35.

144. On Adler, see his obituaries in the *Mitteilungen vom DIGB,* no. 63 (1904): 3–8, and in *GA,* 19 September 1904.

145. For biographical information on Kahn, see the Arthur Kahn collection, *Nachrufe* file, ALBI AR-C 3100. Kahn was a prolific writer; his economic jeremiads include the pamphlets *Hin zur Scholle* (Berlin, 1912); and *Der Weg zur wahren Emanzipation* (Berlin, 1915). This combination of Orthodoxy and economic self-criticism was admittedly idiosyncratic; Orthodox Jews tended to look favorably on commercial occupations, as they were thought to be more conducive to religious observance than others. Mordechai Breuer, *Jüdische Orthodoxie im Deutschen Reich, 1871–1918* (Frankfurt am Main, 1986), 199.

146. Unlike Kahn, Moses has received serious biographical attention: Daniel S. Nadav, *Julius Moses und die Politik der Sozialhygiene in Deutschland* (Gerlingen, 1985).

147. On Moses's political journalism, see Marjorie Lamberti, *Jewish Activism in Imperial Germany* (New Haven, 1978), 35–37, 47, 75–76, 90, 94–95. For one of Moses's economic broadsides, see *Das Handwerk unter den Juden. Vortrag gehalten im Verein selbstständiger Handwerker jüdischen Glaubens* (Berlin, 1902).

148. Secondary literature on these projects is scarce; see E. G. Lowenthal, "The Ahlem Experiment," *LBIYB* 14 (1969): 165–81; Tamar Bermann, *Produktivierungsmythen und Antisemitismus* (Vienna, 1973), 57–59; and the connecting

narrative passages in Friedrich Homeyer, *Beitrag zur Geschichte der Gartenbau-schule Ahlem 1893–1979. Dokumentarische Bearbeitung* (Hannover, 1980). Both the APA and the Ahlem school published detailed annual reports, and the history of Ahlem is nicely summarized in Eugen Katz, *Die Alexander und Fanny Simon'sche Stiftung zu Hannover. Ihre Ziele und ihre Arbeiten von 1907–1914* (Hannover, 1914).

149. Gustav Tuch, *Referat betreffend Beteiligung deutscher Juden an heimischer Landwirtschaft, gehalten am 24. Oktober 1897* (Berlin, 1897); idem, *Innere Kolonisation*, n.p., 1897; Kahn, *Hin zur Scholle!* (Berlin, 1912); A. M. Simon, *Sollen sich Juden in Deutschland dem Handwerk, der Gärtnerei, und der Landwirtschaft widmen?* (Berlin, 1902); idem, *Die Erziehung zur Bodenkultur und zum Handwerk: Eine Soziale Frage* (Berlin, 1904); Katz, *Die Simon'sche Stiftung*.

150. "Verlierende Volkskraft," attached to the *Satzungen* of the APA (Verein für die Förderung der Bodenkultur unter den Juden in Deutschland), Berlin, 1898. See also Kahn, *Hin zur Scholle!* 19; and "Zum Projekt einer jüdische Gartenstadt bei Berlin," undated flyer (probably 1914) in CZA, A12/7. Ironically, Jewish activists situated in German Jewry's rural heartland in the southwest expressed an opposite view of urbanization as a positive force that promoted embourgeoisement. Such were the views of a study of 1900, sponsored by the B'nai B'rith in Mannheim. See Monika Richarz, "Die soziale Stellung der jüdischen Händler auf dem Lande am Beispiel Süwestdeutschlands," in *Jüdische Unternehmer in Deutschland im 19. Und 20. Jahrhundert*, ed. Werner E. Mosse and Hans Pohl (Stuttgart, 1992), 280.

151. Segall himself had been born in Posen. For biographical information on him, see Werner Röder and Herbert Strauss, eds., *Biographisches Handbuch der deutschsprächigen emigration nach 1933* (Munich, 1980–83), 1: 685.

152. *IDR*, 10 October 1913, 433–43 (a presentation of the Centralverein's initiative and its rationale) and 443–49 (Segall's comments).

153. On positive images of the Ostjude in Imperial and Weimar Germany, see Steven Aschheim, *Brothers and Strangers: The East European Jew in German and German Jewish Consciousness, 1800–1923* (Madison, 1982). For an idealization of the rural Jew in fiction, see the discussion of the Orthodox novelist Pinchas Kohn in Michael Brenner, "East and West in Orthodox German-Jewish Novels (1912–1934)," *LBIYB* 37 (1992): 309–23.

154. Verein ehemaliger Ahlemer, *21er Bericht,* Hannover, 1913.

155. Katz, *Die Simon'sche Stiftung,* 31–32; Ahlem school to Ruppin, 5 March 1911, CZA L2/21/V; Land- und Lehrgutgesellschaft in Hannover to Otto Warburg, 24 March 1911, CZA L2/21/II; general correspondence between Simon'sche Stiftung and Ruppin in CZA L2/147 and 148.

156. See the correspondence between, inter alia, Bodenheimer, Tuch, and Simon, in CZA A/15/II/5 and A15/II/8.

157. On these figures, see Derek J. Penslar, *Zionism and Technocracy: The Engineering of Jewish Settlement in Palestine* (Bloomington, Ind., 1991), chaps. 2–4 passim.

158. On agrarian romantic sentiment in Imperial Germany, see Klaus Bergmann, *Agrarromantik und Grossstadtsfeindschaft* (Meisenheim am Glan, 1970); and Wolfgang Krabbe, *Gesellschaftsveränderung durch Lebensreform* (Göttingen,

1974). On internal colonization, see William Hagen, *Germans, Poles, and Jews: The Nationality Conflict in the Prussian East, 1772–1914* (Chicago, 1980), chap. 5. For references to the German environment by the Jewish agrarians, see Gustav Tuch, *Schulgarten* (Berlin, 1898); idem, *Innere Kolonisation*, 10–15; the 1906 report of the APA, 5–6; and its 1913 report, 4–5.

159. Ironically, these schools were often opposed by master artisans, who saw in them an encroachment on their authority. See Derek S. Linton, *"Who Has the Youth, Has the Future": The Campaign to Save Young Workers in Imperial Germany* (Cambridge, 1991), 69–97.

160. Fritz Stern, *The Politics of Cultural Despair: A Study in the Rise of the Germanic Ideology* (Berkeley, 1961), 172–74.

161. *Mitteilungen vom DIGB*, no. 9 (1881): 55; no. 24 (1889): 1–2, 6–7, 25–28; no. 33 (1892): 17–19. The vocational programs of the Allianz zu Wien were similarly motivated. See the 1890 *Jahresbericht*, ix.

162. *Mitteilungen vom DIGB*, no. 45 (1897):2–4; see also no. 24 (1889): 25–28.

163. Statistical data on the work of the Düsseldorf and other vocational societies were tabulated by Adler and printed in no. 24 (1889) and no. 45 (1897) of the *Mitteilungen vom DIGB*. For statistics on the Prussian society, see also Marcus Adler, *Chronik der Gesellschaft zur Verbreitung der Handwerke und des Ackerbaues unter den Juden im Preussischen Staate* (Berlin, 1898), 57.

164. Between 1884 and 1912 the DIGB's Handicrafts Department assisted all of 376 apprentices: *Mitteilungen vom DIGB*, no. 80 (1912): 36.

165. *Mitteilungen vom DIGB*, no.9 (1881): 54; no. 10 (1882): 36; no. 13 (1884): 14; *AZdJ*, 29 May 1908, 253–54.

166. Moses, *Das Handwerk unter den Juden*, 11; W. Pohlmann, *Die Juden und die körperliche Arveit* (Berlin, 1894), 14–15.

167. Jacob Toury, "Ostjüdische Handarbeite in Deutschland vor 1914," *BLBI* 6 (1963): 81–91.

168. Maretzki, "Die Leistungen des Ordens," 38–39; "Die Frauen und die Orden," 86–87.

169. Shulamit Volkov, *The Rise of Popular Antimodernism in Germany* (Princeton, 1978), 17, 197–203, 247–56, 296.

170. Dr. J. Löwenberg, Freie israelitische Vereinigung, *Mitteilungen der Ausschüsse*, 43; *Mitteilungen vom DIGB*, no. 9 (1881): 55.

171. Cf. Robert Gellately, *The Politics of Economic Despair* (London, 1974).

172. *GA*, 14 March 1904.

173. Norbert Kampe, "Jews and Antisemitism in Universities in Imperial Germany (I)," *LBIYB* 30 (1985): 357–94.

174. *Mitteilungen vom DIGB*, no. 13 (1884): 14–15; Simon, *Die Erziehung zur Bodenkultur*, 5; Katz, *Die Simon'sche Stiftung*, 6–7.

175. In 1896 these occupations accounted for 22 of the 41 apprentices supported by the DIGB's Abteilung für Handwerk und technische Gewerbe; 17 of the 35 graduates of the Düsseldorf Verein; 53 of the 144 apprentices in Beuthen; and 19 of 44 in Cassel. Most of the rest were bakers, bookbinders, furriers, upholsterers, and painters. *Mitteilungen vom DIGB*, no. 45 (1897): 8–9, 13, 16, 20. In 1907, 42 of the 171 members of Berlin's Verein selbständiger Handwerker jüdischen Glaubens were tailors. *GA*, 6 January 1907.

176. Narcisse Leven, *Cinquante ans d'histoire: L'Alliance Israélite Universelle (1860–1910)* (Paris, 1920), 2: 357. The leaders of the Russian Jewish vocational society ORT were well aware of this problem. Leon Shapiro, *The History of ORT* (New York, 1980), 56–57.

177. See Heinz-Dietrich Loewe, *The Tsars and the Jews* (Chur, Switzerland, 1993), 37, 71, 89, 93.

178. E.g., in 1909–10, of applicants for aid from the Stettin provincial office, there were 120 merchants and 116 craftsmen; the following year there were 76 craftsmen and 53 merchants. In Bochum in 1911, 341 petitioners were craftsmen, 119 were laborers, and 115 were merchants. In Fürth-Nürnberg in 1910, 1,215 were merchants and tradesmen and 426 were workers and craftsmen. Report of 26 January 1912, documenting activities of thirteen provincial offices, in SAH JG 483.

179. I. Koralnik, "Zur analyse der strukturellen Wandlungen im deutschen Judentum 1895–1925," *Jüdische Wohlfahrtspflege und Sozialpolitik*, Neue Folge, 1931, 6–14.

180. Volkov, *Rise of Popular Antimodernism*, 313–19. Jewish artisans in Vienna and London encountered similar problems; see *NZ*, 18 August 1899, 330–31; and Feldman, *Englishmen and Jews*, 209–10.

181. Moses, *Das Handwerk unter den Juden*, 17–18; *Zur Geschichte des "Vereins selbständiger Handwerker jüdischen Glaubens" zu Berlin. Ein Gedenkblatt zum X. Stiftungsfeste am 2. Dezember 1905* (Berlin, 1905), 6; Louis Wolff, *Handwerk im Judentum. Entwicklung und Aufstieg. Aus den Reden und Schriften von Louis Wolff (1909–1934)* (Berlin, 1935), 35–41. Relations between Jewish artisans and the communal leadership were poor in Frankfurt am Main and Kassel as well as in Berlin but smooth in Hamburg, Cologne, and Hannover. Zentralverband selbstständiger jüdischer Handwerker Deutschlands, *III. Verbandstag. Köln 1913: Verhandlungsbericht* (Berlin, 1913), 31–35.

182. Quoted in Maretzki, *Geschichte*, 183.

183. Efron, *Defenders of the Race;* Mitch Hart, "Social Science and National Identity: A History of Jewish Statistics, 1880–1930" (Ph.D. dissertation, Stanford University, 1994).

184. Hart, *Social Science,* chap. 1.

185. H. L. Eisenstadt, "Sozialpolitik der Juden in der Gegenwart," *Literaturblatt der Jüdischen Rundschau* 4, nos. 2–3 (27 March and 3 April 1908). During the Weimar Republic, the conflation of population and social policy was common among Jews and Gentiles alike. Claudia Prestel, "Bevölkerungspolitik in der jüdischen Gemeinschaft in der Weimarer Republik—Ausdruck jüdischer Identität?" *Zeitschrift für Geschichtswissenschaft*, no. 8 (1993): 685–715.

186. *JC*, 4 March 1881, 9–10.

187. Verein für jüdische Statistik, ed., *Jüdische Statistik* (Berlin, 1903), 7–22. On Jacobs, see Efron, *Defenders of the Race,* chap. 4.

188. *JC*, 19 February 1904, 13; 9 February 1906, 20–21.

189. See Alfred Nossig's comments in the report from the Hauptversammlung des Vereins für Statistik der Juden, 2 March 1910, reproduced in *ZDSJ* 6, no. 5 (1910): unnumbered pages at end of issue.

190. *GA*, 30 November 1903.

191. Rüdiger Vom Bruch, *"Weder Kommunismus noch Kapitalismus":*

Bürgerliche Sozialreform in Deutschland vom Vormärz bis zur Ära Adenauer (Munich, 1985), 130–37.

192. Maretzki, *Geschichte,* 187; idem, "Die Leistungen des Ordens," 51.

193. See the testimonial to Maretzki by Bruno Blau in *ZDSJ* 9, no. 1 (January 1913): 1–2.

194. Julius Moses, "Statistische Erhebungen über die Berufswahl der jüdischen Jugend in Landgemeinden Badens," in *Jüdische Statistik,* 202–8; Maretzki, *Geschichte,* 245–50.

195. The relationship between social science and Jewish identity that I describe here was manifested as well by early feminists, such as those analyzed by Judith Walkowitz in London's Men's and Women's Club, founded in 1885. Olive Schreiner's desire to write a comprehensive book on women from "a historical, biological, and sexological perspective" led her and like-minded women to produce feminist tracts in which scientific data were invoked to support a sociopolitical agenda and heighten collective identity. Judith R. Walkowitz, *City of Dreadful Delight: Narratives of Sexual Danger in Late-Victorian London* (Chicago, 1992), 135–69; quote is from 165.

196. Arthur Cohen, "Georg von Mayr und die Statistik," *ZDSJ* 7, no. 3 (March 1911): 33–36, emphasis in original.

197. For biographical sketches of Cohen, see the *Jüdisches Lexicon* (Berlin, 1927–30), 1: 1418; and Wininger, *Grosse Jüdische National-Biographie,* 1: 561.

198. Efron, *Defenders of the Race,* 168.

199. Friedrich Ollendorf, "Die Zentralwohlfahrtsstelle der deutschen Juden," *Zedaka: Zeitschrift der jüdischen Wohlfahrtspflege,* July 1928, 3. On the ongoing inability of German Jewry to organize politically, see Jacob Toury, "Organizational Problems of Germany Jewry: Steps towards the Establishment of a Central Organization (1893–1920)," *LBIYB* 13 (1968): 57–90.

200. Ludger Heid, "Melocho welo Zedoko: 'Arbeit, nicht Wohltätigkeit für osjüdische Proletarier im Ruhrgebiet," in *Zedaka: Jüdische Sozialarbeit im Wandel der Zeit. 75 Jahre Zentralwohlfahrtsstelle der Juden in Deutschland,* ed. George Heuberger (Frankfurt am Main, 1992), 80. See also Hagit Lavsky, *Before Catastrophe: The Distinctive Path of German Zionism* (Detroit, 1996), 38.

201. Michael Brenner, "The Jüdische Volkspartei: National-Jewish Communal Politics during the Weimar Republic," *LBIYB* 35 (1990): 219–43. Similar developments took place in Vienna in 1933, when the communal leadership passed from Liberals to Nationalists, who aspired to change the Kultusgemeinde into a "people's community" with expanded social welfare services. Harriet Pass Freidenreich, *Jewish Politics in Vienna, 1918–1938* (Bloomington, Ind., 1991), 148.

202. For biographical information on Caspary and Timendorfer, see Georg Herlitz and Bruno Kirschner, eds., *Jüdisches Lexicon* (Berlin, 1927–30), 1: 1281; 4:951. Segal did emigrate in 1933 to Palestine, where he worked for Kupat Holim.

203. Jakob Segall, "Die gegenwärtige Lage der jüdischen Wohlfahrtspflege in Deutschland," *Zedaka,* December 1925, 2–5; Ollendorf, "Die Zentralwohlfahrtsstelle," 4, 7.

204. Young-Sun Hong, *Welfare, Modernity, and the Weimar State, 1919–1933* (Princeton, 1998), 72–73.

205. Compare Alfred Berger's published lecture in *Jüdische Arbeits- und Wan-*

derfürsorge 1, nos. 1–2 (1927): 7–11, with the estimates in the same volume of the journal, nos. 3–4 (1927): 77.

206. Hans Golsar, "Jüdische Sozialpolitik," *Zedakah,* January 1921, 3–6; I. Koralnik, "Die beruflichen und sozialen Wandlungen im deutschen Judentum," *Jüdische Wohlfahrspflege und Sozialpolitik,* Neue Folge, 1 (1930): 15–23, 80–89; 2 (1931): 72–79; and Max Kreutzberger, "Zum Begriff einer jüdischen Sozialpolitik," *Jüdische Wohlfahrtspflege und Sozialpolitik,* Neue Folge, 2 (1931): 1–6, 131–39, 358–67. For a recent overview, see Abraham Barkai, "Juden als sozioökonomische Minderheitsgruppe in der Weimarer Republik," in *Juden in der Weimarer Republic,* ed. Walter Grab and Julius Schoeps (Stuttgart, 1986), 330–46.

207. Avraham Barkai, "Zur Wirtschaftsgeschichte der Juden in Deutschland," *TAJDG* 20 (1991): 200–204; Hart, "Social Science," 74–78.

208. From the statement of purpose for the periodical *Jüdische Arbeits- und Wanderfürsorge* 1, nos. 1–2 (1927): 1–2.

209. I. Koralnik, "Die beruflichen und sozialen Wandlungen im deutschen Judentum," 17. On this theme, see also Alfred Marcus, *Die wirtschaftliche Krise der deutschen Juden* (Berlin, 1931), 160–63.

210. Kreutzberger, "Zum Begriff einer jüdischen Sozialpolitik."

211. E.g., Marcus, *Wirtschaftliche Krise.*

212. Kahn to Felix Warburg, 9 January 1922, AAJJDC AR21/32 50b. One encounters the same sense of humility and humiliation in Austria. The *Jahresbericht* of the Allianz zu Wien for 1929–30 remarked sadly that unlike past eras, when Austrian and German Jewry was prosperous and secure and generously assisted oppressed Jews in the East, the two had become victim to political persecution and economic collapse and were now lumped with Romania and Hungary as "lands of persecution" in the philanthropic publications of American, English, and French Jews (5–7).

213. On the economic plight of German Jewry under Nazi rule, see Avraham Barkai, *From Boycott to Annihilation: The Economic Struggle of German Jews, 1933–1943* (Hanover, N.H., 1989).

214. Kellner, *Reshito shel tikhnun hevrati klal-yehudi,* 14. See also 1–2; and idem, *Le-ma'an Tsiyon. Ha-hit'arvut ha-klal-yehudit bi-metsukat ha-yishuv, 1869–1882* (Jerusalem, 1977), 12–15.

Chapter Six. From Social Policy to Social Engineering, 1870–1933

1. On the origins of "emancipationist" Jewish politics, see Jonathan Frankel, " 'Ritual Murder' in the Modern Era: The Damascus Affair of 1840," *Jewish Social Studies* 3 (1997): 1–16; and idem, *The Damascus Affair: "Ritual Murder," Politics, and the Jews in 1840* (Cambridge, 1997).

2. See the stimulating discussion in Ezra Mendelsohn, *On Modern Jewish Politics* (New York, 1993).

3. For an excellent analysis of the relationship among the Alliance's political strategies, educational policies, and underlying ideologies, see Aron Rodrigue,

French Jews, Turkish Jews: The Alliance Israélite Universelle and the Politics of Jewish Schooling in Turkey, 1860–1925 (Bloomington, Ind., 1990).

4. Moshe Rinott, *Hevrat ha-'ezrah liyehudei Germaniyah biyetsirah u-vema'avak* (Jerusalem, 1971), 26.

5. Theodor Herzl, *Der Judenastaat* (Berlin, 1920), 24. The literature on Weizmann's wartime negotiations with the British is immense; the best recent treatment is Jehuda Reinharz, *Chaim Weizmann: The Making of a Statesman* (Oxford, 1993).

6. Georg Herlitz, *Das Jahr der Zionisten* (Jerusalem, 1949), 139.

7. Rodrigue, *French Jews, Turkish Jews,* 23; Zosa Szajkowski, "Conflicts in the Alliance Israélite Universelle and the Founding of the Anglo-Jewish Association, the Vienna Allianz, and the Hilfsverein," *Jewish Social Studies* 19, nos. 1–2 (1957): 44, 49; Hilfsverein der deutschen Juden, *Achter Bericht,* 1910, 9.

8. Szajkowski, "Conflicts," 39–42.

9. Herzl, *Der Judenstaat,* 10.

10. For a useful, nonscholarly history of the JCA, see Theodore Norman, *An Outstretched Arm: A History of the Jewish Colonization Association* (London, 1985).

11. Leonard Robinson and Frank Rosenblatt to Herbert Lehman, 26 July 1922, AAJJDC, AR21/32/104.

12. E.g., the resolutions passed in the wake of the meeting of the United Jewish Campaign in Philadelphia, 12 and 13 September 1925, AAJJDC AR21/32/508.

13. Compare Yehuda Bauer, *My Brother's Keeper: A History of the American Jewish Joint Distribution Committee* (Philadelphia, 1974), 17–22; with American Jewish Joint Distribution Committee, *Thirty Years: The Story of the J.D.C.* (New York, 1945). In the 1940s the Joint's National Council numbered some 5,200 activists drawn from the communal leadership. But this was only the base of a pyramid, at the top of which stood an elite group of at most a half-dozen men who ran the day-to-day operations of the Joint and set its course. The quote is from Bauer, *My Brother's Keeper,* 26.

14. Leon Shapiro, *The History of ORT* (New York, 1980).

15. Bernard Kahn to Herbert Lehman, 21 November 1923, AAJJDC AR21/32/105.

16. Compare the narratives of the Woodbine, New Jersey, Agricultural School, the JCA's Palestinian colonies, and the Argentinian project, in Samuel Joseph, *History of the Baron de Hirsch Fund* (New York, 1935), 48, 70–78; Derek J. Penslar, *Zionism and Technocracy: The Engineering of Jewish Settlement in Palestine* (Bloomington, Ind., 1991), 27–33; and Haim Avni, *Argentina and the Jews: A History of Jewish Immigration* (Tuscaloosa, Ala., 1991).

17. Louis Oungre to Herbert Lehman, 23 October and 10 November 1923, AAJJDC AR21/32/105.

18. Compare Ehud Luz, *Parallels Meet: Religion and Nationalism in the Early Zionist Movement 1882–1914* (Philadelphia, 1988), with Jacob Kellner, *Le-ma'an Tsiyon. Ha-hit'arvut ha-klal yehudit bi-metsukat ha-yishuv 1869–1882* (Jerusalem, 1977), chap. 3, and Rinott, *Hevrat ha-'ezrah,* 22–23.

19. Quote is from Anglo-Jewish Association, *Annual Report,* 1893–95, 8. See

also the reports for 1874–75, 6; 1887–88, 68 ff. and 124; 1910–11, 5–7, and 42. On the IAzW, see its *Jahresbericht* for 1874 and the historical overview in its 1913 *Jahresbericht*, 8–12.

20. Aron Rodrigue, *De l'instruction à l'émancipation: Les enseignants de l'Alliance Israélite Universelle et les juifs de l'Orient, 1860–1939* (Paris, 1989), 89–95.

21. Narcisse Leven, *Cinquante ans d'histoire: L'Alliance Israélite Universelle (1860–1910)* (Paris, 1920), 2:290–94.

22. Ibid., 403.

23. Ibid., 319–30.

24. Rodrigue, *French Jews, Turkish Jews*, 110.

25. Alliance Israélite Universelle, *Bulletin*, 1884 (1), 35; see also 1878 (2), 17; and 1886 (1), 35.

26. The school in Tunis, and at times the one in Salonica, cost more but served far more pupils. In 1886 the Tunis school served 993 pupils at a cost of 73,480 francs (74 francs each), whereas Jerusalem cost 36,000 francs for 160 pupils (225 francs each). A decade later the budget and number of students at Tunis was about the same, but the budget for the Jerusalem school climbed to 63,241 francs for 249 pupils (254 francs each). Ibid., 1883 (1), 39–40; 1883 (2), 45; 1886 (2), 36, 40; 1896, 96.

27. Anglo-Jewish Association, *Annual Report*, 1901–2, 36; 1902–3, 45; 1908–9, 38; 1911–12, 43; 1912–13, 37; 1914–15, 27.

28. Ibid., 1910–11, 44–45.

29. Ibid., 1897, 103; 1902, 184.

30. Ibid., 1910–11, 6–7, 39.

31. Ernst Feder, *Politik und Humanität. Paul Nathan, Ein Lebensbild* (Berlin, 1929), 85–90, 97–99.

32. Anglo-Jewish Association, *Annual Report*, 1902, 184, 188; *GA*, 17 November 1907.

33. Alliance, *Bulletin*, 1902, 184–85; also 1898, 106–8; 1900, 132.

34. Norman, *An Outstretched Arm*, 161.

35. Haim Avni, "Hevrat IKA ve-ha-tsiyonut," in *Ha-tsiyonut u-mitnagdeihah ba-ʿam ha-yehudi*, ed. Michel Abitbol and Haim Avni (Jerusalem, 1990), 125–46; Yaʿakov Goldstein and Batsheva Stern, "PIKA—Irgunah u-mataroteihah," *Cathedra* 59 (1991): 102–26.

36. Compare Penslar, *Zionism and Technocracy*, 27–33, with Yoram Mayorek, "Emil Meyerson ve-reshit ha-meʿuravut shel hevrat IKA be-Eretz Yisraʾel," *Cathedra* 62 (1991): 67–79.

37. JCA Paris to James Rosenberg, 21 September 1923, AAJJDC AR21/32/104.

38. Wininger, *Grosse jüdische National-Biographie* (Czernowitz, 1925–36), 3: 389–91. See also Kaminka's remarks at the First Zionist Congress, *Stenographisches Protokoll der Verhandlungen des Zionisten-Kongresses* (Vienna, 1897), 110–12, 170–75.

39. Archives of the Leo Baeck Institute New York (ALBINY), Bernard Kahn Archive, Box no. 1.

40. For biographical information on Kahn, see the "Biographische Notizen" (typed ms., dated 1936) and Shalom Adler-Rudel's long obituary, in the 10, 17,

and 24 June 1955 issues of *Allgemeine,* ALBINY, Bernard Kahn Archive, Box no. 1; and the biographical sketch by Joseph van Gelder in AAJJDC AR21/32/50b.

41. Throughout the 1920s Kahn's salary climbed from $7,500 to $12,000. He, like other favorites of the banker and longtime JDC chairman Felix Warburg, received occasional, unexpected transfers of $5,000 to use as a discretionary account. James Rosenberg to Bernard Kahn, 19 January 1922; Bernard Flexner to Kahn, 18 February 1924; Felix Warburg to Kahn, 15 October 1926, in AAJJDC AR21/32/50b.

42. The Joint's Palestinian expenditures amounted to $8 million out of $74 million. Joseph Hyman to W. K. Wasserman, 18 March 1928, YIVO Archives, New York, RG 358/26.

43. David da Sola Pool to JDC Reconstruction Committee, 22 March 1922, AAJJDC AR21/32/297.

44. Da Sola Pool to JDC Reconstruction Committee, 19 September 1921, AAJJDC AR21/32/297.

45. I document the links between the proletarian radicalism of the Second Aliyah *halutzim* and the bourgeois social-reformism of the ZO's settlement officers in *Zionism and Technocracy,* esp. chap. 4.

46. See Kellner, *Le-ma'an Tsiyon,* chap. 3, esp. 88; Penslar, *Zionism and Technocracy,* 13–18.

47. IAzW, *Jahresbericht,* 1882, 98.

48. The phrase "selected human material" was used by Meyerson in a speech of 1898. Yoram Mayorek, "Emil Meyerson ve-reshit ha-me'uravut shel hevrat IKA be-Eretz Yisra'el," *Cathedra* 60 (1991):84.

49. Ruppin, so far as I know, never received a reply to his petition to the antisemitic politician Otto Böckel; Ford was not impressed by Rosenberg's gesture. Compare Allan Laine Kagedan's discussion of Rosenberg in *Soviet Zion: The Quest for a Russian Jewish Homeland* (New York, 1994), 49–56, with my treatment of Ruppin in *Zionism and Technocracy,* 83–84.

50. In AAJJDC AR21/32/534.

51. From p. 20 of the galley proofs of his account of his 1926 trip to Russia, in AAJJDC AR21/32/535.

52. The alliance between bourgeois and proletarian Jews was not limited to Palestine. In 1882 middle-class Jews in Germany and Austria supported Odessa and Kiev's Am Olam groups, some of whom went on to form a colony in Vineland, New Jersey. Like the pioneers on the first Zionist collectives, the Am Olam refused to introduce private landholding, which, they claimed, resulted in a "terrible exploitation of the landless proletariat." Only cooperative principles were considered "wise and suitable, especially in a new country." Cited in Frankel, *Prophecy and Politics,* 94–95.

53. On Revisionist Zionist social thought, see Ya'akov Shavit, *Me-rov li-medinah: ha-tenua'h ha revizionistit, ha-tokhnit ha-hityashvutit, ve-ha-ra'yon ha-hevrati 1925–1935* (Tel Aviv, 1983); idem, *Jabotinsky and the Revisionist Movement* (London, 1988); Raphaella Bilsi Ben-Hur, *Every Individual a King: The Social and Political Thought of Ze'ev Vladimir Jabotinsky* (Washington, D.C., 1993).

54. Herzl used it in *Der Judenstaat,* as did Maurice de Hirsch in his essay, "My Views on Philanthropy," *North American Review* 416 (July 1891), reproduced in Joseph, *History of the Baron de Hirsch Fund,* 275–77.

55. According to George Mosse, before World War I the term "human material" had negative connotations because it appeared to "den[y] the human spirit." The term gained currency during the interwar period as a result of the "mechanization of all aspects of life." See George Mosse, *Fallen Soldiers* (New York, 1985), 179. If so, then the Zionists were ahead of their time. Yet let us recall the late Amos Funkenstein's observation that Zionist concepts of "human material" were offset by a romantic streak asserting human ineffability. Amos Funkenstein, "Zionism, Science, and History," in *Perceptions of Jewish History* (Berkeley, 1993), 347–50.

56. Despite its conceptual continuity from the Ottoman period to the early years of the Israeli state, "selective immigration" ceased to determine Zionist immigration policy after 1929, when the political crises of the Yishuv, followed by the increasing persecution of European Jewry during the 1930s, stimulated efforts to bring in as many immigrants as possible. Thus invocation of "selective immigration" came to signify elite status and nostalgia for an abandoned social vision. Aviva Halamish, "A Critical Analysis of the Term 'Selective Immigration' in Zionist Theory, Practice, and Historgioraphy," paper delivered at the conference "The Centenary of Political Zionism," Jerusalem, 19 May 1997.

On Zionist concepts of the need for selective immigration, see Margalit Shilo, "Tovat ha-aretz o-tovat ha-ʿam? Yahesah shel ha-tenua ʿh ha-tsiyonit le-ʿaliyah bitekufat ha-ʿaliyah ha-sheniyah," *Cathedra* 46 (1987): 109–22; Moshe Mossek, *Palestine Immigration Policy under Sir Herbert Samuel* (London, 1978); Yehiam Vaitz, *Mudaʾut ve-hoser onim—Mapai le-nokhah ha-shoah 1943–45* (Jerusalem, 1994), chap. 5; Tom Segev, *The Seventh Million: The Israelis and the Holocaust* (New York, 1993), 113–22.

57. The history of the conferences held between 1869 and 1882 is narrated in detail in Jacob Kellner, "Philanthropy and Social Planning in Jewish Society (1842–1882)" (Ph.D. dissertation, Hebrew University of Jerusalem, 1973). Details of post-1903 relief work may be found in the IAzW, *Jahresberichte*, 1904, 7; 1906, 9–12.

58. Leven, *Cinquante ans d'histoire*, 2: 357–61; Jewish Colonization Association, *Le Baron Maurice de Hirsch et la Jewish Colonisation Association* (Paris, 1936), 44–46.

59. Kurt Grunwald, *Türkenhirsch* (Jerusalem, 1969), 123; also 76–85. See also Shalom Adler-Rudel, "Moritz Baron Hirsch: Profile of a Great Philanthropist," *LBIYB* 8 (1963): 42–48; and the recent provocative article by Daniel Gutwein, "Herzl ve-ha-plutokratiah ha-yehudit," *Tsiyon* 62 (1998):47–74.

60. Derek J. Penslar, "Technical Expertise and the Creation of the Rural Yishuv, 1882–1948," *Jewish History*, forthcoming; idem, "Theodor Herzl and the Origins of Jewish Social Policy," in *Theodor Herzl: Visionary of the Jewish State*, ed. Gideon Shimoni and Robert S. Wistrich (Jerusalem, 2000), 215–16.

61. The issue of the commission of experts takes up most of the famous three-page memorandum to the Russian Choveve Tsiyon that Hirsch penned in August 1891. The document is reproduced in Grunwald, *Türkenhirsch*, 123 ff.

62. American Jewish Joint Distribution Committee, *Thirty Years*, 14. There is a similar description in Joseph Hyman, *Twenty-five Years of American Aid to Jews Overseas* (New York, 1939), 16.

63. Warburg's diary for May 1927, typescript ms., in AAJJDC AR21/32/534.

Hyman's account, dated 27 December 1928, is in the same file. See also the comments about Rosen in the letter of the American Relief Administration to James Rosenberg, 5 September 1922, AAJJDC AR21/32/52a; and paeans to Rosen by Warburg, Lehman, and Rosenberg, dated between 31 December 1924 and 25 March 1925, AAJJDC AR21/32/508.

64. Yigal Elam, *Ha-sokhnut ha-yehudit: shanim rishonot* (Jerusalem, 1990), 81–82, 91–92.

65. Haim Avni, *Argentina: "ha-aretz ha-ye'udah": Mif'al ha-hityashvut shel ha-Baron de Hirsh be-Argentinah* (Jerusalem, 1983), 65. See also Joseph, *History of the Baron de Hirsch Fund*, 40–42.

66. Jacob Kellner, *Immigration and Social Policy: The Jewish Experience in the U.S.A., 1881–1882* (Jerusalem, 1979), 56.

67. Derek J. Penslar, "Hashpa'ot tsorfatiyot 'al ha-hakla'ut ha-yehudit be-eretz yisra'el, 1870–1914," *Cathedra* 62 (December 1991): 54–66.

68. Penslar, *Zionism and Technocracy*, chaps. 3, 4.

69. See Alon Gal, "Brandeis' Views on the Upbuilding of Palestine, 1914–23," *Studies in Zionism*, no. 6 (1982): esp. 229–30, 234–35; and Ben Halpern, *A Clash of Heroes: Brandeis, Weizmann, and American Zionism* (New York, 1987), 210–36. On American Progressive-era concepts of efficiency and scientific management, see William Akin, *Technocracy and the American Dream: The Technocratic Movement, 1900–1941* (Berkeley, 1977).

70. Seeking the long-term well-being of Palestine's inhabitants, the PEC combined profitable loans, such as those made to the Palestine Potash Company, with losing propositions, such as loans to the Histadrut construction company Solel Boneh. See the Palestine Economic Corporation's first and fourth annual reports, covering 1926 and 1930, respectively, in AAJJDC AR21/32/320.

71. *XL. Jahresbericht der Israelitischen Allianz zu Wien erstattet an die XL. ordentliche Generalversammlung am 16. April 1913 nebst einem Rückblick auf die vierziegjährige Wirksamkeit des Vereines 1872–1912* (Vienna, 1913), 12–18; see also the organization's 1891 *Jahresbericht*, ix–x.

72. Hilfsverein der deutschen Juden, *Erster Geschäftsbericht (1901–1902)* (Berlin, 1903), 20–24; *Dritter Geschäftsbericht (1904)*, 1905, 13–43; *Viertes Geschäftsbericht (1905)*, 1906, 13–49.

73. Alliance Israélite Universelle, *Bulletin*, 1869 (2), 16–19.

74. Kellner, *Immigration and Social Policy*, 8–9.

75. IAzW, *Jahresbericht*, 1880, 73–82; 1904, passim; 1910, 5.

76. Anglo-Jewish Association, *Annual Report*, 1897–98, 43–45.

77. Hyman, *Twenty-five Years*, 16–26, 34–54; Norman, *An Outstretched Arm*, 166–200.

78. Between 1918 and 1933 the ZO expended $9,521,000 on agricultural settlement; this sum amounted to two-thirds of the budget for immigration and agricultural and urban settlement and almost one-third of the total ZO budget (excluding land purchase) over this period. Nachum Gross and Jacob Metzer, *Finance and the Jewish Economy in Interwar Palestine* (Jerusalem, 1977), 52–53, 57. (Gross and Metzer's figures are given on an annual basis in Palestine pounds; I converted them to dollars using the exchange rates in R. L. Bildwell, *Currency Conversion Tables* [London, 1970].)

79. Hagit Lavsky, *Before Catastrophe: The Distinctive Path of German Zionism* (Detroit, 1996), 243.

80. The figure for Argentina, from the 1913 JCA annual report, is reproduced in Avni, *Argentina and the Jews*, 61.

81. Joseph Hyman to Felix Warburg et al., 13 May 1925, AAJJDC AR21/32/508.

82. Bauer, *My Brother's Keeper*, 61–65.

83. Hyman to Warburg et al., 13 May 1925, AAJJDC AR21/32/508; and Bernard Kahn, "My Trip to Russia," typewritten ms. in YIVO Archive, RG358/21, 6–7. When Felix Warburg visited the Agro-Joint colonies, he was very impressed by Tel Chai, mainly because it had nicely irrigated fields and its settlers spoke Hebrew rather than Yiddish, which, he wrote, is "not to my liking." Warburg's diary of his journey to the Soviet Union, entry dated 15 May 1927, AAJJDC AR21/32/534.

84. For the number of Agro-Joint employees, see Rosen to James Rosenberg, 28 July 1936, AAJJDC AR21/32 510.

85. See Rosen to a Miss Adlerstein, AAJJDC AR21/32/52a; and the obituary press release in AR21/32/3188.

86. On 5 November 1927 Hoover attended a dinner, hosted by Felix Warburg for the American German Jewish elite, and made a short speech praising the work of the Agro-Joint. See AAJJDC AR21/554. See also Hoover's public letter to Rosenberg (who contributed heavily to Hoover's presidential campaign) in the *New York Herald Tribune*, 23 September 1928.

87. Minutes of meeting of JDC Executive Committee, 17 June 1924, YIVO RG 358/17, esp. 2, 10–13; Rosenberg to Rosen, 23 January 1925, AAJJDC AR21/32/508; Marshall to Rosenberg, 19 March 1925, AAJJDC AR21/32/508.

88. "[T]he safety of their funds being their first consideration, they find that for the present they have already invested sufficient funds in Russia." Rosen to JDC Board of Trustees, 31 December 1924, AAJJDC AR21/32/508; see also Rosenberg to Warburg, 2 May 1928, YIVO RG 358/26; Leonard Cohen of the JCA to Warburg, 4 July 1928, AAJJDC AR21/32/59.

89. Cable of Rosen to Rosenberg, 17 February 1925, AAJDC AR21/32/508.

90. Grower to Rosen, 20 February 1925, AAJDC AR21/32/508; report by Grower of 1926 or 1927, typed ms., AAJDC AR21/32/534.

91. Rosenberg to Rosen, 10 May 1928, YIVO RG 358/26.

92. Bauer, *My Brother's Keeper*, 61–65, 88.

93. Margalit Shilo, *Nisyonot be-hityashvut: Ha-misrad Ha-eretz-yisra'eli 1908–1914* (Jerusalem, 1988); Gershon Shafir, *Land, Labor, and the Origins of the Israeli-Palestinian Conflict, 1882–1914* (Cambridge, 1989); Penslar, *Zionism and Technocracy;* Zev Sternhell, *The Founding Myths of Israel* (Princeton, 1997).

94. Elam, *Ha-sokhnut ha-yehudit*, 74.

95. Kahn to JDC, New York, 1 July 1925, AAJJDC AR21/32/508.

96. Correspondence between W. K. Wasserman and Joseph Hyman, 10 and 18 March 1928, YIVO RG 358/26.

97. Correspondence about Brainin's South Africa fund-raising tour of 1929 and the anger it provoked among Zionists is in AAJJDC AR21/323/540.

98. *Urteil des Zionistischen Ehrengerichts in der Sitzung vom 7 Oktober 1929,*

CZA L14/12; Naomi Caruso and Janice Rosen, eds., *The Canadian Story of Reuben Brainin* (Montreal, 1993–96), 1:1–7, 2:113–15.

99. From Rosen's address to the Council of Jewish Federations and Welfare Funds, Philadelphia, 8 February 1937, AAJJDC AR21/32/52a. See also Rosen's remarks at the ASJFSR—Agro-Joint Joint Directors' Meeting of 27 January 1938, cited in the 20 September 1938 report of the Secretary to the JDC Executive, in AAJJDC AR21/32/545.

100. René Fülöp-Miller, *Geist und Gesicht des Bolschewismus* (Zurich, 1926), 387–89.

101. Kagedan, *Soviet Zion*, 77–78, 80–83. See also Antje Kuchenbecker, "Ein 'Rotes Palästina' im Fernen Osten der Sowjetunion—Die Verbannung einer Idee: Die Auseinandersetzung um ein autonomes jüdisches Siedlungsgebiet in der frühen UdSSR," *Archiv für Sozialgeschichte* 37 (1997): 268–79.

102. Rosen at JDC Executive meeting of 17 June 1924, in YIVO RG358/17. See also Hyman to Warburg, Lehman, Marshall, and Roseberg, 13 May 1925, AAJJDC AR21/32/508.

103. Bauer, *My Brother's Keeper*, 66–67, 81–86, 90–98.

104. Rosen to James Rosenberg, 11 December 1937, AAJJDC AR21/32/52a.

105. On Birobidzhan, see Benjamin Pinkus, *The Jews of the Soviet Union: The History of a National Minority* (Cambridge, 1988), 71–76, 191–94; and Robert Weinberg, *Stalin's Forgotten Zion: Birobidzhan and the Making of a Soviet Jewish Homeland: An Illustrated History 1928–1996* (Berkeley, 1998).

106. Rosen to Hyman, 7 February 1939, AAJJDC AR21/32/52a.

107. Information on Rosen's post-1940 activities may be found in the *American Jewish Year Book* for 1939–40, 381–82; 1940–41, 44–47; 1941–42, 335; 1950, 523–24.

108. There are dozens of handwritten letters by Rosen from this period in AAJJDC AR21/32/52a. He mentions his Jewish ancestry in a letter to Felix Warburg, dated 7 September 1948.

109. Unknown employee of Domincan Republic Settlement Association to Rosen, penciled date of August 1940, in AAJJDC AR21/32/52a.

110. Memorandum by Joseph Hyman, 11 July 1928, AAJJDC AR21/32/554.

Epilogue

1. Institute of Jewish Affairs of the World Jewish Congress, *European Jewry Ten Years after the War* (New York, 1956); Shmuel Almog, "Produktivizatsiyah, proletarizatsiyah, ve-'avodah 'ivrit," in *Temurot ba-historiyah ha-yehudit ha-hadashah: Kovets ma'amarim shai li-Shmuel Ettinger* (Jerusalem, 1987), 69–70.

2. Institute of Jewish Affairs of World Jewish Congress, *European Jewry Ten Years after the War,* 128, 130–32; Bernard Wasserstein, *Vanishing Diaspora: The Jews in Europe since 1945* (Cambridge, Mass., 1996), 11, 24–27, 32.

3. The concept of "middleman minorities" is developed in Hubert M. Blalock, Jr., *Toward a Theory of Minority-Group Relations* (New York, 1967) 79–84; Edna Bonacich, "A Theory of Middleman Minorities," *American Sociological Review* 38 (1973): 583–94; and Edna Bonacich and John Modell, *The Economic Basis*

of Ethnic Solidarity: Small Business in the Japanese American Community (Berkeley, 1980).

4. "Indonesia Turns Its Chinese into Scapegoats," *New York Times,* 2 February 1998, A3. The responses of the ethnic Chinese to the hostility directed against them include apologetics, similar to those issued by the subjects of this book, and, in language reminiscent of medieval Jewish sumptuary legislation, calls to cease wearing expensive jewelry or having showy public celebrations of holidays and festivals.

5. Wasserstein, *Vanishing Diaspora,* 8–20, 45–46, 51–56, 82.

6. On the importance of this concept for the fin de siècle, see Shulamit Volkov, "Antisemitism as a Cultural Code," *LBIYB* 23 (1978): 25–45.

7. "The Golden Age of U.S. Jews," *Ha-aretz,* 8 August 2000.

8. Cited in Sander Gilman, *Smart Jews: The Construction of the Image of Jewish Superior Intelligence* (Lincoln, 1996), 19, 234.

9. Cited in Sally Bedell Smith, "Empire of the Sons," *Vanity Fair,* January 1997, 117.

10. Jack Wertheimer, "Jewish Organizational Life in the United States since 1945," *American Jewish Year Book* 95 (1995): 3–98; "Grass Roots Seem to Be Withering," *Jewish Forward,* 12 February 1998; "Charities, Shifting Focus, Are Starting New Drive for Jewish Renaissance," *Jewish Forward,* 8 February 1999; "Policy-Makers Scrambling to Identify Right Strategy as Religion, Families Wax," *Jewish Forward,* 2 July 1999.

11. Benjamin Barber, *Jihad vs. McWorld* (New York, 1998).

12. Bonacich and Modell, *Economic Basis of Ethnic Solidarity,* 256–59. Quote is from 259.

Bibliography

Archives

Archives of the American Jewish Joint Distribution Committee, New York
Archives of the Leo Baeck Institute, New York
Central Archive for the History of the Jewish People, Jerusalem
Central Zionist Archive, Jerusalem
Hamburg Staatsarchiv
YIVO Archive, New York

Primary Source Periodicals
(individual articles not cited separately)

Adolf Brülls populär-wissenschaftlich Monatsblätter
Archives Israélites
Allgemeine Zeitung des Judentums
Ephemeriden der Menschheit
Fortnightly Review
General-Anzeiger für die gesamten Interessen des Judentums
Ha-Me'asef
Im Deutschen Reich
Der Israelit
Die Israelitische Familienblatt
Jahrbuch für jüdische Geschichte und Literatur
Jedidja
Jewish Chronicle
Jüdische Wohlfahrtspflege und Sozialpolitik
Jüdische Arbeits und Wanderfürsorge

Die Jüdische Presse
Monatsscrift für die Geschichte und Wissenschaft des Judentums
Mitteilungen vom Deutsch-Israelitischen Gemeindebund
Nathanael
Die Neuzeit
Der Orient
Ost und West
Preussischer Jahrbücher
Revue des Études Juives
Sulamith
Univers Israélite
Zeitschrift für die Demographie und Statistik der Juden
Zeitschrift für die Geschichte der Juden in Deutschland
Zedaka: Zeitschrift der jüdischen Wohlfahrtspeflege

Monthly and Annual Reports of Jewish Philanthropic Organizations (not cited separately)

Alliance Israélite Universelle
Anglo-Jewish Association
B'nai B'rith, Grossloge für Deutschland
Deutsches Central-Komitee für die russischen Juden
Freie Israelitische Vereinigung
Hilfsverein der deutschen Juden
Israelitische Allianz zu Wien
Verein für die Beförderung der Ackerbau unter den Juden Deutschlands
World Zionist Organization
Zentralverband selbstständiger jüdischer Handwerker Deutschlands

Books and Articles

Accampo, Elinor A., Rachel G. Fuchs, and Mary Lynn Stewart, eds. *Gender and the Politics of Social Reform in France, 1870–1914.* Baltimore, 1995.

Adams, Thomas McStay. *Bureaucrats and Beggars: French Social Policy in the Age of the Enlightenment.* New York, 1990.

Adler-Rudel, Shalom. "Moritz Baron Hirsch: Profile of a Great Philanthropist." *LBIYB* 8 (1963):29–69.

Adler, Marcus. *Chronik der Gesellschaft zur Verbreitung der Handwerke und des Ackerbaues unter den Juden im Preussischen Staate.* Berlin, 1898.

Akin, William. *Technocracy and the American Dream: The Technocratic Movement, 1900–1941.* Berkeley, 1977.

Albert, Phyllis Cohen. "Ethnicity and Jewish Solidarity in 19th-Century France." In *Mystics, Philosophers, and Politicians: Essays in Jewish Intellectual History in Honor of Alexander Altmann,* edited by Jehuda Reinharz and Daniel Swetschinksi, 249–74. Durham, 1982.

————. "L'intégration et la persistance de l'ethnicité chez les juifs dans la France moderne." In *Histoire politique des juifs de France,* edited by Pierre Birnbaum, 221–43. Paris, 1990.

Alderman, Geoffrey. "English Jews or Jews of the English Persuasion? Reflections on the Emancipation of Anglo-Jewry." In *Paths of Emancipation: Jews, States, and Citizenship,* edited by Pierre Birnbaum and Ira Katznelson, 128–56. Princeton, 1995.

Aldrich, Howard E., and Roger Waldinger. "Ethnicity and Entrepreneurship." *Annual Review of Sociology* 16 (1990): 111–35.

Almog, Shmuel. "Produktivizatsiyah, proletarizatsiyah, ve-'avodah 'ivrit." In *Temurot ba-historiyah ha-yehudit ha-hadashah: Kovets ma'amarim shai li-Shmuel Ettinger,* 41–70. Jerusalem, 1987.

Altmann, Alexander. *Moses Mendelssohn.* Philadelphia, 1973.

Altmann, Berthold. "Jews and the Rise of Capitalism." *Jewish Social Studies* 5 (1943): 163–86.

American Jewish Joint Distribution Committee. *Thirty Years: The Story of the J.D.C.* New York, 1945.

Anchel, Robert. *Napoléon et les juifs.* Paris, 1928.

Anderson, Benedict. *Imagined Communities: Reflections on the Origin and Spread of Nationalism.* London, 1983.

Anon. *"Betteln und Hausiren ist hier verboten." Eine Studie zur sozialen Frage.* Frankfurt am Main, 1890.

Anon. *Die Gewerbesscheu in Israel in ihren Ursachen und Folgen.* Vienna, 1841.

Aquinas, Thomas. "On the Ethics of Trading." In *Main Currents in Western Thought: Readings in Western European Intellectual History from the Middle Ages to the Present,* edited by Franklin Baumer, 88–91. New York, 1952.

Aschheim, Steven. *Brothers and Strangers: The East European Jew in German and German Jewish Consciousness, 1800–1923.* Madison, 1982.

Augustine, Dolores L. *Patricians and Parvenus: Wealth and High Society in Wilhelmine Germany.* Oxford, 1994.

Avni, Haim. *Argentina: "ha-aretz ha-ye'udah": Mif'al ha-hityashvut shel ha-Baron de Hirsh be-Argentina.* Jerusalem, 1983.

————. *Argentina and the Jews: A History of Jewish Immigration.* Tuscaloosa, Ala., 1991.

————. "Hevrat IKA ve-ha-tsiyonut." In *Ha-tsiyonut u-mitnagdeihah ba-'am ha-yehudi,* edited by Michael Abitbol and Haim Avni, 125–46. Jerusalem, 1990.

Baer, Yitzhak. *Galut.* New York, 1947.

————. "Ha-historiyah ha-hevratit ve-ha-datit shel ha-yehudim." *Tsiyon* 3, no. 4 (1938): 277–99.

Bar, Arie, ed. *The Jewish Press That Was: Accounts, Evaluations and Memories of Jewish Papers in Pre-Holocaust Europe.* Tel Aviv, 1980.

Barber, Benjamin. *Jihad vs. McWorld.* New York, 1998.

Barkai, Avraham. "Between Deutschtum and Judentum: Ideological Controversies Inside the Centralverein." In *In Search of Jewish Community: Jewish Identities in Germany and Austria, 1918–1933,* edited by Michael Brenner and Derek J. Penslar, 74–91. Bloomington, Ind., 1998.

————. *From Boycott to Annihilation: The Economic Struggle of German Jews 1933–1943*. Hanover, N.H., 1989.

————. "Ha-yahadut, ha-yehudim, ve-hitpathut ha-kapitalism." In *Dat ve-kalkalah: yahasei gomlin,* edited by Menachem Ben-Sasson, 53–63. Jerusalem, 1995.

————. "Juden als sozio-ökonomische Minderheitsgruppe in der Weimarer Republik." In *Juden in der Weimarer Republik,* edited by Walter Grab and Julius Schoeps, 330–46. Stuttgart, 1986.

————. *Jüdische Minderheit und Industrialisierung: Demographie, Berufe, und Einkommen der Juden in Westdeutschland, 1850–1914.* Tübingen, 1988.

————. "Temurot ba-kalkalat yehudei Germaniyah bi-tekufat ha-ti'us." In *Yehudim ba-kalkalah,* edited by Nachum Gross, 267–82. Jerusalem, 1985.

————. "Zur Wirtschaftsgeschichte der Juden in Deutschland." *TAJDG* 20 (1991): 195–214.

Baron, Salo. "The Economic Views of Maimonides." In *Essays on Maimonides,* edited by Salo Baron, 127–264. New York, 1941.

————. *The Jewish Community.* 2 vols., Philadelphia, 1942.

————. "Levi Herzfeld, the First Jewish Economic Historian." In *History and Jewish Historians,* 322–44. Philadelphia, 1964.

————. *Social and Religious History of the Jews.* 3 vols. New York, 1937.

————. "Zur ostjüdischen Einwanderung in Preussen." *Zeitschrift für die Geschichte der Juden in Deutschland* 3 (1931): 193–202.

Bartal, Israel. " 'Ha-model ha-mishni'—Tsorfat ke-makor hashpa'ah be-tahalikhei ha-modernizatsiah shel yehudei mizrah Eyropah (1772–1863)." In *Ha-mahpekhah ha-tsorfatit ve-rishumah,* edited by Yeramiel Cohen, 271–85. Jerusalem, 1991.

————. "Mordechai Aaron Günzburg: A Lithuanian Maskil Faces Modernity." In *From East and West,* edited by Francis Malino and David Sorkin, 126–47. Oxford, 1990.

Bartal, Israel, and Yosef Kaplan. " 'Aliyat 'aniyim mi-Amsterdam le-Eretz Yisra'el." *Shalem* 6 (1992): 175–93.

————. "Le-an halakh tseror ha-kesef? Ha-bikoret ha-maskilit 'al hebeteihah ha-kalkaliyim shel ha-hasidut." In *Dat ve-kalkalah: yahasei gomlin,* edited by Menachem Ben-Sasson, 375–85. Jerusalem, 1995.

————. " 'Tokhnit ha-hityashvut' mimei masa'o ha-sheni shel Montefiori le-Eretz Yisra'el (1839)." In Bartal, *Galut ba-aretz,* 100–160. Jerusalem, 1994.

Barzilay, Isaac E. "Smolenskin's Polemic against Mendelssohn in Historical Perspective." *Proceedings of the American Academy for Jewish Research* 53 (1986): 11–48.

Bauer, Yehuda. *My Brother's Keepers: A History of the American Jewish Joint Distribution Committee.* Philadelphia, 1974.

Beck, Hermann. "The Social Policies of Prussian Officials: The Bureaucracy in a New Light." *Journal of Modern History* 64 (June 1992): 263–89.

Ben-Hur, Raphaella Bilski. *Every Individual a King: The Social and Political Thought of Ze'ev Vladimir Jabotinsky.* Washington, D.C., 1993.

Ben Israel, Menasseh. *To His Highnesse the Lord Protector of the Commonwealth of England, Scotland, and Ireland: The Humble Addresses of Menasseh ben Israel.* London, 1655.

Ben-Sasson, Haim Hillel. "The Middle Ages." In *A History of the Jewish People,* edited by Shmuel Ettinger, 385–723. Cambridge, Mass., 1976.

Benayoun, Chantal, Alain Medam, and Pierre-Jacques Rojtman, eds. *Les juifs et l'économique: Miroirs et mirages.* Paris, 1992.

Bendavid, Lazarus. *Etwas zur Characteristick der Juden.* Leipzig, 1793.

———. "Selbstbiographie." In *Bildnisse jetzlebender Berliner Gelehrten mit ihren Selbstbiographien. Erste Sammlung,* edited by S. Lowe, 3–72. Berlin, 1806.

———. "Über Geld und Geldeswerth." In *Aufsätze verschiedenen Inhaltes,* 80–104. Berlin, 1800.

Bergmann, Klaus. *Agrarromantik und Grossstadtsfeindschaft.* Meisenheim am Glan, 1970.

Berkhofer, Robert J., Jr. *The White Man's Indian: Images of the American Indian from Columbus to the Present.* New York, 1978.

Berkovitz, Jay. *The Shaping of Jewish Identity in Nineteenth-Century France.* Detroit, 1989.

Bermann, Tamar. *Produktivierungsmythen und Antisemitismus.* Vienna, 1973.

Berr, Beer Isaac. *Réfléxions sur la régénération complète des juifs en France.* Paris, 1806.

Biale, David. "Confessions of a Historian of Jewish Culture." *Jewish Social Studies,* n.s.1, no. 1 (1994): 40–51.

Bieber, Hugo, ed. *Heinrich Heine. Confessio Judaica.* Berlin, 1925.

Bildwell, R. L. *Currency Conversion Tables.* London, 1970.

Birnbaum, Max. "Moses Mendelssohn, der Seidenfabrikant." *Jüdisches Gemeindeblatt der jüdischen Gemeinde zu Berlin* 19 (1929): 452–54.

Birnbaum, Pierre. "Antisemitism and Anticapitalism in Modern France." In *The Jews in Modern France,* edited by Francis Malino and Bernard Wasserstein, 214–23. Hanover, N.H., 1985.

———. *Anti-Semitism in France: A Political History from Leon Blum to the Present.* Oxford, 1992.

———. *The Jews of the Republic: A Political History of State Jews in France from Gambetta to Vichy.* Stanford, Calif., 1996.

———. "Le role limité des juifs dans l'industrialisation de la societé française." In *Les juifs et l'économique: Miroirs et mirages,* edited by Chantal Benayoun, Alain Medam, and Pierre-Jacques Rojtman, 163–77. Paris, 1992.

Birnbaum, Pierre, and Ira Katznelson, eds. *Paths of Emancipation: Jews, States, and Citizenship.* Princeton, 1995.

Black, Euguene C. *The Social Politics of Anglo-Jewry, 1880–1920.* New York, 1988.

Blalock, Hubert M., Jr. *Toward a Theory of Minority-Group Relations.* New York, 1967.

Bloom, Herbert. *The Economic Activities of the Jews of Amsterdam in the Seventeenth and Eighteenth Centuries.* Williamsport, Pa., 1937.

Bodian, Miriam. "Ha-yazamim ha-yehudim be-Berlin, hamedinah ha-absolutistit, ve-'shipur matsavam shel ha-yehudim' be-mahatsit ha-shniyah shel ha-me'ah ha-yod-tet." *Tsiyon* 49 (1984): 159–84.

————. *Hebrews of the Portuguese Nation: Conversos and Community in Early Modern Amsterdam*. Bloomington, Ind., 1997.

Bogen, Boris. *Jewish Philanthropy*. New York, 1917.

Böhlich, Walter, ed. *Der Berliner Antisemitismusstreit*. Frankfurt am Main, 1965.

Bonacich, Edna. "A Theory of Middleman Minorities." *American Sociological Review* 38 (1973): 583–94.

Bonacich, Edna, and John Modell. *The Economic Basis of Ethnic Solidarity: Small Business in the Japanese American Community*. Berkeley, 1980.

Bonfil, Robert. *Jewish Life in Renaissance Italy*. Berkeley, 1994.

Bornstein, Aharon. *Ha-kabtsanim: Perek be-toldot yehudei Germaniyah*. Jerusalem, 1992.

————. "Lidhot o-liklot? Piteronim le-ba'ayat ha-'aniyim ha-yehudim ha-navadim be-Germaniyah 1900." In *Spiegel Lectures in European Jewish History*, no. 8. Tel Aviv, 1988.

————. "Mi-kabtsanim le-dorshei 'avodah: navadim yehudim 'aniyim be-Germaniyah, 1869–1914." Ph.D. dissertation, Tel Aviv University, 1987.

————. "The Role of Social Institutions as Inhibitors of Assimilation: Jewish Poor Relief System in Germany, 1875–1925." *Jewish Social Studies* 50 (1988–93): 201–22.

Bourdieu, Pierre. *Distinction: A Social Critique of the Judgment of Taste*. Cambridge, Mass., 1984.

Bouwsma, William. "Anxiety and the Formation of Early Modern Culture." In *After the Reformation*, edited by Barbara Malament, 215–46. Philadelphia, 1980.

Boyer, John. *Cultural and Political Crisis in Vienna: Christian Socialism in Power, 1897–1918*. Chicago, 1995.

Braude, Benjamin. "Les contes persans de Menasseh Ben Israël: Polémique, apologétique et dissimulation à Amsterdam au XVIIe siècle." *Annales* 49, no. 5 (1994): 1107–38.

————. "The Myth of the Sephardi Economic Superman." Unpublished ms.

Brenner, Michael. "East and West in Orthodox German-Jewish Novels (1912–1934)." *LBIYB* 37 (1992): 309–23.

————. "The Jüdische Volkspartei: National-Jewish Communal Politics during the Weimar Republic." *LBIYB* 35 (1990): 219–43.

————. *The Renaissance of Jewish Culture in Weimar Germany*. New Haven, 1996.

Brentano, Lujo. "Judentum und Katpitalismus." In *Der Wirtschaftende Mensch in der Geschichte. Gesammelte Reden und Aufsätze*, 426–90. Leipzig, 1923.

Breuer, Mordechai. *Jüdische Orthodoxie im deutschen Reich, 1871–1918. Die Sozialgeschichte einer religiöser Minderheit*. Frankfurt am Main, 1986.

vom Bruch, Rüdiger, ed. *"Weder Kommunismus noch Kapitalismus." Bürgerliche Sozialreform in Deutschland vom Vormärz bis zur Ära Adenauer*. Munich, 1985.

Brucker, Gene, ed. *Two Memoirs of Renaissance Florence: The Diaries of Buonaccorso Pitti and Gregorio Dati*. New York, 1967.

Bruer, Albert A. *Geschichte der Juden in Preussen (1750–1820)*. Frankfurt am Main, 1991.

Buxtorf, Johannis. *Synagoga Judaica noviter restaurata. Das ist. Erneuerte jüdische Synagog, oder Juden-Schul*. Frankfurt am Main, 1738 (1st ed. 1603).

Byrnes, Robert. *Antisemitism in Modern France*. New Brunswick, N.J., 1950.

Callahan, William J. *Honor, Commerce, and Industry in Eighteenth-Century Spain*. Boston, 1972.

Campbell, Joan. *Joy in Work, German Work: The National Debate, 1800–1945*. Princeton, 1993.

Carlebach, Julius. *Karl Marx and the Radical Critique of Judaism*. London, 1978.

Caro, Georg. *Sozial- und Wirtschaftsgeschichte der Juden im Mittelalter und der Neuzeit*. 2 vols. Hildesheim, 1964.

Caruso, Naomi, and Janice Rosen, eds. *The Canadian Story of Reuben Brainin*. 2 vols. Montreal, 1993–96.

Cesarani, David. *The "Jewish Chronicle" and Anglo-Jewry, 1841–1991*. Cambridge, 1994.

Chapman, Stanley D. "Merchants and Bankers." In *Second Chance: Two Centuries of German-speaking Jews in the United Kingdom,* ed. Werner Mosse et al., 336–46. Tübingen, 1991.

Chase, Malcom. *The People's Farm: English Radical Agrarianism, 1775–1840*. Oxford, 1988.

Chazan, Robert. *European Jewry in the First Crusade*. Berkeley, 1987.

———. *Medieval Stereotypes and Modern Antisemitism*. Berkeley, 1997.

Clark, Chris. *The Politics of Conversion: Missionary Protestantism and the Jews in Prussia, 1728–1945*. Oxford, 1995.

Cohen, George. *The Jews in the Making of America*. Boston, 1924.

Cohen, Jeremy. *The Friars and the Jews: The Evolution of Medieval Anti-Judaism*. Ithaca, 1983.

Conze, Werner. "Vom 'Pöbel' zum 'Proletariat.' " In *Moderne deutsche Sozialgeschichte,* edited by Hans-Ulrich Wehler, 111–36. Cologne, 1966.

Corti, Egon. *The Reign of the House of Rothschild*. London, 1928.

———. *The Rise of the House of Rothschild*. London, 1928.

Daalder, Haans. "Dutch Jews in a Segmented Society." In *Paths of Emancipation: Jews, States, and Citizenship,* ed. Pierre Birnbaum and Ira Katznelson, 37–58. Princeton, 1995.

Dahbour, Omar, and Micheline R. Ishay, eds. *The Nationalism Reader*. Atlantic Highlands, N.J., 1995.

Dambacher, Ilsegret. *Christian Wilhelm von Dohm*. Frankfurt am Main, 1974.

Davis, Natalie Zemon. "Religion and Capitalism Once Again: Jewish Merchant Culture in the Seventeenth Century." *Representations* 59 (1997): 56–84.

———. *Women on the Margins: Three Seventeenth-Century Lives*. Cambridge, Mass., 1995.

de Roover, Raymond. *Business, Banking, and Economic Thought in Late Medieval and Early Modern Europe*. Chicago, 1974.

———. "The Concept of the Just Price: Theory and Economic Policy." *Journal of Economic History* 18 (1958): 418–34.

———. *San Bernardino of Siena and Sant'Antonio of Florence: Two Great Economic Thinkers of the Middle Ages*. Boston, 1967.

de la Vega, Joseph. *Confusion de Confusiones 1688: Portions Descriptive of the Amsterdam Stock Exchange.* Edited and translated by Hermann Kelenbenz. Boston, 1957.

Deutsch-Israelitischer Gemeindebund. *Hat das Judenthum dem Wucher Vorschub geleistet?* Leipzig, 1879.

De Vries, B. W. *From Pedlars to Textile Barons: The Economic Development of a Jewish Minority Group in the Netherlands.* Amsterdam, 1989.

Dickey, Laurence. "Historicizing the 'Adam Smith Problem': Conceptual, Historiographical, and Textual Issues." *Journal of Modern History* 58 (1986): 579–609.

von Dohm, Christian K. Wilhelm. *Über die bürgerliche Verbesserung der Juden.* 2 vols. Berlin, 1781–83; rpt, Hildesheim, 1973.

Don, Yehuda. "Patterns of Jewish Economic Behavior in Central Europe in the Twentieth Century." In *Jews in the Hungarian Economy, 1760–1945,* edited by Michael Silber, 247–73. Jerusalem, 1992.

Dubin, Lois. *The Port Jews of Hapsburg Trieste.* Stanford, Calif., 1999.

Duprat, Catherine. *"Pour l'amour de l'humanité": Le temps des philanthropes; La philanthropie parisienne des Lumières à la monarchie de juillet.* Paris, 1993.

Efron, John. *Defenders of the Race: Jewish Doctors and Race Science in Fin-de-Siècle Europe.* New Haven, 1994.

Egmond, Florike. "Contours of Identity: Poor Ashkenazim in the Dutch Republic." *Dutch Jewish History* 3 (1993): 205–25.

Eisen, Arnold M. "Rethinking Jewish Modernity." *Jewish Social Studies,* n.s., 1, no. 1 (1994): 1–21.

Eitzen, D. Stanley. "Two Minorities: The Jews of Poland and the Chinese of the Philippines." *Jewish Journal of Sociology* 10, no. 2 (December 1968): 221–40.

Elam, Yigal. *Ha-sokhnut ha-yehudit: Shanim rishonot.* Jerusalem, 1990.

Elbogen, Ismar, and Eleonore Sterling. *Die Geschichte der Juden in Deutschland.* Frankfurt am Main, 1988.

Eley, Geoff. "Nations, Publics, and Political Cultures: Placing Habermas in the Nineteenth Century." In *Culture/Power/History: A Reader in Contemporary Social Theory,* edited by Nicholas B. Dirks, Geoff Eley, and Sherry B. Ortner, 297–335. Princeton, 1994.

Eliav, Mordechai. *Erets Yisra'el ve-yishuvah ba-meah ha-yod-tet, 1777–1917.* Jerusalem, 1978.

———. *Ha-hinuch ha-yehudi be-Germaniyah biymei ha-haskalah ve-ha-emantsipatsiah.* Jerusalem, 1961.

Ellenson, David. *Rabbi Esriel Hildesheimer and the Creation of a Modern Jewish Orthodoxy.* Tuscaloosa, Ala., 1990.

Elon, Amos. *Founder: A Portrait of the First Rothschild and His Time.* New York, 1996.

Eloni, Yehuda. "Die umkämpfte nationaljüdische Idee." In *Juden im Wilmenischen Deutschland, 1890–1914,* edited by Werner Mosse and Arnold Paucker, 633–88. Tübingen, 1976.

Elukin, Jonathan. "The Eternal Jew in Medieval Europe: Christian Perceptions of Jewish Anachronism and Racial Identity." Ph.D. dissertation, Princeton University, 1994.

Endelman, Todd M. "English Jewish History." *Modern Judaism* 11 (1991): 91–109.

———. *The Jews of Georgian England, 1714–1830*. Philadelphia, 1979.

Erb, Rainer. " 'Jüdische Güterschlächterei' im Vormärz. Vom Nutzen des Stereotyps für wirtschaftliche Machtstrukturen, dargestellt an einem Westfälishen Gesetz von 1836." *International Review of Social History* 30 (1985): 312–41.

———. "Warum ist der Jude zum Ackerbürger nicht tauglich? Zur Geschichte eines antisemitischen Stereotyps." In *Antisemitismus und Jüdische Geschichte. Studien zu Ehren von Herbert A. Strauss,* edited by Rainer Erb and Michael Schmidt, 99–120. Berlin, 1987.

Erb, Rainer, and Werner Bergmann. *Die Nachtseite der Judenemanzipation.* Berlin, 1989.

Etkes, Imanuel. "Immanent Factors and External Influences in the Development of the Haskalah Movement in Russia." In *Toward Modernity: The European Jewish Model,* edited by Jacob Katz, 13–32. New Brunswick, N.J., 1987.

———. *Rabbi Israel Salanter and the Musar Movement.* Philadelphia, 1993.

Ettinger, Shmuel. "The Beginnings of the Change in the Attitude of European Society towards the Jews." *Scripta Hierosolymitana* 7 (1961): 193–219.

Faber, Eli. *Jews, Slaves, and the Slave Trade: Setting the Record Straight.* New York, 1998.

Faierstein, Morris, ed. and trans. *The Libes Briv of Isaac Wetzlar.* Atlanta, 1996.

Feder, Ernst. *Politik und Humanität. Paul Nathan, Ein Lebensbild.* Berlin, 1929.

Feiner, Shmuel. "Mendelssohn and 'Mendelssohn's Disciples': A Re-examination." *LBIYB* 40 (1995): 135–67.

———. "Yizhak Euchel: Ha-ʿyazamʾ shel tenuaʿt ha-haskalah be-germaniyah." *Tsiyon* 52, no. 4 (1987): 427–69.

Feldman, David. *Englishmen and Jews: Social Relations and Political Culture, 1840–1914.* New Haven, 1994.

Felsenstein, Frank. *Anti-Semitic Stereotypes: A Paradigm of Otherness in English Popular Culture, 1660–1830.* Baltimore, 1995.

Ferguson, Niall. *The House of Rothschild: Money's Prophets, 1798–1848.* New York, 1998.

Finley, M. I. "Aristotle and Economic Analysis." In *Articles on Aristotle 2: Ethics and Politics,* edited by Jonathan Barnes, Malcom Schofield, and Richard Sorabji, 140–58. London, 1977.

Fishman, David E. *Russia's First Modern Jews: The Jews of Shklov.* New York, 1995.

Fox-Genovese, Elizabeth. *The Origins of Physiocracy: Economic Revolution and Social Order in Eighteenth-Century France.* Ithaca, 1976.

Frankel, Jonathan. "Crisis as a Factor in Modern Jewish Politics, 1840 and 1881–1882." In *Living with Antisemitism: Modern Jewish Responses,* edited by Jehuda Reinharz, 42–58. Hanover, N.H., 1987.

————. *The Damascus Affair: "Ritual Murder," Politics, and the Jews in 1840*. Cambridge, 1997.

————. "Jewish Politics and the Press: The 'Reception' of the Alliance Israélite Universelle." *Jewish History*, forthcoming.

————. *Prophecy and Politics: Socialism, Nationalism, and the Russian Jews, 1862–1917*. Cambridge, 1981.

————. " 'Ritual Murder' in the Modern Era: The Damascus Affair of 1840." *Jewish Social Studies* 3 (1997): 1–16.

Freidenreich, Harriet Pass. *Jewish Politics in Vienna, 1918–1938*. Bloomington, Ind., 1991.

Frevert, Ute. *Women in German History: From Bourgeois Emancipation to Sexual Liberation*. New York, 1988.

Friedländer, David. *Akten-stücke, die Reform der jüdischen Kolonien in den Preussischen Staaten betreffend*. Berlin, 1793.

————. *Briefe über die Moral des Handels*. Berlin, 1817.

————. *Über die Verbeserung der Israeliten im Königreich Polen*. Berlin, 1819.

Friedman, Menachem. "Mikhtavei hamlatsah le-kabtsanim—'Ketavim': Le-ba'yat ha-navadim be-Germaniyah ba-meah ha-yod-het." *Mikhael* 2 (1973): 34–51.

Frisch, Ephraim. *An Historical Survey of Jewish Philanthropy from the Earliest Times to the Nineteenth Century*. New York, 1924.

Fritzsch, Theodor [F. Roderich-Stoltheim]. *Die Juden im Handel und das Geheimnis ihrer Erfolgen*. Steglitz, 1913.

————. *Geistige Unterjochung. Zugleich ein Antwort an Dr. G. Loner und Prof. Werner Sombart*. Leipzig, 1911.

Fuchs, Rachel. *Abandoned Children: Foundlings and Child Welfare in Nineteenth-Century France*. Albany, N.Y., 1984.

Fülop-Miller, René. *Geist und Gesicht des Bolschewismus*. Zurich, 1926.

Funkenstein, Amos. "The Dialectics of Assimilation." *Jewish Social Studies*, n.s. 1, no. 2 (1994): 1–14.

————. *Perceptions of Jewish History*. Berkeley, 1993.

Furet, François, ed. *A Critical Dictionary of the French Revolution*. Cambridge, Mass., 1989.

Gagliardo, John G. *From Pariah to Patriot: The Changing Image of the German Peasant, 1770–1840*. Lexington, 1969.

Gal, Alon. "Brandeis' Views on the Upbuilding of Palestine, 1914–23." *Studies in Zionism*, no. 6 (1982): 211–40.

Gartner, Lloyd P. *The Jewish Immigrant in England, 1870–1914*. London, 1960.

Geiger, Abraham. *Nachgelassene Schriften*. Edited by Ludwig Geiger. Berlin, 1875.

Gelber, N. M. "Mendel Lefin-Satnover ve-hatsa'otav le-tikun oreh hayim shel yehudei Polin bifnei ha-seim ha-gadol (1788–1792)." *Abraham Weiss Jubilee Volume*, 271–301. New York, 1964.

Gellately, Robert. *The Politics of Economic Despair*. London, 1974.

Gerber, Barbara. *Jud Süss. Aufstieg und Fall im frühen 18. Jahrhundert*. Hamburg, 1990.

Geremek, Bronislaw. *Poverty: A History.* Oxford, 1994.

Gilchrist, J. *The Church and Economic Activity in the Middle Ages.* New York, 1969.

Gille, Bertrand. *Histoire de la Maison Rothschild.* 2 vols. Geneva, 1965–67.

Gilman, Sander. *Jewish Self-Hatred.* Baltimore, 1986.

———. *Smart Jews: The Construction of the Image of Jewish Superior Intelligence.* Lincoln, 1996.

Ginzburg, Carlo. *The Cheese and the Worms.* Baltimore, 1980.

Glanz, Rudolf. *Geschichte des niederen jüdischen Volkes in Deutschland.* New York, 1968.

———. "The Rothschild Myth in America." *Jewish Social Studies* 19 (1957): 3–28.

Godechot, Jacques. "La révolution française et les juifs." In *Les juifs et la revolution française,* edited by Bernhard Blumenkranz and Albert Soboul, 47–70. Paris, 1976.

Goldberg, Sylvie-Anne. *Crossing the Jabbok: Illness and Death in Ashkenazi Judaism in Sixteenth- through Nineteenth-Century Prague.* Berkeley, 1996.

Goldscheider, Calvin, and Allan Zuckerman. *The Transformation of the Jews.* Chicago, 1984.

Goldstein, Ya'akov, and Batsheva Stern. "PIKA—Irgunah u-mataroteihah." *Cathedra* 59 (1991): 102–26.

Graetz, Heinrich. *Geschichte der Juden.* 3d ed. Leipzig, 1894.

———. *The Structure of Jewish History and Other Essays.* Translated and edited by Ismar Schorsch. New York, 1975.

Graetz, Michael. " 'Aliyato u-shkia'to shel sapak ha-tsava ha-yehudi: Kalkalah yehudit be- 'itot milhemah." *Tsiyon* 56, no. 3 (1991): 255–74.

———. "Jews in the Modern Period: The Role of the 'Rising Class' in the Politicization of Jews in Europe." In *Assimilation and Community: The Jews in Nineteenth-Century Europe,* edited by Jonathan Frankel and Steven J. Zipperstein, 156–76. Cambridge, 1992.

———. *The Jews in Nineteenth-Century France: From the French Revolution to the Alliance Israélite Universelle.* Stanford, Calif., 1996.

Graser, J. B. *Das Judenthum und seine Reform.* Bayreuth, 1828.

Gray, Marion. "From the Household Economy to 'Rational Agriculture': The Establishment of Liberal Ideals in German Agricultural Thought." In *In Search of Liberal Germany: Studies in the History of German Liberalism from 1789 to the Present,* edited by Konrad H. Jarausch and Larry Eugene Jones, 25–54. New York, 1990.

Grayzel, Solomon. "The Jews' Function in the Evolution of Medieval Life." *Historia Judaica* 6 (1944): 3–26.

Green, Nancy L. "To Give and to Receive: Philanthropy and Collective Responsibility among Jews in Paris, 1880–1914." In *The Uses of Charity: The Poor on Relief in the Nineteenth-Century Metropolis,* edited by Peter Mandler, 197–226. Philadelphia, 1990.

———. "The Modern Jewish Diaspora: East European Jews in New York, London, and Paris." In *Comparing Jewish Societies,* edited by Todd Endelman, 113–34. Ann Arbor, 1997.

———. *The Pletzl of Paris: Jewish Immigrant Workers in the Belle Epoque.* New York, 1986.

Greenblatt, Stephen. *Marvelous Possessions: The Wonder of the New World.* Chicago, 1991.

Grégoire, Henri Baptiste. *Enquiry Concerning the Intellectual and Moral Faculties, and Literature of Negroes.* Brooklyn, N.Y., 1810.

———. *Essai sur la régénération physique, morale, et politique des juifs.* Metz, 1789.

Grimmer-Salem, Erik, and Roberto Romani. "The Historical School, 1870–1900: A Cross-National Reassessment." *History of European Ideas* 24 (1998): 267–99.

Gross, Nachum. "Entrepreneurship of Religious and Ethnic Minorities." In *Jüdische Unternehmer in Deutschland im 19. Und 20. Jahrhundert,* edited by Werner E. Mosse and Hans Pohl, 11–23. Stuttgart, 1992.

Gross, Nachum, and Jacob Metzer. *Finance and the Jewish Economy in Interwar Palestine.* Jerusalem, 1977.

Grunwald, Kurt. "Lombards, Cahorsins, and Jews." *Journal of European Economic History* 4, no. 1 (1975): 393–98.

———. *Türkenhirsch.* Jerusalem, 1969.

Guggenheim, Yaakov. "Meeting on the Road: Encounters between German Jews and Christians on the Margins of Society." In *In and Out of the Ghetto: Jewish-Gentile Relations in Late Medieval and Early Modern Germany,* edited by R. Po-Chia Hsia and Hartmut Lehmann, 125–36. Washington, D.C., 1995.

Guttmann, Julius. *Die wirtschaftliche und soziale Bedeutung der Juden im Mittelalter.* Breslau, 1907.

Gutwein, Daniel. "Beyn sotsiyologiyah shel mi'ut le-etikah datit: Livehinat ha-te'oriyah shel ha-'ilit ha-kalkalit ha-yehudit be-Germaniyah." *Tsiyon* 55 (1990): 419–47.

———. *A Divided Elite: Economics, Politics, and Anglo-Jewry, 1882–1917.* Leiden, 1992.

———. "Economics, Politics, and Historiography: Hayyim D. Horowitz and the Interrelationship of Jews and Capitalism." *Jewish Social Studies,* n.s. 1, no. 1 (1994): 94–114.

———. "Herzl ve-ha-plutokratiah ha-yehudit." *Tsiyon* 62 (1998): 47–74.

———. "Kapitalism, pariyah-kapitalism, u-mi'ut: Ha-temurot be-teyoriah ha-yehudit shel Marx 'al reka' ha-diyun be-me'afyenei ha-kalkalah ha-yehudit." In *Dat ve-kalkalah: yahasei gomlin,* edited by Menachem Ben-Sasson, 65–76. Jerusalem, 1995.

Habermas, Jürgen. *The Structural Transformation of the Public Sphere.* Cambridge, Mass., 1989.

Hagen, William. *Germans, Poles, and Jews: The Nationality Conflict in the Prussian East, 1772–1914.* Chicago, 1980.

Hahn, Bruno. *Die wirtschaftliche Tätigkeit der Juden im fränkischen und deutschen Reich bis zum zweiten Kreuzzug.* Freiburg, 1911.

Halpern, Ben. *A Clash of Heroes: Brandeis, Weizmann, and American Zionism.* New York, 1987.

Hamburger, Ernest. "Jews in Public Service under the German Monarchy." *LBIYB* 9 (1964): 206–38.

———. *Juden in öffentlichen Leben Deutschlands*. Tübingen, 1968.

Hanak, Peter. "Jews and the Modernization of Commerce in Hungary, 1760–1848." In *Jews in the Hungarian Economy, 1760–1945,* edited by Michael Silber, 23–39. Jerusalem, 1992.

Hardtwig, Wolfgang. "Strukturmerkmale und Entwicklungstendenzen des Vereinswesens in Deutschland, 1789–1848." In *Vereinswesen und bürgerliche Gesellschaft in Deutschland,* edited by Otto Dann, 11–50. Munich, 1984.

Harris, James. *The People Speak! Anti-Semitism and Emancipation in Nineteenth-Century Bavaria*. Ann Arbor, 1994.

Hart, Mitch. "Social Science and National Identity: A History of Jewish Statistics, 1880–1930." Ph.D. dissertation, Stanford University, 1994.

Häusler, Wolfgang, "Toleranz, Emanzipation, und Antisemitismus. Das österreichische Judentum des bürgerlichen Zeitalters (1782–1918)." In *Das österreichische Judentum,* edited by Anna Drabeck et al., 83–140. Vienna, 1974.

Heid, Ludger. "Melocho welo Zedoko. 'Arbeit, nicht Wohltätigkeit' für ostjüdische Proletarier im Ruhrgebiet." In *Zedaka: Jüdische Sozialarbeit im Wandel der Zeit. 75 Jahre Zentralwohlfahrtstelle der Juden in Deutschland,* edited by George Heuberger, 79–92. Frankfurt am Main, 1992.

Hekscher, Eli F. *Mercantilism*. London, 1934.

Hennig, Hansjoachim. "Soziales Verhalten jüdischer Unternehmer in Frankfurt und Köln zwischen 1860 und 1933." In *Jüdische Unternehmer in Deutschland im 19. Und 20. Jahrhundert,* edited by Werner E. Mosse and Hans Pohl, 247–70. Stuttgart, 1992.

Herbert, Ulrich. *A History of Foreign Labor in Germany, 1880–1980*. Ann Arbor, 1990.

Herlitz, Georg. *Das Jahr der Zionisten*. Jerusalem, 1949.

Herlitz, Georg, and Bruno Kirschner, eds. *Jüdisches Lexicon*. Berlin, 1927–30.

Hertzberg, Arthur. *The French Enlightenment and the Jews*. Philadelphia, 1968.

———. *The Jews in America*. New York, 1997.

Herxheimer, Salomon. *Predigten und Gelegenheitsreden*. 2d ed. Leipzig, 1857.

Herzfeld, Levi. *Handelsgeschichte der Juden des Alterthums*. Braunschweig, 1894.

Herzig, Arno. "Die Anfänge der deutsch-jüdischer Geschichtsschreibung in der Spätaufklärung." *TAJDG* 20 (1991): 59–76.

———. "Die Juden in Hamburg 1780–1860." In *Die Juden in Hamburg 1590 bis 1990,* edited by Arno Herzig, 61–76. Hamburg, 1991.

Herzl, Theodor. *Der Judenstaat*. Berlin, 1920.

Heywood, Colin. *Childhood in Nineteenth-Century France*. Cambridge, 1988.

Hilger, Marie-Elisabeth. "Probleme Jüdischer Industriearbeiter in Deutschland." In *Juden in Deutschland. Emanzipation, Integration, Verfolgung und Vernichtung. 25 Jahre Institut für die Geschichte der deutschen Juden, Hamburg,* edited by Peter Freimark, Alice Jankowksi, and Ina Lorenz, 304–25. Hamburg, 1991.

Himmelfarb, Gertrude. *The Idea of Poverty: England in the Early Industrial Age*. New York, 1983.

————. *Poverty and Compassion: The Moral Imagination of the Late Victorians*. New York, 1991.

Hintze, Otto. *Acta Borussica: Die Preussische Seideindustrie im 18. Jahrhundert*. 3 vols. Berlin, 1892.

von Hippel, Gotlieb. *On Improving the Status of Women*. Translated and edited by Timothy Sellner. Detroit, 1979.

Hirsch, Marcus. *Kulturdefizit am Ende des 19. Jahrhunderts*. Frankfurt am Main, 1893.

Hirsch, S. R. *Commentary on the Pentateuch, vol. II: Exodus*. New York, 1971.

Hoffman, Moses. *Der Geldhandel der deutschen Juden während des Mittelalters bis zum Jahre 1350*. Altenberg, 1910.

————. *Judentum und Kapitalismus. Eine kritische Würdigung von Werner Sombarts "Die Juden und das Wirtschaftsleben."* Berlin, 1912.

Hohmann, Joachim S. *Geschichte der Ziegeunerverfolgung in Deutschland*. Frankfurt am Main, 1988.

Holländer, Ludwig. *Die sozialen Voraussetzungen der antisemitischen Bewegung in Deutschland*. Berlin, 1909.

Homberg, Herz. *Ben Jakir. Über Glaubenswahrheiten und Sittenlehren für die israelitische Jugend*. Vienna, 1814.

————. *Benei Zion. Ein Religiös-moralisches Lehrbuch für die Jugend israelitischer Nation*. Vienna, 1812.

————. *Imrei Shefer*. Vienna, 5566 [1803–4].

Homeyer, Friedrich. *Beitrag zur Geschichte der Gartenbauschule Ahlem 1893–1979. Dokumentarische Bearbeitung*. Hannover, 1980.

Hong, Young-Sun. *Welfare, Modernity, and the Weimar State, 1919–1933*. Princeton, 1998.

Horowitz, Elimelech. " 'Ve-yihiyu 'aniyim (hagunim) benei beytekhah': Tsedakah, 'aniyim, u-fikuah hevrati be-kehilot yehudei Eyropa bein yemei ha-beinayim le-reshit ha-'et ha-hadashah." In *Dat ve-kalkalah: yahasei gomlin*, edited by Menachem Ben-Sasson, 209–31. Jerusalem, 1995.

Hsia, R. Po-Chia. *The Myth of Ritual Murder*. New Haven, 1988.

————. "The Usurious Jew: Economic Structure and Religious Representations in an Anti-Semitic Discourse." In *In and Out of the Ghetto: Jewish-Gentile Relations in Late Medieval and Early Modern Germany*, edited by R. Po-Chia Hsia and Hartmut Lehmann, 161–76. Washington, D.C., 1995.

Hunt, Lynn. *The Family Romance of the French Revolution*. Berkeley, 1992.

————. *Politics, Culture, and Class in the French Revolution*. Berkeley, 1984.

Hyman, Joseph. *Twenty-five Years of American Aid to Jews Overseas*. New York, 1939.

Hyman, Paula. "The Dynamics of Social History." *Studies in Contemporary Jewry* 10 (1994): 93–111.

————. *The Emancipation of the Jews of Alsace*. New Haven, 1991.

————. *Gender and Assimilation in Modern Jewish History*. Seattle, 1995.

————. *The Jews in Modern France*. Berkeley, 1998.

————. "Joseph Salvador: Proto-Zionist or Apologist for Assimilation?" *Jewish Social Studies* 34 (1972): 1–22.

Institute of Jewish Affairs of the World Jewish Congress. *European Jewry Ten Years after the War*. New York, 1956.

Isaak, Joseph. "Authentische Berechnung, was eine Judengemeinde von 26 Haushaltungen (im Reichsdorf Gochsheim) jährlich zum Unterhalt ihrer bettelnden Glaubensgenossen beytragen muss." *Journal von und für Franken,* 1. Band (Nürnberg, 1790): 435–46.

———. "Fortgesetzte Betrachtungen über die Betteljuden, mit einigen dahin abzweckenden Vorschlägen in vorzüglicher Hinsicht auf das Hochstift Würzburg und die in demselbigen liegenden ritterschaftlichen Orte." *Journal von und für Franken,* 2. Band (Nürnberg, 1791): 606–19.

———. *Unmassgebliche Gedanken über Betteljuden und ihre bessere und zweckmässigere Versorgung.* Nürnberg, 1791.

Isler, Moses. *Rückkehr der Juden zur Landwirtschaft. Beitrag zu der Geschichte der landwirtschaftlichen Kolonisation der Juden in verschiedener Länder.* Basel, 1929.

Israel, Jonathan. *European Jewry in the Age of Mercantilism, 1550–1750.* 2d ed. Oxford, 1989.

Israelitische Allianz zu Wien. *XL. Jahresbericht der Israelitischen Allianz zu Wien erstattet an die XL. ordentliche Generalversammlung am 16. April 1913 nebst einem Rückblick auf die vierziegjährige Wirksamkeit des Vereines 1872–1912.* Vienna, 1913.

Jellinek, Adolph. *Der jüdische Stamm: Ethnographische Studien.* Vienna, 1869.

———. *Der jüdische Stamm in nichtjüdischen Sprichwörtern.* 3 vols. Vienna, 1881–86.

Jersch-Wenzel, Stefi. *Jüdische Bürger und Kommunale Selbstverwaltung in Preussischen Städten 1808–1848.* Berlin, 1967.

———. "Minderheiten in der bürgerlichen Gesellschaft: Juden in Amsterdam, Frankfurt, und Posen." In *Bürgertum im 19. Jahrhundert. Deutschland im europäischen Vergleich,* edited by Jürgen Kocka, 392–420. Munich, 1988.

Jewish Colonization Association. *Le Baron Maurice de Hirsch et la Jewish Colonisation Association.* Paris, 1936.

Joseph, Samuel. *History of the Baron de Hirsch Fund.* Philadelphia, 1935.

Jost, Isaak Marcus. *Geschichte der Israeliten seit der Zeit der Maccabäer bis auf unsere Tage.* 10 vols. Berlin, 1820–47.

Jüdischen Glaubens-Gemeinde zu München. *Beleuchtung der Petition welche (angeblich) der bürgerliche Handelstand der königliche Haupt- und Residenz-Stadt München, in Betreff des Verfalls des Handels, und der Abstellung der denselben untertragenden Missbräuche und Beeinträchtigungen, unterm 13. April 1810 an die erste Stände-Versammlung des Königreiches Baiern vergeben hat.* Munich, 1819.

Just, Michael. *Ost-und südosteuropäische Amerikawanderung 1881–1914.* Stuttgart, 1988.

Kagedan, Allan Laine. *Soviet Zion: The Quest for a Russian Jewish Homeland.* New York, 1994.

Kahn, Arthur. *Hin zur Scholle!* Berlin, 1912.

———. *Der Weg zur wahren Emanzipation.* Berlin, 1915.

Kampe, Norbert. "Jews and Antisemitism in Universities in Imperial Germany (I)." *LBIYB* 30 (1985): 357–94.

Kaplan, Marion. *The Jewish Feminist Movement in Germany: The Campaigns of the Jüdischer Frauenbund, 1904–1938.* Westport, Conn., 1979.

————. *The Making of the Jewish Middle Class: Women, Family, and Identity in Imperial Germany*. Oxford, 1991.

————. "Tradition and Transition: The Acculturation, Assimilation, and Integration of Jewish Women in Imperial Germany." *LBIYB* 27 (1982): 3–36.

Kaplan, Yosef. "The Jewish Profile of the Spanish-Portuguese Community of London during the 17th Century." *Judaism* 41, no. 3 (1992): 229–40.

————. "Netivah shel ha-yahadut ha-sefaradit ha-ma'aravit el ha-modernah." *Pe'amim* 48 (1991): 85–103.

————. " 'Olamo ha-dati shel soher benle'umi yehudi bi-tekufat ha-merkantilism: Mevuhat ha-'osher shel Avraham Yisra'el Pereira." In *Dat ve-kalkalah: Yahasei gomlin*, edited by Menachem Ben-Sasson, 233–51. Jerusalem, 1995.

————. "The Portuguese Community in Seventeenth-Century Amsterdam and the Ashkenazic World." *Dutch Jewish History* 2 (1989): 23–46.

————. "The Portuguese Community of Amsterdam in the 17th Century: Between Tradition and Change." In *Society and Community*, edited by A. Haim, 142–71. Jerusalem, 1991.

Karniel, Joseph. *Die Toleranzpolitik Kaiser Josephs III*. Gerlingen, 1985.

Katz, David S. *The Jews in the History of England, 1485–1850*. Oxford, 1994.

————. *Philo-Semitism and the Readmission of the Jews to England, 1603–1655*. Oxford, 1982.

Katz, Eugen. *Die Alexander und Fanny Simon'sche Stiftung zu Hannover. Ihre Ziele und ihre Arbeiten von 1907–1914*. Hannover, 1914.

Katz, Jacob. *Exclusiveness and Tolerance: Jewish-Gentile Relations in Medieval and Modern Times*. New York, 1961.

————. *From Prejudice to Destruction: Antisemitism, 1700–1933*. Cambridge, Mass., 1980.

————. "Hirhurim 'al ha-yahas ben dat le-kalkalah." *Tarbitz* 62 (1991): 99–111.

————. *Jews and Freemasons in Europe, 1723–1939*. Cambridge, Mass., 1970.

————. *Out of the Ghetto: The Social Background of Jewish Emancipation, 1770–1870*. New York, 1973.

————. "Pra'ot 'Hep-Hep' shel shnat 1819 be-Germaniyah 'al reka'n ha-histori." *Tsiyon* 38 (1973): 62–115.

————. *Tradition and Crisis: Jewish Society at the End of the Middle Ages*. New York, 1993.

————. ed. *Toward Modernity: The European Jewish Model*. New Brunswick, N.J., 1987.

Kayserling, Meyer. *Bibliothek Jüdischer Kanzelredner*. Breslau, 1885.

————. *Ludwig Philippson. Eine Biographie*. Leipzig, 1898.

————. *Der Wucher und das Judenthum*. Budapest, 1893.

Kellner, Jacob. *Immigration and Social Policy: The Jewish Experience in the U.S.A., 1881–1882*. Jerusalem, 1979.

————. *Le-ma'an Tsiyon: Ha-hit'arvut ha-klal-yehudit bi-metsukat ha-yishuv, 1869–1882*. Jerusalem, 1977.

————. "Philanthropy and Social Planning in Jewish Society (1842–1882)." Ph.D. dissertation, Hebrew University of Jerusalem, 1973.

————. *Reshito shel tikhnun hevrati klal-yehudi: Ha-hit'arvut ha-memusedet bi-metsukat yehudei Russiyah be-reshit shenot ha-shiv'im shel ha-me'ah ha-19.* Jerusalem, 1974.

Kieval, Hillel. "Caution's Progress: The Modernization of Jewish Life in Prague, 1780–1830." In *Toward Modernity: The European Jewish Model*, edited by Jacob Katz, 71–106. New Brunswick, N.J., 1987.

Kilian, Hendrikje. *Die Jüdische Gemeinde in München 1813–1871. Eine Grossstadt-gemeinde im Zeitalter der Emanzipation.* Munich, 1989.

Klausner, Ph. *Prozess gegen die jüdischen Wucherer Marcus Loeb von Mainz und Hirsch/Süsser von Würzburg.* Mannheim, 1883.

Kleiman, Ephraim. "An Early Modern Hebrew Textbook of Economics." *History of Political Economy* 5 (1973): 339–58.

Klier, John. *Imperial Russia's Jewish Question, 1855–1881.* Cambridge, 1995.

————. *Russia Gathers Her Jews: The Origins of the Jewish Question in Russia, 1772–1825.* De Kalb, Ill., 1986.

Klimkiewing, Ronald. *Der Wucher und seine Folgen. Beleuchtungen der Vorgänge im Falle Samuel Horowitz aus Lemberg.* 2d ed. Czernowitz, 1891.

Kouri, E. I. *Der deutsche Protestantismus und die soziale Frage 1870–1919.* Berlin, 1984.

Krabbe, Wolfgang. *Gesellschaftsveränderung durch Lebensreform.* Göttingen, 1974.

Krefetz, Gerald. *Jews and Money: The Myths and the Reality.* New Haven, 1982.

Krohn, Helga. *Die Juden in Hamburg, 1848–1918.* Hamburg, 1974.

Kuchenbecker, Antje. "'Ein 'Rotes Palästina' im Fernen Osten der Sowjetunion — Die Verbannung einer Idee. Die Auseinandersetzung um ein autonomes jüdisches Siedlungsgebiet in der frühen UdSSR." *Archiv für Sozialgeschichte* 37 (1997): 268–79.

Kuhn, Arthur. "Hugo Grotius and the Emancipation of the Jews in Holland." *Publications of the American Jewish Historical Society* 31 (1928): 173–80.

Kurrein, Adolf. *Die sociale Frage im Judenthume.* Mülheim am Rhein, 1890.

Kuznets, Simon. "Economic Structure and Life of the Jews." In *The Jews: Their History, Culture, and Religion*, edited by Louis Finkelstein, 2: 1597–1661. New York, 1960.

Lamberti, Marjorie. *Jewish Activism in Imperial Germany.* New Haven, 1978.

Landes, David. "The Jewish Merchant." *LBIYB* 19 (1974): 11–24.

Landesberger, Julius. "Jüdische Ackerwirthe zu südpreussischer Zeit." *Historische Monatsblätter für die Provinz Posen* 1, no. 12 (December 1900): 177–83.

Landwehr, Rolf and Rüdiger Baron, eds. *Geschichte der Sozialarbeit. Hauptlinien ihrer Entwicklung im 19. und 20. Jahrhundert.* Weinheim-Basel, 1983.

Langewiesche, Dieter. "Liberalismus und Judenemanzipation im 19. Jahrhundert." In *Juden in Deutschland. Emanzipation, Integration, Verfolgung, und Vernichtung. 25 Jahre Institut für die Geschichte der deutschen Juden*, edited by Peter Freimark, Alice Jankowski, and Ina S. Lorenz, 148–63. Hamburg, 1991.

Langmuir, Gavin. *Toward a Definition of Antisemitism.* Berkeley, 1990.

Lavsky, Hagit. *Before Catastrophe: The Distinctive Path of German Zionism.* Detroit, 1996.

Lazarus, Morritz. *Juden als Ackerbauern. Ein Beitrag zur Lösung der sozialen Frage der Juden in Galizien.* Lemberg, 1885.

————. *Treue und Frei. Gesammelte Reden und Vorträge über Juden und Judenthum.* Leipzig, 1887.

Lederhendler, Eli. *The Road to Modern Jewish Politics: Political Tradition and Political Reconstruction in the Jewish Community of Tsarist Russia.* Oxford, 1988.

Le Goff, Jacques. *Your Money or Your Life: Economy and Religion in the Middle Ages.* New York, 1988.

Lessing, Michael Benedict. *Die Juden und die öffentliche Meinung im preussischen Staat.* Altona, 1833.

Lestschinsky, Jakob. *Das jüdische Volk im neuen Europa.* Prague, 1934.

————. *Das wirtschaftliche Schicksal des deutschen Judentums.* Berlin, 1932.

Leven, Narcisse. *Cinquante ans d'histoire: L'Alliance Israélite Universelle (1860–1910).* 2 vols. Paris, 1920.

Levi, Primo. *The Mirror Maker.* New York, 1989.

Levin, Mordechai. "De'ot ve-helikhot kalkaliyot ba-masoret: Behinat torato shel Sombart le-or sifrut ha-musar ve-ha-zikhronot." *Tsiyon* 46 (1978): 235–63.

————. *'Erkhei hevrah ve-kalkalah ba-ideologiyah shel tekufat ha-haskalah.* Jerusalem, 1975.

Levine, Hillel. *Economic Origins of Antisemitism.* New Haven, 1991.

Liberles, Robert. "Emancipation and the Structure of the Jewish Community in the Nineteenth Century." *LBIYB* 31 (1986): 51–67.

————. "The Historical Context of Dohm's Treatise on the Jews." In *Das deutsche Judentum und der Liberalismus — German Jewry and Liberalism,* 44–69. St. Augustin, 1986.

Liebersohn, Harry. "Discovering Indigenous Nobility: Tocqueville, Chamisso, and Romantic Travel Writing." *American Historical Review* 99 (June 1994): 746–66.

Liebesschuetz, Hans. "Max Weber's Historical Interpretation of Judaism." *LBIYB* 9 (1964): 41–68.

Liedtke, Rainer. *Jewish Welfare in Hamburg and Manchester, c. 1850–1914.* Oxford, 1998.

Lindenfeld, David F. *The Practical Imagination: The German Sciences of State in the Nineteenth Century.* Chicago, 1997.

Linton, Derek S. *"Who Has the Youth, Has the Future": The Campaign to Save Young Workers in Imperial Germany.* Cambridge, 1991.

Lipman, V. D. *A Century of Social Service, 1859–1959: The Jewish Board of Guardians.* London, 1959.

————. *A History of the Jews in Britain since 1858.* Leicester, 1990.

Little, Lester. *Religious Poverty and the Profit Economy in Medieval Europe.* Ithaca, 1978.

Littman, Jacob. *The Economic Role of Jews in Medieval Poland: The Contributions of Yitzhak Schipper.* Lanham, Md., 1984.

Loewe, Heinz-Dietrich. *The Tsars and the Jews.* Chur, Switzerland, 1993.

Lorenz, Ina. "Die jüdische Gemeinde Hamburg 1860–1943." In *Die Juden in Hamburg 1590 bis 1990,* edited by Arno Herzig, 77–100. Hamburg, 1991.

———. "Zehn Jahre Kampf um das Hamburger System (1864–1873)." In *Die Hamburger Juden in der Emanzipationsphase 1780–1870,* edited by Peter Freimark and Arno Herzig, 41–82. Hamburg, 1989.

Lotan, Giora. "The Zentralwohlfahrtstelle." *LBIYB* 4 (1959): 185–207.

Lowenstein, Steven M. *The Berlin Jewish Community: Enlightenment, Family and Crisis, 1770–1830.* New York, 1994.

———. "Jewish Upper Crust and Berlin Jewish Enlightenment: The Family of Daniel Itzig." In *From East and West: Jews in a Changing Europe, 1750–1870,* edited by David Sorkin and Francis Malino, 182–201. Oxford, 1990.

———. "The Pace of Modernization of German Jewry in the 19th Century." *LBIYB* 21 (1976): 41–56.

———. "The Rural Community and the Urbanization of German Jewry." *Central European History* 13, no. 3 (1980): 218–35.

Lowenthal, E. G. "The Ahlem Experiment." *LBIYB* 14 (1969): 165–81.

Lowenthal, Marvin, trans. *The Memoirs of Glückel of Hameln.* New York, 1977.

Luther, Martin. "On the Jews and Their Lies." In *Works,* vol. 47, edited by Franklin Sherman, 121–306. Philadelphia, 1971.

Luz, Ehud. *Parallels Meet: Religion and Nationalism in the Early Zionist Movement, 1882–1914.* Philadelphia, 1988.

Magnus, Shulamit S. *Jewish Emancipation in a German City: Cologne, 1798–1871.* Stanford, Calif., 1997.

Mahler, Raphael. *Hasidism and the Jewish Enlightenment.* Philadelphia, 1985.

———. *A History of Modern Jewry, 1780–1815.* London, 1971.

Mannheimer, Isaak Noah. *Gottesdienstliche Vorträge bei der Wochenabschnitte des Jahres.* Vienna, 1835.

Marcus, Alfred. *Die wirtschaftliche Krise der deutschen Juden.* Berlin, 1931.

Maretzki, Louis, ed. *Festschrift zur Feier des zwanzigjährigen Bestehens des U.O.B.B. Herausgegeben von der Gross-Loge für Deutschland. 20. März 1902. Redigiert von San.-Rath. Dr. Maretzki.* Berlin, 1902.

———. *Geschichte des Ordens Bnei Briss in Deutschland, 1882–1907.* Berlin, 1907.

———. *Das Wesen und die Leistungen des Ordens U.O.B.B.* Berlin, 1911.

Markel, Howard. *Quarantine! East European Jewish Immigrants and the New York City Epidemics of 1892.* Baltimore, 1997.

Marrus, Michael. *The Politics of Assimilation: A Study of the French-Jewish Community at the Time of the Dreyfus Affair.* Oxford, 1972.

Marx, Roland. "La régénération économique des juifs d'Alsace." In *Les juifs et la Révolution Française,* edited by Bernhard Blumenkranz and Albert Soboul, 105–20. Paris, 1976.

Mathias, Peter, and Sidney Pollard, eds. *The Cambridge Economic History of Europe.* 8 vols. Cambridge, 1989.

Mayer, Sigmund, *Ein jüdischer Kaufmann.* Vienna, 1912.

———. *Die Wiener Juden. Kommerz, Kultur, Politik, 1700–1900.* Vienna, 1918.

Mayorek, Yoram. "Emil Meyerson ve-reshit ha-meʿuravut shel hevrat IKA be-Eretz Yisraʾel." *Cathedra* 62 (1991): 67–79.

McCagg, William O., Jr. *A History of Habsburg Jews, 1670–1918*. Bloomington, Ind., 1989.

———. "Jewish Wealth in Vienna, 1670–1918." In *Jews in the Hungarian Economy, 1760–1945*, edited by Michael Silber, 54–91. Jerusalem, 1992.

McNally, David. *Political Economy and the Rise of Capitalism: A Re-interpretation*. Berkeley, 1989.

Meek, Ronald. *Social Science and the Ignoble Savage*. London, 1976.

Melton, James van Horn. *Absolutism and the Eighteenth-Century Origins of Compulsory Schooling in Prussia and Austria*. Cambridge, 1988.

Mendelsohn, Ezra. *On Modern Jewish Politics*. New York, 1993.

———. "Should We Take Notice of Berthe Weill? Reflections on the Domain of Jewish History." *Jewish Social Studies*, n.s. 1, no. 1 (1994): 22–39.

Mendelssohn, Moses. *Gesammelte Schriften*. Leipzig, 1843.

Mendes-Flohr, Paul. "Werner Sombart's 'The Jews and Modern Capitalism.' " *LBIYB* 21 (1979): 87–107.

Mevorah, Baruch. " 'Ikvoteihah shel 'alilat Damasek be-hitpathutah shel ha-'itonut ha-yehudit ba-shanim 1840–46." *Zion* 23–24 (1958–59): 46–65.

Meyer, Michael. *The Origins of the Modern Jew*. Detroit, 1972.

———, ed. *German-Jewish History in Modern Times*. 4 vols. New York, 1996–97.

Michman, Jozeph. *Dutch Jewry during the Emancipation Period: Gothic Turrets on a Corinthian Building*. Amsterdam, 1995.

Mintz, Matityahu. *Ber Borochov: Ha-ma'agal ha-rishon, 1900–1906*. Tel Aviv, 1976.

———. "He'erah arukah be-shulei havat-da'ato shel Derzhavin mi-shnat 1800." In *Ben Yisra'el le-umot: Kovetz ma'amarim shai li-Shmuel Ettinger*, 103–12. Jerusalem, 1987.

———. "Nesigat ha-Rotchildim mi-milvat April 1891 le-Russiyah min ha-hebet ha-yehudi." *Tsiyon* 54 (1989): 401–35.

Miron, Dan. *Bein hazon le-emet: Nitzanei ha-roman ha-'ivri ve-ha-yidi ba-me'ah ha-19*. Jerusalem, 1979.

Mitchell, B. R. *European Historical Statistics, 1750–1975*. New York, 1980.

Mitzman, Arthur. *Sociology and Estrangement*. New Brunswick, N.J., 1973.

Moeller, Horst. "Aufklärung, Judenemanzipation und Staat. Ursprung und Wirkung von Dohms Schrift 'Über die bürgerliche Verbesserung der Juden." *Deutsche Aufklärung und Judenemanzipation (TAJDG*, Beiheft 3) (Tel Aviv, 1979): 119–54.

Montesquieu, Charles de Secondat. *The Spirit of Laws*. Cincinnati, 1886.

Moore, Deborah Dash. *B'nai B'rith and the Challenge of Ethnic Leadership*. Albany, N.Y., 1981.

More, Thomas. *Utopia*. New York, 1974.

Moses, Julius. *Das Handwerk unter den Juden. Vortrag gehalten im Verein selbstständiger/Handwerker jüdischen Glaubens*. Berlin, 1902.

Mosse, George. *Fallen Soldiers*. New York, 1985.

———. *German Jews beyond Judaism*. Bloomington, Ind., 1985.

Mosse, Werner. *The German-Jewish Economic Elite: A Socio-Cultural Profile.* Oxford, 1989.

―――. *Jews in the German Economy: The German-Jewish Economic Elite, 1820–1935.* Oxford, 1987.

―――. "Judaism, Jews, and Capitalism: Weber, Sombart, and Beyond." *LBIYB* 24 (1979): 3–15.

―――. "Die Juden in Wirtschaft und Gesellschaft." In *Juden im Wilhelmischen Deutschland, 1890–1914,* edited by Werner Mosse and Arnold Paucker, 57–113. Tübingen, 1976.

Mosse, Werner, and Hans Pohl, eds. *Jüdische Unternehmer in Deutschland im 19. und 20. Jahrhundert.* Stuttgart, 1992.

Mossek, Moshe. *Palestine Immigration Policy under Sir Herbert Samuel.* London, 1978.

Muhlstein, Anka. *Baron James: The Rise of the French Rothschilds.* New York, 1982.

Myers, David N. "The Fall and Rise of Jewish Historicism: The Evolution of the Akademie für die Wissenschaft des Judentums (1919–1934)." *Hebrew Union College Annual* 63 (1992): 107–44.

―――. *Re-inventing the Jewish Past: European Jewish Intellectuals and the Zionist Return to History.* New York, 1995.

Na'aman, Shlomo. "Jewish Participation in the Deutscher Nationalverein (1859–1867)." *LBIYB* 24 (1989): 81–93.

Nadav, Daniel S. *Julius Moses und die Politik der Sozialhygiene in Deutschland.* Gerlingen, 1985.

Nathans, Ben. "Beyond the Pale: The Jewish Encounter with Russia, 1840–1900." Ph.D. dissertation, University of California at Berkeley, 1995.

Necheles, Ruth. *The Abbé Grégoire, 1787–1831.* Westport, Conn., 1971.

Nelson, Benjamin. *The Idea of Usury.* 2d ed. Chicago, 1969.

Nipperdey, Thomas. *Deutsche Geschichte 1800–1866.* Munich, 1987.

―――. *Religion im Umbruch. Deutschland, 1870–1918.* Munich, 1988.

Niremberg, David. *Communities of Violence: Persecution of Minorities in the Middle Ages.* Princeton, 1997.

Norman, Theodore. *An Outstreched Arm: A History of the Jewish Colonization Association.* London, 1985.

Novak, David. "Economics and Justice: The Jewish Example." In *Jewish Social Ethics,* 206–24. New York, 1992.

Oelsner, Toni. "The Place of the Jews in Economic History as Viewed by German Scholars." *LBIYB* 7 (1962): 183–212.

―――. "Wilhelm Roscher's Theory of the Economic and Social Position of the Jews in the Middle Ages." *YIVO Annual of Jewish Social Science* 12 (1958–59): 176–95.

Opalski, Magdalena, and Israel Bartal. *Poles and Jews: A Failed Brotherhood.* Hanover, N.H., 1992.

Pagden, Antony. *The Fall of Natural Man.* Cambridge, 1982.

Pearce, Roy Harvey. *Savagism and Civilization: A Study of the Indian and the American Mind.* Berkeley, 1988.

Penslar, Derek J. "Hashpaʿot tsorfatiyot ʿal ha-haklaʾut ha-yehudit be-eretz yisraʾel 1870–1914." *Cathedra* 62 (December 1991): 54–66.

———. "Technical Expertise and the Creation of the Rural Yishuv, 1882–1948." *Jewish History*, forthcoming.

———. "Theodor Herzl and Jewish Social Policy." In *Theodor Herzl: Visionary of the Jewish State*, edited by Gideon Shimoni and Robert S. Wistrich, 215–26. Jerusalem, 2000.

———. *Zionism and Technocracy: The Engineering of Jewish Settlement in Palestine*. Bloomington, Ind., 1991.

Philipp, Alfred. *Die Juden und das Wirtschaftsleben. Eine Antikritisch-Bibliographische Studie zu Werner Sombart. "Die Juden und das Wirtschaftsleben."* Strasbourg, 1929.

Philippson, Johanna. "Ludwig Philippson und die Allgemeine Zeitung des Judentums." In *Das Judentum in der Deutschen Umwelt*, edited by Hans Liebesschütz and Arnold Paucker, 243–91. Tübingen, 1977.

Philippson, Ludwig. *Über die Resultate in der Weltgeschichte. Sechs Vorlesungen*. Leipzig, 1860.

Piette, Christine. *Les juifs de Paris (1808–1840)*. Québec, 1983.

Pinkney, David H. *Napoléon III and the Rebuilding of Paris*. Princeton, 1958.

Pinkus, Benjamin. *The Jews of the Soviet Union: The History of a National Minority*. Cambridge, 1988.

Pinkus, Felix. *Studien zur Wirtschaftsstellung der Juden*. Berlin, 1905.

Pohlmann, W. *Die Juden und die körperliche Arbeit*. Berlin, 1894.

Poliakov, Léon. *The History of Antisemitism*. 4 vols. New York, 1974–75.

———. *Jewish Bankers and the Holy See*. London, 1977.

Pollins, Harold. "German Jews in British Industry." In *Second Chance: Two Centuries of German-speaking Jews in the United Kingdom*, edited by Werner Mosse et al., 362–77. Tübingen, 1991.

Posener, S. "The Social Life of the Jewish Communities in France in the 18th Century." *Jewish Social Studies* 7 (1945): 195–232.

Prawer, S. S. *Heine's Jewish Comedy: A Study of His Portraits of Jews and Judaism*. Oxford, 1983.

Prelinger, Catherine. *Charity, Challenge, and Change: Religious Dimensions of the Mid-Nineteenth-Century Women's Movement in Germany*. New York, 1987.

Prestel, Claudia. "Bevölkerungspolitik in der jüdischen Gemeinschaft in der Weimarer Republik—Ausdruck jüdischer Identität?" *Zeitschrift für Geschichtswissenschaft*, no. 8 (1993): 685–715.

———. "Weibliche Rollenzuweisung in jüdischen Organisationen. Das Beispiel des Bnei Briss." *BLBI* 85 (1990): 51–80.

———. "Zwischen Tradition und Moderne—Die Armenpolitik der Gemeinde zu Fürth (1826–70). *TAJDG* 20 (1991): 135–62.

Prochaska, F. K. *Women and Philanthropy in Nineteenth-Century England*. Oxford, 1980.

Pulzer, Peter. *Jews and the German State: The Political History of a Minority, 1848–1933*. London, 1992.

———. *The Rise of Political Antisemitism in Germany and Austria*. Rev. ed. Cambridge, Mass., 1988.

Puskas, Julianna. "Jewish Leaseholders in the Course of Agricultural Development in Hungary, 1850–1930." In *Jews in the Hungarian Economy, 1760–1945*, edited by Michael Silber, 106–23. Jerusalem, 1992.

Rachel, Hugo, and Paul Wallich. *Berliner Grosskaufleute und Kapitalisten*. 2 vols. Berlin, 1938.

Raeff, Marc. "The Well-Ordered Police State and the Development of Modernity in Seventeenth- and Eighteenth-Century Europe." *American Historical Review* 80 (1975): 1221–43.

Ramazzini, Bernardino. *Essai sur les maladies des artisans, traduit du Latin de Ramazzini, avec des notes et des additions*. Paris, 1777 (*Diseases of Workers* [New York: 1964]).

Raniach, Anson. "Social Knowledge, Social Risk, and the Politics of Industrial Accidents in Germany and France." In *States, Social Knowledge, and the Origins of Modern Social Policies*, edited by Dietrich Rueschemeyer and Theda Skopcol, 48–79. Princeton, 1996.

Raphael, Freddy. *Judaisme et capitalisme: Essai sur la controverse entre Max Weber et Werner Sombart*. Paris, 1982.

Rappaport, Mordeché. *Christian Wilhelm von Dohm. Der Gegner der Physiokratie und seine Thesen*. Berlin, 1908.

Ravid, Benjamin. *Economics and Toleration in 17th-Century Venice: The Background and Context of the Discorso of Simone Luzzato*. Jerusalem, 1978.

Reich, Ignaz, ed. *Beth Lechem. Jahrbuch zur Beförderung des Ackerbaues, Handwerk und der Industrie unter den Israelitien Ungarns*. Pest, 1871.

Reinharz, Jehuda. *Chaim Weizmann: The Making of a Statesman*. Oxford, 1993.

———. *Fatherland or Promised Land: The Dilemma of the German Jew, 1893–1914*. Ann Arbor, 1975.

Reinhold, Hanoch. "Yosef Salvador: Hayyav ve-de'otav." *Tsiyon* 9 (1941): 109–41.

Richarz, Monika. *Jewish Life in Germany: Memoirs from Three Centuries*. Bloomington, Ind., 1991.

———. "Jewish Social Mobility in Germany during the Time of Emancipation (1790–1871)." *LBIYB* 20 (1975): 69–77.

———. "Die soziale Stellung der jüdischen Händler auf dem Lande am Beispiel Südwestdeutschlands." In *Jüdische Unternehmer in Deutschland im 19. Und 20. Jahrhundert*, edited by Werner E. Mosse and Hans Pohl, 271–83. Stuttgart, 1992.

Richter, Anke. "Das jüdische Armenwesen in Hamburg in der 1. Hälfte des 19. Jahrhunderts." In *Die Hamburger Juden in der Emanzipationsphase (1780–1870)*, edited by Peter Freimark and Arno Herzig, 234–54. Hamburg, 1990.

Rinott, Moshe. *Hevrat ha-'ezrah liyehudei Germaniyah biyetsirah u-ve-ma'avak*. Jerusalem, 1971.

Röder, Werner, and Herbert A. Strauss, eds. *Biographisches Handbuch der deutschsprächigen Emigration nach 1933*. 3 vols. Munich, 1980–83.

Rodrigue, Aron. *French Jews, Turkish Jews: The Alliance Israélite Universelle and the Politics of Jewish Schooling in Turkey, 1860–1925*. Bloomington, Ind., 1990.

———. *De l'instruction à l'émancipation: Les enseignants de l'Alliance Israélite Universelle et les juifs de l'Orient, 1860–1939*. Paris, 1989.

Roehrlich, Wilhelm. *Wucher und Intoleranz. Zugleich eine Antwort auf die Schrift von W. Marr, "Der Sieg des Judenthums über das Germanenthum."* Zurich, 1879.

Rohrbacher, Stefan, and Michael Schmidt. *Judenbilder. Kulturgeschichte antijüdischer Mythen und antisemitischer Vorurteile.* Hamburg, 1991.

Rose, Paul. *Revolutionary Antisemitism in Germany from Kant to Wagner.* Princeton, 1990.

Rosman, M. J. *The Lord's Jews: Magnate-Jewish Relations in the Polish-Lithuanian Commonwealth during the Eighteenth Century.* Cambridge, Mass., 1990.

Rozenblit, Marsha. "Jewish Assimilation in Hapsburg Vienna." In *Assimilation and Community: The Jews in Nineteenth-Century Europe,* edited by Jonathan Frankel and Steven J. Zipperstein, 225–45. Cambridge, 1992.

———. "Jewish Ethnicity in a New Nation-State: The Crisis of Identity in the Austrian Republic." In *In Search of Jewish Community: Jewish Identities in Germany and Austria, 1918–1933,* edited by Michael Brenner and Derek J. Penslar, 134–53. Bloomington, Ind., 1998.

———. *The Jews of Vienna, 1867–1914: Assimilation and Identity.* Albany; N.Y., 1983.

Ruderman, David B. *Jewish Thought and Scientific Discovery in Early Modern Europe.* New Haven, 1995.

Ruppin, Arthur. *The Jew in the Modern World.* London, 1934.

Rürup, Reinhard. "Emancipation and Bourgeois Society." *LBIYB* 14 (1969): 67–91.

———. *Emanzipation und Antisemitismus.* Göttingen, 1975.

———. "The Tortuous and Thorny Path to Legal Equality: 'Jew Laws' and Emancipatory Legislation in Germany from the Late Eighteenth Century." *LBIYB* 31 (1986): 3–33.

Sachsse, Christoph, and Florian Tennstedt. *Geschichte der Armenfürsorge in Deutschland.* Stuttgart, 1980.

Salvador, Joseph. *Histoire des Institutions de Moïse et du peuple hébreu.* Paris, 1828.

———. *Loi de Moïse ou Système religieux et politique des Hébreux.* Paris, 1822.

Schnee, Heinrich. *Die Hoffinanz und der moderne Staat.* 6 vols. Berlin, 1953–67.

Schorsch, Ismar. *From Text to Context: The Turn to History in Modern Judaism.* Hanover, N.H., 1994.

———. *Jewish Reactions to Antisemitism in Germany, 1871–1914.* New York, 1972.

Schwartz, Howard Eilbert. *The Savage in Judaism.* Bloomington, Ind., 1990.

Schwartzfuchs, Simon. *Napoléon, the Jews, and the Sanhedrin.* London, 1979.

Scott, H. M., ed. *Enlightened Absolutism: Reform and Reformers in Later Eighteenth-Century Europe.* Ann Arbor, 1990.

Segall, Jakob. *Die beruflichen and sozialen Verhältnisse der Juden in Deutschland.* Berlin, 1912.

Segev, Tom. *The Seventh Million: The Israelis and the Holocaust.* New York, 1993.

Segre, Dan. "The Emancipation of the Jews in Italy." In *Paths of Emancipation: Jews, States, and Citizenship,* edited by Pierre Birnbaum and Ira Katznelson, 206–37. Princeton, 1995.

Shafir, Gershon. *Land, Labor, and the Origins of the Israeli-Palestinian Conflict, 1882–1914*. Cambridge, 1989.

Shanahan, W. O. *German Protestants Face the Social Question*. South Bend, Ind., 1954.

Shapiro, James. *Shakespeare and the Jews*. New York, 1996.

Shapiro, Leon. *The History of ORT*. New York, 1980.

Shatzmiller, Joseph. *Shylock Reconsidered: Jews, Moneylending, and Medieval Society*. Berkeley, 1990.

Shavit, Ya'akov. *Jabotinsky and the Revisionist Movement, 1925–1948*. London, 1988.

———. *Me-rov li-medinah: Ha-tenua'h ha revizionistit, ha-tokhnit ha-hityashvutit, ve-ha-ra'yon ha-hevrati 1925–1935*. Tel Aviv, 1983.

Sheenan, Bernard W. *Seeds of Extinction: Jeffersonian Philanthropy and the American Indian*. Chapel Hill, 1973.

Sheehan, James. *German Liberalism in the Nineteenth Century*. Chicago, 1978.

———. "Liberalism and the City in 19th-Century Germany." *Past and Present* 51 (1971): 116–37.

Shell, Marc. *Money, Language, and Thought*. Baltimore, 1982.

Sherman, A. J. "German-Jewish Bankers in World Politics: The Financing of the Russo-Japanese War." *LBIYB* 28 (1983): 59–73.

Shilo, Margalit. *Nisyonot be-hityashvut: Ha-misrad Ha-eretz-yisre'eli 1908–1914*. Jerusalem, 1988.

———. "Tovat ha-aretz o-tovat ha-'am? Yahsah shel ha-tenua'h ha-tsiyonit le-'aliyah bitekufat ha-'aliyah ha-sheniyah." *Cathedra* 46 (1987): 109–22.

Shoemaker, Robert, and Mary Vincent, eds. *Gender and History in Western Europe*. London, 1998.

Shohat, Azriel. *'Im hilufei ha-tekufot*. Jerusalem, 1960.

Shucker, Stephen A. "Origins of the 'Jewish Problem' in the Later Third Republic." In *The Jews in Modern France,* edited by Frances Malino and Bernard Wasserstein, 135–80. Hanover, N.H., 1985.

Schüler-Springorum, Stephanie. "Assimilation and Community Reconsidered: The Jewish Community in Königsberg, 1871–1914." *Jewish Social Studies,* n.s. 5, no. 3 (1999): 104–31.

Shulvass, Moses A. *From East to West: The Westward Migration of Jews from Eastern Europe during the Seventeenth and Eighteenth Centuries*. Detroit, 1971.

Simon, A. M. *Die Erziehung zur Bodenkultur und zum Handwerk. Eine Soziale Frage*. Berlin, 1904.

———. *Sollen sich Juden in Deutschland dem Handwerk, der Gärtnerei, und der Landwirtschaft widmen?* Berlin, 1902.

Smith, Anthony. *The Ethnic Origins of Nations*. Cambridge, Mass., 1986.

Smith, Bonnie. *Ladies of the Leisure Class: The Bourgeoisie of Northern France in the Nineteenth Century*. Princeton, 1981.

Smolenskin, Peretz. "Et la-ta'at." In *Ma'amarim,* 2:231–323. Jerusalem, 1925–26.

Sombart, Werner. *The Jews and Modern Capitalism*. New Brunswick, N.J., 1982.

———. *Judentaufen*. Munich, 1912.

Sorkin, David. "The Case for Comparison: Moses Mendelssohn and the Religious Enlightenment." *Modern Judaism* 14 (1994): 121–38.

———. "Enlightenment and Emancipation: German Jewry's Formative Age in Comparative Perspective." In *Comparing Jewish Societies,* edited by Todd Endelman, 89–112. Ann Arbor, 1997.

———. "The Impact of Emancipation on German Jewry: A Reconsideration." In *Assimilation and Community: The Jews in Nineteenth-Century Europe,* edited by Jonathan Frankel and Steven Zipperstein, 177–98. Cambridge, 1992.

———. *Moses Mendelssohn and the Religious Enlightenment*. Berkeley, 1996.

———. "Religious Reforms and Secular Trends in German-Jewish Life: An Agenda for Research." *LBIYB* 40 (1995): 169–84.

———. *The Transformation of German Jewry*. Oxford, 1987.

Stampfer, Shaul. "The Geographic Background of East European Jewish Migration to the United States before World War I." In *Migration across Time and Nations: Population Mobility in Historical Contexts,* edited by Ira A. Glazier and Luigi de Rosa, 220–30. New York, 1986.

Stanislawski, Michael. *Tsar Nicholas I and the Jews, 1825–55*. Philadelphia, 1983.

Steckelmacher, M. *Randbemerkungen zu Werner Sombarts "Die Juden und das Wirtschaftsleben."* Berlin, 1912.

Stegmann, Dirk. *Die Erben Bismarcks. Parteien und Verbände in der Spätphase des Wilhelminischen Deutschlands. Sammlungspolitik 1897–1918*. Cologne, 1970.

Stein, Siegfried. "The Development of the Jewish Law on Interest from the Biblical Period to the Expulsion of the Jews from England." *Historia Judaica* 17 (1955): 18–29.

———. "Interest Taken by Jews from Gentiles: An Evaluation of Source Material (14th to 17th Centuries)." *Journal of Semitic Studies* 1 (1956): 141–64.

———. "Die Zeitschrift 'Sulamith.' " *Zeitschrift für die Geschichte der Juden in Deutschland* 7 (1937): 193–226.

Steinmetz, George. *Regulating the Social: The Welfare State and Local Politics in Imperial Germany*. Princeton, 1993.

Stern, Fritz. *Gold and Iron: Bismarck, Bleichröder, and the Building of the German Empire*. New York, 1977.

———. *The Politics of Cultural Despair: A Study in the Rise of the Germanic Ideology*. Berkeley, 1961.

Stern, Selma. *The Court Jew*. Philadelphia, 1950.

———. *Der preussische Staat und die Juden*. 4 vols. Tübingen, 1971.

Sternhell, Zev. *The Founding Myths of Israel*. Princeton, 1997.

———. "The Roots of Popular Antisemitism in the Third Republic." In *The Jews in Modern France,* edited by François Malino and Bernard Wasserstein, 103–34. Hanover, N.H., 1985.

Sternhell, Zev, with Mario Sznajder and Maia Asheri. *The Birth of Fascist Ideology: From Cultural Rebellion to Political Revolution*. Princeton, 1994.

Stow, Kenneth R. *Alienated Minority: The Jews of Medieval Latin Europe*. Cambridge, Mass., 1992.

Szajkowski, Zosa. "Conflicts in the Alliance Israélite Universelle and the Founding of the Anglo-Jewish Association, the Vienna Allianz, and the Hilfsverein." *Jewish Social Studies* 19, nos. 1–2 (1957): 29–50.

————. "The European Attitude to East European Jewish Immigration (1881–1893)." *Proceedings of the American Jewish History Society* 41 (1951–52): 127–62.

————. "Jewish Participation in the Sale of National Property during the French Revolution" (1952). Reprinted in *Jews and the French Revolutions of 1789, 1830, and 1848*, 475–500. New York, 1970.

————. *Poverty and Social Welfare among French Jews (1800–1800)*. New York, 1954.

Tal, Uriel. "German-Jewish Social Thought in the Mid-Nineteenth Century." In *Revolution and Evolution: 1848 in German-Jewish History*, edited by Werner Mosse, Arnold Paucker, and Reinhard Rürup, 299–328. Tübingen, 1981.

Täubler, Eugen. "Die Entwicklung der Arbeit des 'Gesamtarchivs' und der Versuch einer methodologischen Gliederung und Systematisierung der jüdischen Geschichtsforschung" (1911). In *Aufsätze zur Problematik jüdischer Geschichtsschreibung 1908–1950*, 9–20. Tübingen, 1977.

————. *Zur Handelsbedeutung der Juden in Deutschland vor Beginn des Städtewesens*. Breslau, 1916.

Terpstra, Nicholas. "Apprenticeship in Social Welfare: From Confraternal Charity to Municipal Poor Relief in Early Modern Italy." *Sixteenth-Century Journal* 25, no. 1 (1994): 101–20.

Teveth, Shabtai. *Ben-Gurion: The Burning Ground, 1886–1948*. New York, 1987.

Toland, John. *Reasons for Naturalizing the Jews in Great Britain and Ireland, On the same foot with all other Nations. Containing also, A Defence of the Jews against all Vulgar Prejudices in all Countries*. London, 1714.

Toury, Jacob. "Die bangen Jahren (1887–91). Juden in Deutschland zwischen Integrationshoffnung und Isolationsfurcht." In *Juden in Deutschland. Emanzipation, Integration, Verfolgung und Vernichtung*, edited by Peter Freimark, Alice Jankowski, and Ina S. Lorenz, 164–85. Hamburg, 1991.

————. "Der Eintritt der Juden ins deutsche Bürgertum." In *Das Judentum in der Deutschen Umwelt 1800–1850*, edited by Hans Liebeschütz and Arnold Paucker, 139–242. Tübingen, 1977.

————. "Emanzipation und Judenkolonien in der öffentlichen Meinung Deutschlands (1775–1819)." *TAJDJ* 11 (1982): 17–53.

————. "The Jewish Question: A Semantic Approach." *LBIYB* 11 (1966): 85–106.

————. *Die jüdische Presse im Österreichischen Kaiserreich 1802–1918*. Tübingen, 1983.

————. "Die jüdische Schneider Hamburgs, 1848–54." *TAJDG* 1 1972): 101–18.

————. "Manual Labour and Emigration—Records from Some Bavarian Districts, 1830–1854." *LBIYB* 16 (1971): 45–62.

————. "Organizational Problems of German Jewry: Steps towards the Establishment of a Central Organization (1893–1920)." *LBIYB* 13 (1968): 57–90.

————. "Ostjüdische Handarbeiter in Deutschland vor 1914." *BLBI* 6 (1963): 81–91.

————. *Die politische Orientierungen der Juden in Deutschland.* Tübingen, 1966.

Tribe, Keith. *Governing Economy: The Reformation of German Economic Discourse, 1750–1840.* Cambridge, 1988.

Tsamriyon, Tsemah. *Ha-Me'asef: K'tav ha-'et ha-rishon be-'ivrit.* Tel Aviv, 1988.

Tuch, Gustav. *Innere Kolonisation.* Berlin, 1897.

————. *Referat betreffend Beteiligung deutscher Juden an heimischer Landwirtschaft, gehalten am 24. Oktober 1897.* Berlin, 1897.

————. *Schulgarten.* Berlin, 1898.

Ulbricht, Otto. "Criminality and Punishment of the Jews in the Early Modern Period." In *In and Out of the Ghetto: Jewish-Gentile Relations in Late Medieval and Early Modern Germany,* edited by R. Po-Chia Hsia and Hartmut Lehmann, 49–70. Washington, D.C., 1995.

Vaitz, Yehiam. *Muda'ut ve-hoser onim—Mapai le-nokhah ha-shoah 1943–45.* Jerusalem, 1994.

van Leeuwen, Marco H. D. "Arme Amsterdamse joden en de strijd om hun integratie aan het begin van de negentiende eeuw." In *De Gelykstaat der Joden. Inburgering van een minderheid,* edited by Hetty Berg et al., 55–66. Amsterdam, 1996.

van Horn Melton, James. *Absolutism and the Eighteenth-Century Origins of Compulsory Schooling in Prussia and Austria.* Cambridge, 1988.

van Rahden, Till. "Die Grenze vor Ort—Einbürgerung und Ausweisung ausländischer Juden in Breslau 1860–1918." *TAJDG* 27 (1998): 47–69.

————. "Mingling, Marrying, and Distancing: Jewish Integration in Wilhelmian Breslau and Its Erosion in Early Weimar Germany." In *Jüdisches Leben in der Weimarer Republik/Jews in the Weimar Republic,* edited by Wolfgang Benz, Arnold Paucker, and Peter Pulzer, 197–222. Tübingen, 1998.

Verein für jüdische Statistik. *Jüdische Statistik.* Berlin, 1903.

Verein selbstständiger Handwerker jüdischen Glaubens zu Berlin. *Zur Geschichte des "Vereinselbstständiger Handwerker jüdischen Glaubens" zu Berlin. Ein Gedenkblatt zum X. Stiftungsfeste am 2. Dezember 1905.* Berlin, 1905.

Vierhaus, Rudolf. *Germany in the Age of Absolutism.* Cambridge, 1988.

Vital, David. *The Origins of Zionism.* New York, 1975.

————. *A People Apart: The Jews in Europe, 1789–1939.* New York, 1999.

Volkov, Shulamit. "Antisemitism as a Cultural Code." *LBIYB* 23 (1978): 25–45.

————. *Jüdisches Leben und Antisemitismus im 19. Jahrhundert.* Munich, 1990.

————. *The Rise of Popular Antimodernism in Germany.* Princeton, 1978.

————. "The Written Matter and the Spoken Word." In *Unanswered Questions: Nazi Germany and the Genocide of the Jews,* edited by François Furet, 33–53. New York, 1989.

Wachtel, Friedrich. *Das Judenthum und seine Aufgabe im neuen deutschen Reich.* Leipzig, 1871.

Waetjen, Hermann. *Das Judentum und die Anfänge der modernen Kolonisation. Kritische Bemerkungen zu Werner Sombarts "Die Juden und das Wirtschaftsleben."* Berlin, 1914.

Wahrmund, Adolf. *Das Gesetz des Nomadenthum und die heutige Judenherrschaft*. 2d ed. Berlin, 1892.

Walkowitz, Judith R. *City of Dreadful Delight: Narratives of Sexual Danger in Late-Victorian London*. Chicago, 1992.

Wasserman, Henry. "The 'Fliegende Blätter' as a Source for the Social History of German Jewry." *LBIYB* 28 (1983): 93–138.

———. "Jews and Judaism in the *Gartenlaube*." *LBIYB* 23 (1978): 47–60.

———. "Jews, 'Bürgertum,' and 'Bürgerliche Gesellschaft' in a Liberal Era (1840–1880)" (Hebrew). Ph.D. dissertation, Hebrew University, 1979.

Wasserstein, Bernard. *Vanishing Diaspora: The Jews in Europe since 1945*. Cambridge, Mass., 1996.

Weatherall, David. *David Ricardo: A Biography*. The Hague, 1976.

Weber, Max. *Gesammelte Aufsätze zur Religionssoziologie*. Tübingen, 1920.

———. *The Protestant Ethic and the Spirit of Capitalism*. New York, 1958.

Weinberg, Robert. *Stalin's Forgotten Zion: Birobidzhan and the Making of a Soviet Jewish Homeland: An Illustrated History, 1928–1996*. Berkeley, 1998.

Weinryb, Bernard (Sucher Dov). *Der Kampf um die Berufsumschichtung*. Berlin, 1936.

Weissbach, Lee Shai. "The Jewish Elite and the Children of the Poor: Jewish Apprenticeship Programs in Nineteenth-Century France." *Association for Jewish Studies Review* 12, no. 1 (1987): 123–42.

———. "*Oeuvre Industrielle, Oeuvre Morale*: The Sociétés de Patronage of Nineteenth-Century France." *French Historical Studies* 15 (1987): 99–120.

Wertheimer, Jack. "Jewish Organizational Life in the United States since 1945." *American Jewish Year Book* 95 (1995): 3–98.

———. *Unwelcome Strangers: East European Jews in Imperial Germany*. New York, 1987.

Wessely, Moses. *Hinterlassene Schriften*. Berlin, 1798.

Wessely, Naphtali Herz. *Divrei shalom ve-emet*. Warsaw, 1886.

———. *Wörte der Wahrheit und des Friedens an die gesammten jüdischen Nation*. Vienna, 1782.

Wiener, Max. "The Concept of Mission in Traditional and Modern Judaism." *YIVO Annual of Jewish Social Science* 2–3 (1947–48): 9–24.

Wigler, Jacob Samuel. "Isaac de Pinto: Sa vie est ses oeuvres." Ph.D. dissertation, University of Amsterdam, 1923.

Wilson, Stephen. *Ideology and Experience*. East Rutherford, N.J., 1982.

Wininger, S. *Grösse jüdische National-Biographie*. Czernowitz, 1925–36.

Winkopp, Peter Adolph. *Über die bürgerliche und geistliche Verbesserung des Mönchwesens*. Gera, 1783.

Wischnitzer, M., trans. and ed. *The Memoirs of Ber of Bolechow*. New York, 1973.

Wistrich, Robert S. *The Jews of Vienna in the Age of Franz Joseph*. Oxford, 1990.

Wolf, Gerson. *Geschichte der Juden in Wien (1156–1876)*. Vienna, 1876.

———. *Joseph Wertheimer. Ein Lebens- und Zeitbuch*. Vienna, 1868.

———. *Studien zur Jubelfeier der Wiener Universität*. Vienna, 1865.

Wolff, Louis. *Handwerk im Judentum. Entwicklung und Aufstieg. Aus den Reden und Schriften von Louis Wolff (1909–1934)*. Berlin, 1935.

Woolf, Stuart. *The Poor in Western Europe in the Eighteenth and Nineteenth Centuries*. London, 1986.

World Zionist Organization. *Stenographisches Protokoll der Verhandlungen des Zionisten-Kongresses*. Vienna, 1897.

Yerushalmi, Yosef Haim. "Assimilation and Racial Antisemitism: The Iberian and the German Models." *Leo Baeck Memorial Lecture* 26 (1982).

———. *From Spanish Court to Italian Ghetto: Isaac Cardoso, a Study in 17th-Century Marranism and Jewish Apologetics*. Seattle, 1971.

———. *Zakhor*. New York, 1989.

Zalkind-Hourwitz, M. *Apologie des juifs en réponse à la question: Est-il des moyens de rendre les Juifs plus heureux et plus utiles en France?* Paris, 1789; rpt. 1968.

Zinberg, Israel. *A History of Jewish Literature*. 12 vols. Cleveland, 1972–78.

Zipperstein, Steven J. "Haskalah, Cultural Change, and Nineteenth-Century Russian Jewry: A Reassessment." *Journal of Jewish Studies* 34 (1983): 191–207.

Zunz, Leopold. "Grundlinien zu einer künftigen Statistik der Juden." *Zeitschrift für die Wissenschaft des Judenthums* 1 (1822; rpt. 1976): 523–32.

Index

Abrahams, Israel, 145, 178
Academy for the Science of Judaism, 172
Adams, John Quincy, 39
Adler, Cyrus, 217
Adler, Marcus, 209
Agriculture: after emancipation, 129–30; APA's promotion of, 210–12, 315n150; Aristotelian praise of, 15; Dohm on, 28; eastern European Haskalah on, 81, 82; Friedländer on, 78; Grégoire on, 28; Homberg on, 79; Jews' disconnection from, 66–67, 146, 213; physiocratic support of, 26–27; Pietists on, 24; the poor's occupational role in, 111–12; social morality's derivation from, 86, 87–88, 210; Soviet collectivization of, 251; state's promotion of, 39–40; utopian fantasies of, 16, 266n16; vocational training in, 206, 207, 210–11, 212
Agro-Joint: Crimean project of, 246–47, 325n86; as failure, 250–52, 253; Rosenberg on, 239; Ukrainian project of, 247–49; Zionist opposition to, 237, 242. *See also* The Joint
Agudat Yisra'el, 226
Ahlem agricultural school, 208, 210, 211
AJA (Anglo-Jewish Association), 196, 225–26, 227, 231, 233
Akten-stücke (collection of petitions), 77–78
Algeria, 111, 231

Aliens' Act (1905, England), 143
Allgemeine Armenanstalt (Hamburg), 101
Die Allgemeine Zeitung des Judentums (newspaper), 85, 118; "industrial schools" proposal in, 100; on social ideals, 86, 87, 186; subscribers to, 264–65n7; Tobiad family's story in, 140, 297n51; vagrancy proposal in, 103
Alliance Israélite Universelle, 104, 106, 196, 218; apprentice relocations by, 234–35; and immigration crisis, 198–99, 200; international politics of, 225–28; membership of, 227; vocational schools of, 231, 232–33, 234, 299n70, 321n26
Alsace, 32, 46, 65–66, 99, 121, 127
Ambrose of Milan, 17, 53
American Jewish Congress, 249
American Jewish Historical Society, 171
American Jewish Joint Distribution Committee: on Birobidzhan project, 252; conspiratorial paradigm of, 257; management structure of, 228–29, 320n13; on Orthodoxy, 229–30; Palestinian project of, 237–38, 322n42; post–World War II relief from, 256; technical expertise of, 241–42, 243. *See also* Agro-Joint
American Jewish Joint Reconstruction Foundation, 228
American Relief Administration, 228
American Society for Jewish Farm Settlements in Russia (ASJFSR), 248, 253

Compositor: Binghamton Valley Composition
Text: 10/13 Galliard
Display: Galliard
Printer and binder: Haddon Craftsmen, Inc.